The Hist-
The Church O

From The Time Of Its Being Fir   ,iscover'D By
The Portuguezes In The Year 1501 : Giving An
Account Of The Persecutions And Violent Methods
Of The Roman Prelates, To Reduce Them To The
Subjection Of The Church Of Rome

Michael Geddes, Aleixo de Menezes

Alpha Editions

This edition published in 2021

ISBN : 9789354481499

Design and Setting By
Alpha Editions
www.alphaedis.com
Email - info@alphaedis.com

TO THE

Right Reverend Father in GOD,

GILBERT,

By Divine Providence Lord Biſhop
of *SARUM*, and Chancellor
of the moſt Noble Order of the
GARTER.

May it pleaſe your Lordſhip,

WHatever your Thoughts may
be of all that can be called
mine in this Work, I am certain you
will approve of the deſign I had in
* 3   making

*making it publick; which was to fa-
tisfie the World, That there has always been a confiderable visible
Church upon Earth, that never believed the* Doctrines of the Pope's
Supremacy, Purgatory, Tranfubftantiation, Adoration of Images,
Auricular Confeffion, *&c. To which
good End, if this Treatife fhould any
ways contribute (as I am perfuaded it
muft) I am then fecure, that for that
Reafon alone you will pardon any Miftakes I may have made in putting it
together; as alfo the Prefumption of
inviting you to read it, by prefixing
your great Name to it; a thing I
fhould never have ventured to have
done, had I not found by experience
your Lordfhip's Candor and Goodnefs
to be equal, to the known exactnefs of
your*

The Dedication.

your Judgment. I beg your Lordſhip's
Bleſſing, and am,

My Lord,

Your Lordſhip's moſt humble

and moſt obliged Servant,

MICHAEL GEDDES,

─────────────────────

A

A
TABLE

OF THE

Principal Matters contained in the

HISTORY

OF THE

Church of *Malabar*.

A Table of the History.

** 3

* * 4   A

A TABLE

OF THE

CONTENTS

OF THE

DECREES

OF THE

Synod of *Diamper*.

Det.

A Table of the Decrees.

A Table of the Decrees.

A Table of the Decrees.

ACTION VIII.

A Table *of* the Decrees.

ACTION IX.

Of the Reformation of Manners, p. 388

Dec.

A Table of the Decrees.

A

A
Short History
OF THE
Church of *MALABAR:*

*From the time of its being firſt Dif-
covered by the* Portuguezes, *in the
Year* 1501. *until the Celebration
of the following Synod in the
Year* 1599.

THE Country of *Malabar* begins at *Cananor,* a Town in the Northern *Latitude*
of 11 degrees and 20 minutes, and
ends at Cape *Comorim,* in the Northern
Latitude of 7 degrees and $\frac{2}{3}ds$.

It contains divers Kingdoms, as *Cochim, Travancor, Gundaca, Pimenta, Margate,* &c. and a-
bounds with Ports, as *Calecut, Cale, Cochim, Cou-
lam,* &c. Moſt of its Princes and Nations are
Heathens, and extreamly ſuperſtitious in the Wor-

a   ſhip

ship of *Pagods*, of which there are several a-
mong them of incredible Riches.

The *Serra* or *Gate*, as the Natives call it, is a
Ridge of Mountains running 200 Leagues from
North to South, the South end whereof is inha-
bited by Christians, who call themselves the *Christians of St. Thomas*, upon the account of their having first been converted to the Christian Faith
by the Apostle of that Name. They have always, or at least for 1300 years, been under the
Patriarch of *Babylon*, who, as their *Meterane* or
Arch-Bishop died, took care to send them another, who resided still among them, and was
had in great Reverence both by Christians and
Infidels. As for the Doctrines and Customs of
this Church, I shall referr the Reader to the Accounts he will meet with of them in the following History.

The first news of this ancient, but remote
Church, was brought to *Europe* by *Pedral-
vares Cabral*, who putting into *Cranganor* in the
year 1501. and meeting there with several of
those Christians, he perswaded two of them, who
were Brothers, to come along with him to *Portugal*, where the eldest, whose Name was *Matthias*, died at *Lisbon*; and the other, whose Name
was *Joseph*, went first to *Rome*, and from thence
to *Venice*, where, upon his information, a Tract
was publish'd in *Latin* of the State of the Church
of *Malabar*, and is printed at the end of *Fascicu-
lus Temporum*.

The

The year following the Chriftians of *St. Tho-mas* hearing of *Don Vafco da Gama* being at *Co-chim,* with a confiderable Fleet of Ships , fent fome of their Body to let him know, that under-ftanding that he was a Subject of a Chriftian King, they beg'd the favour of him to take them under his Mafters Protection, that fo they might be de-fended againft the Oppreffions and Injuries which were done them daily by *Infidel* Princes, and for a lafting Teftimony of their having put them-felves under the King of *Portugal,* they fent his Majefty a Rod tipp'd at both ends with Silver, with three little Bells at the head of it, which had been the Sceptre of their Chriftian Kings , for fuch they are reported to have had formerly, tho' upon no very good grounds, fo far as I can per-ceive.

The Admiral *Vafco da Gama,* not being in a condition at that time, to do any more for them, gave them a great many good words, promifing them, in his Mafters name, the favour and pro-tection they had defired, and which he was fen-fible they ftood in great need of.

In the year 1505 two Chriftians, who were fa-mous for their great skill in cafting great Guns, and whom, for that reafon, *Don Vafco da Gama* had taken along with him to the *Indies,* ran o-ver to the *Samorim* , and were the firft that in-troduc'd the ufe of Artillery among the *Malabars:* For the *Venetians* forefeeing that their great *In-dian* Trade would be utterly ruin'd, by the new Paffage that was difcover'd to the *Indies* by the

Cape

Cape of Good Hope, if the _Portugueze_ shou'd once get any footing in those parts, are said to have sent those two Engineers, who were their natural born Subjects, into the _Portugueze_ service, on purpose to go over to the _Indians_, to teach them the use of Great Guns, and other Fire-arms, that they might be the better able to oppose the _Portuguezes_.

But after this forementioned Complement of the Admiral, we hear no more of these Christians, till about the Year 1545, the _Portuguezes_ being all that while too busie in making new Conquests, and the Friars, who were sent thither, too much employed in building and providing commodious Seats for their Convents, to attend to any foreign Business, of what nature soever.

This 40 Years neglect of a Christianity, which was just under their Noses, puts me in mind of what a Minister of State said of the _Portugueze_ Zeal in the _Indies_.

" Vana es Senor
" (_speaking_ to Philip
" IV.) la Opinion que
" entre Nationes tudas
" tienen Portuguezes de
" Religiosos por las con-
" versiones Orientales :
" Aquilas conquiftas las
" Emprendio la codi-
" cia , no la Religion,
" las conversiones se

It is a vain conceit, if it please your Majesty, (speaking to _Philip_ IV.) _that the World has entertain'd of the Zeal of the_ Portuguezes _upon account of the Conversions that have been made by them in the_ Indies, _for it was Covetousness and not Zeal that engaged them to make all_

Hizi-

" Hizieron por obra *thofe Conquefts. The Con-*
" divina y charidad de *verfions that have been*
" perfonas religiofas par- *made there were perform-*
" ticulares, el commun *ed by the Divine Power,*
" y direction de la co- *and the Charity of a few*
" rona attendio a de- *particular Friars, the Go-*
" predar Reynos y Ci- *vernment and Crown ha-*
" dades, alli avia mas *ving no other aim therein,*
" dilatados converfio- *but the robbing of King-*
" nes a donde avia *doms and Cities; and*
" mas que hartar la co- *there were ftill the great-*
" dicia, y alla eran *eft Converfions where there*
" hombres obftinados, *was moft to gratify their*
" donde no avia que *Covetoufnefs. But where*
" robar, *concluding:* y *there was nothing to be*
" ceffa Religion quan- *had, there the People were*
" do no fe fique la co- *Obdurate, and not to be*
" dicia, y que no en- *wrought upon. And fo we*
" tran en el cielo to- *fee their Zeal expired*
" dos los, que dizen fe- *quickly in all places, where*
" nor abrid nos. *it was not animated by*
Covetoufnefs, and how
they who had nothing elfe
to fay but, 𝕷𝖔𝖗𝖉 𝖔𝖕𝖊𝖓 𝖚𝖓=
𝖙𝖔 𝖚𝖘, *were not thought*
fit to enter into Heaven.

Manuel de Faria alfo in the Third Tome of
his *Afia Portuguefa,* after having reckoned up
the Errors (as he calls them) of the Chriftians
of St. *Thomas,* makes the following Reflection

upon his Countrymen's having been so long in reducing them to the *Roman* Church.

"Gran lastima es oir "que uviesse esto in "frente de los Portu- "guesses en la India a "los cien annos de su "assistancia en ella; y "lo que es mas a los "mesmos oios de pre- "lados en Goa. La "verdad es que destos "eran los Mercadores "que Christo hallo en "el Templo y echo del "açote.

It is a shameful thing (saith he) *that this Church should continue an Hundred Years in the Neighbourhood of the* Portuguezes *without being reduced to the* Roman *Faith , and which makes it still the worse, under the Eye of the Bishops of* Goa; *but the truth is, those Merchants whom Christ whipp'd out of the Temple, were such as these.*

Tho' after all, the *Portuguezes* Negligence in this matter was nothing so scandalous as the Violences they afterwards made use of in the reducing of them.

In the Year 1544. the Cross and other *Reliques* of St. *Thomas*, which have since made such a Noise in the World, were found at *Meliapor*, the *Legend* whereof in short is, *That the* Portuguezes *as they were pulling down an old Chappel in order to rebuild it, met with a vast Stone some Foot underground, which having lifted up with great ease, they found all the Earth under it stain'd deep with Blood, that appear'd very fresh, and thereon a Cross excellently*

lently well cut, after the fashion of that of the Mi-
litary Order of Aviz *in* Portugal, *and over it a*
Dove or Peacock (for the learned are not agreed
which 'twas) *and above that a bloody Dagger.*
There was also an Inscription on the Stone, but in
Letters that no Body knew what to make of. There
was a Cross of the same Saint, and found much
after the same manner by the Portuguezes *in* Meliapor *in the Year* 1522. *with this Inscription :*
𝕬𝖙 𝖙𝖍𝖊 𝖙𝖎𝖒𝖊 𝖜𝖍𝖊𝖓 Thomas 𝖋𝖔𝖚𝖓𝖉𝖊𝖉 𝖙𝖍𝖎𝖘 𝕿𝖊𝖒𝖕𝖑𝖊,
𝖙𝖍𝖊 𝕶𝖎𝖓𝖌 𝖔𝖋 Meliapor 𝖒𝖆𝖉𝖊 𝖍𝖎𝖒 𝖆 𝕲𝖗𝖆𝖓𝖙 𝖔𝖋 𝖙𝖍𝖊
𝕮𝖚𝖘𝖙𝖔𝖒𝖘 𝖔𝖋 𝖆𝖑𝖑 𝖙𝖍𝖊 𝕸𝖊𝖗𝖈𝖍𝖆𝖓𝖉𝖎𝖟𝖊𝖘 𝖙𝖍𝖆𝖙 𝖜𝖊𝖗𝖊
𝖇𝖗𝖔𝖚𝖌𝖍𝖙 𝖎𝖓𝖙𝖔 𝖙𝖍𝖆𝖙 𝕻𝖔𝖗𝖙, 𝖜𝖍𝖎𝖈𝖍 𝕯𝖚𝖙𝖞 𝖜𝖆𝖘 𝖙𝖍𝖊
𝕿𝖊𝖓𝖙𝖍 𝖕𝖆𝖗𝖙 𝖔𝖋 𝖙𝖍𝖊 𝕲𝖔𝖔𝖉𝖘. *With this Cross were*
also found the Bones of St. Thomas, *which were*
reckoned by all the World before to have been lodged
at Edessa. *There was also found an ancient Record*
of St. Thomas's *having converted the King of* Meliapor (who it's like was the Prince that gave
him the forementioned Grant) *by drawing a great*
piece of Timber ashore, which the King and St.
Thomas *both pretended a right to, after all the*
King's Elephants, *and all the Wit of Man were*
not able so much as to wag it. A Prophecy of St.
Thomas *was also found in the same Treasure, de-*
claring that whenever the Sea shou'd come up to
Meliapor, *which was then Twelve Leagues from it,*
a Nation shou'd come from the West, which shou'd
preach the very same Faith that he had preached.

And to put all this *Indian* Treasure together,
for it is pity any of it should be loft, the Bones
of the Three Kings were found in the fame

Grave with thofe of the Apoftle, which were
known to be theirs, by an ancient *MS.* which
gave the following account of them. *The King
of* Nubia *and* Arabia *was* Melchior, Baltafar *was
King of* Goli *and* Saba, Gafpar *was King of* Tur-
fi, Infula, *and* Grifola *or* Malabar, *where the Body of St.* Thomas *lieth, by whom they were all
three confecrated Bifhops, and were afterwards martyr'd with him.* I leave the Examination of the
truth of this *MS.* to the City of *Cologne,* whofe
concern it is.

Among other things there was a Copper plate
found, with the following Donation engraved
upon it: *This is the Teftimony of Alms, by which
Paradife is acquired, and which all the following
Kings, who fhall diftribute the faid Alms, fhall
certainly obtain: Whereas they that fhall refufe to
give them, fhall be Six Thoufand Years with Worms
in Hell.* This Imprecation is literally ufed by
the ancient Kings of *Spain* in moft of their charitable Donations; but whether the *Spanifh* Kings
had it from the *Indian,* or the *Indian* from the
Spaniard, is not certainly known.

In the Year 1645. *Dom Joan Dalbuquerque* the
firft Arch-Bifhop of *Goa,* being afhamed, it's
like, of their talking fo much in *Europe,* and
doing fo little in *India* in the matters of Religion, fends one *Vincent,* a *Francifcan* Friar, of
which Order the Arch-Bifhop himfelf was, to
Cranganor, to try what he could do towards the
reducing of thofe Chriftians to the obedience
of the *Roman* Church. The Labours of this
fin-

fingle Friar are fo ftrangely magnified by the *Portuguezes*, that it looks as if it were done on purpofe to excufe their not employing of more Hands in a Work, which here in *Europe* they pretended was their chief Bufinefs in the *Indies*. For he is faid not only to have preached daily in their Churches, which were built after the fafhion of the *Pagod* Temples, but alfo to have built feveral Churches among them after the *Latin* way; and at laft, by the order of the Vice-Roy and Archbifhop, upon his having inform'd them of the fmall fuccefs that his preaching had had among them, to have erected a College at *Cranganor* in the Year 1546. in order to the inftructing of their Sons in the Learning and Ufages of the *Latin* Church.

By the way, It is fomewhat ftrange how Friar *Vincent*, who is not faid to have had the gift of Tongues, no more than the Jefuite *Xavier*, who himfelf complained, That for want of it he was forc'd to prattle more like a Child, than preach like an Apoftle among the *Infidels*, fhou'd commence fo powerful a Preacher among the *Malabars*, the very firft Year of his being in the *Indies*; a Year being a very fhort time for a Man to make himfelf fo far Mafter of a ftrange Language, as to be able to Preach therein to any purpofe.

But tho' the Chriftians of St. *Thomas* did not deny to fend their Sons to this College, feveral of whom, after their having been taught *Latin*, were Ordained Priefts, according to the *Roman* Rites:

Rites: Yet this had little or no effect as to the reducing of that Church to the Papal Obedience, to which they still continued so averse, that they treated those Natives with the same disregard that they did the other *Latin* Priests.

Thus matters continued with the Church of *Malabar* till the Year 1587. when the Jesuits i-magining the reason why this Christianity was so little benefitted by having several of their Sons bred in the College at *Cranganor*, was their not being taught *Chaldee* or *Syriack*, which is the Language all their Offices are in, did thereup-on erect a new College, which was built at the sole charge of *Antonio Guedes Morales*, at a place called *Chanota*, or *Vaipicotta*, a Village inha-bited by those Christians, and which is about a League from *Cranganor*.

But notwithstanding the Jesuits, by educa-ting several of the *Malabars* in the *Chaldee* Tongue, and instructing them thorowly in the *Latin* Faith, did qualify them to serve the *Roman* Church in her Pretensions. Yet all this signified very little, none that had been educated by them daring so much as to mutter the least Word against any of their ancient Doctrines, or in favour of the *Roman*, or to alter any thing in their Offices, or forbear praying for the Bishop of *Babylon* as their Patriarch, in the *Mass*.

Wherefore the *Portuguezes* finding that these Christians were not by any thing that Friars could say or do to them, to be perswaded out of their ancient Faith, or to forsake their present

fent Bifhop to fubmit themfelves to the **Pope**, a-
gainft whom they were fo poffeffed, that they
cou'd not endure fo much as to hear him named, refolved, at laft, to try other methods
with them, that is, to try what Violence would
do, the Method to which Popery, where-ever it
is, owes both its Propagation and Eftablifhment.

And that they did not betake themfelves to
this courfe fooner, we are not to imagine was
in the leaft owing to their temper, or to any
difpofition that was in them, to try firft what
fair and gentle means would do ; for they muft
know nothing of the *Spirit of Popery*, that can
imagine it to be capable of any fuch thing, but
it was owing purely to the circumftances of their
Affairs ; for that before their Government had
fpread it felf, and taken a good root in thofe
Parts, it would not have been fafe for them to
have made ufe of thofe rude and boifterous Methods for the reduction of thefe Chriftians, which
we fhall fee they did afterwards, when they had
in a manner gotten that whole Countrey into
their own Power : In purfuance of the forementioned Refolution, the *Portuguezes* determined to have their Bifhop, to whofe prefence a-
mong them they attributed their conftancy in
their ancient Faith, feized in order to fend him
to *Rome*, which was executed accordingly.

Their Bifhop at that time (for they had but
one of that Order among them) was one *Mar
Jofeph*, who, according to ancient Cuftom, had
been fent thither by *Mar Audixa*, Patriarch of
Babylon.

Babylon. He is acknowledged by the *Portuguezes* to have reformed divers Abuses in that Church, and to have put things in a much better order than he found them in. *Mar Joseph* being brought Prisoner from *Cochim* to *Goa*, was Embarked upon the first Ships that went to *Portugal*, with an intent of sending him to *Rome* ; but being arrived at *Lisbon*, he, by his Addrefs and appearances of an extraordinary Sanctity, did fo far infinuate himfelf into the favour and good opinion of *Dona Caterina*, who was Queen Regent at that time, and of the Infanta *Dona Maria*, that he was fent back by the next Ships to *Goa*, with the Queen Regents Letters, ordering him to be permitted to live quietly in his Bifhoprick , he having promifed the Cardinal Infante *Don Anrique*, who was at that time *Inquifitor-General*, and the Pope's Legate *à latere* to the Crown of *Portugal*, to do all that was in his power towards the reducing of his Diocefs to the *Roman* obedience.

In the Year 1552, one *Tum Siud*, or *Simon Salacan*, a Monk of the Order of St. *Pachomius*, who pretended to have been chofe Patriarch of *Moful* , or *Seleucia Parthorum*, or *Babylon*, for they are all the fame by the whole Clergy of *Perfia* and *Affyria*, came to *Rome* and fubmitted himfelf to the Pope ; by whom, according to fome, he was confecrated a Bifhop, tho' others will have it, that he had only his Eaftern Confecration confirmed, and afterwards received the *Patriarchal Pallium*. He prefented Letters and a
Con-

Confeſſion of Faith to the *Pope*, which he pretended were ſent by all the Eaſtern Biſhops : In
the Letters the *Pope's* Supremacy was exalted as
high, as if they had been writ by a Paraſite
Canoniſt ; which Letters, together with the Confeſſion of Faith, were done into Latin and Printed by *Maſius* : He gave out alſo, that he was
attended by Seventy Perſons of note as far as
Jeruſalem, and from thence only by Three, whereof one died by the way, and another remained
ſick in the Journey ; and the third, whoſe name
was *Calaſi*, came with him to *Rome*. *Tum Siud*,
after he was diſmiſſed at *Rome*, inſtead of returning to *Babylon*, went and lived in an ob-
ſcure place called *Charamet* or *Amed*, where in a
ſhort time he was put to death by the *Mahometans* ; and, as it is ſaid, at the inſtigation of
the *Chriſtians* of thoſe Parts, who, to the great
diſcredit of the pretenſions he had made at *Rome*,
would never own him nor his Authority. But
this ill Succeſs did not hinder another Monk of
the ſame Order, whoſe name was *Abd Jeſu* or
Hebed, who had writ ſeveral Books in defence of
Neſtorianiſm, from coming to *Rome* with the ſame
pretenſions, in the Year 1562 ; and he could never have come in a better time, by reaſon of
the Council of *Trent* being then ſitting, to which
he was ſent with great Solemnity to repreſent
nothing leſs than all the *Chaldean* Biſhops, having
before at *Rome* in their Name, made the ſub-
miſſion of that whole Church to the *Pope* : This
method of making a noiſe with *Mock-Prelates*,
                                                    had

had been made great ufe of by fome former *Popes.* So *Eugenius* the IV. maintained his tottering reputation againft the Council of *Bafil*, by an appearance of *Græcians* and *Armenians* in the Council of *Florence:* And *Paul* the III. graced his Tranflation of the Council from *Trent* to *Bolongia*, which was fo ftoutly oppofed by the Emperor and *Spanifh* Bifhops, by fending one *Stephen* to *Bolognia* with the fplendid Title of the *Armenian Patriarch.*

This Humor was carried on by one *Elias*, who likewife pretended to be chofe Patriarch of *Babylon*; he fent feveral *Nuncio's* to the Pope with the Submiffion of the *Babylonifh* Church, and a Confeffion of Faith; but thefe *Nuncio's* fpoiled their bufinefs by over-acting their Parts; for it having been difcovered, that the better to fupport their Pretence of the *Chaldæan* Church agreeing with the Church of *Rome* in all things, they had tore feveral Pages out of their Church-Offices, they were difmiffed with difgrace.

However this did not difcourage *Elias* (as indeed what will a hungry Monk?) from fending one *Adam Camara*, his pretended Arch-Deacon, to *Rome*, three Years after that misfortune; who, together with his Patriarch's Letter, delivered to the Pope a Book of his own compofing, concerning the Reconciliation of the *Chaldæan* Church to the *Roman*, which he defired might be diligently examined. In his Letter he told *Paul* V. *That let Hereticks do what they will, he for his part was refolved never to go againft the Holy Precepts of*

the

the Apostles and Orthodox Fathers, who had all af-firmed the See *of great* Rome *to be the Head of all other* Sees, *but would always confess that the* Roman Church *was the Mother of all the other Churches in the World, and that all that did not own her to be so, were accursed.* It's obfervable, that this *Elias* had a ftretch of Courtfhip beyond his begging Predeceffors; which was his affuring the Pope, That all their Clergy anciently had their Orders immediately from *Rome*, and that that Cuftom continued, till feveral that were going to *Rome* on that Errand were murdered by the way; which having feveral times happened, the Pope when he came to hear of it, did of his free Grace fay, *Let us ordain them a Patriarch; and not only so, but permit them to chuse him, that so they may not perish thus by the way :* And thus, faid good *Elias*, we received all the Authority we pretend to from *Rome*, and not from our felves, as they pretend to do; (and the greater Wretches they) who trample upon the Canons of the Apoftles, and the Laws of the Fathers. It is from this blind Story that the *Roman* Doctors have endea-voured to perfuade the World, that all the *Ba-bylonish* Bifhops do own, that they derived their Power of Ordination from the *Western* Fathers, meaning the Bifhops of *Rome*, no doubt.

Now what crude Stuff is this, that thofe hun-gry Monks ferved up to the Pope, and was as greedily fwallowed at *Rome*, there being not the leaft Colour of Truth in any part of the Story. For as to the ancient Cuftom that is fo confident-

ly

ly affirmed, it is plainly contradicted by the 33d
Arabick Canon of the Council of *Nice*, which
tho' not the genuine Canons of that Council,
are yet very ancient.   The Canon runs thus :

> Canon 33. *Let the See of* Seleucia, *which is
> one of the* Eastern *Cities, be honoured likewise,
> and have the Title of* Catholicon, *and let the
> Prelate thereof, ordain Arch-Bishops as the o-
> ther Patriarchs do, that so the Eastern Chri-
> stians who live under Heathens, may not be
> wronged by waiting the Patriarch of* Antioch's
> *leisure, or by going to him, but may have a way
> opened to them to supply their own Necessities ;
> neither will any injury be done to the Patriarch
> of* Antioch *thereby, seeing he has consented to
> its being thus, upon the Synod's having desired
> it of him.*

From which Canon it is plain, That the Church
of *Seleucia* or *Babylon* was anciently subject to the
Patriarch of *Antioch*, who of all the Patriarchs
was their nighest Neighbour.   So that if the *Chaldæan* Bishops do own that they derived all their
Authority from the *Western* Fathers, as is pretended they do, they must mean by the *Western*
Fathers, the Bishops of *Antioch*.

And as to its being said, That the *Chaldæan* Bishops do to this day own that they had their Ordinations from the *Western* Fathers, meaning the
Bishops of *Rome*, the falshood of that Pretence
appears evidently, not only from what has been
said

faid, but from the whole Tenor of the following
Synod, and of all the late Reports of the *Portuguezes* concerning that Church : As it does likewife, That all thofe Patriarchs of *Babylon*, who
came to *Rome*, notwithftanding the great Noife
they made in this Part of the World, were mere
Impoftors, never owned by the Churches they pretended to be Patriarchs of. Father *Simon* fpeaking of this in the 93 Page of his *Hiftoire Critique*,
confeffeth their magnifying the Pope's Power as
they did, to have been a piece of grofs Flattery,
but withal, will have it to have been Pardonable
in fuch poor Wretches, who would not otherwife have been fuffered to have approached the
Pope, to whom they came into *Europe* on purpofe
to make their Court ; for, as he obferves upon
the fame occafion, few or none of the Oriental
Prelates ever applied themfelves to the Pope, but
for the promoting of fome particular Intereft,
which was one reafon why the reunions they pretended to make did not laft long. But tho' for
fome time thefe *mock Prelates* being fupported by
the Pope, made a fhift to keep the face of a
Church at *Charamet*, none of them ever daring to
go to *Moful*, yet after a little time the true *Chaldæan* Prelates obliged them to leave *Charamet* ;
from whence they retired to *Zeinalback*, a yet
remoter Place on the borders of *Perfia*, where
from little, in a fhort time, they dwindled to
nothing.

The Prelates of *Babylon* we fee were anciently
ftiled Bifhops of *Seleucia*, a City not far from

A   *Ctefiphon*

Ctesiphon; from whence it was that *Simon*, who suffered Martyrdom under *Sapor* is stiled Bishop of *Seleucia* and *Ctesiphon*, of which City we meet with this following Account in *Strabo*. Babylon *was anciently the Metropolis of* Assyria, *which now* Seleucia *of* Tigris *is, near to which is a great Village called* Ctesiphon, : ˙re *the Kings of* Parthia *used to spend the Winter* ¹ *spare* Seleucia, *that it might not be continually op* *ffed with Soldiers and* Scythians : *but notwithstanding this Change of the Metropolis, as the Country all about is still called* Babylon, *so the Natives, tho' Born in the very City of* Seleucia, *are still called* Babylonians *from the Region, and not* Seleucians.

In the *Bibliotheca Patrum*, there is a Treatise of Paradise translated out of *Syriack* into *Latine*, by *Masius*, writ by one *Moses Bar Cepha*, who is stiled Bishop in *Bethraman* and *Bethleno*, and *Curator of the Ecclesiastical Affairs of the Mozul* or *Seleucia Parthorum*. This *Moses* flourished in the Tenth Century.

But it is time to leave these *Sham Prelates*, who run so fast to *Rome* of their own accord, and return to the true ones, who were forc'd to go thither much against their Wills.

After the Christians of the *Serra* had heard of their Arch-Bishop's being sent a Prisoner to *Portugal*, despairing of ever seeing him again, they sent secretly to *Mar Simeon*, Patriarch of *Babylon*, desiring him to order them a new Arch-Bishop, who straightways sent them one *Mar Abraham*, who having gotten into the *Serra* in a disguise, guife, notwithftanding the great care the *Portu-guezes* had taken to have intercepted him, he was received by the whole Church as their Bifhop, with great joy. But he had not been long there, before he had the news of *Mar Jofeph's* being returned to *Goa*, where having prefented the Letters he had brought along with him, he was permitted to go back to his Bifhoprick.

The Arch-Bifhop of *Goa* who had writ to *Portugal*, that they fhould by no means ever fuffer *Mar Jofeph* to return to the *Indies*, was not without ftrong jealoufies of his having prevaricated in all that he had promifed; and what did very much confirm him therein, was, that *Mar Jofeph* when he defired him to take fome Friars along with him to preach the *Roman* Doctrines in his Bifhoprick, did not only deny to do it, but furthermore pretended, that it was reveal'd to him the Night before, that it was no ways convenient. The Arch-Bifhop being netled at this pretence, told him with great heat, That he had better Revelation from the Scriptures of his not being the Paftor whom God would have to feed his Sheep, but a Wolf in Sheep's cloathing, of whom our Saviour had faid, *That they were to be known by their Fruits*, and that their *Highneffes* would quickly be fenfible how much they had been impofed upon by him.

Notwithftanding all this, he was permitted to go to his Bifhoprick, tho' for no other reafon, its like, but to give birth to a Schifm, by which means the *Portuguezes* hoped to be able to com-

pafs

pafs. their ends upon that Church the eafier, *Divide & impera*, being a piece of Policy that is well underftood, and has been much practi-fed by the *Roman* Church. And if this was their drift in fending him back to his Diocefs, they were not out in their Policy, for *Mar Joseph* was not fooner in the *Serra*, than the whole Bi-fhoprick was divided, fome adhering to *Mar A-braham*, and others to *Mar Joseph*, as their true Prelate.

But *Mar Joseph* finding *Mar Abraham's* Party to be much the more numerous, by reafon of the Communication he had had with the *La-tins*, did thereupon betake himfelf to the courfe that all diftrefled People, who preferr their own Intereft to that of the Publick, take, and com-plains to the *Portuguezes* of *Mar Abraham*, not only as an Ufurper, but as a moft bitter Enemy to the *Roman* Church.

The *Viceroy*, who was glad of this occafion, ftraightways difpatch'd an Order to the Governour of *Cochim*, to have *Mar Abraham* apprehended, and to fend him Prifoner to *Goa*, in order to fend him to *Rome*, which was executed accor-dingly. But the Ship whereon *Mar Abraham* was Embarked, being forced by ftrefs of Weather into *Mazambique*, a Port belonging to the *Portu-guezes* in the Southern Coafts of *Africk*, he made a fhift to efcape, and by the way of *Melindo* and *Ormus*, to get to the Patriarch of *Babylon*, from whom having received new Briefs to Fortifie his Title, he refolved to return to his Bifhoprick;
but

but having afterwards confidered better on the matter, and being fenfible, that if he went thither without the *Pope*'s Order, that the *Portuguezes* would quickly make the Serra too hot for him, he altered his Mind, and refolved to try his Fortune at *Rome*, and to take a Journey thither over Land ; being come to *Rome*, after having abjured his ancient Faith, and reconciled himfelf to the Church, and promifed to reduce that of *Malabar* to its obedience, he obtained of *Pius* the Fourth, all fuch *Briefs* as were any ways necef-fary, having alfo the Title of *Arch-Bifhop*, which he and his Predecellors had enjoyed, given him therein.

But being at *Venice*, in his way home, the Divines there difcovering, as it is faid, both from the Nature of the Opinions that he had abjured, and from his own Confeffion, that he had never been lawfully Ordained, did oblige him to receive all *Orders*, from the *firft tonfure* to the *Priefthood*. He was ordained *Prieft* by the Bifhop of *St. Salvador* and Confecrated a *Bifhop* by the Patriarch of *Venice*.

This *Venetian* Confecration, if it is not a down-right *Naggs-Head* Story, is a Scurvy refle&ion upon the *Pope*'s Infallibility, who herein was not only deceived in a *matter of Fa&*, in giving *Briefs* to one, as an Arch-Bifhop, who really was not at all in *Holy Orders*, but he muft alfo have been deceived in a *matter of Do&rine*, in being Ignorant, that fome of the Opinions which had been Abjured before him by *Mar Abraham*, were of

A 3   fuch

such a nature as to incapacitate him for *Orders.*

While *Mar Abraham* was in this Voyage, *Mar Joseph* finding himself in the quiet Possession of his whole Bishoprick, did not forbear to profess and teach the Doctrines he had abjured in *Portugal.* The Bishop of *Cochim*, who was his next Neighbour, having heard thereof, acquainted the Arch-Bishop of *Goa* therewith, and he *Don Anrique*, the Cardinal Infante, who at that time Governed *Portugal* in the Minority of his Nephew *Don Sebastian*, and the Cardinal informed the Pope of the whole matter.

These repeated Tyrannies of the *Portuguezes* in the *Indies*, of dragging ancient Bishops thus out of their own Country and Diocess, and tumbling them so about the World, I cannot but reckon among those violent Injustices for which *Manuel de Faria* in the very last words of his *Asia Portuguesa*, tells us, God has punished them so visibly. The observation is so remarkable, and to this day so litterally true, as I have been told by several intelligent *Portuguezes*, that I shall set it down in the Author's own words.   " Ponderacion muy
" notable ay en esto, y es, que dequanta persona
" passaran a la India ya como Governadores, ya
" como Capitanes, ya como Mercadores, aunque
" esto ultimo siempre fue de todos : y de quantos
" destos alcançaran groessissimas haziendas, no se
" ve oy in el Reyno de Portugal ninguna casa o
" Mayo razgo que se fundasse con ellas, o lo me-
" nos que sea cosa de importancia : ni tam poco
" ay en la India alguna casa grande desta calidad :
                                              " aun-

" aunque tambien aya avido allá Portugueſes q
" iuntaron mucho y uvo algunos de a million,y de
" dos milliones y de a tres,y a un de a quatro,ye'l no
" luzirſe a nadie conſiderablemente tanta hazien-
" da como tantos iuntaron,ſe hade entendar, que
" fue,y es,y ſera pero por una de dos razones,o por
" ambas, la primera porq' permetiendo Dios eſte
" viaie ſolo para dilatar ſu nombre, y verdedero
" culto, eſtos navigantes trataron por la mayor
" parte de lo material de la ſacrilega codicia, co-
" metiendo muchas maldades, para hartarſe, en
" vez de tractar de la religion : y otra porq' lo
" mas deſto fue ganado por medios injuſtos de ti-
" ranias, robos, y toda ſuerte de inſolencia, como
" conſta de muchos lugares deſtas Hiſtorias.
*It is remarkable, that among all the Perſons who have
gone to the* Indies, *whether as Governours, Captains,
or Merchants, of which ſort moſt of them were in
truth, there has not been one that has raiſed a Family of any conſideration out of the Goods they have
got in thoſe Parts, either there or in* Portugal, *tho'
there have been ſeveral of them that have got there,
one, two, three, or four Millions. Now, that nothing that's conſiderable of all theſe vaſt Treaſures,
ſhould any where appear, muſt be for one or both of
theſe two Reaſons, firſt, that whereas God permitted
the Diſcovery of this Voyage, only for the propogation
of his Name, and true Worſhip (but not by ſuch
barbarous Methods as the forementioned I dare
ſay) theſe Travellers have, for the moſt part, purſued
the ends of a Sacrilegious Covetouſneſs, committing
many Injuſtices to fill their Coffers, inſtead of having*

any

any regard to Religion; the other *is,* because the most of those Riches were gained by the unjust means of *Tyrannies, Robberies, and all sort of Insolencies,* of which you have many Instances in the foregoing History.

Pius V. upon this Issued forth a *Brief,* bearing date the 15th. of *January* 1567. directing it to *Dom Jorge,* Arch-Bishop of *Goa,* and commanding him to use all diligence to have *Mar Joseph* forthwith Apprehended and sent to *Rome,* in pursuance whereof he was seized, and sent Prisoner to *Portugal.,* upon the first Ships that went, whence he was carried to *Rome,* where he died.

Neither were the Violences they made use of to Convert *Infidels,* any whit inferior to those they exercised upon the poor *Chaldæan* Christians, by which they came to provoke the *Infidel* Princes to that degree, that they had like to have lost all that they had in the *Indies* by it. For the *Hidalcaon* who Besieged *Goa* in the Year 1570. both in his Letters to the Viceroy *Don Luis d' Ataide,* and in the Speech he made to his Captains, when he first communicated to them his design of driving the *Portuguezes* out of the *Indies,* gave those Violences for the chief cause of his War. Those Letters and Speech being too long to be here Inserted, I shall only set down so much of them as relates directly to this matter.

In his first Letter to the *Viceroy,* after having complained of some other Grievances, he tells him, *That he was certainly informed that at* Ormus,

Dio,

Dio, Chaul, *and all the other* Portugueze *Ports, his Subjects Ships were all strictly searched, and all the Boys and Girls that were found Aboard, of whatsoever Quality,* Abyssines *or* Mahometans, *were forcibly carried ashoar, and there detained from their Parents or Masters. This,* saith he, *is a matter that I cannot but be extreamly offended with ; neither can I judge otherwise of your permitting such Violences, but that you have a mind to break with me, for if you had not I cannot be perswaded that your People durst presume to commit such Insolencies :* He goes on. *Let it suffice that no difference can happen between us, but what gives me great displeasure, and that I am both a Brother and an Allie of the King of* Portugal, *and do esteem you as my particular Friend, to put a stop to this matter, that so my Subjects may have no further cause to complain thereof. Besides, I am confident the King of* Portugal *will not thank any, that shall be instrumental in making a Breach between me and him, by compelling my Subjects thus against their Wills to turn* Christians, *a practice,* saith he, *that's abominable in the sight of all the World ; nay, I am confident that* Jesus Christ *himself, the God whom you adore, cannot be well pleased with such Service as this : Force and Compulsion in all such Cases, being what God, Kings, and all the People of the World do abominate. The work of turning People from one Religion to another, if it be not done by the Divine Inspiration, and the immediate Will of God can never be sincere, neither can* Converts *have any inward respect for a Religion, which they are compelled to Profess. I do therefore intreat you to see*
that

that this matter be speedily redressed, but especially that of taking Peoples Children from them by violence, which is a thing I stand amazed at, and am in duty bound to see remedied.

In his second Letter he thanks the *Viceroy* for an Order he had sent to *Ormus*, and the other *Portugueze* Ports, prohibiting all such Violences, but at the same time tells him, *That his Order was not in the least regarded; for that the* Portuguezes *notwithstanding it, went on still in their former Courses,* to which he tells him, *If there were not a speedy and effectual stop put, it must necessarily beget a War betwixt him and the* Portuguezes ; adding, *That as he knew that neither God, nor wise Kings, took any delight in Discords, so he was certain that there was no Religion in the World, that justified the forcing of People from one Religion to another.*

And in his Speech to his Captains he tells them, *The* Portuguezes *at first came among us, under the notion of Merchants, promising to help us to several Goods that we wanted, but that afterwards by making of trifling Presents to some weak Princes and other Arts, they had obtained leave to build Store-Houses for their Wares upon the Coast ; but that instead of Ware-Houses, they had built Fortresses, by which means they had strengthned themselves so in* India, *both by Sea and Land, that it was more than time for the Natives to look about them, and to join together to extirpate such cruel Tyrants and Ravagers of so many Kingdoms, and Enemies to the general quiet and commerce of the World ; and that for one*
                                        thing

thing especially, which was what no patience was able to endure, their compelling the Indians *in all places, where they had Power, to change their Religion.*

In this Affair the *Christian* and *Mahometan*, of which Sect this *Hidalcaon* was, seem to have changed Parts, the *Mahometan* writing therein like a *Christian*, and the *Christians* behaving themselves like *Mahometans*.

> *Pudet hæc opprobria nobis*
> *Vel dici potuisse.*

About this time the *Dominican Friars*, under pretence of building a Convent, built a Fortress at *Solor*, into which, as soon as it was finished, the *Viceroy* put a strong Garrison: There were perpetual Bickerings betwixt this Garrison and the Natives, in most of which, some of the *Friars*, as they were Converting those *Infidels*, with Swords in their hands, suffered Martyrdom.

We read of a famous *Portugueze Missionary* about this time, it was one *Fernando Vinagre*, who, tho' a Secular Priest, Commanded the Squadron that was sent to the assistance of the King of *Tidore*; in which occasion he is said to have behaved himself both like a great Captain, and a great Apostle, and to have appeared one day in *Armour*, and another in a *Surplice*, and to have Baptized several in his Armour, with his *Surplice* over it. In these *a la Dragoon* Conversions, he was seconded by his Admiral *Antonio Galvam*, who with the assistance of Captain *Francisco da Castro*,

Castro, is said to have Converted five Kings in the
Island of *Mazacar*; and tho' he was really no other
than a *St. Ruth*, yet he is said by the *Portugueze*
Historians to be another *St. Paul*, in Governing
all that came under his Power both with his Sword
and with his Voice, *A Sword and Voice*, say they,
worthy of a glorious Eternity. It was this *Antonio*
that first discovered the King of *Portugal*'s special
Title to the *Clove*, which, for having five Points,
he said, had the King of *Portugal*'s Arms, which
are the five Wounds of Christ stamp'd upon it.

The same Author tells us, and approves of
what an *Indian* said of the *Portuguezes*, when in
the height of their Triumphs: *Let them alone*,
said the *Indian, for they will quickly come to lose
that as Covetous Merchants, which they have gained
as admirable Soldiers ; they now Conquer* Asia, *but
it will not be long before* Asia *will Conquer them*.

The Emperor of *Persia* is reported by the same
Author to have made the same Prediction, who
being told by the *Portugueze* Ambassador, when
he asked him how many of the Governours of
the *Indies* Heads his Master had chopped off,
that he had not taken off one, replied, *If that is
true, it is not possible the* Portuguezes *should hold
the* Indies *long*.

About this time the *Portuguezes* were driven
out of the Island of *Ito* by the *Natives*. They
were stirred up to do it by a Speech made by
one *Gemulio*, a considerable *Native*, wherein he
told the *Portuguezes* in a full Assembly of them,
That if they Preached to others that there was a God

in

*i*n Heaven, *who obſerved all that was done on Earth,
and would certainly Reward all Good, and Puniſh
all Evil-Deeds, without believing it themſelves, or
without practiſing what they believed, they were certainly guilty of the Abomination, which ſuch a God
muſt deteſt above all others :* He likewiſe told them,
*They were Strangers come from the very Skirts of the
World, and will you,* ſaith he, *who are the Off-
ſpring of the Shades, which the Sun leaves when it
goes down, preſume to Tyrannize over us, who entertained you ſo kindly, and have been ſo long a Sanctuary to you? If theſe be the Cuſtoms of your Country, you muſt know they are what we Abominate;
return, return therefore to your native darkneſs, or
your ancient Habitations, where the want of Light
will hide your Actions, and do you not come hither
to commit them in the very apple of the Eye of the
Sun, as it riſeth out of his brighteſt Cradle.* You
preach Chriſt Crucified *to us, and at the ſame time
Crucifie thoſe you have perſwaded to believe in him.
You will make others to be* Chriſtians, *without appearing to be ſuch your ſelves. You muſt know we
are not ignorant of what you have done to the King
of* Xael, *and how you rewarded his great kindneſs
and Civility to you, with Violences and Outrages,
and his Subjects good turns with diſhonouring their
Wives : We know likewiſe how you have uſed the
Queen of* Aram, *whom, after ſhe had loſt both her
Kingdom and Husband to ſecure you, you have
diſhonourably thrown off, as one who could be of no
further uſe to you. Be gone therefore immediately
out of this Iſland, and hereafter don't you preſume to*
ſet

set your Foot, or so much as cast your Eye upon it.
The Historian who relates this, tho' a *Portugueze,*
makes this reflection upon it, *Thus we lose Places
by our Insolencies, which we gained by our Valour.*

When *Mar Abraham* returned to *Goa* over
Land, by the way of *Ormus,* and found *Mar
Joseph* Shipped off for *Portugal,* thereupon he
flattered himself with the hopes of meeting with
nothing to molest him in the Possession of his
Bishoprick ; but he quickly found himself deceived, for having presented the Pope's *Briefs,* and
other Papers he brought along with him to the
Arch-Bishop, the *Portuguezes* not having the same
reason to permit him to return to the *Serra,* as
they had when they permitted *Mar Joseph,* which,
as I have observed, was done on purpose to give
rise to a Schism, he was told, that before they
would put him in Possession of his Bishoprick,
they must first have both the *Briefs* and his *Informations* strictly examined, that so they might be
satisfied he had not imposed upon his *Holiness.*

Wherefore, tho' resolved whatever came on't,
never to let *Mar Abraham* go out of their hands,
yet that they might not seem to refuse to pay a
due respect to the *Pope's Briefs* ; the Arch-Bishop
and others, after having examined all his Papers,
found several flaws in them, which were declared
to be sufficient to justifie their detaining of him :
This is no more than what the *Canonists* can do,
and do daily in the clearest cases, it being impossible to have any Matrimonial or other cause drawn
up, or worded so accurately, that the *Canonists,*
and

and efpecially if the Pope defire it, will not find feveral Nullities in. Upon the publication of the nullity of the *Pope's Briefs*, as having been obtained by mifinformation, poor *Mar Abraham*, inftead of being fent back in Triumph to his Bifhoprick, as he expected, was, after all the Pains he had been at, confined to the *Dominican* Convent at *Goa*, there to remain till fuch time as the *Pope's* Anfwer came to the *Arch-Bifhop's* Information of his Cafe.

Mar Abraham, being fenfible that to be confined till that came, was the fame thing as to be condemned to be a Prifoner for Life, refolved, let what would be the Iffue, to try to make his efcape, which, after feveral unfuccefsful Attempts, he did, at laft, upon an *Holy Thurfday* at Night, while the *Friars* were all imployed in the Chapel, and having gotten over to the Continent, he pofted away to *Malabar*, where he was received with great Joy and Feftivity by all the Chriftians, who having two of their Arch-Bifhops Prifoners among the *Portuguezer*, defpaired of ever feeing another *Babylonifh* Bifhop among them.

The *Viceroy* and *Arch-Bifhop* were much troubled at *Mar Abraham's* having made his efcape thus, and writ ftraightways to the Bifhop of *Cochim*, and all the Governours upon the Coaft of *Malabar*, to have him apprehended if he was above Ground ; but *Mar Abraham* knowing how it would be, took care to keep himfelf, as far as he could, out of their reach, never adventuring to vifit any of the Churches that were in the Neighbourbourhood of *Cochim*, or of any other *Portugueze* Garrison.

But tho' after this *Mar Abraham* is said, in all his Letters to the *Portuguezes* to have still profesfed himself a *Romanist*, and not only so, but to have re-ordained all that had been ordained by him formerly; yet it is certain, that in all things else he acted quite otherwise in his Diocess, where he continued not only to preach his old *Doctrines*, but in his Prayers still named the Bishop of *Babylon* as his Patriarch.

Gregory XIII. being informed of this by the *Arch-Bishop* of *Goa*, and other Prelates of the *Indies*, issued forth a *Brief*, bearing date the 28th. of *November*, 1578. directing it to *Mar Abraham*, and commanding him therein to repair to the next Provincial Council that should be Assembled at *Goa*, to assist at it, and to observe all the Decrees that should be made therein, relating to his Bishoprick, and that he might not excuse his not obeying this *Brief*, by pretending that he could not do it with safety; the *Pope* likewise sent him *Letters of safe Conduct*, to go and come without being any ways molested.

In pursuance whereof *Dom Vicente da Fonseca*, a *Friar*, of the Order of *St. Dominick*, and *Arch-Bishop of Goa*, having called a Provincial Council, which was the third of *Goa*, ordered the forementioned *Brief* to be intimated to *Mar Abraham*, and together with the *Pope's*, his own, and the Viceroy's *Letters of safe Conduct*, to be sent to him.

Mar

Mar Abraham, having well confidered the matter, and perceiving how difficult it would be for him to efcape being Dragoon'd by the *Portuguezes*, whofe power increafed daily in thofe Parts, if he fhould difobey this Summons, determined, whatever came on it, to repair to the Council, at which he affifted, and was obliged once more to Abjure, and make a profeffion of the *Roman* Faith, promifing withal, to fee all the Decrees made in that *Synod*, in relation to his Bifhoprick, punctually executed, and to fend in all the Heretick Books in his Diocefs to be burned or amended ; and having confeffed, that in *the Ordination of Priefts* there was no Wine in the Cup, which he delivered into their hands, together with the Hoft, he was commanded to Ordain all that he had Ordained before over-again.

Now if this, of there being no Wine in the Cup, which was delivered into the hands of thofe who were Ordained *Priefts*, was the only ground whereon the *Romanifts* founded the invalidity of the *Chaldæan* Orders, as it is the only thing they have been pleafed to inftance in, what a ftretch was this to invalidate the Orders of a whole Church by? But for *Canonifts* and *Schoolmen* by Subtilties invented on purpofe to fupport a late Error, or to ferve a prefent turn, to wound Chriftianity in its very Vitals, is a practice too common to be wondred at. I am fure the Church of *Rome* has much more reafon to apprehend that the Sacrilege of denying the Cup to the Laity

B   in

in the Sacrament, may make her Communion imperfect and ineffectual, than that this alone should make Ordinations so.

But after all this stir, the Doctrine of the delivering the Bread and Cup into the hands of those who are to be ordained Priests, being essential to Orders, is so far from being true, that it is owned to be a Novelty by all the Modern Learned Divines of the Church of *Rome*, and is moreover contradicted by her daily Practice, who, as all the World knows, allows the *Greek Orders* to be good, in the Collation whereof she knows, the Bread and Cup is not put into the hands of those who are ordained Priests.

It is true, the Council of *Florence*, in her Instructions to the *Armenians*, seems to have doted into the same Error with this of the *Portuguezes*, in making that new Ceremony essential to *Orders*. But let that be as it will, it is certain that both the present practice of the *Roman* Church, and all her truly Learned *Sons*, the Modern *Schoolmen* not excepted, do condemn it as an Error; for which I shall only quote two of her most eminent Schoolmen, and one of her ablest Criticks.

Cardinal *Lugo*, in his 2 Disp. *de Sacramentis*, saith as followeth, *Aliunde autem habemus, non porrectionem panis & vini determinatè requiri ex divinâ institutione, cum Græci absque illâ porrectione ordinentur; ergo fatendum est Christum solum voluisse pro materiâ aliquod signum proportionatum hoc vel illud.*

And

And *Becanus*, in the third part of his Scholastical Divinity, *Chap.* 26. of the Sacrament of Order, has as follows: *Concilium Florentinum in instructione Armenorum solum meminit materiæ accidentalis, quæ ab Ecclesiâ fuit instituta,* which was the delivering of the Bread and Cup, *non autem substantialis, quam Christus præscripsit,* which is the imposition of hands, *Quia hæc ex Scripturis & antiquis Patribus erat satis cognita, non autem illa. Addo, si hoc argumentum valeret, posse optimè retorqueri ita, Antiqua concilia non assignant aliam materiam nisi impositionem manuum, ergo,* &c. He concludes thus, *Nota antiqua concilia assignâsse materiam à Christo institutam, Florentinum verò mateam assignâsse, quam Ecclesia introduxit,* that is the *Latin* only. By this one may see, that the Church of *Rome* is not so uniform a Body as she pretends to be, being thus inconsistent with her self in a thing of so high a nature, as that, *of what is,* and *what is not essential to Orders:* and we may see likewise, how she will break thorow all ancient Doctrines and Rules, rather than not disgrace all Bodies of Christians, which deny her Obedience, by unchurching them by some subtilty or other; and indeed, thorow the clearest evidences of matter of Fact, as she does in the case of the Orders of the *Church of England.* And furthermore, how apt she is to look upon her own novel Inventions as the main Substantials of Religion.

To whom I shall only add *Morinus,* whose judgment in a case of this nature is of more

weight

weight, than that of the whole Tribe of School-men. Who in the 1 *Chap.* of his firſt Exercitati-on, *De Sacris Ordinationibus,* ſaith, *Nemo, ut mi-hi videtur, dubitare poteſt, antiquos Latinos, à quibus accepimus & Ordinationes, & quod ſacerdo-tes ſumus, legitimè & validè ſacerdotes conſecraſſe, & cætera ſacrarum Ordinationum munia contuliſſe: Eadem antiquorum Græcorum ratio. Certiſſimum enim eſt & evidentiſſimum, neminem Ordinationes Græcas criminari poſſe, quin crimen in Latinas re-dundet, cum utrique mutuo alterius Ordinationes pro-baverint: Græcuſque apud Latinos, & Latinus a-pud Græcos ſine ullâ unquam Ordinationis querelâ ſacra Myſteria celebraverit: pari veritatis evidentia certum eſt recentiores Latinos in hunc uſque diem le-gitimas Ordinationes celebraſſe & celebrare, eadem ratio hodiernorum Græcorum, cum ut ex iis quæ manifeſtiſſimè* ὰ αὐτοψία *quadam demonſtrata ſunt, ab antiquis non differant, eoſque publicè in ſuis Or-dinibus miniſtrantes ſuſcipiat Eccleſia Romana, ſem-perque ſuſceperit.* And in his ſeventh Exercitati-on, ſpeaking of the delivering the Bread and Cup into the hands of thoſe that are ordained Prieſts, he acknowledgeth it to be a late Cere-mony in the *Roman* Church. *Antiqui Rituales Latini, non ſecus ac Græci, iſtam inſtrumentorum traditionem nobis non exhibent: Quidquid ſpectat ad illam materiam & formam ab iis abeſt. Duo ritus Ordinationis editi, unus Romæ in ſancti Gre-gorii ſacramentario ex Bibliotheca Vaticanâ, alter Pa-riſiis ab Hugone Mainardo, ex Bibliothecâ Corbeienſi, iſta omnia nobis non repræſentant duo antiquiſſimi*

Peta-

*Petaviani literis uncialibus scripti qui præ cæteris
eminent, duo alii secundum istos antiquissimi &
egregiè splendidéque scripti, qui ampli sunt, & multa
Ordinationibus illis exhibent, quæ videri possunt
non necessaria, quorum unus est Rotomagensis, alter
Rhemensis.* Tres alii, *quorum primus Senonensis
est, dno alii Corbeienses, unus à Rodrado scriptus,
nunc vertitur annus octogentesimus primus, alter a.
Rotaldo præcedente multo junior, sed copiosissimus,
qui quæcunque noverat ad Ordinationes pertinere, iis
ditavit Sacramentarium suum ;* denique unus è Bibliothecâ Thuanâ *perantiquus, & alter Bellovacensis.*
In all which ancient *Rituals,* he faith, there is a
profound filence of this Ceremony.

The Council being ended, *Mar Abraham* returned to his Bifhoprick, where he obferved nothing of what he had promifed and fwore, fave
that of ordaining his Priefts again the third time,
at which Ordinations there were feveral *Jefuites,*
who were skilled in the *Syriack* Tongue, that affifted to fee that nothing was omitted that was
effential.

Not long after a Letter of *Mar Abraham* to the
Patriarch of *Babylon* was intercepted, wherein he
informed him of his having been at a Council of
the Bifhops of the *Indies* at *Goa,* whither he had
gone purely out of fear of the *Portuguezes, who,* he
faid, *were over his Head, as a Hammer over an Anvil :*
but when he was there, that he had delivered
in a Profeffion of his Faith, which none of the
Latin Bifhops were able to contradict, profeffing

B 3. him-

himself to his Patriarch a Dogmatist of the *Chaldæan* Faith.

Mar Abraham being grown ancient and very much broke, by the long and unintermitting Persecutions of the *Portuguezes*, was willing to have a *Coadjutor* from *Babylon*, who might, after his Death, also succeed him in his Bishoprick, and accordingly had one *Mar Simeon* sent to him by the Patriarch of *Babylon*.

Mar Simeon was no sooner fixed in the *Serra*, but, finding the People, by reason of his never having had anything to do with the *Latins*, to have a much greater Affection for him than they had for *Mar Abraham*, who, tho' to his Sorrow, had been so much among them, he was encouraged to set up for sole Bishop, and having fixed his *See* at *Carturte*, one of the principal Towns of the Christians of St. *Thomas*, was much favoured by the Queen of *Pimenta*, in whose Territories *Carturte* is.

These two Bishops fell presently to fulminate their Excommunications one against another, to the great disturbance of the whole Diocess, and *Mar Abraham* finding his Adversary to gain ground of him daily, complains of him to the Viceroy and Arch-Bishop of *Goa*, desiring them to drive *Mar Simeon* out of the *Serra*, who was not only an Intruder, but a bitter Enemy to the *Latin* Faith.

The Viceroy, tho' he had no great kindness for *Mar Abraham*, yet considering that he was Bishop of the *Serra*, by the Pope's appointment,

re-

refolved, if it were poffible, to eafe him of his Adverfary, and underftanding that it would be a difficult thing for him to get *Mar Simeon* into his hands by open force, he employed fome *Francifcan* Friars to inveigle him with fair promifes to go to *Rome*, and get the Pope's *Brief* for the Bifhoprick, without which he could never expect to enjoy it peaceably.

Mar Simeon having firft conftituted one *Jacob*, a Parifh Prieft his *Vicar General* during his Abfence, was perfwaded by the Friars to go along with them to *Cochim*, from whence he was fent to *Goa*, and from *Goa* upon the firft Ships to *Portugal*, and from thence to *Rome*, where, after having been examined by the *Inquifition*, he was declared by Pope *Sixtus* V. not to be in Holy Orders, and was with that Sentence upon him fent by the Cardinal St. *Severiana* to *Philip* the Second, who put him into the hands of *Dom Aleixo de Menezes*, whom he was then fending to *Goa*, to be Arch-Bifhop of that place.

Arch-Bifhop *Menezes*, inftead of carrying him along with him to the *Indies*, which was what *Mar Simeon* expected, confined him to a *Francifcan* Convent in *Lisbon*, from whence he is faid to have wrote Letters by every Fleet, that went to the *Indies* to his Vicar-General *Jacob*, and in all his Letters to have ftill ftiled himfelf *Metropolitan of the Indies*, and to have profefs'd the *Chaldæan* Doctrines; thefe Letters were found by Arch-Bifhop *Menezes* in the *Serra*, when he vifited it, by whom they were fent to the chief Tribunal of

the

the General *Inquisition* of *Portugal*, where if they found *Mar Simeon* alive, they doubtless made him change his *Franciscan* Prison for that of the *Inquisition*, where they would take care he should write no more such Letters.

Dom Matthias, Arch-Bishop of *Goa*, having in the Year 1590. called another Provincial Council, did, in conformity to *Gregory* XIII's *Brief*, Summon *Mar Abraham* to repair to it, who being sensible how ill he had complied with what he promised in the former Council, returned no other Answer to the Summons, but a Saying, which, he said, was a Proverb in his Country, *That the Cat that bites a Snake is afraid of her Cord*, intimating thereby, that he durst not trust the *Portuguezes* and *Latin* Bishops any more : After which he dissembled no longer, but in all things declared himself to be of the *Chaldæan* Faith.

Clement VIII. being informed of all this, dispatched a *Brief*, bearing date the 27th. of *January* 1595. wherein he Commanded *Dom Aleixo de Menezes*, Arch-Bishop of *Goa* to make Inquisition into the Crimes and Errors of *Mar Abraham*, and in case he found him guilty of such things as he had been accused of, to have him apprehended and secured in *Goa*, as also to appoint a Governour or *Vicar-Apostolical* of the *Roman* Communion over his Bishoprick, and upon *Mar Abraham*'s Death to take care that no Bishop coming from *Babylon* should be suffered to enter into the *Serra* to succeed.

This

This Brief was delivered to the Arch-Bishop before he went to the *Indies,* by virtue whereof, and in obedience to the Pope's Commands, he made Inquisition into the Crimes and Errors of *Mar Abraham,* and finding him guilty of all that he had been accused of, he sent him his Process without Summoning him to appear at *Goa,* by reason of his having been Bed-rid for some time.

The Arch-Bishop furthermore understanding by the Informations he had taken, that *Mar A-braham,* in conjunction with all the Christians of his Diocess, had sent to the Patriarch of *Babylon* for another *Coadjutor,* Commanded those of *Ormus* and of all other places that lay in the way, under grievous Censures, to stop all *Chaldæan, Persian,* or *Armenian* Ecclesiasticks that should come towards the *Indies* without his Pass. This Order was so punctually executed, that one who came to *Ormus* with the Title of the Arch-Bishop of the *Serra,* was discovered in a disguise, and sent home again. There were several others of those Priests and Bishops who attempted to get into the *Serra* in the Habit of Mariners, were stopt, to the great Grief of the Christians of St. *Thomas,* who, the more they saw their Clergy Persecuted, respected them the more, and grew every day more zealous for their ancient Doctrines and Rites.

The Arch-Bishop being much encouraged by the Success of this diligence, laid the matter of the reduction of this Church to the obedience of the *Roman,* much more to Heart than any of his
Pre-

Predeceſſors had ever done. The firſt he applied himſelf to was *Jacob*, whom *Mar Simeon* had left his *Vicar General*, to whom he writ a long Letter, paſſionately entreating him to throw away the Commiſſion he had from *Mar Simeon*, who was Convicted at *Rome* of not being in Holy Orders, and to ſubmit himſelf to the *Papal Authority* ; making him large Promiſes of what he would do for him, if he complied with his deſires. But *Jacob*, who died preſently after, was deaf to all the Arch-Biſhop could ſay to him, making it his whole buſineſs to enflame his Flock againſt the *Latins*, and their Doctrines.

The Arch-Biſhop did not neglect at the ſame time to write earneſtly to *Mar Abraham*, as alſo to the *Arch-Deacon*, who is the only *Dignitary* in that Church under the Biſhop, and who is employed by him as his *Vicar General*, calling upon them to purge their Dioceſs of the Errors wherewith it had been ſo long infected, and to reduce it to the *Roman* Obedience.

St. *Francis*, about this time, deſtroyed a whole Fleet of *Jores* to the *Portugueze*, who, tho' he was not ſeen by any of the *Portuguezes* in the Fight, which was very bloody on both ſides, yet a Cook who belonged to a *Capuchin* Convent not far off, having hid himſelf in the Ruines of their Church, ſaw a Friar in his own Habit Board the Fleet of *Jores*, one after another, whom he ſo terrified with his very look, as to put them all to flight immediately, and purſued them out of ſight : This formidable Friar was afterwards
diſ-

difcovered to be St. *Francis* ; but tho' the Hiſto-
rian has not been pleaſed to tell us how it came
to be known certainly, he tells us it was an Action very proper for St. *Francis* , who was the
lively Image of *Chriſt*, to appear thus and confound the Enemies of *Chriſtianity*, by ſaying,
It is I. Now, if this Story did not rebuild the
Capuchins ruined Church , the *Portuguezes* were
not ſo grateful as they uſe to be in ſuch caſes.
But this was nothing to what their own St. *An-*
thony did for them five or ſix Years afterwards
in a Land Battle, wherein he was ſeen by ſeveral,
where the greateſt fury of the Battle was, Mow-
ing down whole Squadrons of the Enemy, and
at the ſame time extinguiſhing the Fire of the E-
nemies Artillery with the Sleeve of his Sacred
Habit. There were ſeveral *Portuguezes*, its true,
fell in this Fight, but they muſt have been killed
by ſomething elſe than Fire-Arms, or at leaſt
than Cannon.

In the Year 1584. there came a famous *Ama-*
zon to *Goa*, who had been drove out of her
Country by the *Hidalcaon* ; her name was *Abehi* ;
ſhe had Fought in ſeveral Battles to admiration ;
and tho' when ſhe came to *Goa*, ſhe was 62 years
of Age, ſhe is reported to have had a great deal
of Wit, and the ruines of an exquiſite Beauty ;
ſhe pretended to have buſineſs of great moment
to communicate to the Viceroy, but the Inqui-
ſition, no body knew why, put a ſtop to the Ne-
gotiation ; which, after having kept her Pri-
ſoner for ſome time, baniſhed her to *Ormus*,
from

from whence having made her escape, she went to the Great *Mogul's* Court.

In the Year 1593. the Bull of *Cruzada* was first brought into the *Indies* by *Francisco Faria*, a *Dominican* Friar; and indeed considering how great a Revenue that Bull is to the Pope in *Spain* and *Portugal*, it is very much that it did not find its way into the *Indies* sooner.

When the Arch-Bishop was visiting the City of *Damaon*, he received Letters of the 16th. of *Feb.* 1597. from the Viceroy *Matthias Dalbuquerque*, advising him of the Death of *Mar Abraham*. On the same day he received this news, he in obedience to the Pope's *Brief*, constituted *Francisco Roz*, a *Jesuite*, and who was afterwards made Bishop of the *Serra*, Governour and *Vicar-Apostolical* of the said Diocess.

The *May* following the Arch-Bishop being returned to *Goa*, a Consultation was held about the Affairs of the Church of the *Serra*, where it was unanimously agreed; that notwithstanding the Pope in his *Brief* had commanded none to be made Governour or *Vicar Apostolical* of the Diocess, but what was of the *Roman* Communion, it was convenient to nominate the present Arch-Deacon to it, which they did, joining *Francisco Roz*, and the Rector of the *Jesuites-*College of *Vaipicotta*, in Commission with him. But it being required of the Arch-Deacon, that he shou'd subscribe the Profession of Faith made by *Pius* IV. before he had his Patent he declined doing it, pretending he was not satisfied
with

with having two joyned with him in Commiffion.

The Arch-Bifhop, tho' he was fenfible that it
was the Subfcription that ftuck with him chiefly,
thought fit to diffemble, fo far as to feem to believe him, and by a new Patent conftituted him
the fole Governour of the Bifhoprick.

The Arch-Deacon accepted of this Patent, but
at the fame time declared, That it gave him no
Authority but what he had before; but when
he was called upon to Subfcribe the forementioned Profeffion of Faith, he defired four Months
to confider of it, hoping by that time a Bifhop
might be fent them by the Patriarch of *Babylon,*
when the four Months were expired. Being urged a frefh to Subfcribe, he told them flatly, that
he would never do it, nor fubmit to the *Roman*
Church, which he was fure had nothing to do
with the Apoftolical Church of St. *Thomas,* no
more than that of St. *Thomas* had to do with the
Roman. And not being fatisfied with having
made this Declaration as to himfelf, he furthermore affembled a Synod of moft of the Priefts,
and moft fubftantial Chriftians at *Angamale,* the
Metropolis of the Diocefs, where they all fwore
to ftand by their *Arch-Deacon,* in the defence of
the ancient Faith they and their Fore-fathers had
been bred up in, fo as not to fuffer the leaft alte-
ration to be made therein, nor ever to admit of
any Bifhop, but what fhould be fent them by
the Patriarch of *Babylon* ; of all which they made
a publick Inftrument, and having Sworn to maintain

tain it with their Lives and Fortunes, ordered it
to be publifhed thorow the whole Diocefs.

After the meeting of this Synod, the Chriftians of St. *Thomas* came to be fo far enraged againft
the *Latins*, for what they had done to deftroy
their ancient Faith, and for their having treated
fo many of their Arch-Bifhops, fo barbaroufly as
they had done, that they would fuffer no *Latin*
Prieft to officiate in their Churches, nor fo much
as to live among them. Two *Jefuites*, one at
Angamale, and another at *Carturte*, having very
narrowly efcaped being murdered by them. The
Jefuites, and other *Latin* Priefts, were fo far intimidated, by the fury that Synod had put that
whole Chriftianity into, that for fome time
none of them were found fo hardy, as to venture to go among them.

The news of this great and unexpected Heat,
as it did ftrangely afflict the Arch-Bifhop, who
had fet his Heart fo much on the reducing of
thofe Chriftians; fo it was the thing that made
him refolve to go in Perfon to the *Serra* to try
what his Prefence and Authority would do.

Not only the Viceroy, but the whole Clergy
and Laity, and particularly the whole Chapter of
Goa, together in a body, did all they could, as
it is faid, to diffwade him from fo dangerous an
enterprife, but tho' he was deaf to all the Re-
monftrances of his Friends, yet upon a War
breaking out fuddenly in the Year 1598. betwixt
the Kings of *Mangate* and *Paru*, in whofe Territories moft of thefe Chriftian Churches ftand,
he

he thought fit to put off his Journey for that Year, fatisfying himfelf with writing a Letter to the Arch-Deacon to perfwade him to reconcile himfelf and his Church to that of *Rome*, and acquainting him with his Intentions to vifit all the Churches in the *Serra* in Perfon, fo foon as the forementioned War was over, which he believed would be very fpeedily.

The Arch-Deacon, when he received this Letter, dreading nothing fo much as the Arch-Bifhop's coming in Perfon among them, declared that he had refufed to Subfcribe the forementioned Profeffion of Faith, for no other reafon, but becaufe he was Commanded to do it before the Rector of the *Jefuites* College of *Vaipicotta*, with whom and his whole Order he pretended to be juftly diffatisfied, giving the Arch-Bifhop to underftand at the fame time, that if he would order any other Prieft or Friar to take his Subfcription, that he was ready to make it.

But the Arch-Bifhop looking upon this only as a Trick to throw an *Odium* upon the whole Order of *Jefuites*, and that for no other reafon, but becaufe they were the moft induftrious in the reduction of thofe Chriftians to the *Roman* Faith, would not comply with the Arch-Deacon's Requeft, in naming fome body elfe to take his Subfcription ; for which Conduct the Arch-Bifhop was very much blamed, moft People, and efpecially the other Orders of Friars murmuring againft him, as one grown fo fond of the *Jefuites*, as to lofe the reduction of fo many thoufand Souls,

Souls, rather than difpleafe the *Jefuites.*

But the *Jefuites*, who facrifice all Interefts
and Obligations to the Honour of their Order,
have requited the Arch-Bifhop but very ill for
this his great kindnefs for them, in having reported this Affair fo here in *Europe*, as to rob him
of that which he efteemed his chief Glory, to
wit, the Reduction of this Church to the *Roman*
Faith.

For in the Hiftory of the *Jefuites* in the *Indies*,
publifhed by *Pieire du Jarri*, a *Jefuite*, and printed at *Bourdeaux*, in the Year 1608. we have all
that is faid by the *Portuguezes* of *Mar Abraham*,
and his Arch-Deacon's great averfion to the
Roman Church, and particularly to the whole Order of *Jefuites*, flatly contradicted; for in that
Hiftory we are told that *Mar Abraham* had fuch
an extraordinary kindnefs for the *Jefuites*, that
for fome time before his Death, he put himfelf
fo entirely into their hands, as to be governed
by them in all things; and that the Arch-Deacon
George had fuch an high Opinion of their worth,
as to declare to all the World, that without their
aid and affiftance, he fhould not know after the
Arch-Bifhop's Death, how to Govern the Diocefs.
It is furthermore faid, that *Mar Abraham*, when
he was upon his Death-bed called the Rector of
the College of *Vaipicotta* to him, and having all
his Clergy about him, declared, that he committed his Flock to the Bifhop of *Rome*, as the chief
Paftor and Prelate of the whole Church, and
Commanded the Arch-Deacon, and all his Priefts,

to

to obey the *Jesuites*, whom his *Holiness* had sent
to cultivate that Vineyard in all things, and to
be sure to follow the Doctrines that they taught,
which were the whole truth, and nothing but
the truth; after which Charge he is said furthermore to have beseeched and conjured the Rector,
by *the love of Christ*, and the *great friendship* there
had been always between them, to take care of
the Government of his Church after his Death,
and to have ordered an authentick instrument
to be made of all this to remain as a Testimony
of his last Will, and of the Faith he died in.

The same History furthermore tells us, That
this Church was so far reconciled to the Pope,
in the Year, 1596. that when the *Jubile* of
Clement VIII. was published among them by the
Jesuites, they gave his *Holiness* a thousand Blessings for it, and took a singular pleasure in pronouncing his Name; and that during the whole
time of the *Jubile*, they were at Church from
Morning to Night, without taking any refection,
and were so zealous to confess themselves to the
Fathers, that they waited in the Church till Midnight in great Crowds to do it. Now according to this report of things, the Arch-Bishop,
when he came into the *Serra*, had little more to
do than to open his Arms to embrace a People,
who, being beforehand prepared by the *Jesuites*,
were ready to throw themselves into them.

But to leave Romance, and return to History,
having only observed by the way, that it is visible from this gross misrepresentation of those

C   As-

Affairs, how little regard is to be had to the *Jesuites* Reports of their Feats in the *Indies*; since to support a Story purely invented for the Honour of their Order, they do not boggle to pretend to have an authentick instrument of the truth of it, and that drawn up by the Order of a dying Prelate.

But a thing happened at this time, which, tho' in it self not considerable, did abundantly manifest how little disposed the Clergy of this Church was to submit to the *Pope*.

A Boy, that went to School to the *Jesuites* at *Vaipicotta*, having been taught by them to name the Pope in his Prayers before the Patriarch of *Babylon*, being over-heard doing it in the Church by some of the *Malabar* Priests, was, after they had beat him severely, turned out of the Church; they spoke also to his Father to whip him out of praying for the Pope, who, they said, was none of their Prelate, nor had any thing to do with them. The Arch-Bishop being informed thereof, writ immediately to the Arch-Deacon, commanding him to make Examples of those impudent Hereticks, for what they had said and done to the Boy: which the Arch-Deacon was so far from doing, that he Honoured them the more for it. By the way, the *Jesuites*, teaching their Scholars to pray for the Patriarch of *Babylon*, tho' after the Pope, is one instance, among others, of their Conscience, in those Parts, being subservient to their Policy.

But

But the World continuing still to blame the Arch-Bishop for not putting the Affairs of the *Serra* into some other hands than those of the *Jesuites*, against whose order that whole Church was so much incensed, he was obliged at last, tho' contrary to his Inclination, to send a *Francifcan* Friar to the Arch-Deacon, with authority to take his Subscription to the *Roman* Creed, and to require him to punish the Priests, who had beat the Boy for naming the Pope in his Prayers.

The Arch-Deacon having nothing to object against the *Francifcan* Friar, and being extreamly defirous, if it was possible, to keep the Arch-Bishop from coming into the *Serra*, tho' he refused to Subscribe the Creed of *Pius* IV. yet condescended to Subscribe a Confession of Faith, wherein he professed himself a *Catholick*, and that he believed *as the Church believed*, but without naming the *Roman*, or acknowledging the Pope as universal Pastor of the Church; he is furthermore said, upon the Arch-Bishop's signifying his dissatisfaction at the ambiguous Profession he had made, to have given his consent publickly to that of *Pius* IV. being read to him in *Portugueze*, of which he did not understand a Syllable. But let that be as it will, it is certain that he continued still to teach, that the Pope was the head of his own Church, but had nothing to do with that of St. *Thomas*.

The

The Arch-Bishop not being able to brook such things any longer, fix'd a day for his going towards the *Serra*, and when the Viceroy and the whole Clergy beg'd of him not to expose his Person to such visible danger, they could have no other answer from him but this, *That his life was but too secure in this case, seeing he had never merited enough to entitle him to the Honour of being a Martyr.* However, left his Humility might deceive him in passing a Judgment upon himself, he did not think fit to trust too much to his want of Merits; and for that reason went attended with a good Guard, he had also a Commission to treat with all the Princes of *Malabar*, about Peace and War, and particularly to engage the *Samorin* to assist the *Portugueze* to take *Cunahle*, a Fortress lately possessed by a company of *Mahometan* Pyrates, who did very much disturb the *Portugueze* Trade upon that Coast. This Nest of Pyrates, was first built by one *Pate Marca*, a *Mahometan*, who having in a short time enriched it strangely with the Spoils of the *Portuguezes*, both by Sea and Land, left it at his Death to his Nephew *Mahomet Cunahle Marca*. This *Mahomet* was Governour, or rather Prince of it at this time; and as he was nothing inferior to his Uncle in Courage or Conduct, so he had Fortified the place so as to make it absolutely one of the strongest Garrisons in the *Indies*, neither did he insult the *Portuguezes* only, but the *Malabars* also, and particularly the *Samorim*, in whose Country *Cunahle* stood, and who had given
leave

leave to his Uncle to fortifie that place, on purpose to incommode the *Portugueze*.

And tho' the *Portugueze* Historians will have
it, that he took this Affair of *Cunable* only in the
way to his Visitation; yet by the course of his pro-
cedure, one would be tempted to think, that
it was what principally carried him to those
Parts.

On the 27*th*. of *December*, 1598. the Arch-
Bishop Embarked upon a Gally Commanded by
Don Alvaro de Menezes, and on the day of *Epiphany*, arrived at the Bar of *Cunable*, where he
joined the whole *Portugueze* Armada, Commanded by the Viceroy's Brother, he was saluted
with all the Guns and Musick of the Fleet;
and having called a Council of War, and heard
the several Opinions of all the Captains concerning the best way to take *Cunable*, he dispatched the resolution they had come to thereon, to the
Council of State at *Goa*; a most Apostolical beginning of a Visitation. After having put the Siege of
Cunable into a good Posture, he departed with
a good Convoy to *Cananor*, where he continued
16 days, and then sailed to *Cochim*, where he
was splendidly received by the Governour and
the whole City, at the Stairs they had made on
purpose for him to Land at.

Next day, when the Magistrates of the City
came to Complement him at his House, he acquainted them with his design of reducing the
Christians of St. *Thomas* before he returned to

Goa, defiring their affiftance therein, which they frankly promifed him.

The day following His *Grace* having called the common Council of the City together, re-commended the enterprife of *Cunahle* to them, whom he made fo fenfible of how great impor-tance it was to their City above all others, to have that Fortrefs wrefted out of the hands of the *Mahometan* Pyrates, who had lately made themfelves Mafters of it, that they immediately caufed 150 Men to be Raifed and Armed at their own Charge, whom, together with a great quantity of all forts of Ammunition, they fent upon five ftout Ships to joyn the *Armada* before *Cunahle*; the Arch-Bi-fhop alfo, to give the more life to the enterprife, fent one of the beft of his own *Manchua's* or Yachts, mann'd with his own menial Servants, along with them.

The King of *Cochim* was much troubled to hear of the Arch-Bifhop's being fo hot upon the re-duction of *Cunahle*, being fenfible that a Peace betwixt the *Portuguezes* and the *Samorim*, with-out whofe affiftance by Land, it wou'd be hard for them to reduce that Fortrefs, muft be the Con-fequence of the enterprife. And as there had been nothing, the Kings of *Cochim* had been always more careful to hinder fuch a Peace, which they than did on purpofe to keep the *Portuguezes* in a clofer dependance upon them; fo the prefent King fol-lowing the wife meafures of his Anceftors, en-deavour'd, by a Stratagem, to deftroy the Con-fidence he faw the *Portuguezes* had already repo-
fed

fed in the *Samorim*. To which end he fent
his *Chief Juftice*, and one *Joan de Miranda*,
a Gentleman of *Cochim*, to wait upon the *Arch-
Bifhop* and to acquaint his *Grace* from him, that
he had received certain advice from fome Spies
he had in the *Samorim* Cabinet-Council, that that
Prince, whenever the *Portuguezes* Landed, inftead of joyning with them, had determined
to cut them all off in revenge of the many Injuries they had done his Anceftors, of which
danger he thought himfelf obliged, both as a
Friend and a Brother in Arms to the King of
Portugal to advife him.

The *Arch-Bifhop*, who underftood the In-
trigues of Princes, as well as any Man living,
returned the King his Thanks for his Intelligence,
but withal fent him word, that they were refolved to truft the *Samorim* in this occafion; and
the rather, becaufe they did not want Power to
be revenged on all that fhould deceive the King
of *Portugal* either in Peace or War.

The King, when he found his Plot had not
fucceeded according to his expectation, refolved
to divert the *Samorim* from fending an Army to
Cunahle, by making a War prefently upon the
Caimal, or Prince of *Corugeira* his Friend and
Allie : and having with incredible expedition
got an Army of 60000 Men together, he fent
to let the *Arch-Bifhop* know, that before he
marched he defigned to wait upon him. The
Arch-Bifhop, tho' he did not go over his Threfhold
to meet the King, received him, when he came,

with great Civility; and after the Complements were over, acquainted him firft, with his Intention of vifiting all the *Chriftian Churches* in the *Serra*, in order to reduce them to the true Chriftian Faith, from which they had very much fwerved; telling him, that fince great numbers of thofe Churches were within his Territories, he expected his affiftance in fo good a work; of which being affured by the King, the *Arch-Bifhop* went on and told him, that there was another thing that he muft not deny him, and that was to put off his War with the *Caimal* till *Cunahle* was taken; the King gave many reafons why he could not deferr it; but the *Arch-Bifhop* preft him fo hard upon the point, that before they parted, he made him promife to disband his Army.

The *Arch-Bifhop* having put the Affairs of the Siege in a good pofture, begun to apply himfelf to the reduction of the Chriftians of St. *Thomas*, and the firft ftep he made towards it, was to fend to the *Arch-Deacon* to come and fpeak with him at *Cochim*. But after having expected him fome days, and finding that he neither came himfelf, nor returned him any anfwer, he concluded, as well he might, that he was afraid to venture himfelf in that City; whereupon he fent him a Letter of *fafe Conduct*, fwearing he would not queftion him about any thing that was paft.

The *Arch-Deacon*, upon this occafion, Affembled a great number of *Caçanares*, and other con-

confiderable Chriftians to confult together what was beft to be done.   It was agreed on all hands, that the *Arch-Deacon* fhou'd go and wait upon his *Lordſhip*, who was a Perfon of that Authority as to be able to undo them all at once, by depriving them of their *Pepper*-Trade, if they fhould difoblige him, and befides, he was able to oblige their Kings, who were all very much at his Devotion, to Sacrifice all their Lives and E-ftates to his difpleafure ; and what made them the willinger to comply with him therein, was, their being confident that they fhould be quickly rid of his Company, fince Winter was at hand, which they thought would certainly call him to *Goa.*

Upon all which Confiderations it was agreed, That they fhould give way to his faying of *Maſs*, and his Preaching in their Churches, which their Books told them was a common Civility, that is every where paid to Bifhops, tho' out of their own Dioceffes ; but as for any Acts of Jurifdiction, fuch as Vifiting, Conferring Orders, Excommunicating, and the like, if he fhould pretend to exercife any fuch Acts, as it was to be feared he would, that they fhou'd then put him off as well as they cou'd with delays, until he returned to *Goa,* which they thought he would in two Months at fartheft ; by which means they might, without embroiling themfelves with fo powerful a Prelate, wait till they had a Bifhop fent them by the Patriarch of *Babylon,* to whom they had writ for one ; of all which they made a publick

lick Inftrument, and for their further Security, brought together a Body of 3000 brave Men, who were all well Armed; the Chriftians of St. *Thomas* being, by much, both the ftouteft and beft Firemen in the *Indies*, as the *Portuguezes* knew very well, which made them be the more zealous to reduce them to the *Roman Church*, in order to make them Subjects to the King of *Portugal*.

The *Arch-Bifhop* fent alfo at the fame time to fome of their *Paniquais*, fome of which have 4000, fome 6000 Men at their Command, to come and fpeak with him at *Cochim*; but they, inftead of going thither, took an Oath folemnly to make themfelves *Amouços*, after the Cuftom of the *Malavars*, againft him, in cafe he offer'd any violence to their *Arch-Deacon*, or to any other of their Priefts. When the *Malavars* devote themfelves to be *Amouços* for any caufe, they defend it to the laft drop of their Blood, without either fear or wit.

With two of thefe *Paniquais*, and 3000 Men well Armed, the *Arch-Deacon* came to wait upon the *Arch-Bifhop* at *Cochim*. *Don Antonio de Noronha*, the Governour of the City, met them without the Gates, and conducted them to the *Arch-Bifhop*'s Palace. The *Arch-Deacon*, when he came before the *Arch-Bifhop* kneeled down and kifs'd his Hand, as did all the other *Caçanares* that were in his Company; the two *Paniquais* were alfo prefented to his *Lordfhip* by the *Arch-Deacon*, who when the *Arch-Bifhop*, and the *Governour*,
and

and the *Arch-Deacon* came to sit down, placed themselves at the Elbows of the *Arch-Bishop's* Chair, where they stood all the while with their broad Swords naked over his Head. The door of the Room where they were being shut, to keep out the Crowd, those that stood without imagining that it was done to make their *Arch-Deacon* a Prisoner, said to one another, this is the time to die for our *Arch-Deacon*, and for the Church of St. *Thomas*, but being assured that their *Arch-Deacon* was in no danger, they were quieted.

After the hubbub was over, and they had discoursed together for some time, it was agreed, that the *Arch-Bishop* should go next day to *Vaipicotta*, which upon the account of its having a College of *Jesuites* in it, should be the first Church he should Visit, and that the *Arch-Deacon* with his *Caçanares*, should repair thither immediately.

The *Arch-Bishop* having furnished himself with all Necessaries for his Voyage, embarked with all his Retinue upon seven *Tones* or *Gallies*, and *Roque de Mello Pereyro*, who had been Governour of *Malaca*, attended him with two *Gallies* more, and *Joan Pereyra de Miranda*, who was afterwards Governour of *Cranganor* with one.

Being arrived at *Vaipicotta*, he was conducted by the *Jesuites*, and their Scholars, and the whole Village to the Church, where, with his *Mitre* on his Head, and his *Crosier* in his hand, he gave them a long Sermon. His Text was, *He that*

enter-

entereth not in by the door, &c. on which words he told them at length, *That none were true Pastors, but what entered in by the door of the* Roman *Church, and were sent by the Pope, who was Christ's Vicar; which none of their former Prelates having been, who had been all sent to them by the Schismatical Bishops of* Babylon, *they were all Thieves and Murderers of the Flock.* When he had done his Sermon, he bid them come next day to the Church to be confirmed, which some did; to whom, after he had confirmed them, he told the news of *Purgatory,* a place most of them had never heard of before.

All this while no *Arch-Deacon* appeared, who came not to *Vaipicotta,* till two days after the arrival of the *Arch-Bishop.* He had delayed his coming on purpose, that he might not by his presence, seem to consent to any of those things, which he knew the *Arch-Bishop* would offer to do at that place.

Tho' the *Arch-Bishop* knew well enough what it was that had made the *Arch-Deacon* loiter so behind, yet he dissembled so far as to receive him very kindly, treating with him about the course he was to take in the reduction of the Church, who seemed to approve of every thing that was proposed to him.

The *Arch-Bishop* went daily to *Matins* and *Vespers,* which were sung by those of the Seminary in *Chaldee,* but coming to understand at last, for he understood *Chaldee* no more than he did *Malavar,* that they prayed therein for the Patriarch

arch of *Babylon*, ftiling him the *Univerfal Paftor of the Church*, a Title that all Patriarchs, as well as the Pope, have affumed to themfelves for fome Hundred of Years (nay, by what *Gregory* I. has faid of that Title, I do not know but the Pope might be one of the laft that affumed it) he refolved not to permit fo wicked a thing to be done any longer, notwithftanding all that the good *Jefuites*, who out of Policy had all along complyed with it, could fay to diffwade him; and fo having one Evening, without communicating his defign to any one, called all the *Jefuites*, Mafters of the Seminary, and the *Arch-Deacon*, and his *Caçanares*, together at his Lodgings, having firft made a Speech to them to prove, *That the* Pope *was the only Head of the Church on Earth, and that the Bifhop of* Babylon *was a Heretick and Schifmatick*, he pulled out of his Pocket an Excommunication *latæ fententiæ*, commanding his Secretary to read it with an audible Voice, and his Interpreter to declare it to thofe that did not underftand *Latin*, in *Malavar*, by which he Commanded, *That no Perfon Secular or Ecclefiaftick do from henceforward prefume to pray for the* Patriarch of Babylon. He Commanded the *Arch-Deacon* and *Caçanares* to fign it, and finding the *Arch-Deacon* had a great mind to have fhuffled it off, he faid to him, *Sign it, Father, for it is full time the Axe were laid to the Root of the Tree*; to which the *Arch-Deacon* returned no anfwer, but Signed it without faying a word, as did all the other *Caçanares*, after which

it

it was fixed to the Gates of the Church.

The Chriſtians of the Village, when they came to hear of what had been done, run, as if they had been Mad, in a Body to the *Arch-Deacon's* Lodgings, where, with one voice, they ſet up a moſt lamentable howl, crying out, *That the Arch-Biſhop of* Goa, *with his* Portuguezes *was come to deſtroy their Religion, and had affronted their* Patriarch, *by whom they had been Governed for above* 1200 *Years* ; and after having exclaimed againſt the *Arch-Biſhop* at a moſt bitter rate, and bewailed their great Miſery, in having Strangers come among them to deſtroy the Religion they had been born and bred in, they told their *Caſſanares*, that if they would but give way to it, they would either Sacrifice their Lives in defence of their Religion, or be revenged on thoſe that had affronted it.

But the *Arch-Deacon* having made a ſign, that he deſired to be heard, they all held their Peace, he told them, *There was a time for all things, and that that was not a time for Revenge, but Diſſimulation* ; *that it was true he had Signed the Excommunication, but that he did it purely out of Fear,* for they were to conſider, that, beſides the Strength the Arch-Biſhop *had brought along with him, he had engaged the King of* Cochim, *in whoſe Country they were, to protect him in all he did, and who, if they ſhould offer any affront to the* Arch-Biſhop, *would certainly revenge it on their Lives and Eſtates. As to himſelf, he was reſolved to die in defence of the Religion of his Country, ſooner than conſent to the*
intro-

introduction of Popery ; adding, *The* Portuguezes, *if they liked their own Religion, might live in it, in* God's *Name, and he knew no Body that would trouble them for it ; but that he saw no reason why they should thus disturb and persecute People in their own Country, because they will not turn* Papists, *or change their* old Religion *for theirs, and that as to the* Arch-Bishop, *the thing that made him so furious to destroy the Authority of the* Patriarch of Babylon *was, that he might make himself Primate of the* Indies ; *to which he hoped, none of the Christians of* Malabar *would ever consent, or would ever be perswaded to forsake their* old Religion *for that of* Popery. At this they all gave a great shout, crying, *They would lose their Lives, and all they had in the World, before they would do it.* But none of the forementioned *Amoucos* being among them, it's like, at that time they went no further.

The *Portuguezes* upon this uproar, did not forbear to blame the *Arch-Bishop,* for having published such an *Excommunication,* contrary to the advice of all that were about him, advising him to hasten aboard his Galleys if he would secure his Person ; he told them, *He was so far from repenting for what he had done, that were it to do again, he would do it, and that instead of retreating to* Cochim, *he would go next Morning to* Paru.

Paru is the *Metropolis* of a Kingdom, wherein the noblest Body of all the Christians of St. *Thomas* lives, but withal, the most violent against *Popery,* as they had sufficiently manifested on several occasions ;

cafions; for tho' *Don Jorge du Cruz*, and *Don Joan du Cruz*, both Natives of the Country, had been fent by the *Portuguezes* to *Rome* in the time of *Gregory* XIII. who had done them great Honours there, and had granted them many *Indulgences* for their Churches, and withal, a Privileged Altar therein, yet their Countrymen did not only flight all thofe *Indulgences*, but would not fo much as fuffer them, tho' of two of the nobleft Families in the Country, to officiate in any of their Churches, and at laft forc'd them to leave the Kingdom, their own Brethren and Kinsfolk, having the firft hand in their expulfion.

The Chriftians of *Paru*, tho' thus affected to the *Roman* Church, had, according to the forementioned Agreement, prepared great *Feftivities* for the reception of the *Arch-Bifhop*, hoping, by fuch Complements, to have kept him from doing any bufinefs; but, having the Night before he came, heard of what he had done at *Vaipicotta* to their Patriarch, they turned all their *Feftivities* into *Arms*, and were fo much incenfed againft him, that when he Landed, he was met by eight or ten Perfons only that waited on the *Arch-Deacon*.

The *Arch-Bifhop*, tho' he read trouble and dejection in all their Countenances, feemed to take no notice of it, but with his *Crofs* carried before him went directly to the Church, which, contrary to Cuftom, he found full of Armed Men, without fo much as one Woman or Child amongft mongſt them ; whereupon, being apprehenſive leſt his Guards and Servants, if they continued aſhoar, might come to Blows with the *Malavars*, whom he ſaw ſo much diſpoſed to Quarrel, he Commanded them all aboard except two Prieſts, who were to aſſiſt at the Offices.

The *Arch-Biſhop* having put on his *Pontificals*, and given his Bleſſing to the Congregation, made a long diſcourſe to them, ſhewing them , *That there was but one true Religion*, *which was the* Roman, *and that all Chriſtians were under an indiſpenſable obligation to ſubmit themſelves to the* Pope. After he had done his Sermon, which laſted an hour and an half, and explained to them the Doctrine of the Sacrament of *Confirmation*, and then called upon them to come to it; the Congregation, tho' they had heard him till then very quietly, began to cry out with great fury, *That they would never be Confirmed by him, that being a thing that none of their Prelates had ever uſed, and that it was no Sacrament of Chriſt's Inſtitution, but an Invention of the* Portuguezes *to make them their Slaves, by* ſetting a Mark on their Foreheads, *and* giving them a Box on the Ear, which is what all the *Roman* Biſhops do in *Confirmation, and tho' the* Daſtards *in* Vaipicotta *had been ſo tame as to ſuffer themſelves to be buffered and enſlaved by him, they would never endure it, nor ſuffer him to touch their Beards, or their Wives Faces ; that he might go home in a good hour to his* Portuguezes, *and let them alone with their Religion, and if he did continue to diſturb them thus, it ſhould*

D *coſt*

coſt him dear. The *Arch-Biſhop* heard all this with great patience, and ſitting down, endeavoured to convince them of the Truth of the Sacrament of *Confirmation*; but when he perceived that they were the worſe, rather than the better for what he ſaid to them, having muſtered all his Courage together, he roſe up, and having advanced two ſteps with his *Croſier* in his hand, he told them with great heat, *That the Faith he Preached to them was the Faith of* Chriſt *and St.* Thomas, *and was believed by all Chriſtians, and that he was ready to die to confirm the truth of it*; but they being as ready to die for their Religion as he was, or pretended to be, for his, that Argument had no effect at all upon them. He furthermore challenged all thoſe that *Talked againſt the* Roman *Faith by Night in Corners, to come forth, if they durſt, to diſpute with him publickly*; which the *Arch-Deacon*, who the Night before had aſſembled moſt of the conſiderable Chriſtians of *Paru* together, and had made them promiſe never to throw off the *Patriarch* of *Babylon*, taking to himſelf, he roſe up in a paſſion, and having asked aloud *who they were that taught Hereſies in the dark, and that Preached no where but in Corners*, flung out of the *Church*, and going into the Town picked up eight or ten Boys, whom he preſented to the *Arch-Biſhop* to be confirmed by him, pretending, that with all that he was able to do, he could perſwade no more to come: The *Arch-Biſhop* having confirmed theſe Boys, returned to his Gallies very angry, and

and finding there was nothing more to be done
at *Paru*, he determined to Sail next Morning to
Mangate, to fee how thofe *Chriftians* ftood affected.

When he came to the Church of *Mangate*, a
Town chiefly inhabited by Chriftians, he found
the Church filled with Houfhold Goods and Women, by reafon of the War that was then on foot
between the Kings of *Mangate* and *Paru*. After
having comforted the Chriftians for the Loffes
they had fuftained, and given them his Bleffing,
he began to Preach againft the Errors they had
been Educated in. But having advice that there
were fome *Amouços* coming after him from *Paru*,
he went ftraightways aboard his Gallies, and row-
ing away before Night, he arrived next Morning at *Cheguree*, a place belonging to his Friend
the King of *Cochim* ; where having fent afhore an
Order to the *Caçanares* and *Chriftians* to meet
him at the Church, he had word fent him,that the
Church doors were all fhut, and there was neither Man, Woman, nor Child, to be feen in
the whole Village ; he was informed at Night,
that the *Arch-Deacon* was in the Town, but
that he had fhut himfelf up in a Houfe, and was
refolved never to fee his *Lordfhip* again.

The *Portuguezes* that were in his Train, as well
Ecclefiafticks as Seculars, were at him perpetually
to give over this enterprife, and not to expofe
his Perfon and Dignity (as he did) to no purpofe ;
but inftead of returning any anfwer to their

D 2   Impor-

Importunities, he retired all alone to his *Cabin*, where he wrote a long Letter to the *Arch-Deacon*, in which he swore that he remembred nothing that was past, and that he had no design of doing him any harm, and if he would but do him the favour to come and speak with him once more, he did not doubt but that he should be able to convince him of his Errors, promising with all to do great things for him, if he would but entirely submit himself to the *Roman* Church.

This Letter was delivered the same Night to the *Arch-Deacon*, who having read it, called the *Caçanares* together, and told them, that it being a scandalous thing in them to decline treating with the *Arch-Bishop* above-board, about the Affairs of Religion, he was for their going to wait upon him to hear what he could say, but with such a Guard, that it should not be in his Power to make them Prisoners. Having all agreed to this Proposition, they sent to the *Arch Bishop* to let him know, That if he would be pleased to come ashoar, they would wait upon him: The *Arch-Bishop* sent them back word, That the Sun was too hot to stand in, and desired them therefore to come aboard his Galley, which lay with her *Stern* on ground. The *Arch-Deacon* and *Caçanares* seeing the Galley quite surrounded by their People ventured to go aboard; where being come, they were conducted to the *Arch-Bishop's* Cabin, where they found him with all his Priests, *Jesuites*, and several Gentlemen expecting them. After some discourse, the *Arch-*
                                                                    Deacon

Deacon told the *Arch-Bifhop*, *That it was true they had not received his* Grace *fo courteoufly as might have been expected, nor indeed as they intended to have done,* had he not fallen fo foul upon their Patriarch, *whom, tho' he had been pleafed to call an Excommunicate Heretick,* they knew to be both a *Catholick and a moft holy Man, and endeavoured to introduce feveral Novelties into the* Serra, *which they and their Forefathers had never fo much as heard of before.* To all which the *Arch-Bifhop* anfwered, *That he was fure they were not ignorant of the* Patriarch *of* Babylon's *being a Profeffed* Neftorian, *and not to trouble them with any Arguments to prove that all* Neftorians *muft be Hereticks, he would only ask them one fingle Queftion,* which was, *Whether they believed the Gofpel of St.* John? They told him *they did, and would die rather than deny any thing that was revealed in it. Well then,* faid the *Arch-Bifhop, pray tell me, how you can reconcile what St.* John *faith,* The word was made Flefh, and dwelt among us, *with what your Patriarchs and Bifhops have taught you, to wit,* that the Word did not make it felf Flefh, and that Chrift was not God, and that God did not make himfelf Man, *for do you not fing in your Churches upon the Feaft of the Nativity, that the Word did not make it felf Flefh, as the unbelieving* Romans *teach, but did only dwell in Chrift as in a Temple.*

The *Arch-Deacon* returned no anfwer to this, but paffing to another point, faid to the *Arch-Bifhop, Your* Grace *would fain perfwade us likewife, that none can be faved out of the Obedience of the*

D 3　　　　　Ro

Roman *Church*, which is what *St.* John *no where
faith, that ever I could fee*; *befides, we have in our*
Archives *a Letter of St.* Caius, *Bifhop of* Rome,
*wherein he confeffeth that he had nothing to do with
the Church of* Babylon, *no more than the Church of*
Babylon *had to do with his Church. We have alfo
another Letter, which is called in our Books the*
Letter of the Lord's-day, *becaufe it is faid upon
that day to have fallen down from Heaven, wherein the fame Truth is affirmed.* Here the *Arch-Bifhop*
run into a long difcourfe of the Primacy of
St. *Peter*, and of the *Pope's* being his Succeffor,
and *Chrift's Vicar* upon Earth; after which they
came at laft to this Agreement, That as to matters
of Faith, a Synod fhould be called to determine
them; and that in the mean while the *Arch-Bifhop* might, if he pleafed, give the Bleffing, and
Preach in any of their Churches, but fhould not
be received in them as their Prelate, but as a
Bifhop that was a Stranger, neither fhould he
pretend to *Confirm*, or do any other Epifcopal
Act within that Diocefs. This Agreement was
Signed by the *Arch-Bifhop* and the *Arch-Deacon*,
and all the *Caçanares* who were prefent, with a
Declaration that the Synod fhould be Celebrated
before *Whitfuntide*, and that the *Arch-Deacon*
fhould no longer ftir up the People againft him,
nor go attended with fuch Troops of Armed
Men as he had done formerly.

This Agreement being Signed, the *Arch-Bifhop* fet Sail for *Canhur*, whither the *Arch-Deacon*
went by Land, not daring to truft himfelf by
Wa-

Water, where he would have been in the Power
of the *Portuguezes.*

At *Canhur* he was received very friendly by
the *Chriſtians,* who had been told by the *Arch-
Deacon,* that he did not pretend to come among
them as their Prelate, but only as a Stranger, but
tho' he kept to his Agreement ſo far as not to offer to do any thing but give the Bleſſing and
Preach, yet in his *Sermon,* which was a very long
one, he talked ſo much of the *Roman Church,*
and its *Supremacy,* and of the obligation all
Churches were under to ſubmit to it, that the
whole Congregation were much offended with
him ; the *Arch-Deacon* was likewiſe diſcontented
with it, and being Sick, or at leaſt pretending he
was, returned to *Cheguree* to be cured ; and the
Arch-Biſhop having other work on his hands, was
willing enough to diſmiſs him ; who, in purſu-
ance of the Inſtruction he brought with him from
Goa, was obliged to haſten to *Coulaon,* a Fortreſs
belonging to the *Portuguezes,* to ſee in what
condition it was, and to take ſome courſe to
have the Fort the King of *Travancor* was building in its Neighbourhood, and would much incommode it, demoliſhed.

On the firſt of *March* he ſet Sail for a Caſtle
that is within two Leagues of *Cochim,* where the
Governour and Biſhop of the City met him, to
whom having communicated his Deſigns, he
Sailed directly for *Porcoa,* where the King of the
Country had been ſome days expecting him ; he
went to a Church that was there in the Evening,

where

where he was kindly received by the *Christians* ; the King, who professed a great Friendship for the *Portuguezes*, having Commanded them, upon pain of his displeasure, to comply with the *Arch-Bishop* in all things. After having Preached, he went to Lodge at the House of the *Caçanar*, whither the King came at Night to visit him ; the *Arch-Bishop* entertained him very friendly, and thanked him for the kindness he had shewed to the *Christians* of St. *Thomas*, and their Churches, and for having cleared his Coast of Pyrates : the King, after some Complements desired to be admitted to the Honour of being a *Brother in Arms* to the King of *Portugal*, as the King of *Cochim* had been : The *Arch-Bishop* told him, that was an Honour the King of *Portugal* never did to any King, before he had merited it by some signal Service ; however, he promised to do all that lay in his Power to help him to it.

Next Morning the *Arch-Bishop* went to Church, where he said *Mass*, and afterwards confirmed the whole Congregation, notwithstanding his late solemn Promise to the contrary, as indeed none but Fools will ever expect, that *Papists* will observe any such Promises longer than the first opportunity they have to break them.

From *Porcoa* he sailed directly to *Coulaon*, where, under pretence of visiting a Church that stood near the Fort the King of *Travancor* was building, he took a view of the Fort, and finding it was near finished, and would in a few days have a Garrison put in it, he immediately dispatched

patched away a Meſſenger to the Captain-General of the Fleet and Troops that were before *Cunahle*, to come forthwith with his whole *Armada*
to demoliſh the ſaid Fort, which, if he came quickly, he might do with great eaſe, for that he
would find none in it but Workmen.

Now you muſt know that the *Arch-Biſhop*,
when he was laſt at the Bar of *Cunahle*, notwithſtanding that the King of *Travancor* and the *Portuguezes* were at that time in Peace, had left a
private Order with the General, that ſo ſoon as
he was Maſter of *Cunahle*, he ſhould ſet Sail immediately with the whole *Armada*, and demoliſh
this Fort, which, by reaſon of *Cunahle's* not being
yet taken, had not been executed.

But while the *Arch-Biſhop* was expecting the
Captain-General, he received the bad news of a
great ſlaughter of *Portuguezes* in an Attack they
had made upon *Cunahle*, and that the Captain-
General was retired to *Cochim* to have his wounded Men cured; from whence he intended to
come and wait upon him for further Orders.

The *Arch-Biſhop* was extreamly troubled at this
News, as well upon the account of the great
numbers of Perſons of Quality that had been
killed in the Action, as becauſe he feared it would
very much hearten the Kings of *Malabar*, who
had till then ſtill looked upon the *Portuguezes* as
Invincible. Wherefore, to prevent the ill effects
that the true News of this Defeat might have upon the Minds of the Princes of *Malabar*, he diſpatched Letters immediately to all of them to
acquaint

acquaint them with the great Victory the *Portuguezes* had obtained before *Cunahle* ; and tho' he acknowledged, that it was purchased with the Blood of several brave Men, among whom were some of his own Kindred, who were very dear to him, yet he did not doubt but that they would infallibly carry the Place, at the next Attack they made.

These tricks of the *Arch-Bishop* coming so thick, one upon the neck of another, for here we have no fewer than three of them in less than a Fortnight, puts me in mind of what *Manuel de Faria* saith of him in the 3*d.* Tome of his *Asia Portuguesa*, which I shall give the Reader in his own words, " Este illustre Prelado estuviera yo por ventura " en el numero de los santos, si no passara a " Espanna a donde le quito esta gloria , en la " opinion mortal, la deficil del acierto en el " maneio de los grandes puestos que vinoa ocupar, " o fuessen solicitudos, o fuessen ofrecidos. *This Illustrious Prelate, had he never returned to* Spain, *had, in all probability, been made a Saint before this time, where, thro' the difficulty there is in the managery of high Posts, whether offered to him or procured by Sollicitations, he lost all the Glory he had acquired in the* Indies *in the Opinion of the World.*

His High Posts in *Spain*, which the Author saith he does not know whether he procured by Sollicitations or not, were the *Primacy of Braga,* and *Viceroyship of Portugal*, under *Philip* III. for two Years, and the *Presidentship* of the *Council of State*

State of *Portugal* at *Madrid,* in which Office and
Court he died.

What his Miscarriages were in *Spain,* whereby
he is said to have forfeited his Glory, I have not
been able to learn; but whatever they were, one
would think that the violating of a solemn Agreement openly, within a Week after it was made,
and the ordering a Fort belonging to a Prince,
that was in Peace with them, to be treacherously
demolished, and the dispersing of notorious
Falshoods only to serve a turn, ought to be no
very good title to *Saintship.* But the *Arch-Bishop,*
if he could have had hands to have executed it,
had served the King of *Travancor* a much worse
trick than this, when he was upon his Visitation
that was after the Synod. We are told of a lively thing spoke by a *Portugueze* Captain, that was
very brave, but had scarce Bread to eat, who,
in this Siege, having seven of his Teeth struck out
with a Musquet-Bullet, after he had wiped his
Mouth said, *The* Mahometan *had done him no
Injury, and had known doubtless he had no need of
Teeth.* But to return to the Story.

The *Arch-Bishop,* after having sent this false
News about, and having sent to the Queen of
Changanate, to let her know, that he should not
be able to meet her according to his Promise,
until he returned; Sailed in great haft to *Cochim,*
to conferr with the Captain-General, and to
consult whether it would not be convenient to
make an absolute Peace with the *Samorim,* and
the rather because he had been so true to his
                                         Word,

Word, in carrying on the Siege of *Cunahle.* It was agreed on all hands that such a Peace would be convenient at that time; however, they would not venture to conclude it before they had the *Viceroy's* Opinion of it, to whom they sent the Project.

The *Arch-Bishop,* after he had dispatched this business, Sailed to *Molandurte,* a great place of Christians, where he was received very kindly, which kindness of theirs is said to have cost them dear; for the King of *Cochim,* to whom *Molandurte* belongs, being grown extreamly jealous that the *Arch-Bishop,* under a pretence of reducing the Christians of St. *Thomas* to the obedience of the *Roman Church,* designed to bring them under the obedience of the Crown of *Portugal,* as it is plain he did from the 24*th Decree* of the last *Action* of the following *Synod,* for this very reason laid a great Tribute upon them, which they have not been able to this day to shake off; and furthermore Commanded them, upon pain of Death, to repair to *Angamale* to their *Arch-Deacon,* who being there, and having heard, it's like, of the *Arch-Bishop's* having violated their Agreement within less than a Week after it was made, begun to thunder out Excommunications against him, writing to all his Churches to have nothing more to do with him, and to all the Princes of *Malabar,* to have a care of him as a Person that had ill designs upon their Subjects.

While

While the *Arch-Bishop* was at *Molandurte*, where he confirmed and exercised all Episcopal Acts, he received Letters from the *Viceroy* approving his Project of Peace with the *Samorim*, and desiring him to return to *Vaipim* to Sign it, which he did in great haste, as did the Governour and Bishop of *Cochim* also, who both met him there.

This Peace was much promoted on the *Samorim* side by his Nephew and first Minister *Uniare Cherare*, who, notwithstanding he had been privately Christned by Father *Roz*, had leave to continue to Profess himself a Heathen still, the better to enable him to serve the *Portuguezes*, which he did effectually, both by communicating to them daily all the Secrets of his Uncles Cabinet-Council, whereof he was President, and by disposing him to have a good opinion of the *Portuguezes*; which was what he would not have been in a capacity to have done, but would have been immediately disgraced, and turned out of all, had he discovered himself to have been a Christian so soon as he was Baptized. And as for the *Arch-Bishop*, we find he was so far from condemning either the Prince or the Jesuite for this scandalous dissimulation, that after the Celebration of the Synod he confirmed and anointed the Prince therein, by giving him the Sacrament of *Chrism* or *Confirmation*, with the same Secresie, and the same Dispensation as the Jesuite had given him that of Baptism.

After

After he had difpatched the Peace, Signed to the Captain-General, he fet Sail for *Diamper*, the ancient Seat of feveral of the Bifhops of the *Serra*, where meeting with feveral that had a mind to take Orders, there having been no Ordination in the Bifhoprick for two Years, he gave notice that he intended to conferr Orders on the *Saturday* before the *Fifth Sunday* in *Lent*.

He writ alfo to the *Arch-Deacon* to come and affift at the Solemnity ; the *Arch-Deacon* was much concerned at the news, and writ him back word, *That this was contrary to the late Agreement they had made together, and that his doing of it would put an end to the Affair of the Synod, which he feemed to defire fo much, fince the principal point that was to be debated therein was,* 𝔚𝔥𝔢𝔱𝔥𝔢𝔯 𝔥𝔢 𝔴𝔞𝔰 𝔱𝔥𝔢𝔦𝔯 𝔓𝔯𝔢𝔩𝔞𝔱𝔢 𝔬𝔷 𝔫𝔬 ? But the *Arch-Bifhop* fanfying that the *Arch-Deacon* talked of a Synod only to amufe him and gain time, writ him word, that nothing fhould hinder him from Conferring Orders at the time appointed; and not only fo, but that he would exercife all other Acts of Epifcopal Jurifdiction, in obedience to the Pope's *Briefs*, to whom all the Churches of the World were fubject. The *Arch-Deacon* finding he was abfolutely determined to Ordain, defired him, fince he was refolved to do't right or wrong, to Ordain none but *Latins*, for fo they called not only the *Portuguezes*, but all the *Malavars*, who were bred up under the *Jefuites*. The *Arch-Bifhop* fent him word again, that he
would

would Ordain both *Latins* and *Chaldæans*, it being his bufinefs to deftroy that diftinction by
bringing all Chriftians under one head. Upon
this the *Arch-Deacon* finding nothing elfe would
do, ordered an Edict to be publifhed in all the
Churches of the Diocefs, prohibiting all Chriftians, upon pain of Excommunication, *latæ fententiæ*, to receive any Orders from him, with which
he fent another Inftrument, commanding all
Priefts and Chriftian People not to fuffer him to
come into any of their Churches, as alfo not to
be prefent at any of his *Maffes* or *Sermons*.

The *Arch-Bifhop* had Preached two days following, and had confirmed a great many before
thefe Inftruments had reached *Diamper* ; but after
they came once to be publifhed, they put a full
ftop to what went on fo currently before : The
oldeft *Caçanar* of the Church requiring the *Arch-
Bifhop*, upon the receipt of them, to leave the
place, and not to offer to fet his Foot in their
Church any more, nor to Confirm any Body,
which among them, who anointed Children on
the Head when they were Baptized, was an unneceffary Ceremony.

Notwithftanding this, the *Arch-Bifhop* continued
ftill a Preaching, and when the day appointed
for the Ordination was come, Ordained 37 on
it, having firft obliged them to fubfcribe the
Faith of *Pius* IV. and to fwear obedience to
the Pope. After this Solemnity was over, the
Arch-Bifhop determined to pafs the *Holy Week*,
and *Eafter* at *Carturte*, a confiderable Town of
Chri-

Chriftians in the Dominions of the Queen of
Pimenta. He took feveral Churches in his way
thither, at fome of which he met with a kind
Reception, at others the Chriftians would not
fo much as fee him. Being arrived at *Carturte*,
after a dangerous Voyage, on the *Friday* before
Palm-Sunday, he went to Church betimes next
Morning, where having faid *Mafs*, and Preached,
he Commanded the Congregation not to fail to
be at Church next day, for that he had fomething of Importance to communicate to them;
and having the fame Night invited feveral of the
moft confiderable Chriftians of the place aboard
his Galley, by fome means or other; for you
muft underftand he was not fparing of his Money
in this occafion, no more than he was of his
Promifes, he gained two of the moft fubftantial
among them intirely to his Party, who did him
afterwards very great Service: Their Names were
Itimato Mapula, and *Itimane Mapula*.

The *Arch-Bifhop* not knowing but that the *Portuguezes* Mufick might charm the common People,
and reconcile them to the *Latin* Service, to
which they feemed to have a great averfion,
fent for a full Quire from *Cochim*, and on *Palm-
Sunday* had high *Mafs* performed with the fame
Ceremony and Majefty that he could have had
it done at *Goa:* but the *Caçanares* and People
were fo far from being fatisfied with the Mufick
and pompous Ceremony of that Service, that if
they liked it ill before, they liked it a great deal
worfe after that, as in truth none but they that
place

place all Religion in external Performances can
do otherwife, there being no Paffion which that
Service will not excite in its Spectators (which
is all the People are) fooner than Devotion.

The Queen of *Pimenta* being importun'd to
it by feveral Chriftians, and her own Jealoufies,
fent an Order to the *Arch-Bifhop* to leave her
Kingdom in three days upon pain of Death, and
not to trouble her Subjects with his *Novelties*, under which, fhe had reafon to apprehend fome ill
defign againft her State was couched. But the
Arch-Bifhop knew his own ftrength too well to
be frighted away with Paper Threats, and fo fent
the Queen back word pofitively, that he would
not ftir out of her Territories before he had
finifhed the work that had brought him thither,
telling her withal, *That he was ferving her rather
than otherwife in what he was doing, and that her
Anceftors had granted Privileges to the Arch-Bifhop
of the* Serra, *but being* Infidels *had never offered to
concern themfelves in the matters of their Religion;
That if fhe fhould Murther him, fhe muft know, that
fhe Muthered the fecond Man in the* Indies; *and
that his would be the deareft Blood that ever fhe fpilt
in her Life; fince the* Portuguezes, *the Greatnefs
of whofe Power fhe and her Kingdom could not be
but fenfible of, having fo often felt it, would infallibly Revenge his Death to the utmoft.*

What made the *Arch-Bifhop* the ftouter in this
occafion, was his knowing that he had fecured
moft of her *Regedores*, namely him of *Carturte*,
and the Country about it to his Party, whom
he

he had engaged by very rich Prefents to favour and protect him in the execution of his defigns. The *Arch-Bifhop* having thus intimidated the Queen, and bribed her Officers, began to make bolder fteps than he had offered to make before, and fo feeing a *Caçanar* at Church one day, whom he had excommunicated but a little before, for having prefumed to excommunicate him, he fent to him to get him out of the Church, which was no place for an excommunicate Rebel as he was. The *Caçanar* laughed at the Order, and told him very briskly, *That he would not go out of the Church, for that he was none of his Prelate, neither did he value* Roman *Excommunications no more than he did the dirt under his feet; the* Roman *Church having nothing to do with the Church of the* Serra; the *Arch-Bifhop* not being able to bear fuch a publick Affront, and knowing his Party in the Church to be the ftronger, commanded the Service and Mufick to ceafe; and turning towards the place where the *Caçanar* ftood, commanded him to come up to him, which the *Caçanar* refufing to do with great fcorn; he was dragg'd up to him by fome *Caçanares*, and others that he had gained to his Party, and being kept down upon his Knees before him, was commanded to beg his *Lordfhip's* Pardon; he told them refolutely, *He would die before he would do it, or any thing whereby he fhould acknowledge him his Prelate.* The *Arch-Bifhop* perceiving that he was not to be terrified into a compliance, ordered him to be turned out of the Church; the *Caçanar* told him,

him, *He would not be turned out of a Church where he had more to do than he had* ; upon this the whole Church was all in an uproar, fome ftriving to keep him in the Church, and others to thruft him out, but the *Arch-Bifhop's* Party being the ftronger, after a great difturbance, turned out he was.

The Night following feveral *Caçanares* and others, abjured the Patriarch of *Babylon*, and were reconciled to the Church of *Rome* at the *Arch-Bifhop's* Lodgings, which were over the Church. After which the *Arch-Bifhop* was refolved either to make the *Arch-Deacon* bend, or to break with him totaliy ; and fo having all his Converts together, without whofe advife he told them he would never do any thing ; he declared to them that he could no longer bear with the *Arch-Deacon's* Rebellion, and was therefore determined to depofe him, and put another in his place, naming one *Thomas Curia* a near Kinfman of the *Arch-Deacon's*, to be his Succeffor. They all owned that His *Grace* had great reafon to be angry with the *Arch-Deacon* ; but yet feeing he was but a young Man, and had had the ill luck to be in the hands of bad Counfellors, they intreated His *Grace*, before he declared his place void, to allow them fome time to admonifh him in, and to try whether they could not perfwade him to Conformity ; for which they defired but twenty days, promifing, that if he did not fubmit within the time, that they would never own him more, but would fubmit to any

Arch-

Arch-Deacon that His *Grace* should set over them.
Next day they sent six to treat with him, who,
tho' they took a great deal of pains to perswade
him to submit himself to the *Arch-Bishop*, could
not prevail with him to do it.

On *Easter-Eve* the *Arch-Bishop* had a second
Ordination, whereat he Ordained a great many
that had been hindred by the *Regedores* from
coming to the first. The same day *Francisco
Roz*, the *Jesuite*, who was afterwards made Bishop of the *Serra* by the Pope, came to wait
upon the *Arch-Bishop*, who, after *Mass*, told him,
That he could not believe he was in Carturte, *where,
not many Months ago, having a mind to say* Mass,
*he was forced to have the Church doors opened to him
by the Queen's* Regedor, *and where, when he eleva-
ted the Sacrament, the People all shut their Eyes,
that they might not see it ; and beat one of his Scholars for having named the* Pope *in his Prayers ; and
when he shewed them an Image of our* Lady, *cried
out,* 𝔄𝔴𝔞𝔶 𝔴𝔦𝔱𝔥 𝔱𝔥𝔞𝔱 𝔣𝔦𝔩𝔱𝔥𝔦𝔫𝔢𝔰𝔰, 𝔴𝔢 𝔞𝔯𝔢 𝔠𝔥𝔯𝔦𝔰𝔱𝔦𝔞𝔫𝔰,
𝔞𝔫𝔡 𝔣𝔬𝔯 𝔱𝔥𝔞𝔱 𝔯𝔢𝔞𝔰𝔬𝔫 𝔡𝔬 𝔫𝔬𝔱 𝔞𝔡𝔬𝔯𝔢 𝔍𝔡𝔬𝔩𝔰 𝔬𝔯 𝔓𝔞-
𝔤𝔬𝔡𝔰.

On *Easter-day* the *Arch-Bishop* intended to have
a most solemn *Procession*, which the *Heathens*
having notice of, were resolved either to hinder
or disturb it ; but finding they were not strong
enough to do the former, by reason of the *Re-
gedore's* guarding the *Arch-Bishop* as he did, they
hired the most infamous Sorcerer of the whole
Country to kill the *Arch-Bishop* in the *Procession*,
which he undertook to do with a Charm that
had

had never failed him, but as he begun to do his *Tricks* in the *Proceſſion*, he was ſeized on and ſent to Priſon, and a Currier was immediately diſpatched away to the Queen to acquaint her with what had been done : The Queen ſtraight-ways ſent back an Order, that he ſhould be put on the *Caloete*, which is a ſharp Stake faſtned in the Ground, which being ſtuck thorow the Body of the Malefactor, he dies thereon in great tor-ment. But the *Arch-Biſhop* would not give way to his being puniſhed ſo, but condemned him to greater puniſhment, in ſending him to *Cochim* to Row in the Gallies as long as he lived, which ſhews how great the *Arch-Biſhop*'s Power, how-ever he came by it, was at *Carturte*, where he made his firſt great Converſion.

When the Morning-Service was over, the *Arch-Biſhop* was invited by the *Caçanares* to the *Nercha*, which is a Feaſt kept in the Church on certain days, all the Chriſtians that are preſent ſitting down to it. The Biſhop, if preſent, craves the Bleſſing, and in his abſence, the eldeſt Prieſt of the Church. The Biſhop has one half of the Proviſion, the Prieſts a quarter, and the People a quarter among them. In many Churches there are certain Rents dedicated to the maintenance of thoſe Feaſts, which ſeem to be the ſame with the Apoſtolical *Agapæ* or *Love-Feaſts*, I do not know but St. *Paul* might allude to this double Portion that the Biſhop has at theſe Feaſts, when he ſaith, *That they who rule well, and labour in the Word and Doctrine*, are

worthy

worthy of double Honour ; and the rather becaufe he immediately fubjoyns, *Thou fhalt not muzzle the Ox that treadeth out the Corn*, &c. Befides it is evident from St. *Cyprian*, 34 *Ep.* to his Church of *Carthage*, that the Clergy were faid to be Honoured, according to the proportion they had of the Publick Offerings where fpeaking of *Aurelius* and *Cellerinus*, two Confeffors, he writes, *Presbyterii honorem defignaffe nos illis jam fciatis*, & *fportulis iifdem cum Presbyteris honorentur*, & *divifiones menfurnas æquatis quantitatibus partiuntur*.

The *Arch-Bifhop* being tired with the Service of the day, defired to be excufed affifting at the *Nercha*; neverthelefs he had his double Portion fent home. It was a great branch of *Figs*, and feveral Cakes made of *Rice* and *Honey*, with feveral other Difhes dreffed *a la Mode de Malabar*.

In the Evening the *Arch-Bifhop* went and vifited all the Sick in the Town, and gave them both Money and Ghoftly Counfel, the People imagining that this was the common Practice of all the *Roman* Prelates, began to cry them up to the Skies, as much more humble and charitable than the *Chaldean* Bifhop.

On *Eafter-Tuefday* the *Arch-Bifhop* went out to *Nagpili*, a Church about a quarter of a League from *Carturte*, where having Preached, he confirmed a great many, and reconciled feveral *Caçanares* to the *Roman* Church. By the way, it is fomething ftrange too, how the *Arch-Bifhop*, tho' he was able to School their Kings and *Regedores*, who

who all fpoke *Portugueze*, fhould be fo powerful
a Preacher as the *Portugueze* make him to have
been among the *Malavars*, confidering that he neither knew a word of their Language, nor they of his.

Next day the *Arch-Biſhop* fet Sail for *Molandurte*, where, when he arrived, he found the
People much changed from what they were,
when he was there laſt, for they had ſhut the
Church doors againſt him, neither did there fo
much as one ſingle Perſon appear to receive
him at the place where he was to Land, which
was a quarter of a League from the Town.

The *Arch-Biſhop* underſtanding how things
were aſhoar, did not offer to Land for fear of
raiſing a Tumult, but wrote away immediately
to the Governour of *Cochim*, to ſend the King
of *Cochim's* chief *Regedor* to him before *Molandurte*. The King, tho' he did not love to hear
of the Chriſtians of St. *Thomas*, ſubmitting themſelves to the *Arch-Biſhop*, being very ſenſible, if
they were once brought under *Portugueze* Biſhops,
it would not be long before they would be entirely
under the Crown of *Portugal* too, by which
means he ſhould loſe 50000 of the beſt Soldiers
in his Kingdom ; yet at the ſame time he appeared very zealous to promote that work, having
more than once Commanded all his Chriſtian
Subjects in all things to do what the *Arch-Biſhop*
would have them, and accordingly when the Governour ſent him word that the *Arch-Biſhop* deſired to ſpeak with the chief *Regedor* at *Molandurte*,
he immediately ordered him to go and wait on
him.   E 4   When

When the *Regedor* was come, the *Arch-Bishop* complained to him of the vexation his Master had given the Christians of *Molandurte*, for no other reason but for the kind reception they had given him when he was there last. The *Regedor* endeavoured to palliate the matter, and promised to acquaint his Master with what the *Arch-Bishop* had told him, *Who, if any thing were amiss*, he said, *would be sure to redress it, and to give his* Grace *satisfaction*. The *Arch-Bishop* here took him up short, and told him, *That he expected no kindness from his Master, since he had denied him so small a favour, as to order the Musquets that were lodged in the Quire of the Church, to be removed to a proper place, which, tho' he had faithfully promised to do, yet he understood the Musquets were there still.* The *Regedor* told him, *The* Regedor *of the Place, and not his Master, was to blame for that, who, to his knowledge, was ordered to have done it.*

Upon this the *Arch-Bishop* and *Regedor* went to Church together, where the *Regedor*, in his hearing, commanded all the Christians of the place, in the King's Name, to do whatsoever the *Arch-Bishop* should command them. But, tho' he is said, at the same time to have whispered some in the Ear, That the King would rather that they should adhere to their *Arch-Deacon*, and their old Customs, than submit to the *Arch-Bishop*, yet that did not appear in the sudden change that was wrought in their Carriage, by what the *Regedor* had told them publickly; for they
who

who but the day before would not fo much as endure to fee the *Arch-Bifhop*, were, without any other Argument, reconciled to the Church of *Rome*, and him the next day.

From *Molandurte* the *Arch-Bifhop* went a fecond time to *Diamper*, where the chief *Regedor*, according to his promife, met him again. The *Arch-Bifhop* complained to him of the *Regedor*, of the place, who had not only hindred the *Chriftians* from coming at him, but encouraged feveral *Heathens* to deride and threaten him ; as the chief *Regedor* was offering to excufe his Brother, the *Arch-Bifhop* interrupted him, and ftriking the *Cane* he had in his hand three times againft the Ground, bid him in a great fury not *to offer to fpeak to him, for that he knew his Heart well enough, and that he bore an ill will to all Chriftians ; but there's another, faid he, I blame more than you, and that's your Mafter, who, notwithftanding his being Brother in Arms to the King of* Portugal, *fuffers me to be abufed in his Country; but you may tell your Mafter from me, that the King of* Portugal *fhall know how I have been ufed by him, and that it will not be long before he fhall fmart for it.* The *Regedor* defiring to appeafe him, did affure his Grace, *That his Mafter knew nothing of what had been done to him at* Diamper ; *and that fo foon as he was acquainted with it, he would be fure to make Examples of all thofe that had any way affronted his* Grace. This put the *Arch-Bifhop* in a greater Paffion than he was in before ; he faid, *This was all Trick, and that he had treated too*

often

often with Kings, and knew their Tempers too well to be made believe, that they would not ſee themſelves obeyed when they had a mind to it.

The *Regedor* aſſured him a ſecond time, that his Maſter always had, and always would favour his deſigns in the *Serra*, *I ſhall quickly know that,* ſaid the Arch-Biſhop, *for if you be ſincere, you will preſently call all the Chriſtians together, and Command them, in the King's Name to acknow-ledge me as their Prelate, and to unite themſelves to the Church of* Rome. The *Regedor* promiſed to do it preſently, and having called all the Chriſtians together, commanded them before the *Arch-Biſhop* on pain of the King's high diſpleaſure, to obey the *Arch-Biſhop* in all things, aſſuring them withal, that this was His Majeſty's Will, and therefore they ſhould give no credit to any that ſhould whiſper the contrary to them; and thus, by Hectoring and Bribing of Kings and their *Regedores,* the *Arch-Biſhop* made both ſudden and great Converſions.

Having diſmiſſed the *Regedor,* the *Arch-Biſhop* gave them a Sermon, and commanded them to come to Church next Morning to be confirmed by him. Next day after the Confirmation, he told them, *That he had Excommunicated and De-poſed the* Arch-Deacon, *as a Rebel to the* Pope, *who is Chriſt's Vicar on Earth; and that he told them of it on purpoſe that they might have no more Communication with ſuch a Rebel, but might ac-knowledge him for their Prelate.* The People ſeemed to be ſatisfied with what he had done,

and

and to blame the *Arch-Deacon* for his obftinacy.
In the Evening he vifited the Sick, and gave
large Alms to the Widows and Orphans of the
Town, telling them withal, that what he did
was their Prelate's duty, and not to take Money
from them as their former Bifhops had done;
but he forgot to tell them, that whereas their
former Prelates had lived altogether upon Alms,
having no fettled Revenues to maintain them,
by reafon of their living under Princes who
were *Infidels*, that he had above 20000 Crowns
a Year in Rents that were certain. Befides, by
having reprefented what he was doing in the
Serra, as a great Service to the Crown, he had
the Command of the Publick Treafure at *Goa*,
which was never fo great as at this time; the
Viceroy *Don Matthias de Albuquerque* having in
the Year 1597 left 80000 Ducats, and an im-
menfe Summ in Jewels therein.

This *Trick*, for it deferves no better Name,
together with his Hectoring of Kings and their
Regedores as he did, made a great many People
wifh themfelves under *Portugueze* Prelates, who,
they faw, would not fuffer their Princes to Tyrannize over them, but would efpoufe all their
Quarrels, and defend them in their Rights,
which was what the *Chaldean* Prelates were not
able to do.

The *Arch-Bifhop* now having by the forefaid
Methods brought three fuch confiderable places,
as *Carturte*, *Molandurte*, and *Diamper*, befides feveral fmall Villages, under his Obedience; and
being

being alfo fure of all the Churches that are in the Kingdom of *Porca*, *Gundara*, *Marca*, and *Batimena*, whofe Kings had already Commanded all their Subjects to obey him in every thing: The *Arch-Deacon* hearing how things went, began to be fenfible, that it would not be poffible for him to contend with fo powerful an Adverfary much longer ; and that he muft therefore, either fub-mit or be fent a Prifoner to *Portugal*, the *Arch-Biſhop* having fo blocked the *Serra* up to prevent a *Chaldean* Biſhop's coming thither, that it was not poffible for him to make his efcape, if he had a mind to run his Country rather than renounce his Religion.

The *Arch-Biſhop* being informed by a *Caçanar*, that the *Arch-Deacon* was in great perplexity what he had beft to do, writ him a long Letter, wherein among other things he cited him *to ap-pear before the Judgment-feat of God, to anfwer for the Souls that were now burning in Hell, by his ha-ving kept them from being reconciled to the* Roman *Church, out of which there is no Salvation.* To which Letter the *Arch-Deacon* returned an anfwer in a ftrain quite different from what he had writ in formerly.

Before this Letter came to his hand, the *Arch-Biſhop* having done his work at *Diamper*, was failed to *Narame*, a confiderable Village of Chri-ftians, which he found all in Arms, having all bound themfelves with an Oath never to forfake their Religion and *Arch-Deacon*, but to defend them with the laft drop of their Blood ; and fo

when

when the *Arch-Bishop* was ready to Land to go
to Church, they called to him to stay where he
was ; for besides that, the Church doors were
shut, there was not one Person among them,
who would have any Communication with him.
Whereupon the *Arch-Bishop*, according to his
Custom, sent immediately to the *Regedor* of
the Country, which also belonged to the King of
Cochim to come aboard, for that he had something to say to him.

What made the *Arch-Bishop*, making such
great use of Kings and *Regedores*, who were all
Infidels in the Conversion of these Christians to
the *Roman* Church, the more unpardonable, was,
that but a little before he had made the *Arch-
Deacon's interesting of* Infidel *Princes in the Affairs of* Christianity, with which they were not
to be suffered to meddle, the chief Article for
which he deserved to be deposed.

The *Regedor* being come aboard, the *Arch-
Bishop* spoke to him to go ashoar, and do as much
for him at *Narame*, as the chief *Regedor* had
done at *Molandurte* and *Diamper*. The *Regedor*
promised him he would, but when he came
ashoar to cause the Church to be opened, there
was no body left in the Town; for the Christians hearing of his coming, and what his business was, had all hid themselves, that so they
might not be constrained to break the Oath they
had made so lately. The *Arch-Bishop*, when the
Regedor brought him word how it was, was in
a great Passion with him, and would not be perswaded

swaded but that he had underhand fomented this division. But however these Christians came to be incensed against the *Arch-Bishop*, it is certain they were to that degree, that they denied him fresh Provisions for his Money, so that he was forc'd to live upon the *Rice* and *Bisket* that was aboard for some days.

While the *Arch-Bishop* was in this Diet, the *Arch-Deacon*'s Letter came to his hand, the substance whereof was, *That he was overcome at last by the irresistable force of Truth, and was resolved to submit himself to the* Roman *Church, intreating his* Grace *to pardon all the by past Errors of an ignorant Son.*

The *Arch-Bishop* tho' he was extream glad at the news, would not discover that he was, but told the *Caçanar* that brought it very gravely, *That he had been so often deceived by the* Arch-Deacon, *that he did not know how to trust him, and that he never would any more, before he had subscribed the Ten following Articles.*

I. *That he abjured all the Errors of* Nestorius, *and of all his Followers,* Diodorus *and* Theodorus (who, by the way, were both in their Graves before *Nestorius* was ever heard of) *acknowledging them to be cursed* Hereticks, *that are burning in Hell for their Errors.*

II. *That he should confess there was but one* Christian *Law.*

III. *That*

III. *That he should subscribe the Confession of Faith, which he sent to him from* Goa, *when he made him Governour of the Bishoprick.*

IV. *That he should deliver all the Books of the Diocess to be amended or burnt according as they deserved.*

V. *That he should swear Obedience to the* Pope, *as St.* Peter's *Successor, and Christ's Vicar upon Earth, and the Supream Head of all Christians, and of all Bishops, Arch-Bishops, Primates and Patriarchs in the World, so that none can be saved out of his obedience.*

VI. *That he should curse the Patriarch of* Babylon, *as a* Nestorian *Heretick and Schismatick, and swear never to obey him any more in any matter, nor to have any further Commerce or Communication with him by Letters or otherwise.*

VII. *That he should swear never to receive any Bishop or Prelate in the* Serra, *but what should be sent thither by the* Pope, *and to obey whomsoever he sent.*

VIII. *That he should swear to acknowledge and obey him for his true Prelate, as being made so by the* Pope.

IX. *That*

IX. *That he should pass* Olas *or Provisions for the Assembling of a Diocesan Synod, to treat of all such matters, as the Arch-Bishop should think fit, and swear to be present at it himself.*

X. *That he should accompany the* Arch-Bishop *peaceably, wheresoever he went, without any thing of Guards, and should go along with him in his Galley to all the Churches he had a mind to visit.*

These Articles being made and signed by the *Arch-Bishop*, he delivered them to the *Caçanar*, together with a Letter, wherein he bid the *Arch-Deacon*, if he was not fully resolved to subscribe them, allowing him but twenty days to do it in, not to appear before him; and being willing to secure himself of the fidelity of the Bearer, he obliged him, before he dismiss'd him, to swear obedience to the *Roman* Church, making him swear also to return, and never to have any thing more to do with the *Arch-Deacon*, in case he refused to sign the Articles.

Having dismissed this Messenger, the *Arch-Bishop* returned to *Cochim*, where his main business was to get the Governour of the place to joyn with him, to press the King of *Cochim* to assist him cordially in his design of uniting the Church of St. *Thomas* to that of *Rome*; and while he was satisfying the Governour of what

what Importance fuch an Union would be to the *Portugueze* Intereft in the *Indies*, which was what he himfelf had all along as much in his Eye, as the Governour could have for his Heart : The King having heard of his being in Town, came very opportunely to pay him a vifit, in which, before they parted, the King renewed his pro-mife to him of commanding all his Chriftian Subjects to obey him in all things; with which promife the Arch-Bifhop returned well fatisfied to *Cranganor*, in order to fettle the Affair of the Synod.

The day after his arrival there, he had Letters brought him by a *Patamar*, or Currier, from the King of *Samorim*, advifing him of the King of *Cochim's* having begun a War upon the *Caimal* or Prince of *Corugeira* his Allie, to which if a ftop were not put fuddenly, it would necefl孩rily oblige him to withdraw his Army from before *Cunahle*, which was what the King of *Cochim* aimed at. So foon as the *Arch-Bifhop* had read thefe Letters, he difpatched a Currier away im-mediately after the King of *Cochim*, who was already on his March, defiring him not to make a War upon the *Caimal* till after *Cunahle* was taken, fince it could not be done without di-verting the *Samorim* from the Siege of *Cunahle*, who was then before it, expecting the return of the *Portugueze Armada*, which would be with him in the beginning of the Spring, he writ alfo to the Governour of *Cochim*, and the Commiffioners of the *Treafury* to come to

F   him;

him ; whom, after some discourse about the business, he ordered to go after the King of *Cochim*,
and to stop him in his March.

Before the *Arch-Bishop* left *Cranganor*, he received a Letter from the *Arch-Deacon*, wherein he
wrote to him, *That, tho' he was ready to subscribe
all the Articles he had sent him, yet that it was
not possible for him to wait upon His* Grace *in so
short a time as he had fixed.*

The *Arch-Bishop* understanding that the King
of *Mangate*, in whose Country the *Arch-Deacon*
was at that time, was very much against his
submitting to him, sent a Servant of his own
with a splendid Retinue to him, to let him
know, *That, if he should offer to hinder the Arch-
Deacon from coming to him, the King of* Portugal
*should know of it, who was resolved to revenge all
the wrongs that were done to him in the* Serra *to the
utmost of his Power.* The King, who had too
great a dependance on the *Portuguezes*, to provoke one of the *Arch-Bishop*'s Character and Spirit, sent him word, *That the* Arch-Deacon *might
wait upon him when he pleased for all him, and
that he never had any thoughts of hindring him.*
For all that, the *Arch-Deacon* did not come,
having in truth no Stomach to the morsel the
Arch-Bishop had prepared for him. Whereupon the
Arch-Bishop sent a couple of *Jesuites* to him, to
let him know, *That that was his last admonition,
and that if he did not come to him in eight days*
he

he would infallibly depose him and put another in his place.

The Governour and Commiſſioners having prevailed with the King of *Cochim* to deſiſt from the War; the King, in his return home, reſolved to take *Cranganor* in his way. The *Arch-Biſhop* having received advice that he was ready to Land, was civiler to him than he had been formerly, and went to the *Caiz* of the Caſtle to meet him, and after ſome Complements had paſſed on both ſides, they went together to an *Hermitage* that was not far off. Where they diſcourſed alone for a conſiderable time; after which the King called in his chief *Regedor*, and ſeveral of his Nobles, and the *Arch-Biſhop*, the Captain of the Caſtle, and ſome of his own Servants. Before whom the *Arch-Biſhop* thanked His *Highneſs* for having deſiſted from the War of *Corugeira*, promiſing him thanks alſo from the King of *Portugal* for it, but told him withal, *That this muſt not hinder him from acquainting His Highneſs with his being much diſſatisfied at his having uſed him ſo as he had done.* The King deſired His *Lordſhip* to tell for what he was diſpleaſed, there being nothing that he was ſo deſirous of, as to ſatisfie him in all things. The *Arch-Biſhop* told him with a frowning Countenance, *That when his Brother in Arms, the King of* Portugal, *ſent him into the* Serra, *he expected he ſhould have been defended there by His Highneſs, and not only ſo but that he would have aſſiſted him to the utmoſt in the Pious deſign he*

came

came about ; *in confidence of which* Protection *and* Affiftance *it was that he left* Goa *to come into thofe Parts, but that he had found himfelf miferably deceived, there not being a Prince in* Malabar, *in whofe Dominions he had been* (and he had been in the moft of them) *but what had ſhewed him more favour than His* Highneſs, *who had loaded ſome of his Chriſtian Subjects with Taxes, for no other reafon, but for having given him a kind Reception.* Here the chief *Regedor* interpofed, and defired him *to let His* Majefty *know what the Affronts or Injuries were that he had received in any part of his Dominions.*   The *Arch-Biſhop* replied with great paffion, *Sir, There is no Body knows them all better than you do, ſince they were done before your Eyes* ; *however, you were pleafed to wink at them* ; *nay, I do not know but you might have a hand in procuring them* ; *and therefore pray do not you offer to conceal them from your Maſter.*   The King protefted he had never heard of any Injury or Affront that had been put upon His *Lordſhip* in any part of his Territories. The *Arch-Biſhop*, without any Ceremony, told him, *It was not ſo, for that he himfelf had acquainted His* Highneſs *ſeveral times by Letter, of what he ſuffered from his Subjects, but could never have them remedied as he expected, and as they ought to have been by one that owed ſo much to the* Portugueze *as His* Highneſs *did, wherefore,* said he, *for the future I'll complain of none but my own King, for having ſent me from a Palace at* Goa, *where I lived at my eafe and in ſplendor, to wander*
                                                            about

about the Serra, *and be abused as I have been.*
This does not agree very well with what is said
before of his going into the *Serra* purely out of
Zeal and Devotion, and contrary to all that the
Viceroy and others could say or do to hinder him;
but upon his upbraiding the King with his not
having answered his expectations, nor the obligations which he owed to the *Portuguezes*, who, of
a petty Prince, had made him a great Monarch;
the King ask'd him, as well he might, *what his*
Lordship *meant*, desiring him *to instance in what*
particulars he had been thus aggrieved; whereupon
the *Arch-Bishop* told him of what had been done
at *Molandurte* and *Diamper*, and charged him
with having encouraged the *Arch-Deacon* in his
Rebellion, to whom he had granted several *Ollas*
or Provisions, without having granted him one
as yet. The King told him he would treat with
the Governour of *Cochim* about an *Olla* for his
Lordship. This put the *Arch-Bishop* in a much
greater passion than he was in before : for he
reckoned the King slighted him, in saying he
would treat with the Governour about a thing
that was his immediate concern; whereupon he
told his *Majesty*, *That it had been always his custom*
to put him off with delays, that for his own part he
desired none of his Ollas; *and that the Christians of*
St. Thomas, *if they had been true Christians, would*
never have suffered their Kings to have meddled with
matters of Religion; *but especially being* Infidels *and*
Idolaters, *as he was, and who not knowing the true*
God, *Worshipp'd Stocks and Stones, and Devils in-*

F 3   *stead*

stead of him: That for his part he could not but wonder at His Highnes's *taking upon him to favour the* Patriarch *of* Babylon *againſt the* Pope, *who underſtood nothing of the difference between them;* That His Highneſs *would do well therefore to leave his Chriſtian Subjects to him, who was their true Prelate, and not to meddle with matters he did not underſtand: That as for the* Arch-Deacon *he had determined that if he did not come and ſubmit to him by next* Saturday, *to turn him out of his place, and put another into it, and that he could not but look upon the* Arch-Deacon *as an ill Chriſtian, if for no other reaſon, for that of having communicated the* Affairs *of* Chriſtianity *to His* Highneſs, *whom all the World know to be an Infidel.* The King was deſperately angry at what the *Arch-Biſhop* had ſaid of his *Idols;* however being a very wiſe Prince he did not touch upon that ſtring, but told him, His *Lordſhip* might expect the *Arch-Deacon* one *Saturday,* two *Saturdays,* and three *Saturdays.* The *Arch-Biſhop* took the words out of his Mouth, and ſtriking his *Cane* againſt the Ground in great Fury, ſaid, *I will not expect him one, two, and three* Saturdays, *but if I live I will depoſe him if he does not come and ſubmit before the next, and that he deſerved to be Depoſed, if for no other reaſon, for his having intereſted His* Highneſs *in the concerns of* Chriſtianity, *notwithſtanding he knew him to be an* Infidel. The King, who could not help ſtanding amazed at the *Arch-Biſhop* condemning the *Arch-Deacon* ſo much for endeavouring to intereſt him in a thing which

he

he himfelf at the fame time was fwaggering him into, perceiving that the more they talked, the *Arch-Bifhop* grew the more furious, and talked the louder, put on a pleafant Countenance, and told him with great fweetnefs, *That there was nothing he had ever ftudied fo much as to pleafe His Lordfhip.* With this the *Arch Bifhop's* Paffion being fomething mitigated, he replied, *It was what he had always expected from His* Highnefs, *and that he hoped he would not wonder to fee him put into fo great a Paffion, in a cafe wherein Chriftianity was fo much concerned, for the leaft of whofe Intereft he was bound in duty to facrifice his Head.* The King told him, *That if he knew of any that fought after his Head, they fhould not keep their own long upon their Shoulders.* After they had made an end of this hot bufinefs, they talked for fome time of indifferent matters; and when the King was for going, the *Arch-Bifhop* accompanied him to the *Caiz,* where they are faid to have parted very good Friends; which if they did, the King confidering how he had been treated, was certainly the beft natured Prince that ever wore a Crown, and in a very fubftantial point a much better Chriftian than the *Arch-Bifhop.*

This rancounter was of no fmall advantage to the *Arch-Bifhop* in the reduction of that *Chriftianity*; for the King fearing to provoke one of the *Arch-Bifhop's* Character and Temper, fo foon as he had left him, writ away immediately to the *Arch-Deacon* to come and fubmit himfelf to the *Arch-Bifhop*; he writ alfo to the King of *Mangate,*

in

in cafe he found the *Arch-Deacon* not willing to do it, to oblige him to it.

Upon the receipt of this Letter the *Arch-Deacon* fent away immediately to the *Arch-Bifhop*, to let him know, That he was ready to throw himfelf at his *Grace*'s Feet, and to obey all his Commands, and that within the time he had prefixed; but withal, defired to wait upon him fome where elfe than in *Cranganor*, which being a Fortrefs belonging to the *Portuguezes*, he was afraid to truft himfelf in, there being nothing that he dreaded fo much as being fome time or other kidnapped for *Goa*. However the *Arch-Bifhop* complyed fo far with his Fears as to order him to meet him at the *Jefuites*-College in *Vaipicotta*. They met firft in the Church, where the *Arch-Deacon* threw himfelf at the *Arch-Bifhop*'s Feet, with the words of the *Prodigal* in his mouth, *Father, I have finned againft Heaven, and againft thee, and am no more worthy to be called thy Son. I do humbly beg Pardon for all my Errors, which have been great.* The *Arch-Bifhop* lifting him up and embracing him tenderly, told him, all that was paft was forgot; and that God's Mercy in reducing him to the *Catholick Church* was greater than the Malice of the Devil, which had been the caufe of his returning no fooner, that he would certainly have that great Reward that is referved in Heaven for thofe that bring fo many Souls to the purity of the Faith, as he was confident he would do by his Example; that he would therefore have him fubfcribe the Profeffion of

Faith

Faith and ten Articles immediately. The *Arch-Deacon* beg'd to fpeak one word firft with His *Grace* in private, promifing, after that to do whatfoever His *Grace* fhould command him ; and being alone, he told him, That if His *Grace* would have it fo, he was ready to fubfcribe the Profeffion and Articles publickly, tho', with fubmiffion he thought it would be better if he would allow him to do it in private, for the fake of that Chriftianity who were not as yet fo well inftructed as they ought to be ; but that before the meeting of the Synod, at which he promifed to fign them publickly, he hoped to be able to prepare them for the receiving of whatfoever fhould be therein determined, which he believed he fhould be able to do the more effectually, if they knew nothing of his having already fubmitted to the *Roman Church.* The *Arch-Bifhop* anfwered, *That notwithftanding a Profeffion of the Faith was by fo much the better, as it was the more publick, neverthelefs he fo far approved of his Reafon as to difpenfe with his making it openly.* Whereupon they and the Jefuite *Francifco Roz* repaired to the *Arch-Bifhop's* Lodgings, and having fhut the doors, the *Arch-Deacon* kneeled down before a *Crucifix* that ftood on the *Arch-Bifhop's* Table, and laying his hands upon the *Miffal,* fwore to the Ten Articles, and to the Profeffion of Faith, to which the *Arch-Bifhop* obliged him to put his hand, to prevent his denying it afterwards.

Next Morning all the *Caçanares* being called together, the *Arch-Bifhop* acquainted them with his in-

intention of calling a Synod very fpeedily, which they all agreed to. It was then debated where it fhould meet, fome were for its being held at *Angamale*, the *Metropolis* of the Diocefs, but the *Arch-Bifhop* would not hear of its being held there for three Reafons; the firft was, That the Chriftians of *Angamale* were the Chriftians of the whole Bifhoprick that were moft addicted to their old Religion, *Secondly*, It was not in the Dominions of the King of *Cochim*, the Prince of *Malabar* that had the greateft dependance upon the *Portuguezes*; And *Laftly*, Becaufe it was at too great a diftance from the *Portugueze* Garrifon of *Cochim*. It was carried therefore that it fhould be held in the Town of *Diamper*, which was but a little way from *Cochim*, and fhould begin on the 20*th*. of *June*, being the 3*d. Sunday* after *Whitfuntide*.

In purfuance whereof the *Arch-Bifhop* and *Arch-Deacon* did both iffue forth their *Ollas*, commanding all Priefts and Procurators of the People, who were four from every Town, to affemble together at the Town of *Diamper*, on the 20*th*. of *June* next, there to celebrate a Diocefan Synod. The *Ollas* bore date the 11*th*. of *May*, fo that there were fix Weeks allowed for the preparing of bufinefs, which the *Arch-Bifhop* made good ufe of.

Before the *Arch-Bifhop* left *Vaipicotta*, the *Caimal* of *Angamale*, who was called the *black King* of *Malabar*, came to give him a vifit: The *Arch-Bifhop* received him kindly, and at parting prefented him with fome pieces of very rich Cloath; which

which was what he went well furnished withal from *Goa*, having laid out 18000 *Pardaos* in Goods, to make Presents of in the *Serra*. The *Caimal*, who was a boisterous and bloody Prince, was so well pleased with his Present, that he promised the *Arch-Bishop* to see him obeyed in all things.

After which the *Arch-Bishop* returned to *Cranganor*, where he composed the Decrees of the Synod; which were all writ with his own Hand, word for word as they are published. As soon as he had finished them he had them translated out of *Portugueze* into *Malavar*. He likewise Consecrated there a Stone Altar for every Church in the *Serra*, which was what they all wanted.

What remained to be done, after having engaged all the Neighbouring Princes, and their *Regedors* to assist him, was to secure the *Major* Vote in the Synod ; and in order thereunto he Ordained no fewer than fifty Priests on *Trinity-Sunday*, in the Church of *Paru*, which fifty being added to the thirty eight he had Ordained but a little before at *Diamper*, and to those he had Ordained at *Carturte*, who are said to have been many, must make up at least two thirds of the Priests that were present at the Synod, who in all were but 153, of which two thirds the *Arch-Bishop* was secure, having before he Ordained them, made them abjure their old Religion, and subscribe the Creed of *Pius* IV.

He was also industrious to secure to himself the Votes of several of the most considerable among

the

the *Procurators*, by making them great Presents, giving to one of them a Cross set with *Diamonds* of great value, as he did another of equal price, to an old *Caçanar*, who had been a great Companion of Arch-Bishop *Mar Abraham*. Upon which, and the other Precautions made use of by the *Arch-Bishop* to compass his ends in the Synod, Father *Simon* in his 109 Pag. of his *Historie Critique*, makes the following judicious reflection : *All that these methods have hitherto produced, serves only to let the World see by what means the* Roman *Religion has been established in the* East, *which he that knows will not wonder, that all the re-unions which have been made with those People we call* Schismaticks *in those Parts, have been so short lived.*

On the 9th. of *June* the *Arch-Bishop* accompanied with six *Jesuites* and his Confessor, who were all Divines, and several *Caçanares*, arrived at *Diamper*, where he immediately erected a *Junto* of eight of the most popular *Caçanares*, before whom he laid the Decrees, desiring their opinion of them ; and when they came to consider the Decrees relating to manners, he called four of the gravest of the *Procurators* also to be present at the Examination of them ; after some Debates the Decrees were all agreed to by the *Junto*, which, for that reason, was given out to be the Author of them.

On the 20th. of *June* 1199. the Synod was opened, at which solemnity were present the *Dean* and *Chapter* of *Cochim*, with their whole *Quire*, as also the Governour, the Commissioners of the

Trea-

Treafury, and the Chamber of the fame City, and feveral other *Portuguezes* of Quality.

I will detain the Reader no longer from the perufal of the Synod it felf, in which he is not to wonder if he meets with the whole mafs of *Popery*, confidering that all its Decrees were compofed by a Popifh *Arch-Bifhop* who affembled it on purpofe to eftablifh the *Roman* Religion in the *Serra*; in the doing whereof, tho' he was inftrumental in letting the World know more of the Orthodoxy of that Apoftolical Church, than its like they would ever have known of it otherwife, we have reafon to blefs Providence, but none at all to thank him for it, who intended nothing lefs than the making of fuch a happy difcovery.

A Ca-

A Catalogue of the *Vice-Roys* and *Governors* of the *Indies*, from the Year 1505. to the Year 1599.

1 DOn *Francisco de Almeyda.*
    2 *Alphonso de Albuquerque.*
3 *Lope Soares de Albergaria.*
4 *Diego Lopes de Sequeyra.*
5 *Don Duarte de Menezes.*
6 *Don Vasco de Gama Conde de Vidigueyra.*
7 *Don Enrique de Menezes.*
8 *Pedro de Muscarenhas.*
9 *Lope vaz de Sampayo.*
10 *Nuno de Cunha.*
11 *Don Garcia de Noronha.*
12 *Don Estevan de Gama.*
13 *Martin Alphonso de Sousa.*
14 *Don Juan de Castro.*
15 *Garcia de Sa.*
16 *Jorge Cabral.*
17 *Don Alonso de Noronha.*
18 *Don Pedro Muscarenhas.*
19 *Francisco Barreto.*
20 *Don Constantino de Bargança.*
21 *Don Francisco Coutinho Conde de Redondo.*
22 *Juan de Mendiça.*
23 *Don Antonia de Noronha.*
24 *Don Luis de Ataide.*
25 *Don Antonio de Noronha.*
26 *Antonio Moniz Barreto.*
27 *Don Lorenço de Tavara.*
28 *Don Diego de Menezes.*
29 *Don Luis de Ataide Conde de Atouguia.*
30 *Fernando Telles de Menezes.*
31 *Don Francisco Muscarenhas Conde de Santa Cruz.*
32 *Don Duarte de Menezes.*
33 *Manuel de Sousa Coutinho.*
34 *Matias de Albuquerque.*
35 *Don Francisco de Gama Conde de Vidigueyra.*

A Cata-

A Catalogue of the Prelates, Bishops, *and* Arch-Bishops *of* Goa, *and of the* Bishops *of* Cochim, *till the time of the Celebration of the Synod of* Diamper.

THE City of *Goa* was taken by the Vice-Roy *Don Alphonso Albuquerque*, in the Year 1510.

The first Prelate thereof was *Dom Duarte nunez* a *Dominican* Friar, and Bishop of *Laodicea*.

The second was *Dom Fernando Vaqueito*, Bishop of *Auren*.

In the Year 1537. *Goa* was made an Episcopal *See* by Pope *Paul* III. and put under the Metropolitan of *Funchal*, a City in the Island of *Madera*.

The first Bishop thereof was *Don Francisco de Mela*.

The second was *Dom Juan de Albuquerque* a *Franciscan* Friar, who held it above 14 Years. In his time, that is to say, in the Year 1557. it was made a Metropolitan and Primate of all the *Indies* by Pope *Paul* V. who, at the same time, erected an Inquisition at *Goa*.

The second Arch-Bishop was one *Dom Gaspar*, who resigned it after he had held it seven Years.

The third was *Dom Jorge Temudo*, a *Dominican* Friar, who was translated to it from *Cochim*. He Governed it two Years and eight Months, and after his Death *Dom Gaspar* who before resigned it, it, returned to it again and Governed it till he died.

The fourth was *Dom Enrique de Tavara,* a *Dominican* Friar, who was also translated from *Cochim.*

The fifth was *Dom Vicente de Fonseca,* a *Dominican* Friar.

The sixth was *Dom Mattheo,* a Friar of the Order of *Christ,* who was likewise translated from *Cochim.*

The seventh was *Dom Aleixo de Menezes,* an *Austin* Friar, who was Governour General of the *Indies* for three Years, and was afterwards translated to the Primacy of *Braga,* was Governour of *Portugal* for two Years; and after that President of the Council of State of *Portugal* at *Madrid,* where he died.

Cochim was made a Bishoprick in the Year, 1559.
The first Bishop thereof was *Dom Jorge Temudo.*
The second *Dom Enrique de Tavara.*
The third *Dom Mattheo.* These three were all translated to *Goa.*
The fourth was *Dom Andres,* a Discalceat *Franciscan* Friar.

THE

THE
PREFACE
TO THE
READER.

THE following Synod is printed at the end of the History of *Dom Frey Aleixo de Menezes*, Archbishop of *Goa*'s Visitation of the Christians of Saint *Thomas* in the *Serra* or Mountain of *Malabar*, made immediately after the Celebration, and in pursuance of the Order of the said Synod; the History of which Visitation was compos'd by *Antonio de Gouvea*, an *Austin Friar*, and Reader of Divinity in *Goa*, at the Command of the Provincial of his Order in *Portugal*. It contains divers things that are fit for all Protestants to know; namely, the rude and boisterous Methods, that the *Roman* Prelates, where they may do it with safety, make use of in the Reduction of those

G   they

they call *Hereticks*; together with clear Confirmations of the Truth of what we meet with in the Fourteenth, and other Decrees of the Third Action of this Synod; to wit, That the Three great Doctrines of Popery, the *Pope's Supremacy, Transubstantiation,* the *Adoration of Images,* were never believed nor practised at any time in this ancient Apostolical Church; but, on the contrary, were rejected and condemned by her, and that in her Publick Offices. So that upon what we learn from this Synod and History, I think one may venture to say, That before the time of the late Reformation, there was no Church that we know of, no not that of the *Vaudois,* abating that one thing of her being infected with the Heresie of *Nestorius,* of which too she is cleared by one of the *Roman* Communion, that had so Few Errors in Doctrine, as the Church of *Malabar.*

If the Synod I here publish should be well received, as I have reason to hope it will, by all Protestants, and lovers of Truth, upon the account of the clear Discoveries

it

PREFACE.

it makes of the forementioned Popifh Errors, having never been at any time the Doctrines of the Univerfal Church, which we know is confidently affirmed, and much boafted of; and for further fatisfaction in fo important a Matter, the above-named Hiftory fhould be defired , I fhall be ready to tranflate and publifh it with all expedition, alone, and in the fame Volume with this of the Synod; together with the beft Account I can procure of the Church of *Malabar*, and the other Oriental Churches, that were never within the Bounds of the *Roman* Empire; for it is in thofe Churches that we are to expect to meet with the leaft of the Leaven of Popery.

As to the Synod, to prevent all furmifes of its being a Piece either forged by fome Proteftant, or of no Authority in the Church of *Rome*, tho' fet forth by a Member of her Communion; I have, together with the whole Title Page, which tells where, when, and by whom it was printed, tranflated and publifhed all the *Licences* that it came out with: And if any fhould fufpect the Tranf-

G 2   lation,

PREFACE.

lation, if they pleafe, they may fatisfie themfelves of its Fidelity, by having recourfe to
the Original in the *Bodleian Library* at *Ox-
ford*; to which, as the fafeft, as well as nobleft Repofitory of Books in the World, I
defign to give it.

I have here and there added fome fhort
Remarks upon fome Paffages, which will
not, I hope, be unacceptable to the Reader.

The

The DOCTRINES wherein the Church of *Malabar* agrees with the Church of *England*, and differs from that of *Rome*.

1. SHe condemns the Pope's Supremacy.
2. She affirms that the Church of Rome *is* fallen from the true Faith.
3. She denies Transubstantiation, or that Christ's Body and Blood are really and substantially in the Eucharist.
4. She condemns Images, and the Adoration of them as Idolatrous.
5. She makes no use of Oils in the Administration of Baptism.
6. She allows of no Spiritual Affinity.
7. She denies Purgatory.
8. She denies the necessity of Auricular Confession.
9. She knows nothing of Extream Unction.
10. She allows her Priests to Marry as often as they have a mind, and Ordains such as have been married three or four times, and to Widows, without any scruple.
11. She denies Matrimony to be a Sacrament.
12. She holds but two Orders, Priesthood, and Diaconate.
13. She Celebrates in Leavened Bread.
14. She Consecrates with Prayer.
15. She denies Confirmation to be a Sacrament.

In

*In the Account that is given of the Doctrines of
the Church of* Malabar, *in the Eighteenth
Chapter of the First Book of the Visitation,*

SHe is said, 1. Not to adore Images. 2. To
hold but Three Sacraments, Baptism, the Eucharist, and Order. 3. To make no use of Oils.
4. To have had no Knowledge of Confirmation
or Extream Unction. 5. To abhor Auricular
Confession. 6. To hold many enormous Errors
about the Eucharist, insomuch that the Author
of the History saith, he is inclined to believe,
that the *Hereticks* of our Times, meaning Protestants, the revivers of all forgotten Errors, and
Ignorances, might have had their Doctrine a-
bout the Eucharist from them. 7. To Ordain
such as have been married several times, and to
Widows, and to approve of her Priests marrying as often as they have a mind. 8. That she
abhors the Pope and the Church of *Rome* as Anti-
Christian, in pretending to a Superiority and Jurisdiction over all other Churches.

A Dio-

A
Diocesan SYNOD

Of the Church and Bishoprick of

ANGAMALE,

Belonging to the Ancient Christians of St. *Thomas* in the *Serra* or Mountains of *M A L A B A R.*

Celebrated by the most Reverend Lord Dom Frey Aleixo de Menezes, *Archbishop, Metropolitan of* Goa, *Primate of the* Indies, *and the See being vacant, of the above-named Bishoprick, by virtue of two Briefs of the most Holy Father Pope* Clement 8th. *on the third* Sunday. *after* Pentecost, *being the* 20th. *day of* July, *in the Year of our Lord* 1599. *in the Church of* All-Saints, *in the Town and Kingdom of* Diamper, *Subject to the King of* Cothin, *an Infidel ; in which the said Bishoprick, with all the Christians thereunto belonging, submitted it self to the Pope and the Holy* Roman *Church.*

Printed at *Conimbra*, in the Shop of *Diogo Gomez Laureyro*, Printer to the University, in the Year of our Lord, 1606.

THE

THE *Father of the Society of* Jesus *intrusted with the revising of Books in* Conimbra, *having perused the Synod mentioned in the following Petition, and the Inquisition of the said City having upon his Approbation, given Licence to Print the same, we do Order, That after it is Printed, it be, together with the Book Intituled,* The Journey of the Serra *or Mountains, transmitted to this Council, that it may be compared with the Original, and Licensed; without which it shall not be made publick.*

Marcos Teixira,
Ruy Piz de veiga.

I *Have perused this Synod, and to me it appears to be a Work that deserves to be Printed; for besides the sound Doctrine contained therein, it will be of great Use and Consolation to all, and very necessary to the extirpating of the Errors, Schism, and Heresies sown by Hereticks, and particularly the* Nestorians *in the ancient Christianity, planted in the* Indies *by the Apostle St.* Thomas.

Octob. 23*d.* 1605.

Joan Pinto.

B*Y virtue of a particular Commission to us granted in this behalf, by the Council of the General Inquisition of these Kingdoms; having seen the Information of Father* Joan Pinto, Revisor *of this City, we give Licence for the Printing of the Book Intituled,* The Synod, *and the Journey of the* Serra; *provided that after it is Printed, it be sent to the said Council, to be compared with the Original, and to have leave to be made publick.*

Jan. 11. 1606.

Joan Alvarez Brandon.

It may be Printed, *Conimbra,* 25*th.* of *Feb.* 1606.

The Bishop *Conde.*

THE

THE

PUBLICATION and CALLING

OF THE

SYNOD.

DOM Frey Aleixo de Menezes, *by the merey of God, and the Holy* Roman *See, Archbiſhop, Metropolitan of* Goa *, Primate of the* Indies*, and the Oriental Parts,* &c. *To the Reverend in Chriſt , Father* George*, Archdeacon of the Chriſtians of St.* Thomas *in the* Serra *of the Kingdom of* Malabar*, and to all other Prieſts, Curates, Deacons and Subdeacons, and to all Towns, Villages, and Hamlets, and to all Chriſtian People of the ſaid Biſhoprick, Health in our* Lord *Jeſus Chriſt.*

We give you all, and every one of you in particular to underſtand, that the moſt Holy Father Pope Clement VIII. *our Lord Biſhop of* Rome*, and Vicar of our Lord Jeſus Chriſt upon earth, at this time preſiding in the Church of God ; having ſent two*
Briefs

Briefs directed to Us, one of the 27th. of Jan. *in the Year* 1595, *and the other of the* 21st. *of the same Month, in the Year* 1597; *in which, by virtue of his Pastoral Office, and that Universal Power bequeathed to the Supream, Holy and Apostolical Chair of St.* Peter *over all the Churches in the World, by Jesus Christ the Son of God our Lord and Redeemer, he commanded us upon the death of the Archbishop* Mar-Abraham, *to take Possession of this Church and Bishoprick, so as not to suffer any Bishop or Prelate coming from* Babylon, *to enter therein, as has been hitherto the Custom, all that come from thence being Schismaticks, Hereticks, and* Nestorians, *out of the Obedience of the Holy* Roman *Church, and Subject to the Patriarch of* Babylon, *the Head of the said Heresy; and to appoint a Governour or Apostolical Vicar to Rule the said Diocess both in Spirituals and Temporals, until such time as the Holy* Roman *Church shall provide it of a proper Pastor; which being read by us, we were desirous to execute the Apostolical Mandates with due Reverence and Obedience; besides, that the same was incumbent on us of right (the said Church having no Chapter to take care of it during the vacancy of the See) as Metropolitan and Primate of this and all the other Churches of the* Indies, *and the Oriental Parts.*

But perceiving that our Mandate in that behalf had no effect, what we had ordered, not having been obeyed in the said Diocess, so that what our most Holy Father, the Bishop of Rome, *had designed, was like to be frustrated, after having laboured therein for the space of two Years, Schism and Disobedience to*

the

the *Apoftolical See*, *having been fo rooted in that*
Diocefs for a great many Years, that the Inhabi-
tants thereof, inftead of yielding Obedience to the
Apoftolical, and Our Mandates ; on the contrary upon
the intimation thereof, did daily harden themfelves
more and more, committing greater Offences againft
the Obedience due to the Holy Roman *Church ; af-*
ter having commended the Matter to God, and or-
dered the fame to be done through our whole Diocefs,
and after mature Advice, by which Methods the
Apoftolical Mandates might be beft executed ; and
being alfo moved by the Piety of the People, and the
Mercy God had fhewn them in having preferved fo
many thoufand Souls in the Faith of our Lord Jefus
Chrift, from the time that the Holy Apoftle St. Thomas *had Preached to them until this day, natwith-*
ftanding their having lived among fo many
Heathens, and been fcattered in divers places, their
Churches and all belonging to them, having been al-
ways fubject to Idolatrous Kings and Princes, and
incompaffed with Idols and Pagods, and that with-
out holding any correfpondence with any other Chri-
ftians before the coming of the Portuguezes *into*
thefe Parts ; we being likewife defirous that the La-
bours of the Holy Apoftle St. Thomas, *which ftill*
remained among them, fhould not be loft for want of
found Doctrine ; and that the Apoftolical Mandates
might not be fruftrated, did determine, and having
provided for the Government of our own Church
during our abfence, did prepare to go in Perfon to
take Poffeffion of the faid Bifhoprick, to fee if by
our Prefence we might be able to reduce them to

the

the Obedience of the *Holy* Roman *Church, and purge
out the Herefies and falfe Doctrines fown among
them, and introduced by the Schifmatical Prelates,*
and Neftorian *Hereticks that had governed them
under the Obedience of the Patriarch of* Babylon ;
*as alfo to call in and purge the Books containing
thofe Herefies* ; *and according to our Paftoral Duty, fo far as God fhould enable us, to Preach to
them in Perfon the Catholick Truth.*

   *Accordingly going into the faid Bifhoprick, we fet a-
bout vifiting the Churches thereof* ; *but at that time
Satan, the great Enemy of the good of Souls, having
ftirred up great Commotions, and much oppofition
againft this our juft intent, great numbers departing from us, and forming a Schifm againft the Holy*
Roman *Church, after having paffed through many
troubles and dangers, out of all which God of his
great mercy, not remembring our fins and evil deeds,
was pleafed to deliver us, and to grant us an intire
Peace for the Merits of the glorious Apoftle St.*
Thomas *the Patron of this Chriftianity, but chiefly
of his own great Clemency and Mercy, which makes,
that* he doth not delight in the death of a finner,
but rather that he fhould return and live ;
*and by coming all to the light of the Truth, may
joyn with us in the Confeffion of the Catholick Faith,
approving our Doctrine and Intention, and fubmitting
themfelves to the Obedience of the Holy* Roman
Church ; *which being by us obferved, after having
returned Thanks to God, we thought fit, in order
to the compaffing and fecuring of all thofe good
Effects, to affemble a* Diocefan Synod *in fome commodious*

modious place near the middle of the said Diocess, there to Treat of all such Matters as are convenient for the honour of God, the exaltation of the Holy Catholick Faith and Divine Worship, the good of the Church, the extirpation of Vice, the Reformation of the Christians of the said Diocess, and the profit and peace of their Souls; to which end having pitched upon the Town and Church of Diamper,

We do hereby let all the Inhabitants and Christians of the said Bishoprick, as well Ecclesiasticks as Laicks, of what State or Condition soever, to understand, that we do call and assemble a Diocesan Synod in the said Town of Diamper, on the 20th. of June of this present Year 1599, being the Third Sunday after Whitsuntide; and do therefore, by Virtue of holy Obedience, and upon pain of Excommunication, latæ Sententiæ, Command the Reverend the Arch-Deacon of this Diocess, and all the other Priests of the same, that shall not be hindered by Age, or some other just Impediment, to be present in the said Town of Diamper, there with us to celebrate a Diocesan Synod conformable to the Holy Canons: And whereas by immemorial Custom, and a Right introduced into this Diocess from its Beginning, and consented to by all the Infidel Kings of Malabar, the whole Government as it were, and the Cognizance of all Matters wherein Christians are any ways concerned, has belonged to the Church, and the Prelate thereof; and it having likewise been an ancient Custom in the same, to give an Account to the People of whatsoever has been ordained in the

the *Church*, *in order to its being the better observed
by all: We do therefore under the same Precept and
Censure, command all Christians in all Towns and
Villages of this Bishoprick; and where there are no
Villages*, *all that use to assemble together at any
Church as belonging to it*, *immediately upon this
our Pleasure being intimated to them*, *to chuse
Four of the most Honourable, Conscientious, and Ex-
perienced Persons among them, to come in their
Name at the said time*, *to the said Synod*, *with
sufficient Powers to Approve, Sign, Confirm, and
Consult in their Name, so as to oblige themselves
thereby to comply with whatsoever shall be determined in the Synod. And that these Commissioners
may demand or propose whatsoever they shall judge
to be of Importance to the Synod, and for the Spiritual or Temporal Good of their People ; We do grant
free Liberty to all in this Diocess, as well Ecclesiasticks as Laicks, that have any Complaints, Grievances, or Controversies about any such Matters as
are decidable by the Prelate, or other Christians, to
represent the same to the Synod; where they shall
be heard with Patience, and have Justice done
them according to the Sacred Canons, Customs, and
lawful Usages of the Country.*

*And whereas we are informed that there are se-
veral things in this Bishoprick which are the Causes of
great Contentions, we do therefore not only give leave,
but do also admonish and command all that are
concerned in any such Matters, that forbearing
all other ways that are prejudicial to Christianity,*

ty, they do now make use of this just and holy
way of putting an end to all their Debates: *And
since to bring all these things to a good issue the
favour and assistance of God is necessary, from
whom all good things do proceed, and without
whom we can do nothing, wherefore to engage the Divine Clemency by Prayer to be favourable to us,
following the laudable Custom of the Holy Fathers,
and Ancient Councils, we do Admonish, and in
the Name of God earnestly request, all the faithful
Christians of this Bishoprick, from this time forward until the end of the Synod, to exercise themselves with a pure and clean heart, in Fasting,
Alms, Prayer, and other works of Piety, instant-
ly beseeching God to enlighten the Understandings
of all that shall meet together, and so to enflame our
Wills with Divine Love, that we may determine
nothing but what is right, and may observe and
comply with whatsoever shall be Decreed ; taking
for our Intercessor, our Lady the most Holy Virgin Mary, of whose Praise and Honour we are to
Treat particularly ; as also the Glorious Apostle
St. Thomas, the Master, Patron, and Protector
of this Church ; and all the other Saints in Heaven, that so this Synod may begin, and proceed in
Peace and universal Concord, and may end to the
Praise, Honour, and Glory of God our Lord for
ever. And that this our Publication of a Diocesan Synod may come to the knowledge of all
that are concerned, we Will and Command it to
be Read in all the Churches of this Bishoprick to
the People on the Sunday next after the intimation
there-

thereof to the Curates, and after that, to be fix-
ed to the Gates of the Church.

Dated from *Chanotta,* the 14*th.* of *May,* under
our Seal, and the Great Seal of our *Chan-*
cery, and Written by *Andre Cerqueira,* Secretary to the moſt Illuſtrious Archbiſhop
and Primate, in the Year 1599.

Frey Aleixo Arcebispo, Primas.

THE

THE
ACTS and DECREES
OF THE
SYNOD of *Diamper*.

ACTION I.

IN the Name of the moſt Holy and undivided
Trinity, the Father, Son, and Holy Ghoſt, in
the Year of our Lòrd 1599, on the 20*th* of *June*,
being the third *Sunday* after *Whitſuntide*, in the ſeventh Year of the Pontificate of our moſt holy
Lord, *Clement* VIII. the Supreme *Roman* Biſhop,
and in the firſt Year of the Reign of the Catholick King *Philip*, the Second King of *Portugal*, and
Algarves, and of *Malucco*; the Illuſtrious Lord
Dom Franciſco da Gama Conde de Vidigeyra, Admiral of the *Indies*, being Vice-roy in the Town
of *Diamper*, ſubject to the King of *Cochim*, an Infidel and Heathen, in the Church of *All-Saints*,
in the Biſhoprick of *Angamale* of the Chriſtians
of St. *Thomas* in the *Serra* of *Malabar*, the See
being vàcant by the death of the Arch-Biſhop

H   *Ma-*

Mar-Abraham, there affembled in a Diocefan Synod according to the Holy Canons, the moft Illuftrious and moft Reverend Lord *Dom Frey A-
leixo de Menezes*, Arch-Bifhop Metropolitan of
Goa, Primate of the *Indies*, and the Oriental
Parts, together with all the Priefts and Curates
of the faid Bifhoprick; and the Procurators of
all the Towns and Corporations in the fame, with
great Numbers of other Perfons belonging to the
faid Church, and called to the faid Synod by the
moft Reverend Metropolitan : Where, after having given Thanks to God for his having extinguifhed and compofed all the Alterations and
Commotions by which *Satan*, the Enemy to all
that is Good, had endeavoured to hinder the af-
fembling of this Synod; and being all filled with
Joy, to fee themfelves met together to Treat of
things pertaining to the Service of God, the Purity of the Faith, and the Good of Chriftianity
and their own Souls; the moft Illuftrious Metropolitan did celebrate the Solemn Mafs for the
removing of Schifm, as it is in the *Roman* Miffal;
and having preached to the People to the fame
purpofe, the Mafs being ended, he re-invefted
himfelf in his Pontifical Robes, and read the Office for the beginning of a Synod, as it is in the
Roman Pontifical; which being over, and the
Metropolitan feated in his Chair, with all the Ecclefiafticks and Secular Procurators about him in
their order, he told them, That he celebrated
this Holy Synod by Virtue of two Briefs of the
Holy Father our Lord Pope *Clement* VIII. in
                                                    which

which his Holiness had recommended to him the Government of that Church, after the death of the Arch-Bishop *Marabran*, until such time as it should be provided of a Pastor and Prelate; besides, that the same belonged to him as the Metropolitan thereof, and Primate of the *Indies*, and all the Oriental Parts, by the Canons, the See thereof being vacant, and it having no Chapter to take care of it during the vacancy; which Briefs being faithfully translated into the *Malabar* Tongue, were immediately read, and received with that Reverence and Obedience that was due to them: After which the Lord Metropolitan told them, That seeing he had but little knowledge of the *Malabar* Tongue, it was necessary for him to have some faithful Person, and that was well versed in Ecclesiastical Affairs, to relate truly in the Congregations what he should say, or what should be spoke to him: Whereupon *Jacob*, a Priest, and Curate of the Church of *Pallurte* in the said Bishoprick, a Person well skilled both in the *Portugueze* and *Malabar* Languages, was presently pitched upon by common Consent; who being called by the Lord Metropolitan, was charged by him with the Office of Interpreter to himself and the Holy Synod, giving him an Oath at the same time upon the Holy Gospels, well and faithfully to discharge the said Office, and truly and exactly to relate all that should be said by his Lordship or any other Person in the Synod, without any addition or diminution; as also to read in the Congregations

all

all the Decrees and Determinations of the Synod,
which were to be in the *Malabar* Tongue : And
whereas Truth it felf has teftified, That in the
mouth of two or three there is all Truth; therefore for the greater fecurity, there were given to
the faid Interpreter, by the moft Reverend Metropolitan, as Affiftants, the Reverend Fathers,

*He was afterwards
made Bifhop of the
Chriftians of St. *Tho-
mas*.

Francifco Roz, and *Antonio Tof-
cano* of the Society of Jefus
in the College of *Vaipicotta*
in this Diocefs, who being well
skilled in the *Malabar* Tongue , were to obferve all that was related by the Interpreter, and
in cafe he was at any time faulty, to correct him;
there were befides feveral others prefent, Natives
as well as *Portuguezes*, that were well vers'd in
both Languages.

Decree I.

THe Congregation being met, and all placed
according to their Order, the Metropolitan feated in his Chair, faid, In the Name of the
Father, Son, and Holy Ghoft, Three Perfons and
One only True God. *Amen.*

My beloved Brethren , you the Venerable
Priefts, and my moft dear Sons in Chrift, you the
Reprefentatives and Procurators of the People,
Does it pleafe you, that for the Praife and Glory
of the Holy and undivided Trinity, the Father,
Son, and Holy Ghoft, and for the Increafe and
Exaltation of the Catholick Faith, and the Chri-
ftian Religion, of the Inhabitants of this Bifhop-
rick,

rick, and for the deſtruction of the Hereſies and
Errors which have been ſown therein by ſeveral
Hereticks and Schiſmaticks, and for the purging
of Books from the falſe Doctrines contained in
them, and for the perfect Union of this Church
with the whole Church Catholick and Univerſal,
and for the yielding of Obedience to the Supreme
Biſhop of *Rome*, the Univerſal Paſtor of the
Church, and Succeſſor in the Chair of St. *Peter*,
and Vicar of Chriſt upon Earth, from whom you
have for ſome time departed, and for the extirpation of Simony, which has been much practiſed in this Biſhoprick, and for the regulating
of the Adminiſtration of the Holy Sacraments
of the Church, and the neceſſary Uſe of them,
and for the Reformation of the Affairs of the
Church and the Clergy, and the Cuſtoms of all
the Chriſtian People of this Dioceſs; We ſhould
begin a Dioceſan Synod of this Biſhoprick of
the *Serra?* They anſwered, *It pleaſeth us.* Then
the moſt Reverend Metropolitan asked them a-
gain; Venerable Brethren, and moſt beloved Sons
in Chriſt, ſince you are pleaſed to begin a Synod,
after having offered Prayers to God, from whom
all Good proceedeth, it will be convenient, that
the Matters to be treated of appertaining to our
Holy Faith, the Church, the Divine Offices, the
Adminiſtration of the Holy Sacraments, and the
Cuſtoms of the whole People, be entertained by
you with Benignity and Charity, and afterwards
by God's Aſſiſtance complied with, with much
Reverence; and that every one of you ſhould

faith-

faithfully procure the Reformation of such things
in this Synod as you know to be amiss, and if a-
ny that are present shou'd happen to be dissatis-
fied with any thing that shall be said or done
therein, let them without any scruple declare
their Opinion publickly, that so by God's Grace
it may be examined, and all things may be truly
stated as is desired ; but let not Strife or Con-
tention find any room among you to the perverting of Justice and Reason ; neither be ye
afraid of searching after and embracing the Truth.

Decree II.

THe Synod by Virtue of Holy Obedience, and
upon pain of Excommunication to be incurred *ipso facto*, does command all Persons whatsoever, Ecclesiastical and Secular, that have been
called to, and are present at this Synod, not to depart the Town of *Diamper*, where the said Synod is celebrated, without express leave from
the most Illustrious Metropolitan, before the Synod is ended, and they have signed the Decrees
thereof with their own Hand, or till all the rest
are dismiss'd : The Synod does likewise Request
and Command all that have any Matter that is
fitting to be offered to it for the Advancement
of God's Honour, and the Good of the Christians
of this Bishoprick, to acquaint the Metropolitan
therewith, either by Word or Writing, or some
Third Person, that so what is convenient may be
determined therein.

Decree

Decree III.

BE it known and declared to all prefent and abfent, That no prejudice fhall be done, or follow to any Town, Corporation, or Village, as to any Preeminence they may pretend to; by the celebration of this Synod in the Town of *Diamper*; as alfo that no Church, or Perfon fhall fuffer by reafon of the Places they fit in, in this Synod, but fhall have their Rights and Privileges, in the fame ftate and vigour that they were in before; and if any Doubts fhould happen to arife about this or any fuch Matter, let them be brought before the Illuftrious Metropolitan; where both Parties being heard, they fhall have Juftice done them.

Decree IV.

THis Synod knowing that all that is Good is from God, and that every perfect Gift cometh down from the Father of Light, who giveth perfect Wifdom to thofe that with an humble Heart pray for it; and being withal fenfible that the beginning of true Wifdom is the fear of the Lord; we do admonifh and command all Chriftians, as well Ecclefiafticks as Seculars gathered together in this Place, to confefs their Sins with a true contrition for them, and all Priefts to fay Mafs, and others to receive the moft Holy Sacrament of the Altar, befeeching our Lord with humble

and

and devout Prayers for good Succefs to all that
fhall be Treated of in this Synod; to which intent, there fhall be two folemn Maffes faid in the
Church every day during the Seffion of the Synod, one of the *Latins* to the Holy Spirit, and
the other of the *Syrians* to our Lady the Bleffed
Virgin *Mary*, whofe Praife and Honour is to be
particularly Treated of; which Maffes fhall be
faid at fuch hours as to be no hindrance to the
Congregations, which henceforward fhall meet
every day in the Church at Seven in the Morning.
They fhall likewife, *Latins* as well as *Syrians*, e-
very day after Sun-fet Sing the folemn Litanies
of the Church, with a Commemoration of our
Lady for the good intention of the Synod.

Decree V.

THE Synod, for the preventing of fome
Inconveniences that may otherwife happen, and to leave no room for unneceffary and
hurtful Debates, does command by virtue of
Obedience, and upon pain of Excommunication
to be *ipfo facto* incurred, That while the Congregations laft, no Perfon whatfoever, Ecclefiaftick or Secular, prefume to meet together in any
Junctoes with any Perfons, Ecclefiafticks or Seculars, to Treat of any Matters appertaining to the
Synod, or this Church, without exprefs Licence
from the moft Illuftrious Metropolitan; that fo
all that is defired, may be handled publickly,
and in the Congregation, thofe Meetings only
excep-

excepted which are kept by the People in order to their propofing of Matters to be confulted about, according to ancient Cuftom, and the Order of the faid Metropolitan.

ACTION II.

ON the fecond Day after the finging of the *Antiphony*, Pfalm, Prayers, and Hymn, as they are in the *Roman Pontifical*, the moft Reverend Metropolitan being feated in his Chair, faid, Venerable and Beloved Brethren, the Priefts, and you my deareft Sons in Chrift, the Procurators and Reprefentatives of the People, We having done little more Yefterday than celebrate the Divine Offices, and Preach to the People, it is fit we fhould begin to Day to Treat of Matters appertaining to the Synod. In the firft place, of thofe that belong to the Integrity and Truth of our Holy Catholick Faith, and the Profeffion of the fame; which before we go about, I do again admonifh you in our Lord Jefus Chrift, that all fuch things as you fhall judge to ftand in need of Reformation in this Bifhoprick, or any part thereof, may be fignified to us, or to the Congregation, that fo with the Divine favour and affiftance, all things by your Diligence and Charity, may be brought into fo good Eftate as is defired, for the praife of the Name of our Lord Jefus Chrift.

Decree

Decree II.

THat this Synod may in all things Govern it self according to the Directions of the Holy Canons, and tread in the Footsteps of the Holy General Councils, and particularly of the Holy Council of *Trent*, upon the knowledge it has of the Necessities of this Church, and of the diversity of Opinions that have been hitherto therein concerning Matters of our Holy Catholick Faith, and of the Errors contrary thereunto, which have been sowed in this Diocess by Hereticks and Schismaticks: it doth command all Persons Ecclesiasticks and Seculars, called hither, either in their own Name, or in the Name of others, Ecclesiasticks or Laicks, of this Bishoprick, to make Profession and Oath of the following Faith, in the hands of the most Illustrious Metropolitan, President of this Synod: And for the more effectual execution of this Decree, and to provoke others by his own Example, the most Illustrious Metropolitan having robed himself in his Pontificals, but without his Mitre, kneeling down before the Altar, and having laid his hands upon a Cross that was upon a Book of the Gospels, did in his own Name, as the present Prelate and Metropolitan of the Diocess, and in the Name of all the Christians belonging to the same, and every Person thereof, Secular and Ecclesiastick, make Profession and Oath of the Faith following, which was immediately declared to all that were present.

The

The *Profeſſion and Oath of the Faith.*

I N the Name of the moſt Holy and undivided Trinity, the Father, Son, and Holy Ghoſt, one only true God, in the Year of our Lord, 1599, in the Seventh Year of the Pontificate of our moſt Holy Lord *Clement* VIII. Biſhop of *Rome*, in the Town of *Diamper*, in the Kingdom of *Malabar*, in the *Eaſt-Indies*, in the Church of *All-Saints*, on the 21ſt. of *June*, in a Dioceſan Synod of the Biſhoprick of *Serra*, Aſſembled by the moſt Illuſtrious and Reverend Lord *Dom Frey Aleixo de Menezes*, Arch-Biſhop Metropolitan of *Goa*, and the Oriental Parts, and the See being vacant, of the ſaid Biſhoprick ;

I *N.* do of my own free Will, without any manner of force and conſtraint, for the Salvation of my Soul, believing it in my heart, proteſt , that with a firm Faith I do believe, and confeſs, all and every one of the Articles contained in the Symbol of Faith which is uſed in Holy Mother *Roman* Church.

I believe in one God the Father Almighty, Maker of Heaven and Earth, and of all things viſible and inviſible :

And in one Lord Jeſus Chriſt, the only begotten Son of God, begotten of his Father before all Worlds ; God of God, Light of Light, very God of very God, begotten, not made, being of one ſubſtance with the Father, by whom all things were made : Who for

us

us Men, and for our Salvation, came down from
Heaven, and was Incarnate by the Holy Ghost of
the Virgin Mary, *and was made Man, and was*
Crucified also for us under Pontius Pilate; *He*
suffered and was buried, and the third day he rose
again according to the Scriptures, and ascended into
Heaven, and sitteth on the right hand of the
Father, and he shall come again with Glory to
Judge both the Quick and the Dead: whose
Kingdom shall have no end.

And I believe in the Holy Ghost, the Lord and
giver of Life, who proceedeth from the Father, and
the Son, who with the Father and the Son together
is worshipped and glorified, who spake by the Pro-
phets. And I believe one Catholick and Apostolick
Church; I acknowledge one Baptism, for the remissi-
on of Sins; and I look for the Resurrection of the
Dead; and the Life of the World to come.

I do firmly receive and embrace all Apostolical and Ecclesiastical Traditions, and all the Observances and Constitutions of the said Church;
I admit the Holy Scriptures in that sence wherein
it has ever been , and is still held by Mother
Church, to whom it belongeth to judge of the
true Sence and Interpretation of the Holy Scriptures; neither will I either receive or interpret
it but according to the unanimous consent. of
the Fathers.

I do confess likewise, that there are Seven true
and proper Sacraments of the New Testament,
instituted by Christ our Lord, which are all necef-
sary

fary to the health of Mankind, tho' not to every particular Person; they are, Baptism, Confirmation, the Eucharist, Order, Penance, Matrimony, and Extream Unction, which do all confert Grace on those that receive them worthily; and of these seven Sacraments, that Baptism, Confirmation, and Orders, are to be received but once, neither can they be repeated without great Sacrilege.

I admit and receive all the Customs, Rites, and Ceremonies, received and approved of in the *Roman* Church, in the solemn Administration of the said seven Sacraments, and do also receive and embrace all in general, and every thing in particular, that has been defined and declared concerning Original Sin, and Justification, in the Holy Council of *Trent.*

I do likewise confess, that in the *Mass* there is offer'd to God a true and proper Sacrifice of Pardon both for the Quick and the Dead; and that in the most Holy Sacrament of the Eucharist, there is the true, real, and substantial Body and Blood, together with the Soul and Divinity of our Lord Jesus Christ; and that the whole substance of the Bread is by Consecration turned into the Body of Christ, and the whole substance of the Wine into his Blood; which Conversion the Catholick Church calls *Transubstantiation*: Moreover, I do confess, that under each Species Christ is entire, and the true Sacrament is received.

I

I do conſtantly hold and confeſs, that there is a * *Purgatory*, and that the Souls which are cleanſing from their Sins, do receive benefit from the Prayers and Devotions of the Faithful.

I do likewiſe affirm, that † the Souls of the Juſt

---

* **Purgatory.**] *John Fiſher,* Biſhop of *Rocheſter,* in his 18th Article againſt *Luther,* does acknowledge the Doctrine of *Purgatory* to be an Article of Faith of no long ſtanding in the Church. *Multa (inquit) ſunt de quibus in primitivâ Eccleſiâ nulla quæſtio factura fuerat, quæ tamen poſteriorum diligentiâ, ſubortis dubitationibus jam evaſerunt perſpicua. Nemo certè jam dubitat Orthodoxus an Purgatorium ſit, de quo tamen apud priſcos illos nulla, vel quàm rariſſima fiebat mentio, ſed & Græcis ad hunc uſque diem, non eſt creditum Purgatorium eſſe. Legat qui velit Græcorum veterum Commentarios, & nullum (quantum opinor) aut quàm rariſſimum de Purgatorio ſermonem inveniet. Quamdiu enim nulla fuerat de Purgatorio cura; Nemo quæſivit Indulgentias, nam ex illo pendet omnis Indulgentiarum exiſtimatio; quum itaque Pugatorium tam ſerò cognitum ac receptum Eccleſiæ fuerit univerſæ, quis jam de Indulgentiis mirari poteſt quod in principio naſcentis Eccleſiæ nullus fuerat earum uſus, cœperunt igitur Indulgentiæ, poſtquam ad Purgatorii cruciatus aliquando trepidatum eſt.*

† **The Souls of the Juſt.**] This was the common Opinion of the Ancient Fathers; namely, *Irenæus* at the end of his 5th Book; *Juſtin. Quæſt.* 76th. *Tertullian* in his 4th Book againſt *Marcion;* *Origen*

in his 7th Homily upon *Leviticus,* and a great many other places: *Lactantius* in the 21ſt Chap. of his 7th Book; *Victorinus* in his Commentary upon the words, *I ſaw under the Altar;* *Ambroſius* in his 2d Book of *Cain* and *Abel;* *Chryſoſtom* in his 39th Homily upon thoſe words, *If in this life only,* in the 1ſt to the *Corinth.* The Author of the Imperfect Work, in his 34th Homily upon St. *Matthew;* *Auſtin* in his Enarration upon the 36th Pſalm; *Theodoret* in his Commentaries upon the 11th to the *Heb. Oecumenius* in his Commentaries upon the ſame place; *Theophylact* in his Commentaries upon the 23d of St. *Luke;* *Aretho* on thoſe words, *How long, O Lord,* &c. *Euthymius* upon the 23d of St. *Luke;* and *Bernard* in his Sermon upon *All-Saints* day: And to Pope *John* the 22d being charged with having believed this Doctrine, *Bellarmin* returns the following Anſwer, *Joannem hunc 22dum. reverâ ſenſiſſe Animas non viſuras Deum niſi poſt reſurrectionem, cæterum hoc ſenſiſſe quando adhuc ſentire licebat ſine periculo Hæreſis, nulla enim adhuc præceſſerat Eccleſiæ definitio.* Which Confeſſion makes the Doctrines of praying to Saints, and of *Purgatory,* and of Indulgences, to be very new Articles of Faith.

and

and Faithful, which at their departure out of this
Life, have entirely satisfied for the Punishment
due to the Sins that they have committed ; as also
those in *Purgatory* which have made an end of satisfying for their sins according to the Divine Pleasure
and Ordination ; as also those who after Baptism
have committed no Sin , do at the moment of
their death go immediately into Heaven, where
they behold God as he is : And I do condemn,
and anathematize the Heresy of those, who think
that the Souls of the Just are in a Terrestrial Paradise till the day of Judgment ; and that the
Damned are not Tormented any otherwise than
by the certainty they have of the Torments they
are to enter into after the day of Judgment.

And I do confess, and affirm, that the Saints
now reigning with Chrift in Heaven, are to be
Reverenced, and Invoked, and that they offer
Prayers to God for us, whose Relicks are likewise to be reverenced on Earth : And moreover,
that the * Images of our Lord Chrift, and of our
Lady the Glorious Virgin *Mary*, and of all the
other Saints, are to be kept, used, and reverenced, with due Honour and Veneration.

---

* 𝕴𝖒𝖆𝖌𝖊𝖘.] *Gyraldus,* a Learned Papift, in the 18*th* Page of
the Hiftory of the Gods, fpeaking
of Images in the Church of *Rome,*
faith, *At de iftiufmodi magis mu-*
tire poffumus, quam palam loqui, *idcircò fatius ea fuerit Hippocrati &*
Angeronæ confignare ; illud certè non
prætermittam, Nos dico Chriftianos,
ut aliquando Romanos, fuiffe fine Ima-
ginibus in primitivâ, quæ vocatur,
Ecclefiâ.

I

I do alfo believe, that our Lady the moft Holy Virgin *Mary* is the proper and true Mother of God, and ought to be called fo by the Faithful, for having brought forth according to the Flefh, without any pain or paffion, the true Son of God, and that fhe always continued a Virgin, in, and after her Deliverance, having never been defiled by any actual Sin.

I do confefs, that the power of granting Indulgences was left to the Church by our Lord Jefus Chrift; the ufe whereof I do affirm to be healthful and profitable to all Chriftian People.

I do acknowledge the Holy, Catholick, and Apoftolick *Roman* Church to be the Head, Mother and Miftrefs of all other Churches in the World; and do hold all that are not fubject and obedient to her, to be Heretical, Schifmatical, and difobedient to our Lord Jefus Chrift, and his Commands, and to the Order that he left in the Church, and to be Aliens from Eternal Salvation.

I do promife and fwear true Obedience to the Pope, the *Roman* Bifhop, the Succeffor of the Blefled Prince of the Apoftles St. *Peter*, and Vicar of our Lord Jefus Chrift on earth, the Head of the whole Church on earth, and Doctor and Mafter of the fame, and the Father, Prelate, and Paftor of all Chriftians; and do confefs, that all who deny Obedience to the faid *Roman* Bifhop, the Vicar of Chrift, are Tranfgreffors of the Divine Commands, and cannot attain to Eternal Life.

I do without any ſcruple receive, approve, and confeſs all other Matters, defined and declared in the Sacred Canons, and General Councils, and chiefly in the Holy Council of *Trent* ; and do in the ſame manner condemn, rejeƈt, and anathematize every thing that is contrary to the ſame ; together with all Hereſies condemned, rejeƈted and anathematized by the ſaid Church ; Namely, the Diabolical and perverſe Hereſie of *Neſtorius*, together with its perverſe Author *Neſtorius*, and its falſe Teachers * *Theodorus* and † *Diodorus*, and all that have and do follow it, who being perſwaded and ſeduced by the Devil, do impiouſly maintain, That our Lord and Saviour Chriſt

---

* **Theodorus.**] They ſhould not have been ſo hard upon *Theodorus*, for Pope *Honorius*'s ſake, who by Name was condemned together with him by the 5*th*. General Council ; and I am miſtaken, if *Pighius*, and ſome other Popiſh Writers, have not for that very reaſon laboured hard to vindicate *Theodorus*'s Memory.

† **Diodorus.**] *Du Pin* in his 4*th*. Century of Chriſtianity, *p.* 189. ſaith : As to what concerns his Doƈtrine of the Incarnation, we could better judge of it, if we had his Books ; but there is no great probability, that one who was praiſed, eſteemed and cheriſhed by *Meletius*, St. *Baſil*, St. *Gregory Nazianzen*, St. *Epiphanius*, and even by St. *Athanaſius*, and his Succeſſors *Peter* and *Timothy* of *Alexandria* ; who was alſo conſidered in a General Council as one of the moſt Learned and moſt Orthodox Biſhops of all the Eaſt ; and in ſhort, who was Maſter to St. *Chryſoſtom*, ſhould be guilty of ſo groſs an Error as that of *Neſtorius*. 'Tis true, that he had for his Scholar *Theodorus* of *Mopſueſtia*, and that he was accuſed of the ſame Error with *Neſtorius*, and that he was condemned as conviƈted of this Error after his Death in the 5*th*. Council. But beſides, that there have been ſome Perſons who have undertaken to juſtifie him : Yet if it ſhould be granted that he was guilty of this Error, it would not follow that he learned it of his Maſter, ſince we daily ſee Heretical Diſciples who have had Orthodox Maſters. Should not the Faith of St. *Chryſoſtom* rather ſerve to juſtifie *Diodorus*, than the Error of *Theodorus* to condemn him?

I

confifts of Two Perfons, affirming the Divine
Word not to have taken the Flefh into a Unity
of Perfon with it felf, but only to have dwelt
therein as in a Temple, and fo will not fay,
that God was Incarnate, or that our Lady, the
moft Bleffed Virgin *Mary*, was the Mother of God,
but only the Mother of Chrift ; all which I reject, condemn and anathematize as Diabolical Herefies ; and do believe, and embrace, and approve
of all that was determined about this Matter, in
the Council of *Ephefus*, confifting of two hundred Fathers, in which by order of *Celeftine* 1*ft*.
Bifhop of *Rome*, the Bleffed St. *Cyril*, Patriarch
of *Alexandria*, was Prefident, whom I acknowledge to be a Saint now enjoying God, and that
all that blafpheme him are in a ftate of Damnation.

Moreover, I do condemn all that fay, that the
Paffion of our Saviour ought not to be mentioned, and that it is an Injury to him to do it;
on the contrary, I do believe and confefs, that
the Confideration and Difcourfes thereof are holy, and of benefit to Souls.

I do likewife confefs and believe, that in pure
Chriftianity there is only one Law of our Lord
Jefus Chrift, true God, and true Man ; in like
manner as there is no more than one only true God,
one only Faith, and one only Baptifm ; which one
only Law was preached by all the holy Apoftles, and
their Difciples and Succeffors after the fame manner.
I do therefore condemn and reject all thofe who
ignorantly teach, That there was one Law of St.
Thomas,

Thomas, and another Law of St. *Peter*, and that they are so different as not to have any thing to do with one another; as also all other Heresies and Errors condemned by Holy Mother Church. This true and Catholick Faith, out of which there is no Salvation, and which at present I do of my own free Will, profess and truly hold and believe, I shall with the help of God endeavour to keep entire, and undefiled to my last breath; and constantly to hold and profess, and to procure its being held, professed, preached, and taught by all that are subject to me, or that shall be any ways under my care. I *N.* do promise and vow to God, and Swear to this Holy Cross of our Lord Christ : So help me God, and the Contents of this Gospel *.

I do also Promise, Vow and Swear to God, this Cross, and these Holy Gospels, never to receive into this Church and Bishoprick of the *Serra*, any Bishop, Archbishop, Prelate, Pastor or Governour whatsoever, but what shall be imme-

---

* *Pagninus Gaudentius*, a Learned Papist, in his 2d. Book *De Vita Christianorum*, makes this Judicious reflection upon the Church of *Rome's* long Creed. *Mirabitur aliquis, cum tam latè pateant limites Theologiæ Christianæ, Scriptores Vetustissimos, quique floruerunt ante Constantinum, brevi admodum ratione, non multisque effatis complecti præcipua Capita Christianæ Religionis, Summamque Mysteriorum quæ tradita sunt ab Apostolis : Lege Ju-* *stinum, Tertullianum & observa quàm parci sunt, dum referunt quid divinâ fide sentiunt Christianis Sed subsecuta secula tam multa desinierunt, & addiderunt, ut ingentia Volumina nunc nostram complectuntur Theologiam : ei ergo, qui de vitâ Christianorum ante tempora Constantini agit, danda opera est, ut exponat incrementum Dogmatum Catholicorum ; quod tamen nescio annon offensurum sit aures nostras.*

diately

diately appointed by the Holy Apoſtolical See, and the Biſhop of *Rome*, and that whomſoever he ſhall appoint, I will receive and obey as my true Paſtor, without expecting any Meſſage, or having any further dependance upon the Patri- arch of *Babylon*, whom I condemn, reject and anathematize, as being a *Neſtorian* Heretick and Schiſmatick, and out of the Obedience of the Holy *Roman* Church, and for that reaſon out of a ſtate of Salvation : And I do ſwear and promiſe, never to obey him any more, nor to communicate with him in any Matter : All this that I have profeſſed and declared, I do pro- miſe, vow and ſwear to Almighty God, and this Holy Croſs of Chriſt : So help me God, and the Contents of theſe Goſpels. *Amen*.

The moſt Reverend Metropolitan, after ha- ving made this Proteſtation and Confeſſion of Faith, roſe up, and ſeating himſelf in his Chair, with his Mitre on his Head, and the Holy Go- ſpels, with a Croſs upon them in his hands ; the Reverend *George*, Archdeacon of the ſaid Biſhop- rick of the *Serra*, kneeling down before him, made the ſame Profeſſion of Faith, with a loud and intelligible Voice, in the *Malabar* Tongue, taking an Oath in the hands of the Lord Metro- politan, and after him all the Prieſts, Deacons, Subdeacons, and other Eccleſiaſticks that were preſent, being upon their Knees, *Jacob*, Curate of *Pallarty*, and Interpreter to the Synod, read the ſaid Profeſſion in *Malabar*, all of them ſay- ing

ing it along with him ; which being ended, they
all took the Oath in the hands of the Lord Metropolitan, who asked them one by one in particular, Whether they did firmly believe all that
was contained in the Profeſſion ; as alſo whether
they did believe and confeſs all that is believed
and profeſſed by the Holy Mother Church of
Rome, and did reject all that ſhe rejects, and if
they did anathematize the curſed Hereſie of the
Neſtorians, with all its falſities, and all the Au-
thors and Cheriſhers of the ſame ; Namely, the
perverſe *Neſtorius, Theodorus*, and *Diodorus*, together with all their Followers ; and whether
they did acknowledge the Holy *Roman* Church
to be the Mother, and Miſtreſs*, and Head of all the
Churches in the World, and confeſs that all that

* There is no Chriſtian Church
beſides the *Roman*, and a handful
of *Maronites*, who put together,
are not the fourth part of *Chri-
ſtendom*, but what deny this Supremacy, and do with Pope *Gregory* I. condemn it as an Anti-
chriſtian and Heretical Uſurpati-
on. It is nothing ſo much as this
Magiſterial Pride of the *Roman*
Church that makes the Papiſts to
be by much the moſt generally
hated Sect of People in the whole
World ; for not to ſpeak of the
Jews, Mahometans and Heathens,
who hate them infinitely beyond
all other Sects of Religion, the
Greek and *Alexandrian* Chriſtians
have them in ſuch deteſtation, as
to reckon an Altar defiled by a
Roman Prieſt's having celebrated
thereon : And for the *Muſcovites*,
Poſſevinus tells us, their greateſt
imprecation is, I hope, to live to
ſee thee ſo far abandoned, as to
turn Papiſt. The *Abbiſſin* Chriſtians, as *Godinus* tells us, do not
only condemn the *Romaniſts* as
Hereticks, but do affirm, that
they are worſe than *Mahometans*,
and in the 28th. Chap. of the firſt
Book of Archbiſhop *Menezes*'s Viſitation, it is ſaid that the *Chaldean* and *Malabar* Chriſtians did
ſo abhorr the Pope, that they
could not endure ſo much as to
hear him named.

I 3

were

were not obedient to her, were out of a
ſtate of Salvation ; and if they did promiſe and
ſwear true Obedience and ſubjection to the moſt
Holy Father the Pope and Biſhop of *Rome*, as
Univerſal Paſtor of the Church, and Succeſſor
of St. *Peter*, the Prince of the Apoſtles, and Vicar of Chriſt upon Earth, without any manner of
dependance upon the Schiſmatical Patriarch of
Babylon, to whom tho' contrary to Juſtice, they
had hitherto been ſubject ; and if they did promiſe never to receive any other Biſhop into this
Dioceſs, but what ſhall be ſent by the Holy *Roman* Church, by the appointment of our Lord
the Pope, and that whomſoever he ſhall ordain,
they will acknowledge and obey for their Prelate, as becomes true Catholicks, and Sons of the
Church, anathematizing the Patriarch of *Babylon*, as a *Neſtorian* Heretick, out of the Obedience of the Holy *Roman* Church, and promiſing and ſwearing never to obey him more in any
matter, nor to have any further Commerce or
Communion with him in things appertaining to
the Church.

To all which, and every particular, they did
all, and every one of them for themſelves with
their hands upon the Croſs and the Goſpel, ſwear
and proteſt to God by the Holy Goſpel, and the
Croſs of Chriſt. After the Eccleſiaſticks had
made this Profeſſion and Oath, the Procurators
and Repreſentatives of the People, by virtue of
the Powers they had , made the ſame in their
own Name, and in the Name of the People of

the Bifhroprick, as did alfo all the other Chriftians that were prefent.

Decree III.

THe Synod doth command all Priefts, Deacons,
and Sub-Deacons, of this Bifhoprick, that
were not prefent at this Solemnity, to make the
forefaid Oath and profeffion of Faith in the
hands of the moft Illuftrious Metropolitan, at the
Vifitation of their Churches, which he intends to
make fpeedily, or in the hands of fuch as he fhall
depute for thofe that fhall be abfent at the time
of the Vifitation; that fo there may be none in
Holy Orders in this Bifhoprick but what has made
this Profeffion in the manner aforefaid. The
Synod doth likewife declare, That hereafter none
fhall be capable of undertaking any Vicaridge,
or Cure of a Church, until they have made the
faid Profeffion, in the hands of their Prelate, or
of fome Commiffionated by him for that purpofe;
as alfo, that all that take Holy Orders, do firft make
the faid Profeffion in the fame manner; and if
any of the forementioned, which God forbid,
fhall refufe to do it, that they fhall thereupon be
declared Excommunicate, until they comply, and
withal be vehemently fufpected of Herefy, and
be punifhed according to the Sacred Canons.

ACTION III.

BEcause without Faith it is impossible to please God; and the Holy Catholick Faith, without which none can be saved, is the beginning of true Life, and the foundation of all our Good; the Purity thereof being that, that distinguishes Christians and Catholicks from all other People; wherefore the Synod being sensible, that by means of some Heretical Persons, and Books scattered all over this Bishoprick, many Errors and Falsities have been sown therein, with which many are poisoned, and more may be, doth judge it necessary, besides the profession of Faith that has been made, further to declare to the People in some Chapters, the chief Articles of our Holy Catholick Faith, and to point at, and observe the Errors contained in their Books, and to have them Preached against in this Bishoprick, that so knowing the mischief and falsehood of them, they may avoid them.

The

CHAP. I.

The Doctrine of Faith.

OUr Holy Faith, that is believed with one unanimous confent by the Catholick Church
fpread all over the World, is, That we believe
in One only True, Almighty , Immutable, In-
comprehenfible, and Ineffable God, the Eternal
Father, Son, and Holy Ghoft, One in Effence,
and Three in Perfons; the Father not begotten,
the Son begotten of the Father, and of the fame
fubftance with him, and equal to him, and the
Holy Ghoft proceeding eternally from the Father and the Son; not as from two Principals, or
two Infpirations, but from both as from one only
Principal, and one only Infpiration; the Father
is not the Son, nor the Holy Spirit; the Holy
Spirit is not the Father, nor the Son; but the
Father is only the Father, the Son is only the
Son, and the Holy Spirit is only the Holy Spirit,
none of them being before another in Eternity,
nor fuperiour to another in Majefty, nor inferiour to another in Power, but were all without
beginning or end; the Father is he who begot,
the Son is he who was born, and the Holy Ghoft
he who proceedeth, Confubftantial, Equal, alike
Almighty, and alike Eternal. Thefe three Perfons are one only God, and not three Gods, one
only

only Essence and Substance, one Nature, one Immensity, one Principal, one Creator of all things Visible and Invisible, Corporal and Spiritual, who when he pleased, created all things, with his goodness, and would that they should be all very good.

C H A P. II.

FUrthermore; That the only begotten Son of God, who is always with the Father, and the Holy Spirit, Consubstantial to the Father, at the time appointed by the profound Wisdom of the Divine Mercy, for the redeeming of Men from the sin of *Adam*, and from all other sins, was truly Incarnate by the operation of the Holy Spirit, in the pure Womb of our Lady the most Blessed Virgin *Mary*, and in her took our true and intire Nature of Man, that is, a Body and rational Soul, into the Unity of the Divine Person; which Unity was such, that our Lord Jesus Christ is God and Man, and the Son of God, and the Son of Man, in as much as he was the Son of the Blessed Virgin; so that the one Nature is not confounded with the other, neither did the one pass into, nor mix it self with the other; neither did either of them vanish, or cease to be; but in one only Person, or in one Divine Suppositum, there are two perfect Natures, a Divine and Humane, but so that the properties of both Natures are still preserved, there being two Wills, the

the Divine and Humane, and two Operations, Chriſt ſtill continuing one; for as the Form of God does not deſtroy the Form of a Servant, ſo the Form of a Servant does not diminiſh the Form of God; becauſe he who is true God, is alſo true Man: God, becauſe *in the beginning he was the Word, and the Word was with God, and God was the Word:* Man, becauſe *the Word was made Fleſh,* and died among us: God, becauſe by his own Power he ſatisfied five Thouſand Men with five Loaves, and promiſed the Water of Eternal Life to the *Samaritan* Woman, and raiſed *Lazarus* from the Grave when he had been dead four days, and gave ſight to the Blind, cured the Sick, and commanded the Winds and the Seas: Man, becauſe he ſuffered Hunger and Thirſt, was weary in the Way, was faſtned with Nails to the Croſs, and died thereon: Equal to the Eternal Father as to the Divinity, and Inferior to the Father as to the Humanity, and Mortal, and Paſſible.

C H A P. III.

FUrthermore; That the ſame Son of God that was Incarnate, was truly born of the Virgin *Mary,* and had his Sacred Body formed of the pure Blood of the ſame moſt Bleſſed Virgin, and is truly her Son; for which reaſon we confeſs her to be truly the Mother of God, and that ſhe ought to be ſo called and invocated

by

by the whole Catholick Church; for that she
really and truly brought forth according to the
Flesh, tho' without any Pain or Paffion, the true
Son of God, made Man; and that the faid Son
of God Incarnate, truly fuffered for us, and was
truly dead and buried, and in his Soul truly defcended into Hell, or *Limbo*, to redeem the
Souls of the Holy Fathers, which were therein,
and did truly rife again from the dead the third
day, and afterwards for forty days taught his
Difciples, fpeaking with them of the Kingdom
of Heaven, and immediately by his own Power
afcended into the Heavens, where he fits at the
right hand of the Majefty, Glory, and Power of
the Father, from whence he fhall come to Judge
the quick and the dead, and to give to every cne
according to their Works.

CHAP. IV.

FUrthermore; That none that are defcended
from *Adam*, ever were or can be faved by
any other means, than by Faith in the Mediator
betwixt God and Man, our Lord Jefus Chrift,
the Son of God; who by his Blood and Death
reconciled us to the Eternal Father, by having
fatisfied him for our Debts; the Faith before cur
Saviour appeared in the World, being to believe
in him who was to come; as after his appearance,
to believe in him who is come, and by his Blood
and Death has faved us.

CHAP.

CHAP. V.

FUrthermore; That all we who are born of *Adam* by the way of Natural Generation, are born Children of Wrath, with the guilt of Original Sin, incurred by the difobedience of *Adam*, in whom we all finned, and which we all committed in him; for which fin, *Adam* loft for himfelf, and us, Holinefs and Righteoufnefs, and fo that guilt of fin is derived to all of us by Generation, we having all finned in him, as the Apoftle St. *Paul* tells us, that *by one Man Sin entred into the World, and by Sin Death, and fo Death paffed upon all Men, all having finned in him,* but notwithftanding this guilt is derived to us by Generation; neverthelefs our Souls are not derived by Generation as our Bodies are, but are created by God of nothing, and by the Divine Ordination infufed into our Bodies, at the time when they are perfectly formed and orga-nized, and in the inftant in which they are in-fufed into our Bodies, they contract the guilt of Original Sin, which we committed in *Adam*, and for which we were all expelled the Kingdom of Heaven, and deprived of God for ever; but which is now pardoned by Holy Baptifm, by which our Souls are cleanfed from the guilt of that fin, and of Children of Wrath, and Aliens from Glory, we are made the bleffed Sons of God, and Heirs of Heaven; wherein likewife all

our

our other fins and actual tranfgreffions, where there are any, together with all the punifhments due to the fame, are forgiven.

C H A P. VI.

FUrthermore; That the Souls of all thofe that have committed no fin after Baptifm, and of thofe who having committed fins, have done condign Penance, and have made an entire and equal fatisfaction for them, are carried immediately into Heaven, where they behold God, Three and One as he is; and do partake of the Divine Vifion, in proportion to the diverfity of their Merits, fome more perfectly than others, and in the fame manner they who die in any Actual Mortal fin, without having done condign punifhment for it; or only in Original fin, do go ftraightway down into Hell, there to be tormented with Eternal punifhments, though unequal, according to the meafure of their guilt.

C H A P. VII.

FUrthermore; That all Chriftians departing this life in Charity, and having truly repented of the fins they have committed, before they have made full fatisfaction to the Divine Juftice for the fame, are at their death carried into *Purgatory,* where their guilt is purged away by Fire,

Fire, and other punifhments in fuch a fpace of time as by the Divine Ordination is fuitable to their Quality, or until they have entirely fatisfied for them, after which they are carried up into Glory, there to enjoy God; and that in Purgatory the Prayers, Alms, and other Works of Piety that are performed by the Faithful that are alive, for the Faithful that are dead, are profitable to them; but above all, the holy Sacrifice of the Mafs, for their being relaxed from the punifhments that they fuffer, and for the fhortning of their banifhment from Heaven.

CHAP. VIII.

FUrthermore, That at the day of Judgment, our Bodies, tho' crumbled into duft and afhes, fhall be raifed up the fame that they were in this Life, and be reunited to their Souls, thofe of the Righteous to be cloathed with Glory, and to reign with Chrift for ever in the Heavens; and thofe of the Wicked, to be together with their fouls tormented for ever in the Company of Devils in the Eternal and real Fire of Hell.

CHAP.

C H A P. IX.

FUrthermore, That in the beginning, and in
Time God created all things Viſible and Inviſible, Corporeal and Spiritual, and the Empy-
rean Heavens full of Angels, of whom, thoſe that
continued ſubject to God were confirmed in
Grace, enjoying God with all the perfections and
Gifts wherewith they were created, as thoſe
who diſobeyed him fell into Hell, which God ſo
ſoon as they ſinned made for them, where they
are tormented for ever with the rigour of Juſtice; not only with puniſhments of loſs, in being Eternally deprived of the Divine Viſion,
which they were created to have enjoyed, but
with real Fire, and other Eternal Torments alſo; and do tempt men, endeavouring to do them
all the miſchief they are able, out of envy, for
the Bleſſings that are reſerved for the Juſt, and
which they have forfeited by their ſins, and out
of hatred they have for God and his Works,
and that intrinſical Malice they are hardned in.

C H A P. X.

FUrthermore, That the Bleſſed Angels and
Saints that reign with Chriſt in the Heavens
are to be venerated, and invok'd by the Faithful, deſiring of God a Remedy for our wants
through

through their Interceffion.; and of them that
they would intercede for us, which they do
daily by offering up our Prayers and Petitions to God; That the Bodies and Reliques of Saints ought to be had in veneration, in
being carefully kept, kiffed and adored by the
Faithful, and placed under the Holy Altars, and
other confecrated places, upon the account of
their having been lively Members of Chrift, and
the Temple of the Holy Spirit, and becaufe they
are to be raifed again at the day of Judgment,and
and clothed withEternal Giory inHeaven,and God
vouchfafes many Bleflings upon Earth by them.

C H A P. XI.

FUrthermore, That the Images of our Lord
Chrift, and of our Lady the Glorious Virgin
Mary, and of the Holy Angels that are painted
after our manner, and of other Saints which the
Church believes to be in Heaven, ought to be
kept and ufed in all decent places; not only in
the houfes of the Faithful, but chiefly in Churches and Altars, and to be reverenced and adored
with due veneration, and with the fame that is
due to the Perfons they reprefent; not that we
believe that there is any thing of Divinity or*Virtue in them for which they ought to be honoured, or that we put our Hope and Confidence in

*Virtue.] If there is nothing
of Virtue in one Image more than
another, why do People go fo
many hundred miles to pray to
fome particular Images of the

Virgin *Mary*, when there is fcarce
a Church or Chappel in their way,
wherein there is not an Image
of her.

K   them,

them, as the * Heathens did in their Idols; but becaufe the Honour which we pay to them, referrs to what they reprefent, fo that in proftrating our felves before their Images, we adore Chrift, and reverence the Saints, whofe Images they are: In like manner we adore the fign of the Crofs, with the Worfhip of † *Latria*, which is due only to God, becaufe it is a fign reprefenting the Son of God our Lord Jefus Chrift upon the Crofs, and which he himfelf hath told us will be the fign of the Son of Man in the Day of Judgment, and with the fame Worfhip of *Latria* we adore the Images of our Lord Jefus Chrift, becaufe they reprefent him.

* **Heathens**] The Learned Heathens made the very fame declaration concerning their worfhipping of Images.

† **Latria**.] The faying that this *Latria*, or Supream worfhip is only Relative, cannot excufe it from being Idolatrous, without excufing the groffeft Worfhip among the Heathen, it being impoffible in Nature to give any otherWorfhip, than what is relative to an Image, when worfhipped as fuch.

Martinus Perefius Aila, Bifhop of *Guidex* in *Spain*, in the third part of his Book of Traditions, *p.* 223. paffeth a fevere, but juft cenfure upon the Worfhip here eftablifhed. *Cujus doctrina, nullum (quod ego viderim) afferunt validum fundamentum, quod poffit, fideles ad id quod decent obligari. Nam neque Scripturam, neque Traditionem Ecclefiæ, neq; communem fenfum fanctorum, neq; Concilii Generalis d. terminationem aliquam, nec eti-*
am rationem quâ hoc efficaciter fuaderi poffit adducunt. Et p. 226. Certe haud diffimile, imò fortè majus fcandalum infirmis paratur, qui has diftinctiones prorfus ignorant, nec poffunt nifi errando intelligere (ut ego ipfe in multis fimplicibus experimento deprehendi, cum ab eis fcifcitarer, quid de hac re fentirent) in eo quod dicitur eâdem adoratione adorandum effe Imaginem, quâ & rem cujus eft. Nam cum videant fimulachrum operofè fculptum, affabrè expolitum, in eminenti loco templi pofitum, ipfumque à multitudine veneratum, & fuper hæc audiant, quòd eodem honore debeat honorari quo & res cujus eft, colitur, certè in multis fimplicibus periculofiffimus erroris affectus facilè poteft adgenerari, quo putent aliquid Numinis latere in imagine, fic quoq; rei reprefentatæ tum nomen, tum gloriam, ad imaginem facilè poffunt transferre: quod maximè periculofum effe judico.

CHAP.

C H A P. XII.

FUrthermore, the Church profeffeth that every Perfon as foon as he is born, hath a
Guardian Angel given him, whofe bufinefs it is
to excite People to what is good, and to deliver them from many evils which they would o-
therwife have fallen into, which Angel protects
and accompanies People through their whole
lives, doing all it can to keep them from Sin, and
all other Evils, that fo it may bring them to Eternal Life, and is always fuggefting good things to
their Free Will, from which we receive many
Bleffings as well Spiritual as Temporal, notwithftanding we neither fee them, nor underftand how
they do it; and thefe we call our Guardian Angels.

C H A P. XIII.

FUrthermore, That the Catholick Church is
one and the fame all over the World, having
for its Paftor the chief Bifhop of *Rome*, Succeffor
in the Chair of the Bleffed Prince of the Apoftles, St. *Peter*, to whom, and by him to his Succeffors, our Lord Jefus Chrift delivered the full
power of ruling and governing his whole Church;
from whence it is, that the *Roman* Church is the
Head of the whole Church, and the Father, Mafter and Doctor of all Chriftians ; and the Pre-

K 2   late

late of all in common, and of all **Priests**, **Bi-shops**, **Archbishops**, **Primates** and **Patriarchs**, of whatsoever **Church** they are; as also the **Pastor** of all **Emperors**, **Kings**, **Princes** and **Lords**: In a word, of all that are **Christians**, and of all the **Faithful People**. Hence it is, that all that are not under the Obedience of the said *Roman* **Bishop**, the Vicar of Christ upon Earth, are out of a state of Salvation, and shall be condemned to Hell as Hereticks and Schismaticks, for their Disobedience to the Commands of our Lord Jesus Christ, and the Order that he left in his Church.

CHAP. XIV.

FUrthermore, that One and the same God is the Author of the New and Old Testament, of the Prophets, and the Gospels, the Saints of both those Testaments being inspired in the Writing of them with the same Holy Spirit; and so the Catholick Church receives all the Canonical Books of both Testaments, which contain in them nothing but what is infallibly true, and was dictated by the Holy Spirit: To wit, of the Old Testament the five Books of *Moses*, *Genesis*, *Exodus*, *Leviticus*, *Numbers*, *Deuteronomy*; as also *Joshua*, the two Books of *Judges*, *Ruth*, the four Books of *Kings*, the two Books of *Chronicles*, the first Book of *Esdras*, the second which is called *Nehemias*, *Tobit*, *Judith*, *Esther*, *Job*, the Psalms of *David*, being 150, the *Proverbs*, *Ecclesiastes*, clefiaftes, the *Song of Songs*, the Book of *Wifdom*, *Ecclefiaſticus*, the four greater Prophets, *viz. Iſaiah*, *Jeremiah*, *Ezekiel*, *Daniel*; the twelve letter, *viz. Hoſea*, *Joel*, *Amos*, *Obadiah*, *Jonah*, *Micah*, *Nahum*, *Habakkuk*, *Zephaniah*, *Haggai*, *Zechariah*, *Malachi*, and the firſt and ſecond of *Maccabees*; and of the New Teſtament, St. *Matthew*, St. *Mark*, St. *Luke*, and St. *John*, the Acts of the Apoſtles writ by St. *Luke*, the fourteen Epiſtles of St. *Paul*, viz. One to the *Romans*, two to the *Corinthians*, one to the *Galatians*, one to the *Epheſians*, one to the *Philippians*, one to the *Coloſſians*, two to the *Theſſalonians*, two to *Timothy*, one to *Titus*, one to *Philemon*, and to the *Hebrews*; two of the Apoſtle St. *Peter*, three of the Apoſtle St. *John*, one of the Apoſtle St. *James*, one of the Apoſtle St. *Jude*, and the *Revelation* of the Apoſtle St. *John*, all which Books, with all their parts are Canonical, and contain in them nothing but what is infallibly true.

Decree II.

THe Synod declareth, that in the Books of the New Teſtament uſed in this Church, and writ in the *Syrian* or *Syriack* Tongue, there is wanting in the Goſpel of St. *John*, the beginning of the 8*th*. Chapter, the Hiſtory of the Adulterefs that was carried before our Lord Chriſt; as alſo in the 10*th*. of St. *Luke*, where it is ſaid, that *Chriſt ſent ſeventy two Diſciples*, it is ſaid, he *ſent ſeventy Diſciples*; and in the 6*th*. of St.

Mat-

Matthew, the words, *For thine is the Kingdom, the Power, and the Glory for ever*, is added to the end of the Lord's Prayer; there is also wanting in the said Books the second Epistle of St. *Peter*, the second and third Epistles of St. *John*, and that of *Jude*, and the *Revelation* of St. *John*, and in the 4*th*. Chapter of the first Epistle of St. *John*, this Verse is wanting, having been impiously left out, *Qui solvit Jesum, non est ex Deo*; and in the 5*th*. Chapter of the same Epistle, these words are wanting, *There are three that bear Record in Heaven, the Father, the Word, and the Holy Ghost, and these three are One*; and in the Old Testament there are wanting the Books of *Esther*, *Tobit*, and *Wisdom*, all which the Synod commandeth to be translated, and the passages that are wanting to be restored to their Purity, according to the *Chaldee* Copies, which are emended, and the Vulgar Latin Edition made use of by holy Mother Church, that so this Church may have the Holy Scriptures entire, and may use it with all its parts, as it was written, and as it is to be used in the Universal Church; to which end the Synod desireth the Reverend Father *Francisco Roz*, of the Society of Jesus, and Professor of the *Syrian* Tongue in the College of *Vaipicotta* in this Bishoprick, that he would be pleased to take the trouble thereof upon him, for which he is so well qualified by reason of his great skill both in the *Syrian* Language, and the Scripture.

Decree

Decree III.

WHereas the Holy Scriptures are the Pillars that fupport our Holy Faith, and as it were the Foundations whereon it ftands, and wherein the Truth and Purity thereof is to be met with, which has made all Hereticks in their endeavours to deftroy the faid Faith, conftantly and induftrioufly to corrupt the Text of the Divine Scriptures, partly by taking away fuch paffages as did manifeftly contradict their Errors, and by perverting other places fo as to make them * feem to favour them ; which hath alfo happened in this Bifhoprick, through its having been governed by Bifhops who were *Neftorian* Hereticks, and that ufed the fame practices upon the Holy Scriptures, that were in their hands in favour of their Herefies; as in the 20*th.*of the Acts of the Apoftles, where St. *Paul* faith, *Take heed to your felves, and the whole Church, over which the Holy Spirit hath made you Bifhops to rule the Church of God, which he purchafed with his Blood ;* the word God is impioufly changed for

---

* **Seem to favour them.**] It is hard to give any other reafon than this, why the Church of *Rome,* tho' fince the time of the Council of *Trent,* fhe has corrected fome hundreds of Errors in the Vulgar Latin, did not think fit to correct that in the 3*d.* of *Genefis,* which they apply to the Virgin *Mary*; nor that in the 11*th.* of *Ifaiah,* which they make ufe of to promote Pilgrimages to *Jerufalem* ; nor that in the 11*th.*to the *Hebrews,* which feems to make for the Adoration of Images ; nor that in the firft Chapter of the 2*d.* Epift. of St. *Peter,* which feems to give fome countenance to the Invocation of Saints.

that

that of *Christ*, and it is said *that Christ hath
made them to govern his Church, which he purchased with his own Blood* ; because the *Nestorians*,
being instigated by the Devil, will not acknowledge according to the Catholick Truth, that
God suffered and shed his Blood for us ; and in
the fourth Chapter of the first Epistle of St. *John*,
this Verse is left out, *Qui solvit Jesum, non est ex
Deo* ; because it contradicts the *Nestorians*, who
do impiously divide Christ, by making him to
have two Persons ; and in the 3d. Chap. of the
same Epistle, where it is said, *In this we know the
Love of God, because he laid down his Life for us,*
the word *God* is maliciously left out, and that of
Christ put in its stead, saying, *That in this we know
the Love of Christ,* &c. and so it favours the *Nestorian* Heresie, which denies God to have dyed
for us ; and in the 2d. Chap. of the Epistle to the
Hebrews, where the Apostle saith, *We have seen
Jesus for the Passion of his Death crowned with glory and honour, that he by the Grace of God should
taste death for all men* ; the *Surian*, the better to
make a difference of Persons in Christ, which
was what *Nestorius* taught, has impiously added,
*We have seen Jesus for the passion of his death crown-
ed with honour and glory, that the Grace of God,(præ-
ter Deum,* or besides God*) might taste death for
all* ; and in the 6th. of St. *Luke*, where our Lord
Christ saith, *Lend, hoping for nothing again* ; to
favour and justifie their Usury, they have made
it, *Lend, and from thence hope for something :* All
which places being depraved and corrupted by
Here-

Hereticks, the Synod commandeth to be corrected in all their Books, and to be restored according to the Purity and Truth of the Vulgar
Edition used by Holy Mother Church, entreating the most Illustrious Metropolitan forthwith to
visit the Churches of this Diocefs, either in Person, or by some well skilled in the *Syrian* Tongue,
whom he shall be pleased to depute.

Decree IV.

THe Synod being informed that the Christians of this Diocefs, by reason of the
Communication they have with Infidels, and by
living among them, have imbibed several of their
Errors and Ignorances, namely, three that are
the common Errors of all the Infidels of these
parts ; the first is, That there is a * Transmigration of Souls, which after Death go either into the
Bodies of Beasts, or of some other Men ; which
besides that it is a great Ignorance, is also an Error contrary to the Catholick Faith, which teacheth, That our Souls after Death are carried to
Heaven or Hell, or Purgatory, or *Limbus*, according to every ones Merits, and that there is
no such fabulous and false Transmigration.

* **Transmigration.**] This
was not the Doctrine of this
Church, as appears plainly from
what is said in twenty places of
this Synod, of her believing, that
the Souls of the Just departed this
Life, were in a Terrestrial Paradise, where they were to remain
till the day of Judgment.

The

The second is, That all things come neceſſarily to paſs, or through * Fate or Fortune, which
they call the Nativity of Men, who they ſay are
compelled to be what they are, and that there
is no help for it ; which is a manifeſt Error, and
condemned by Holy Mother Church, for as much
as it deſtroys that Liberty of Will, with which
God created us, leaving us in the power of our
own Will, to do Good or Evil, to obey his Holy
Inſpirations and Internal Motions, by which he
excites to Good, or to reſiſt Evil ; ſo that as it depends on his Divine mercy and goodneſs to move
us to Good, ſo it depends on our Free-Will,
whether by his aſſiſtance we will obey thoſe Inſpirations, and will profit our ſelves of his Internal Motions, or of our own free Will refuſe to
do it ; or in a word, do Well, or Ill ; ſo that
if we periſh for doing any thing that is Ill, it
is the fault of our own Free-Will ; as the Catholick Faith teaches us ; and not from the fate of
our Nativity, as the ignorant Heathens will have it.

The third is, † That every one may be ſaved
in his own Law ; all which are Good, and
lead Men to Heaven. Now this is a manifeſt
Hereſy ; there being no other Law upon earth
in which Salvation is to be found, beſides that of

---

* I am very apt to believe that they are here falſely accuſed of attributing all things to Fate, for no other reaſon but becauſe they believed Predeſtination ; which if it was ſo, Arch-Biſhop *Menezes*, who was himſelf an *Auſtin* Fryar, ſhewed but little reſpect to the Memory of his pretended Father, in making Predeſtination and Fate to be equally deſtructive of hu-mane Liberty.

† This is an Error that *Juſtin Martyr, Clemens Alexandrinus*, and others of the Philoſophical Fathers ſeem to have been in.

our

our Saviour Chrift, for that he only teacheth the
Truth ; fo that all that live in any other Sect, are
out of a ftate of Salvation, and fhall be condemned to Hell ; there being no other Name given
to Men, by which we can be faved, but only
the Name of our Lord Jefus Chrift the Son of
God, who was Crucified for us : All which Errors, the Synod commandeth the Vicars and
Preachers often to preach againft in the hearing
of the ignorant People; and all Confeffors to
examine their Penitents concerning them, and
to teach them the Catholick Truth.

Decree V.

THis Synod being informed, that there is a
dangerous Herefy, and very injurious to
our Lord Jefus Chrift, fown and preached through
this Diocefs ; which is, That it is a * grievous fin
fo much as to think or fpeak of our Saviour's Holy
Paffion : and as there are a great many of this
Opinion, fo the doing of it has formerly been
prohibited by impious Cenfures ; all which is a
manifeft Error, and extreamly prejudicial to the
Souls of all faithful Chriftians ; and the fruit and
profit of Souls, arifing from fuch Confiderations,
and Difcourfes, which is very great, as well for that
love and affection which they beget in us, for
our Saviour, who fuffer'd for our Salvation, as

*. **Grievous Sin.**] How does
this confift with their having fo
many Croffes in their Churches,
and Houfes, as they tell us they
had ; or with their adminiftring
the Sacrament of the Euchariſt ;
or with their Preaching that it was
Chrift, and not the Son of God,
that fuffered upon the Crofs.

for

for the Example of those Vertues which were so
Illustrious in his Holy Passion, and the hatred of
Sin, for which he suffer'd so much, and the fear
of the Divine Justice which he so rigorously satisfied, and the confidence of our Salvation by
such a plenteous Redemption; and the use of the
Sacraments, to which he applyed the virtue of
his Holy Passion, and other infinite benefits
which are derived from thence to our Souls,
which Error included another no less prejudicial,
and which is also common among the *Nestorians*;
the condemning of Holy Images; for that if it
were an Impiety to think of the Passion of our
Lord Christ, it must follow that all those things
are unlawful, that move or contribute thereunto; as, the Sign of the Holy Cross; and all
Images of the Holy Passion; all which is a gross
and manifest Heresy : Wherefore the Synod doth
recommend it to all Preachers, Confessors, and
Rectors of Churches, frequently to perswade
their People to the consideration of those Divine Mysteries; and to that end, they shall advise them to the Devotion of the *Rosary* of our
Lady the most Blessed Virgin *Mary*; wherein
are contained all the principal Mysteries of the
Life of our Lord Christ, with profitable Medita-
tions upon them.

Decree VI.

AMong the many Errors sown in this Diocess,
and left in the Books thereof, by the perfidious *Nestorian* Hereticks, there being several
against our Lady, the most Blessed Virgin *Mary*,
the

the Mother of God, the *only* Remedy of Chriftians, the Mother of Mercy, and the Advocate of Sinners, the Queen of Angels. The Synod doth therefore declare, That it is the Doctrine of the Catholick Faith, that the Holy Virgin was never at any time ftained with the guilt of any actual fin; and that it is Pious to believe, that fhe was alfo Conceived without Original Sin; it feeming to be moft agreeable to the Dignity of the Mother of God, that it fhould be fo; tho' it is true, that Holy Mother Church † has not as yet determined any thing about that matter. Furthermore, the Catholick Faith teacheth, that fhe was always, before, in, and after Child-birth, a moft pure Virgin, and that fhe brought forth the Son of God, made Man, without any Pain, or Paffion; having none of thofe things which are common to other Women after Child-birth, nor no need of any created affiftance to help her to bring forth, or afterwards, there being nothing in her but what was pure, the Eternal Word, made Flefh, fpringing out of her Womb, the Clauftrum of her pure Virginity being fhut,

† **Has not as yet determined**] It is much fhe has not, fince the Invention of the Holy Reliques in the Mountains of *Granada*, among which there was a Book in *Arabick* of S. *Cecilius*, who was confecrated Bifhop of *Eliberis* by St. *Peter* and St. *Paul* at *Rome*, with this Title, *De Dono Gloriæ & Dono Tormenti*; in which there is the following Definition of the Immaculate Conception made by all the Apoftles, being met together to Solemnize the Exequies of the Bleffed Virgin: *Illa Virgo* Maria, *Illa Sancta, Illa electa à primo, Originarioque peccato præfervata fuit, & ab omni culpâ libera; atque hæc veritas Apoftolorum Concilium eft, quam qui negaverit, maledictus & excommunicatus erit, & falutem non confequetur, fed in æternum damnabitur :* All which Reliques, and this Book among the reft, were after a fevere and impartial Examination, approved of, and received as genuine, by a late Provincial Synod in *Spain*.

when

when the time, determined in the Confiftory of the Holy Trinity was come, to the great Spiritual Joy and fatisfaction of the faid Bleffed Virgin; for which reafon fhe ought truly to be ftiled the Mother of God, and not only the Mother of Chrift; and that when fhe departed this Life, fhe was immediately carried up into Heaven, where by a particular privilege due to her Merits, fhe enjoys God both in Body and Soul, without waiting for the general Refurrection; there being no reafon why that Body, out of which there was moft Holy Flefh formed, for the Son of God made Man, fhould as other Bodies be diffolved into Duft and Afhes, but that it fhould be immediately exalted and glorified, and placed high above all the Quires of Angels, as Holy Mother Church fings and confeffeth; concerning the whole of which matter, the Impious *Neftorian* Hereticks have fpoke, and writ, even in the Breviaries ufed in this Bifhoprick, a great many Blafphemies and Herefies.

Decree VII.

THe Synod is with great forrow fenfible of that Herefy, and perverfe Error, fown by the Schifmaticks in this Diocefs, to the great prejudice of Souls; which is, That there was one Law of St. *Thomas*, and another of St. *Peter*, which made * two different and diftinct Churches, and

* **Two different.**] By all this which the Synod calls Two Laws, the Chriftians of St. *Thomas* meant only, That the Churches planted by the Apoftles in divers Regions, had nothing of Superiority or Jurifdiction over one another; which is a moft certain and ancient truth.

both

both immediately from Chrift ; and that the one
had nothing to do with the other ; neither did
the Prelate of the one owe any obedience to the
Prelate of the other ; and that they who had followed the Law of St. *Peter*, had endeavoured to
deftroy the Law of St. *Thomas*, for which they
had been punifhed by him ; all which is a
manifeft Error, Schifm, and Herefy, there being but one Law to all Chriftians, which is that
which was given and declared by Jefus Chrift
the Son of God, and preached by the Holy Apoftles
all over the World, as one Faith, one Baptifm,
there being but one Lord of all, and one Catholick and Apoftolick Church, of which our
Lord Chrift, God and Man, who Founded it,
is the only Spoufe ; and one only Univerfal Paftor, to whom all other Prelates owe obedience,
the Pope and Bifhop of *Rome*, Succeffor in the
Chair of St. *Peter*, the Prince of the Apoftles ;
to whom our Lord Jefus Chrift bequeathed that
Supream Authority, and by him to his Succeffors;
which Catholick Doctrine is neceffary to Eternal
Life :   Wherefore the Synod doth command all
Parifh Priefts, and Preachers, to Treat often of
this matter, by reafon of the great need there
is of having this Bifhoprick well inftructed
therein.

Decree

Decree VIII.

FOr that, till the very time of the moſt Illuſtrious Metropolitan entring into this Dioceſs, there was a certain Hereſy twice repeated
in the Holy Sacrifice of the Maſs, and twice more
in the Divine Office, in calling the Patriarch of
Babylon, the Univerſal Paſtor, and Head of the
Catholick Church, in all places, and as often as
they happen to name him ; a Title that is due
only to the moſt Holy Father , the Biſhop of
Rome, Succeſſor of the Prince of the Apoſtles,
St. *Peter*, and Vicar of Chriſt on Earth : the Synod doth therefore command in virtue of Obedience, and upon pain of Excommunication to
be *ipſo facto* incurred, that no Perſon of this Biſhoprick, Secular or Eccleſiaſtical , ſhall from
henceforward preſume, by Word or Writing,
either in the Holy Sacrifice of the Maſs, or in
the Divine Office, or in any other occaſion, to
beſtow that Title on the ſaid Patriarch of *Babylon*, or on any other Prelate, beſides our Lord,
the Biſhop of *Rome* ; and whoſoever ſhall dare to
contravene this Order, ſhall be declared Excommunicate, and held for a Schiſmatick and Heretick, and ſhall be puniſhed as ſuch, according to
the Holy Canons: And whereas the Patriarchs
of *Babylon*, to whom this Church was ſubject,
are *Neſtorians*, the Heads of that curſed Sect,
and Schiſmaticks out of the Obedience of the Holy
Roman Church, and Aliens from our Holy Catholick

lick Faith, and are for that reafon Excommunicate and accurfed; and it not being lawful to
joyn with fuch in the Church in publick as ftand
Excommunicate: Wherefore this Bifhoprick, upon its having now yielded a perfect Obedience
to the moft Holy Father, the Pope, Chrift's Vicar
upon Earth, to which it was obliged by Divine
Authority, and upon pain of Damnation, fhall
not from henceforward have any manner of dependance upon the faid Patriarch of *Babylon*; and the
prefent Synod, does under the faid precept of Obedience, and upon pain of Excommunication to
be *ipfo facto* incurred, prohibit all Priefts, and
Curates, from henceforward to name the faid
Patriarch of *Babylon* in the Holy Sacrifice of the
Mafs, or in any other Divine Office, in the Prayers of the Church, even without the falfe Title
of Univerfal Paftor; but inftead thereof, fhall
name our Lord the Pope, who is our true Paftor,
as alfo of the whole Church, and after him, the
Lord Bifhop of the Diocefs, for the time being;
and whofoever fhall malicioufly and knowingly
act the contrary, fhall be declared Excommunicate, and otherwife punifh'd at the pleafure of his
Prelate, according to his contumacy.

Decree IX.

WHereas all the Breviaries ufed in this Church
are *Neftorian*, and by the commands of
Prelates of the fame Sect, on a certain day the
impious and falfe Heretick *Neftorius* is Commemorated in this Bifhoprick, and a Day is kept to

his Honour, and at other times, *Theodorus, Diodorus, Abbaratho, Abraham, Narfai, Barchauma,
Johanan, Hormifda,* and *Michael,* who are alfo
Neftorian Hereticks, were likewife Commemorated; *Neftorius, Theodorus,* and *Diodorus,* being
commemorated on the *Friday* after the Nativity;
and on the feventh *Friday* after that, *Abraham,*
and *Narfai,* and all the above-named; and all
of them on every *Thurfday* in the Year, in the
faid *Neftorian* Office, and every day in the Holy
Sacrifice of the Mafs, and the Divine Office; and
notwithftanding in fome places they have not of
late named *Neftorius, Theodorus,* and *Diodorus,*
but do ftill continue to name *Abraham, Narfai,
Abba Barchauma, Johanan, Hormifda,* and *Michael,*
in the Blefling that the Prieft gives to the People at the end of the Mafs; wherein they defire
Hormifda to deliver them from evil, being his
Difciples; as alfo on all *Fridays* in the Year they
commemorate as Saints, the faid *Hormifda, Jo-
feph, Michael, Johanan, Barchauma, Barianda,
Rabba Hedfa, Machai, Hixoiau, Caurixo, Avahixo,
Lixo, Xaulixo, Barmun Lixo, Metidor, Cohada
Ifrael, Ezekiah Lixo, David Lixo, Barai Ifrael,
Julianus Haudixo,* &c. who were all *Neftorian*
Hereticks, and as is evident from the faid Mafles,
and from their Lives, Commemorations, and
Praifes, beftowed upon them, the Heads of the faid
Sect. Therefore the Synod in Virtue of Holy Obedience, and upon pain of Excommunication to
be *ipfo facto* incurred, doth prohibit all Priefts,
and Curates, and all other Perfons, as well Se-
cular,

cular, as Ecclefiafticks, in this Diocefs at any time, either in common, or in particular, to commemorate any of the forefaid Hereticks, or to keep a day to them, or to celebrate their Feftivities, with any Solemnity, or to make any mention of them in the Divine Offices, or in the Mafs or any where elfe, or to direct any Prayers to them, either in common, or particular, or to make any Vows, Promifes, Offerings, or any Nercha's to them; or to have their Images either in the Churches, or in their Houfes; and in no wife to give them that Worfhip, and Veneration, which is due to Saints; and that they raze their Names out of their Books, Calendars, and Offices; and that their Maffes be cut out of their Breviaries, and Miffals, and burnt, and their Commemorations extinguifhed, that fo their Memory may perifh among the faithful, all of them having been curfed and excommunicate Hereticks, and condemned by Holy Mother Church, and are * at this time burning in the torments of

* **At this time burning**] This rafh Judgment brings to my mind what the *Conde de Ereicera*, in his Hiftory printed about fourteen years ago at *Lisbon*, faid of King *Charles* having fpent fome time in Devotion upon the Scaffold, that feeing he died a Heretick, that Devotion was of no other benefit to him, but as it prolonged his life a few minutes: But tho' our Princes, for I have reafon to believe they heard of it, did not think fit to refent this Saucinefs, as well as Impiety, fo far as to have the Author queftioned for it; yet it would feem that God would not fuffer it to go long unpunifhed; who a few years after, fuffered that great Minifter to go out of the World after fuch a manner, that they muft have a great deal of Charity indeed, that can think well of the future ftate of his Soul; for the unhappy Man Murthered himfelf; which is a thing that very feldom happens in *Portugal*.

Hell,

Hell, for their Crimes and Heresies, and for their
having been the † followers of such a cursed
Sect; the Synod doth furthermore command,
that instead of them, on the *Friday* next after
the Nativity, St. *Athanasius*, St. *Gregory Nazian-*
zen, St. *Basil*, St. *John Chrysostom*, and St. *Cyril*

---

† ꝼollowers of ſuch] The
Church of *Rome* is not without
Hereticks in her Martyrologies,
and Calendars; for, not to speak
of *Eusebius Cæsariensis*, St. *George*,
Lucifer Calaritanus, *Barsanuphius*,
and others; the Learned *Valesius*,
in his Tract of the *Roman* Martyrology, gives the following Account of *Theodotus* Bishop of *Lao-*
dicea: *Jam vero illa quæ in dicto*
Martyrologio, Adonis sc. & Rosweidi,
leguntur secundo die Novembris. La-
odiceæ Theodoti Episcopi, qui arte
Medicus fuit, descripta sunt ex
Ruffini, lib 7. cap. ult Sed Compi-
lator iste non animadvertit Theodotum
hunc Laodiceæ Episcopum, cujus eo
loco laudationem intexuit Eusebius
Arianarum partium præcipuum fau-
torem fuisse; quippe qui & ab initio
Arianum dogma tutatus est, & post
Nicænum Concilium, conspiratione cum
Arianis facta, Eustathium de Anti-
ochená sede dejecerit; ut scribit
Theodoretus lib. 1. hist. cap. 24.
Hic est Theodotus cui Eusebius libros
suos de Præparatione Evangelicá
nuncupavit; & cujus meminit Suidas
in voce, Ἀπολλιπάει⊙. *Idem quo-*
que Error irrepsit in Martyrologium
Romanum, quod Patrum memoriá,
jussa Sixti quinti editum, & Baronii
notationibus illustratum est; nec satis
mirari possum quonam modo id Baronii

diligentiam fugerit. Furthermore,
The Church of *Rome* has several
Saints in her present Calendars,
and Martyrologies, that were never in being, or were never of
humane race; and here not to
mention St. *Almanakius*, or St. *Al-*
manak, upon the 1st. of *January*;
nor St. *Zinoris*, on the 24th. of
the same Month; on the 24th. of
July, in the present Reformed
Roman Martyrology, it is said,
Amiterni in vestinis Passio Sancto-
rum Militum Octoginta trium; a-
mong whom (as *Baronius* learned-
ly observes) *Florentinus* and *Fælix*
were two of the most Eminent.
Now in the ancient Martyrology
published by *Maria Florentinus*, it
is said upon the same day; *In*
Amiterniná civitate Miliario 83°
ab urbe Romaná via Salutaria nata-
lis Sancti Victori; and in another
ancient one, called *Martinianum*,
it is writ, *In Amiterniná civitate*
Mil. 83 *ab urbe Romana via Salu-*
taria Sancti Victurini; and in the
Queen of *Sweden*'s Martyrology,
is writ, *In Amiterna civitate Mil.*
83 *ab urbe Roma Sancti Victurini*;
and in the *Corbey* Martyrology,
thus; *In Amiternina civitate Mili-*
avio Octogesimo tertio ab urbe Roma
via Salutaria natalis Sancti Victorini
Martyris. So that here we have
of

of *Alexandria*, fhall be Commemorated; and on
the feventh *Friday* following, St. *Aujiin*, St. *Ambrofe*, St. *Gregory*, and St. *Ephrem*, who was mentioned by them among the Hereticks, and on
Wednefdays, *All-Saints* and Confeffors together;
and in the Commemorations of the Divine Offices, and Mafs, they fhall Commemorate all the
forenamed Saints, in the place of the above-mentioned Hereticks; neither fhall any one that fhall
prefume to do the contrary, be abfolved from
the Cenfures he has incurred, until he hath undergone a condign Penance, or fuch a one as his
Prelate fhall think fit to impofe upon him, and
fhall thereupon be obliged to curfe all the faid
Hereticks, and their damnable Sect, and to make
Oath of the Faith publickly, and to fubmit to all
other punifhments that his Rebellion fhall deferve,
and if he is an Ecclefiaftick, he fhall moreover be
fufpended from his Orders, and Benefices, and
punifhed according to the Holy Canons.

Eighty-three *Italian* Miles Canonized, and made Eighty-three
Martyrs, and Souldiers, with their
Captain and Lieutenants Names.
    Again, On the 16th. of *Feb.*
in the prefent Reformed *Roman*
Martyrology, it is faid; *In Ægypto
Sancti Juliani Martyri, cum aliis
quinque Millibus :* Now if this is
the *Julianus* that was *Pamphilius*'s
Companion,as doubtlefs it is, they
muft then have encreafed his

Company mightily,for they were
but five that fuffered with nim in
Ægypt , who it is probable were
Souldiers; and fo the contracted
word *Mil.* came to be taken for
Mille: This makes me fufpect
that there may be fome fuch miftake in St. *Urfula*'s Army of Eleven thoufand Virgins. For fome
of her Saints who were Heathens,
fee the Remarks upon 25 *Decree*,
Act. 8.

L 3   𝕯𝖊𝖈𝖗𝖊𝖊

Decree X.

WHereas the Church of *Angamale*, called the Archbishop's, was built by *Mar-Abraham*, and dedicated to *Hormiſda* the Abbot, commonly called St. *Hormuſio*, who was a *Neſtorian* Heretick, and a great Ring-leader of that Sect, and for that reaſon was abhorred by all Catholicks, who are called *Romans*, as is reported in his Life writ in the *Surian* Tongue, and which was ordained to be burnt by the moſt Illuſtrious Metropolitan, upon the account of the manifold Hereſies and Blaſphemies contained therein, and the many falſe Miracles ſaid to be wrought by him, in confirmation of the *Neſtorian* Sect: Therefore the Synod does in virtue of Obedience, and upon pain of Excommunication, to be *ipſo facto* incurred, prohibit the Obſervation of the two Feſtivities that have been dedicated to his Memory, the one upon the firſt of *September*, the other ſixteen days after *Eaſter*; and the dedicating of any Church to him, commanding the abovenamed Church to be dedicated to St. *Hormiſda* the Martyr, who was alſo a *Perſian*, and whoſe Feſtivity is celebrated upon the 8th. of *Auguſt*, upon which day the Feaſt of the ſaid Church ſhall be obſerved; and on the *Retablo* they are to make the Picture, wherein the Martyrdom of the ſaid Saint ſhall be drawn to the beſt advantage, that ſo the People may learn to what Saint the ſaid Church is dedicated, and all the
Prayers

Prayers and Devotion that ufed to be performed upon the Feftivities of the Heretick *Hormifda,* may be directed to this Glorious Saint.

Decree XI.

SEeing in the Creed, or Holy Symbol of Faith,
ordained by the Sacred Apoftles, and declared
by the Holy Councils, which is fung in the Mafs,
all the principal Myfteries and Articles of our Faith
are contained, it is not fit that any thing fhould be
added to it, or taken from it, but that it fhould
be fung in this Bifhoprick as it is all over the
Univerfal Church; wherefore the Synod doth
Order, that the words which are wanting in the
Creed that is faid in the Mafs be added to it;
where fpeaking of Chrift, it it faid, that he was
born of the Father before all Times, there is
wanting, *God of God, Light of Light, very God
of very God,* that fo it may in all things be conformable to what is fung in the Univerfal Church,
ufing alfo the word *Confubftantial* to the Father,
and not what is faid inftead thereof in the *Surian, Son of the Effence of the Father.*

Decree XII.

NOtwithftanding it is contrary to the Sacred
Canons, That the Children of Chriftians
fhould go to School to Heathen Mafters: Neverthelefs, feeing this Church is under fo many Heathen Kings, who many times will not fuffer any
but

but Infidels to be Schoolmasters; wherefore the Synod doth command and declare, That in all Schools, whether for Reading or Writing, wherein the Masters have *Pagods,* to which they oblige their Children at their coming into the School to pay their Reverence, as the Custom is; that it shall not be lawful for Christian Parents or Guardians to send Christian Children to such Schools, upon pain of being proceeded against as Idolaters; but if there should be any such Schools, wherein the Heathen Masters will consent that Christian Children shall pay no Reverence, nor be obliged to any Heathen Ceremony, in case there is no Christian Master near, they may be sent to such Schools, their Parents instructing them that they must pay no reverence but only to the Master, and that they must use none of the Ceremonies of the Heathen Children, that so they may not * suck in Idolatry as Mothers Milk. Furthermore, the Synod doth earnestly recommend it to all Towns and Villages, to do all that is in their Power to have their Children Educated by Christian Masters, and as for Reading and Writing, to have the Parish-Priests to teach them to do that in their

---

* Suck in Idolatry.] They would have done well to have considered, whether the introducing of the Adoration of Images into a Christianity that was planted amidst Heathens, and under Idolatrous Princes, how Innocent soever it may be in other places, was safe or not in *Malabar,* before they did it, and whether the reconciling them to Images might not dispose them to Heathenism.

Houses:

Houſes: But as to thoſe maſters who do oblige Chriſtian Children to do reverence to their *Pagods*; the Synod in virtue of Holy Obedience, and upon pain of Excommunication to be *Ipſo facto* incurred, doth command all Fathers of Families, and others that have charge of Children, not to conſent to their going to ſuch Schools; and doing the contrary, let them be declared Excommunicate, and be rigorouſly puniſhed by the Prelate, neither ſhall ſuch Children be ſuffered to enter the Church; as to which matter the Vicars and Prieſts ought to be extreamly vigilant, to prevent Childrens being Educated in Idolatry; and where-e'er there is a Chriſtian Schoolmaſter in any Town, or near it, the Children of Chriſtians are not to go to School to Infidels.

Decree XIII.

THe Synod being certainly informed, that there are ſome Chriſtian Schoolmaſters, who to conform themſelves to others, and to have the more Scholars, do ſet up *Pagods* and Idols in their Schools, to which the Heathen Children pay reverence, doth command all the ſaid Schoolmaſters, ſo ſoon as it ſhall be intimated to them, upon pain of Excommunication, to remove the ſaid *Pagods* Idols, and Reverence out of their Schools, and not to give way to Heathen Children, paying any ſuch adoration; and whoſoever ſhall be found guilty thereof, ſhall be declared Excommunicate, and denyed the Communion

of

of the Church, and of all Chriſtians, and dying, ſhall not be buried in holy Ground, nor have Chriſtian Burial, nor have any Prayers ſaid for them, and let this Decree be publiſhed by the Vicars of the Churches to which ſuch do belong.

Decree XIV.

THe Purity of the Faith being preſerved by nothing more than by Books of ſound and holy Doctrine; and on the contrary, there being nothing whereby the Minds of People are more corrupted, than by Books of ſuſpicious and Heretical Doctrines; Errors being by their means eaſily inſinuated into the Hearts of the Ignorant, that read or hear them: Wherefore the Synod knowing that this Biſhoprick is full of Books writ in the *Surian* Tongue by *Neſtorian* Hereticks, and Perſons of other Deviliſh Sects, which abound with Hereſies, Blaſphemies and falſe Doctrines, doth command in virtue of Obedience, and upon pain of Excommunication to be *ipſo facto* incurred, that no Perſon, of what quality and condition ſoever, ſhall from henceforward preſume to keep, tranſlate, read or hear read to others, any of the following Books.

The Book intituled, *The Infancy of our Saviour*, Or *The Hiſtory of our Lady* ; condemned formerly by the ancient Saints, for being full of Blaſphemies, Hereſies, and fabulous Stories, where among others it is ſaid, that the Annunciation of the

the Angel was made in the Temple of *Jerusalem,*
where our Lady was, which contradicts the Gospel of St. *Luke,* which faith, it was made in *Nazareth;* as also that *Joseph* had actually another
Wife and Children, when he was betrothed to
the Holy Virgin ; and that he often reproved the
Child Jesus for his naughty Tricks ; that the
Child Jesus went to School to the Rabbins, and
learnt of them, with a thousand other Fables and
Blasphemies of the same Nature, and things unworthy of our Lord Christ, whereas the Gospel
faith, that the *Jews* were astonished at his Wisdom, asking how he came by so much Learning,
having never been taught ; that the Devil tempted Christ before his Fast of forty days, which is
contrary to the Gospel; that St. *Joseph,* to be satisfied whether the Virgin had committed Adultery, carried her before the Priests, who according to the Law gave her the Water of Jealousie
to drink; that our Lady brought forth with pain,
and parting from her Company, not being able
to go farther, she retired to a Stable at *Bethlehem* ;
that neither our Lady, nor any other Saint is in
Heaven enjoying God, but are all in a Terrestrial Paradise, where they are to remain till the
day of Judgment, with other Errors, too many
to be related : But it is the Synod's pleasure to
instance in some of the chief Errors contained in
the Books that it condemns, that so all may be
satisfied of the reason why they are prohibited
to be read, or kept upon pain of Excommunication, and that all may avoid and burn them
with

with the greater Horror, and for other juft and neceffary refpects.

Alfo the Book of *John Barialdan*, wherein it is faid in divers places, That there were two Perfons, a Divine and Humane, in Chrift, which is contrary to the Catholick Faith, which confeffes one only Divine Perfon: It is alfo faid, That the Names of Chrift and *Emanuel* are the Names of the Humane Perfon only, and for that reafon that the moft fweet Name *Jefus* is not to be adored ; that the Union of the Incarnation is common to all the Three Divine Perfons, who were all Incarnated ; that our Lord Chrift is the adopted, and not the Natural Son of God ; that the Union of the Incarnation is accidental, and is only that of Love betwixt the Divine and Humane Perfons.

Alfo the Book intituled, *The Proceffion of the Holy Spirit* ; wherein it is endeavoured to be proved at large, that the Holy Spirit proceedeth only from the Father, and not from the Son, which is contrary to the Catholick Truth, which teaches, that he proceeds from the Father and the Son.

Alfo the Book entituled *Margarita Fidei*, or *The Jewel of Faith* ; wherein it is pretended to be proved at large, That our Lady, the moft Holy Virgin, neither is, nor ought to be ftiled the Mother of God, but the Mother of Chrift ; that in Chrift there are two Perfons, the one of the Word, and the other of Jefus ; that the Union of the Incarnation is only an accidental Union of Love and Power, and not

a

a fubftantial Union; that there are three diftinct
Faiths, which is divided into three Profeffions,
the *Neftorian*, *Jacobite* and *Roman*; that the *Ne-*
ftorian is the true Faith that was taught by the
Apoftle, and that the *Roman* is falfe and Heretical, and was introduced by force of Arms, and
the Authority of Heretical Emperors, into the
greateft part of the World; that to Excommunicate *Neftorius*, is to Excommunicate the Apoftles and Prophets, and the whole Scripture;
that they that do not believe his Doctrine, fhall
not inherit Eternal Life; that they that follow
Neftorius, received their Faith from the Apoftles,
which has been preferved to this day in the
Church of *Babylon* of the *Syrians*, That *Matrimo-*
ny neither is, nor can be a Sacrament; that the
fign of the Crofs is one of the Sacraments of the
Church inftituted by Chrift; that the Fire of
Hell is Metaphorical, not real; that the *Roman*
Church is fallen from the Faith, condemning it like-
wife for not celebrating in leavened Bread, according to what the Church has received from the A-
poftles, for which it is faid the *Romans* are Hereticks.

Alfo the Book of the Fathers, wherein it is
faid, That our Lady neither is, nor ought to be
called the Mother of God ; that the Patriarch of
Babylon of the *Neftorians*, is the Univerfal Head
of the Church immediately under Chrift; that
the Fire of Hell is not real, but fpiritual; that
it is Herefie to fay, that God was born, or dyed;
that there are two Perfons in Chrift.

Alfo

Alfo a Book of the Life of Abbot *Ifaias*, commented by a *Neftorian*, wherein it is faid, That the Union is common to all the Three Perfons; that St. *Cyril* of *Alexandria*, who condemned *Neftorius*, was an impious Heretick, and is now in Hell, for having taught, that there is but One Perfon in Chrift; whereas, as often as *Neftorius*, *Theodorus* and *Diodorus* are named, they are ftiled Saints, and bleffed; by whofe Authority it is there proved, that the Saints fhall not enjoy God before the day of Judgment; and that till then they fhall be in an obfcure place, which they call *Eden*, near to the Terreftrial Paradife; and that by fo much the worfe as any one has been, he is tormented * the lefs for it in Hell, by reafon of his greater conformity and friendfhip with the Devils; that the Word was not made

---

* **The lefs for it in Hell.**] This of fixing fomething that is juftly abominable to all Mankind, upon her Adverfaries, has been the conftant practice of the Church of *Rome*: So the Emperor *Michael Balbus*, becaufe he was an Enemy to Image-worfhip, is faid to have laughed at the Prophets, not to have believed there were any Devils, and to have placed *Judas* among the Saints; the Templars, upon the Pope and the *French* Kings confpiring together to deftroy their Order, are faid to have obliged all their Novices to blafpheme God, to renounce Chrift, the Virgin *Mary*, and all the Saints in Heaven, to fpit and trample upon the Crucifix, and to declare that Chrift was a falfe Prophet; the *Albigenfes* are faid to have held it lawful to deny their Faith, when interrogated upon it by a Magiftrate, to have held, that promifcuous Venery was lawful, but that Matrimony was Hell and Damnation; that the Souls of Men were as Mortal as their Bodies; that the way of choofing their chief Priefts, was by toffing an Infant from one to another, and that he in whofe hands the Infant expired, had that Office, and that the Devil was unjuftly thrown out of Heaven.

Man,

Man, and that it is Blasphemy to affirm it ; that
Christ conquer'd all the Passions of Sin by a Power derived from God, and not by his own
strength ; that St. *Cyril* was a Heretick in teaching, that there was but One Person in Christ ;
that the Divine and Humane Nature were united in Christ accidentally by Love ; that the
whole Trinity was incarnated ; that God dwelt
in Christ as in a Rational Temple, giving him
power to do all the good things he did ; that
the Souls of the Just will be in a Terrestrial Paradise till the day of Judgment ; that the Wicked when they dye in Mortal Sin, are carried to
a place called *Eden*, where they suffer only by
the sense of the punishments they know they are
to undergo after the day of Judgment.

Also the Book of Synods, wherein there is a
forged Letter of Pope *Caius*, with false Subscrip-
tions of a great many other Western Bishops, directed to those of *Babylon*, wherein it is acknowledged, that the Church of *Rome* ought to be
subject to that of *Babylon*, which with all that
are subject to her, are immediately under Christ,
without owing any reverence to the *Roman* Bishop ; they say likewise, That the *Roman* Church
is *fallen from the Faith*, having perverted the Canons of the Apostles, by the force of Heretical
Emperors Arms ; and that the *Romans* are Hereticks, for not *celebrating in leavened Bread*,
which has been the inviolable Custom of the
Church derived from our Saviour, and his Holy Apostles ; that all the Bishops that followed
Nestorius,

Neſtorius, ought to be much eſteemed, and when named, to be ſtiled *Saints*; and to have their Reliques reverenced : *That Matrimony is not a Sacrament*, that it may be diſſolved for the bad conditions of the Parties : That *Uſury* is Lawful, and there is no Sin in it.

Alſo the Book of *Timothy* the Patriarch, where, in three Chapters, *The moſt Holy Sacrament of the Altar* is blaſphemed; it being impiouſly aſſerted in them, *That the true Body of our Lord Chriſt is not there, but only the Figure thereof.*

Alſo the Letter which they pretend came down from Heaven, called the *Letter of the Lord's day,* wherein the *Roman Church is accuſed of having fallen from the Faith,* and having violated the *Domingo*, or *Lord's-day Letter.*

Alſo the Book called *Maclamatas*; wherein the diſtinction of two Perſons in Chriſt, and the accedental Union of the Incarnation are pretended to be proved at large, and are confirmed with ſeveral falſe and Blaſphemous Similitudes.

Alſo the Book intituled *Uguarda*, or the *Roſe* ; wherein it is ſaid, That there are two Perſons in Chriſt; that the Union of the Incarnation was Accidental; that our Lady brought forth with Pain ; and the Sons of *Joſeph*, which he had by his other Wife, being in company, went for a Midwife to her, with other Blaſphemies.

Alſo the Book intituled *Camiz* ; wherein it is ſaid, That the Divine Word, and the Son of the Virgin are not the ſame; and that our Lady brought forth with Pain.

Alſo

Alfo the Book intituled *Menra* ; wherein it is faid, That our Lord Chrift is only the Image of the Word ; that the Subftance of God dwelt in Chrift as in a Temple ; that Chrift is next to the Divinity ; that Chrift was made the Companion of God.

Alfo the Book of *Orders* ; wherein it is faid, That the Form, and not the Matter, is neceflary to Orders ; and the Forms therein are likewife Erroneous ; that there are only two Orders, *Diaconate* and *Priefthood* ; that Altars of Wood, and not of Stone, are to be Confecrated ; there are alfo Prayers in it for thofe that are converted from any other Sect to *Neftorianifm*, in form of an Abfolution from the Excommunication they had incurred for net having followed *Neftorius*, and of a reconciliation to the Church.

Alfo the Book of *Homilies* ; wherein it is faid, That the *Holy Euchariſt is only the Image of Chrift, and is diſtinguiſhed from him, as an Image is from a true Man ; and that the Body of our Lord Jefus Chrift is not there, nor no where elfe but in Heaven :* That the whole Trinity was Incarnate ; that Chrift is only the Temple of the Divinity, and God only by Reprefentation ; that the Soul of Chrift defcended not into Hell, but was carried to the Paradife of *Eden* ; that whofoever affirms the contrary, errs, and that we therefore err in our Creed : There are therein likewife fome Letters of fome Heretical Synods, in which it is faid, That the Patriarch of *Babylon* is not fubject to the *Roman* Bifhop ; with an Oath to

M   be

be taken to the faid Patriarch, as the Head of the Church, wherein People Swear to obey him, and him only, and not the Bifhop of *Rome*.

Alfo a Book intituled , *An Expofition of the Gofpels*; wherein it is every where pretended to be proved , That there are two Perfons in Chrift, and that Chrift as a pure Creature, was obliged to adore God , and ftood in need of Prayer; that he was the Temple of the moft Holy Trinity; that Chrift's Soul when he died, defcended not into Hell, but was carried to the Paradife of *Eden*; which was the place he pro-mifed to the Thief on the Crofs : That our Lady, the Virgin, deferved to be reproved for having vainly imagined, that fhe was Mother to one that was to be a great King; looking upon Chrift as no other than a pure Man; and prefuming that he was to have a Temporal Empire, as well as the reft of the *Jews* : That the Evangelifts did not Record all Chrift's Actions in Truth as they were, they not having been prefent at fe-veral of them; which was the reafon why they differed from one another fo much: That the Wife Men that came from the *Eaft*, received no favour from God, for the Journey they took ; neither did they believe in Chrift; that Chrift was the adopted Son of God, it being as im-pofiible that he fhould be God's Natural Son, as it is that Juft Men fhould be fo ; that he re-ceived new Grace in Baptifm, which he had not before ; that he is only the Image of the Word ; and the pure Temple of the Holy Spirit; that
                                                        the

the *Holy Eucharist is only the Image of the Body of Christ, which is only in Heaven at the right hand of the Father, and not here on Earth:* That Christ, as pure Man, did not know when the day of Judgment was to be: That when St. *Thomas* put his Hand into Christ's Side, and said, *My Lord, and my God!* he did not speak to Christ; for that he that was raised was not God; but it was only an Exclamation made to God upon his beholding such a Miracle: That the Authority that Christ gave to St. *Peter* over the Church, was the same that he gave to other Priests; so that his Successors have no more Power or Jurisdiction than other Bishops: That our Lady, the Virgin, is not the Mother of God: That the first Epistle of St. *John*, and that of St. *James*, are not the Writings of those Holy Apostles, but of some other Persons of the same Name, and therefore are not Canonical.

Also the Book of *Hormisda Raban*, who is stiled a Saint; wherein it is said, That *Nestorius* was a Saint, and Martyr, and suffered for the Truth; and that St. *Cyril*, who persecuted him, was the Priest and Minister of the Devil, and is now in Hell: *That Images are filthy and abominable Idols, and ought not to be adored;* and that St. *Cyril*, as a Heretick invented and introduced them: There are also many false Miracles Recorded in this Book, which are said to have been wrought by *Hormisda* in confirmation of the *Nestorian* Doctrine; with an Account of what he suffered from the Catholicks, for being obstinate in his Heresy.   M 2   Also

Also the Book of *Lots*, into which they put that they call the *Ring of* Solomon, with a great many more Superstitions, for the choice of good Days to Marry upon, and for several other uses; wherein are contained many Blasphemies, and Heathenish Observances; as also all other Books of *Lots*, and for chusing of Days, the Synod prohibits under the same Censure.

Also the Book written after the manner of † *Flos Sanctorum*; wherein are contained the Lives of a great many *Nestorian* Hereticks, who are there called Saints; and not only that entire Book, but also any of the Lives contained therein, which may be current separately; namely, those of *Abraham*, stiled the *Great*, of *George Abbot Cardeg*, whom they call a Martyr; *Jacob*, *Abban*, *Saurixo*, *Johanan*, *Gauri*, *Raban*, *Sabacat*, *Ocama*, *Daniel*, *Barcaula*, *Raban Nuna*, *Jacob*, *Rabai* the Great, *Dadixo*, *Jomarufia*, *Schalita*,

---

† Flos Sanctorum.] Let their Legends be as fabulous as they will, I am sure they cannot be worse than those of the Church of *Rome*; namely, her *Flos Sanctorum*, which is certainly the dullest Romance that ever saw the Sun.

Melchior Canus, the Bishop of *Canaries*, in his 11th. Book *de Lo eis Theologicis*, gives this just Character of them : *Dolenter hoc dico potius, quàm contumeliose, multò à Laertio severius vitas Philosophorum scriptas, quàm à Christianis vitas Sanctorum; longéque incorruptius & integrius Suetonium res Cæsarum* expofuiffe, quàm expofuerint Catholici; non res dico Imperatorum, fed Martyrum, Virginum, & Confefforum. Illi enim in probis, aut Philofophis, aut Principibus, nec vitia, nec fufpiciones vitiorum tacent, in improbis etiam colores virtutum produnt. Noftri autem plerique vel affectibus inferviunt, vel de induftriâ quoque ità multa confingunt, ut eorum me nimirum non folùm pudeat, fed etiam tædeat. In illo enim Miraculorum monftra fæpiùs quàm vera miracula legas : hanc auream fc. legendac homo fcripfit ferrei oris, plumbei cordis, animi certè parùm feveri & prudentis.*

Ihab,

Ihab, Abimelech the Expofitor, *Abraham,* another *Abraham Natpraya, Jobcarder, John, Ircafca, Neftorius, Jaunam, Barcurra, Raban Gabarona, Schabibi, Barcima, Titus, Raban Sapor, Gregory* the Metropolitan, *George, Monach, Xahucalmaran, Jofeph, Nathanael, Simon Abbot Chabita, Zinai Abbot, Audixo, John Crafcaya, Barcahade, Italaah, John Sahadui, Aha, Xalita, Joanacoreta, Xari,* another *John, Elias, Joadarmah, Ananixo,* another *John, Barhetta, Rabai Simeon, Narfai Naban, Raban Theodorus, Rabai* Doctor, *Abda, Abolaminer, Rabantarfaha* of *Cadarvi, Xuuelmaran, Sergiududa, Xuuealmaran, Dadixo,* another *Abraham, Ezekieldafa, Rabai Perca, David Barnutar, Hormifda, Pition, Salomon Abbot, Raban Machixo,* another *George, Muchiqua,* another *Abraham, Apuimacan, Xaurixo, Ixofauran, Jofedec, Raban Camixo, Bardirta Abbot, Abraham Barmaharail, George Raban, Zliva Abbot, Guiriaco Rabanbaut, Jofeph Abbot, Zaca, Nasbian, Jefus Abbot, Aaron Bucatixo, Afcan,* another *Abraham, Xonxa Abbot, Amanixo Gafraya, Sahedona* Bifhop, *Jofeph, Azaya, Ifahaha* Bifhop, *Jacob,* whom they call a Prophet, *Ixaiahu, Eunuco Ramain, Jobar Malchi:* Who were all *Neftorian* Hereticks, and the chief followers of that curfed Sect, as is evident from their Lives, which are full of Herefies, Blafphemies, and falfe and * fabulous Miracles, with which they pretend to Authorize their Sect.

* **Fabulous Miracles.**] For people not only to condemn that in others, which they themfelves are vifibly and infinitely more guilty of; but to do it with the Air, and affurance of an unqueftionable Innocency, cannot be denied to be no common privilege;

Also the Book called *Parisman*, or the *Persian Medicine*, which is full of Sorceries, teaching certain Methods whereby one may do mischief to their enemies, and may gain Women, and for a great many other lewd and prohibited purposes; there are likewise in it strange Names of Devils, of whom they affirm, that whosoever shall carry the Names of seven of them about him writ in a Paper, shall be in no danger of any Evil: It contains also many * Superstitious Exorcisms for the casting out of Devils; mixing some Godly words with others that are not Intelligible; and with the Invocation of the most Holy Trinity, oftentimes desiring the doing

for were all the false Miracles, that have been pretended to be wrought by all the other Sects of Religion, put together, they would fall infinitely short of what may be met with in any single Saint's Life, or in confirmation of any single Doctrine of the Church of *Rome*; most of which too, are what *Canus* said of them, rather *Monstra Miraculorum* than *vera Miracula*, or any thing else.

* **Superstitious Exorcisms.**] I do not think they had an Exorcism in any of their Books, that was more absurd than that we meet with in the *Sacerdotale Romanum*, printed at *Venice* no longer ago than the Year 1576. where the Priest when he meets with a sullen Devil, that will not tell his Name, nor give any account of himself, is order'd to fall upon him with *Præcipio tibi sub pœnâ Excommunicationis majoris & mino-*

riu, ut respondeas, & dicas mihi Nomen & Diem & Horam exitus tui : I shall not make that reflection upon this Exorcism, which is very obvious at the first hearing of it : It was with some such Exorcism as this, doubtless, that they got out of the Devil that raised the terrible Persecution in *Japan*, that he was sent thi her from *England*, where he had been employed a great many Years in persecuting of *Roman Catholicks*; upon which the Jesuit *Luys Pineyro*, the Writer of the Persecution, makes this grave Remark; That doubtless it is with Devils as it is with Men; that some of them have particular Talents for some particular works; and that this Devil's Talent must doubtless have lain chiefly towards the raising of bloody Persecutions against Catholicks, and the Christian Faith.

of

of lewd things, and enormous fins, joyning the
Merits of *Neftorius* and his followers, many times,
in the fame Prayer with thofe of the bleffed Virgin,
and thofe of their Devils, with thofe of the Holy
Angels; all which is very common in this Diocefs;
moft Curates having this Book, and making ufe of
it to this very day; all which fort of Books the Synod prohibits in this Diocefs under the forementioned cenfures; and whofoever from henceforwards
fhall be found to have any of them, befides the cenfure they have incurred thereby, fhall be feverely
punifhed by their Prelate.

Decree XV.

BUt the forementioned Herefies are not only
to be met with in thefe Books, but are likewife in the Common Prayer, and Breviaries
that they ufe in their Churches, which having
been compofed by *Neftorian* Hereticks, are full
of Blafphemies, Herefies, Fables, and Apocryphal ftories, whereby inftead of praifing God,
they are continually blafpheming him in their
Divine Offices.

In the Book called the *Great Breviary*, it is
faid, That the Divine Word did not affume Flefh,
ignorantly pretending to prove it thus; becaufe
if the Word had affumed Flefh, to what purpofe
was the Holy Spirit's overfhadowing the Virgin?
In the fame Breviary the whole Office of Advent is Heretical, it being every where affirmed
therein, that Chrift had two Perfons, and calling

M 4   him

him continually only the Temple of God; and in the Feaſt of the Nativity, there is a propoſition in one of the ſolemn Antiphona's, that directly contradicts St. *John*, in which it is ſaid, that *the Word was not made Fleſh*, and that all that believe the contrary, are diſobedient to the Church, and are obſtinate Rebels againſt the Faith; ſo that the whole Offices of the Advent and Nativity are little elſe than pure Blaſphemy.

In the Book of Prayers for the great Faſt, it is frequently ſaid, that there were two Perſons, a Divine and Humane in Chriſt. It contains alſo ſeveral Commemorations of *Neſtorius*, and other Hereticks his Followers, affirming *Marndeay*, *Theodorus* and *Diodorus*, and other *Neſtorian* Hereticks, to have been the Followers of St. *Ephrem*.

In the Greater Breviary, which they call *Hudre* and *Gaza*, or *The Treaſure of Prayers*, it is every where ſaid, that there are two Perſons in Chriſt, and one repreſentation of the Son of God; that he is the Image of the Word, and the Temple of the ſame; that the Divine Perſon did enlighten the Humane, and that Chriſt advanced in Grace and Knowledge by degrees; that our Lady never carried God in her Womb, as Hereticks affirm, Chriſt being a Man like to others, and that ſhe ought not to be called the Mother of God, but only the Mother of the ſecond *Adam*; that the whole Trinity aſſumed Humanity, and that St. *Matthew* taught the *Hebrews* ſo; that God did not make himſelf Fleſh, which he only took as

a

a Dwelling to cover his Glory; that God accompanyed Chrift on the Crofs, but had not taken the Humanity, neither was it God that suffered; that the Word of the Father changed it self into Humanity, and by the Son of *Mary* redeemed Mankind; that the Father Eternal took Flesh in the fame manner as the Son; that the Angel delivered his Meſſage to the Virgin in the Temple, and not at *Nazareth* ; that the pains of travail opened the Womb of the Virgin, who brought forth with labour after the manner of other Women ; that * *in the moſt Holy Sacrament of the Euchariſt, there is not the true Body of Chriſt*; with a thouſand more Blaſphemies about

* **In the moſt holy Sacrament.**] The Chriſtians who live ſcattered about *Meſopotamia* and *Aſſyria*, and whoſe Patriarch reſides at the Monaſtery of St.*Raban Hurnez* the *Perſian*, in the *Gordyæan* Mountains, 40 miles above *Niniveh*, tho' *Eutychians*, and for that reaſon Enemies to the *Chaldæan* Chriſtians, do agree with them in denying Tranſubſtantiation, as appears from the following Prayer taken out of their Miſſal, and communicated to me by my Learned Friend Dr. *Hide.* *Angeli & homines laudabunt te, O Chriſte, Sacrificere pro nobis, qui per Sacramenta, quæ ſunt in Eccleſia tua, docuiſti nos, ſecundum magnificentiam tuam, quod ſicut in Pane, & Vino Natura ſunt à te diſtinEta, in Virtute & potentia idem ſunt tecum. Sic etiam Corpus quod à nobis, diſtinEtum eſt à verbo in ſubſtantia,* *cum illo tamen qui accipit illud, adunitum eſt in magnificentia & potentia. Sic credimus & non metuimus ab iniquitate, quod in uno (ſc. una Hypoſtaſi) ſit filius fatemur, & non eſt duo ſicut improbi, (id eſt, ſicut dicunt Neſtoriani) non enim in completionibus Sacrificii, Corpus & Corpus frangimus, ſed unum per fidem, ſicut docuiſti nos in Evangelio tuo, laus tibi qui per Sacramenta tua, inſtruxiſti nos ut lauemus nomen tuum.*

Now I take this Teſtimony againſt Tranſubſtantiation to be much the ſtronger for it's being given by the *Eutychians*, to whoſe Hereſie Tranſubſtantiation, had it been believed, would have given great Countenance ; as indeed I cannot but reckon thoſe Hereticks having no where made uſe of that Doctrine to ſupport their Hereſie, to be a conſiderable Argument of

it ;

it ; that *Nestorius* was a Preacher of Truth ; and
in several places God is praised for having declared the Truth to *Theodorus* and *Diodorus*, who
was Master to *Nestorius* ; and in several Prayers
they beseech God to chastise those that believe
otherwise than *Nestorius*, and his Followers,
whose Faith they say is founded on St. *Peter's*,
and the rest of the Apostles ; Moreover it is
said, that the Holy Virgin, and her Spouse *Joseph*, appeared before the Priests, who could not
tell how she had conceived ; and *that Images are
Idols, and ought not to be adored, nor so much as
kept in Churches or in Houses of Christians* ; there
are likewise Offices of *Nestorius* and his Followers, and Commemorations of several Hereticks.

In the Office for Priests departed, it is sung,
That in the most holy Sacrament of the Altar,
there is only the Virtue of Christ, but not his true Bo-

its not having been believed either by themselves, or by the Orthodox ; for had the latter believed it, tho' they had not done it
themselves, they could not have
failed to have used it as *Argumentum ad hominem*, which is what
they have no where done. It is
true, this is only a Negative Argument, but it is as true, that it is
so circumstantiated as to be of e-
qual force with one that is positive. So again, I do not see how
we could have had a clearer proof
of Transubstantiation, not having
been believed either by the *Mani-*
chees, or the Orthodox, than we
have from the *Manichees* abstain-
ing from the Cup in the Sacrament
for no other reason, but because
they did not think it lawful to
drink Wine, and from the Ortho-
doxes proving against them from
that very Institution that it was
lawful, and endeavouring to convince them by several Arguments,
that it was their Duty to receive
the Cup in the Sacrament ; and
all this without ever so much as
once intimating, that the Liquor in
the Cup, when it came to be received, was Blood and not Wine.

dy

dy and Blood ; all which Books and Breviaries,
tho' they do well deferve to be burnt, for thefe
and other Errors that they contain, yet there
being no other at prefent in this Diocefs, for the
keeping up of Divine Service, and the celebration of Religious Offices, until fuch time as they
fhall be furnifhed with new Breviaries, which
the Synod defires they may fpeedily, and that
fome may be Printed for them at St. *Peter's* in
Rome ; the Synod doth order them to be corre-
&ted and purged from all their Errors, and Commemorations of Hereticks, and the entire Offices
for all fuch ; and the Offices of Advent and the
Nativity to be entirely tore out of their Breviaries and burnt, entreating the moft Illuftrious
Metropolitan to fee it done at his next Vifitation in all the Churches of the Diocefs, commanding all Curates in virtue of Obedience, and upon pain of Excommunication to be *ipfo facto* incurred, to produce the faid Books, and all the
other Books that they have, as well of publick
as of private Ufe, and of Prayers, as well as of
the Mafs, before the faid Lord Metropolitan at
his Vifitation, in order to their being corrected
by Perfons appointed for that work, in conformity to what is here ordained.

Decree XVI.

FOR the prefervation of the Purity of the
Faith, the Synod does command all Priefts,
Curates, and all other Perfons, of whatfoever
Con-

Condition, or Quality, within this Bishoprick, in virtue of Obedience, and upon pain of Excommunication within two Months after the publication thereof shall come to their knowledge, to deliver all the Books they have written in the *Syrian* Tongue, either with their own hands, or by some other Person, to the most Illustrious Metropolitan, which they may do at the Visitation that he intends to hold speedily, or to Father *Francisco Roz*, of the Society of Jesus, Professor of the *Syrian* Tongue in the College of *Vaipicotta*, or to the said College, in order to their being perused and corrected, or destroyed, as shall be thought most convenient, the Books of Common Prayer being excepted, which are to be emended in the form abovesaid; and under the same Precept of Obedience, and pain of Excommunication, the Synod does command, That no Person, of what Condition or Quality soever within this Bishoprick, shall presume to translate any Book into the *Syrian* Tongue, without express Licenfe from the Prelate, with a Declaration of the Book to which it is granted, the Books of Holy Scripture and Psalms only excepted; and until such time as this Church shall be provided with a Bishop, the most Illustrious Metropolitan doth commit the Power of granting all such Licenfes to the Reverend Father *Francisco Roz*, of the Society of Jesus, by reason of his great skill in those Books, and in the *Chaldee* and *Syrian* Languages.

Decree

Decree XVII.

SEeing the Purity of Faith and good Manners doth very much depend on the Doctrine that is preached to the People; wherefore the Synod, being informed that there are several ignorant Curates who do take upon them to preach, and make Difcourfes in publick, wherein they teach several Errors and Herefies that they meet with in Books that they do not underftand, and several fabulous and Apocryphal things, thofe efpecially which they take out of the Book of the *Infancy of our Saviour*, and other Apocryphal and Heretical writings, doth command that none prefume to preach, or make any fet Difcourfe to the People, but who are Licenfed by the Prelate in Writing, who fhall firft examine them diligently, as to their fufficiency and Doctrine, according to the Holy Council of *Trent*; and when there fhall happen to be no Prelate during the vacancy of the See, the moft Illuftrious Metropolitan doth commit the care thereof to the Rector of the Jefuits College of *Vaipaicotta* in this Diocefs, that fo he, and fuch of the Fathers as he fhall name, may make the faid Examinations, of which they fhall give a Certificate fealed by the Rector; and at the next Vifitation the Lord Metropolitan fhall name fuch as fhall appear to him to be moft for the benefit of the People of this Bifhoprick, in order to their being rightly inftructed; and whofoever

shall

shall, without having undergone such an Examination, and without having obtained a Licenfe thereupon, in writing, under the hand of the Bifhop, or Prelate, prefume to preach, or make any Difcourfes to the People, fhall be fufpended from their Office and Benefice for a Year; neverthelefs, all Vicars may in their own Churches make fuch Difcourfes to their People, as they fhall judge neceffary, out of the Holy Scriptures, and other approved Books; to which end the Synod doth earneftly defire, that there may be a Catechifm made in the *Malabar* Tongue, out of which there may be every *Sunday* fomething read to the People: And whereas the Synod is informed that the moft Illuftrious Metropolitan is already about fuch a Work, and has reafon to hope that it may be done by the end of the Vifitation, it doth command, fo foon as it is finifh-ed and publifhed, That all Vicars do every *Sunday* at the time of Offering, or before, or after Mafs, read a Chapter of the fame to the People in conformity to the Orders they fhall receive.

Decree XVIII.

WHereas, through the Ignorance and bad Doctrines of the Priefts of this Diocefs, occafioned by their having been accuftomed to read Heretical and Apocryphal Books, they do many times deliver Errors, and fabulous Stories, in their Sermons, and Admonitions to the People, without knowing what they fay themfelves:

Where-

Therefore, to prevent the Peoples being mif-
taught, the Synod doth command, That whenfoever it fhould be proved to the Prelate,
that any fuch thing has been delivered in publick, or in any Congregation, that the Prelate having drawn up a Form of Recantation in Writing, fhall fend to the faid Curates, or the Perfons that have delivered fuch things, commanding them to retract and unfay the fame in publick, either by reading the faid Recantation, or
by declaring the Contents of it to the People,
and teaching them the Truth; which if any fhall
refufe to do, which God forbid, they fhall be
declared Excommunicate, and fhall be punifhed
according to the Holy Canons, and the quality
of the Matter they delivered; which fhall be
executed with great rigour, if it fhall appear to
have been fpoke with Knowledge and Malice; but
where it fhall be found to have flow'd from Ignorance, and an innocent Mind, it fhall fuffice
that a ready Obedience be paid to the faid Satisfaction and Recantation.

Decree XIX.

THe Synod having been informed of feveral
Meetings that were in this Diocefs, upon
the death of Bifhop *Mar-Abraham,* in which both
publick and private Oaths were taken, againft
yielding Obedience to the Holy *Roman* Church,
feveral Curates, and others, obliging themfelves
never to confent to any change either in the
Govern-

Government of the Bifhoprick, or in matters of
Faith, nor to receive any Bifhop that fhould be
fent to them by the Holy Apoftolical See, or by
any other way, than by the Order of the Schifmatical, Heretical, *Neftorian* Patriarch of *Babylon*,
with feveral other particulars, contrary to the
Sacred Canons, and the Obedience that is due to
the moft Holy *Roman* Pontificate ; doth declare
all * fuch Oaths, or any other taken, or that fhall
be taken in the fame manner, to be void, and
of no force ; and that they do not only not oblige the Confciences of thofe that have taken
them, but that as they were rafhly and malicioufly
taken, fo it is an Impiety and Schifm to keep
them ; denouncing the Sentence of the greater
Excommunication upon all thofe that made them,
or took them ; This Synod having above all o-
ther things promifed and fworn to yield Obedience to the Commands of the Pope, and the
Holy Apoftolical See, according to the Holy Canons, and never to receive any Bifhop or Prelate, but what fhall be fent by the Holy *Roman*
Church, to which it of right belongs to provide
Prelates and Bifhops to all the Churches in the
World, and to receive thofe that he fhall fend,
without any doubt or fcruple, acknowledging
them for the true Prelates and Paftors of their
Souls, without waiting for any other Order,
befides that of the Bifhop of *Rome*, notwithftan-

---

* **Such Oaths.**] We may defend a Church that is not Popifh,
fee by this what doughty Securi- are, in the opinion of Papifts.
ties, Promifes, or Oaths made to

ding

ding any impious Oaths that may have been made
at any time to the contrary.

Decree XX.

THis prefent Synod, together with all the
Priefts and faithful People of this Diocefs,
doth embrace all the Holy General Councils received by Holy Mother Church, believing and
confeffing all that was determined in them, anathematizing, rejecting, and condemning all that
they have rejected and condemned; but efpecially it doth with great Veneration receive and
embrace the firft Holy Council of *Ephefus*, confifting of 200 Fathers, firmly believing all that
was therein determined, and rejecting and condemning whatfoever it condemned; but above
all, the Diabolical Herefy of the *Neftorians*,
which has been for many Years preached and believed in this Diocefs; which together with its
Author *Neftorius*, and all his Followers, the faid
Council did reject , and anathematize; who being taught by the Devil, held that there were
Two Perfons in our Lord Chrift; affirming
alfo, that the Divine Word did not take Flefh,
into the Unity of its Perfon, but only for an
Habitation, or Holy Dwelling, as a Temple;
and that it ought not to be faid, that God was Incarnate, or that he Died, nor that our Lady, the
Glorious Virgin, was the Mother of God, but
only the Mother of Chrift, with other Diabolical Herefies, all which this Synod does condemn,
N   reject,

reject, and anathematize, embracing the Holy
Catholick Faith , in that purity and integrity,
that it is believed, and profeſſed in, by the Holy Mother *Roman* Church, the Miſtreſs of all
Churches, to which in all things it ſubmits it ſelf
according to the profeſſion it has made. Furthermore, this Synod does acknowledge the Glorious *Cyril* Archbiſhop and Patriarch of *Alexandria* , who by Order of the Biſhop of *Rome*,
† preſided in the Holy *Epheſan* Council, to be a
Bleſſed Saint, at this time enjoying God in Heaven ; and that his Doctrine in the ſaid Council
againſt the *Neſtorians*, is Holy, and univerſally
received in the Catholick Church, profeſſing all
that reject it, to be Excommunicated Hereticks.

Decree XXI.

FUrthermore , This preſent Synod, with all
the Prieſts and faithful People of this Dioceſs, doth embrace the laſt * Holy and Sacred
Council of *Trent*, and does not only believe and

† **Preſided.**] St. *Cyril* preſided in the *Epheſan* Council in his
own right, being the only Patriarch that was preſent at it.

* **Holy Council of Trent.**]
Juſtinianus, a Noble *Venetian*, in
the 15th Book of his Hiſtory of *Venice*, gives the following account of
the Holineſs of the *Trent* Council:
*Religionis cauſa in Tridentino Conci-
lio parum proſperos ſucceſſus habebat,
ob diſſentientes animos , cæcamque
Prælatorum ambitionem. Solus autem
Cardinalis Lothoringius, Vir pietatis*

*Studio, & dicendi arte clarus, quæ
ad Dei honorem, & veram Eccleſiæ
reformationem eſſent, ſuadebat ; cui
plerique ex Concilii Patribus, huma-
narum potius rerum, quàm divinarum
curam habentes, refragabantur : va-
riiſque opinionibus Sanctâ Synodo
diſſidente, nil quod rectum, ſanctum,
piumque foret, decerni potuit, omniaque
confuſione, & cæcitate plena erant,
tantaque Prælatos ambitio cœperat,
ut nulla apud eos fidei, Religioniſque
pro verâ Eccleſiæ reformatione ratio
haberetur.*

confeſs

confefs all that was determined and approved of
therein, and reject, and anathematize all that that
Council rejected and condemned; but doth
moreover receive and embrace the faid Council
as to all matters therein determined, relating to
the reformation of the Church, and all Chriftian
People, promifing and fwearing to Govern it
felf according to the Rules thereof, and to obferve the fame Forms that are obferved in the
Catholick Church, and as are obferved in this
Province of the *Indies,* and in all the other Provinces, and Suffragans to the Metropolis of *Goa*;
in order to the removing of all Abufes and Cuftoms that are contrary to the Decrees of the faid
Council of *Trent*; by which only it is refolved
to Govern it felf as to all matters relating to
the Government of the Church, and the Reformation of the Manners of this faithful and Catholick People, any Cuftoms, tho' immemorial, in
this Bifhoprick, to the contrary notwithftanding.

Decree XXII.

THis prefent Synod, together with all the
Priefts and faithful People of this Diocefs,
doth with great fubmiffion, and reverence, fubmit it felf to the Holy, Upright, Juft and Neceffary Court of the Holy Office of the † Inquifition,

---

† 𝕴nquifition.] This agrees
with what *Paul* the IIId. faid of
the Inquifition upon his Death-
bed, that it was the Pillar of the
Church of *Rome*; if he had been
in his Chair he could not have
delivered a greater truth. A Heathen *Roman* Synod would never
have been guilty of calling that an
Upright and Juft Court, which

in

in thefe Parts Eftablifhed ; and being fenfible how
much the Integrity of the Faith depends upon
that Tribunal, it does promife and fwear to be
obedient to all its Commands in all things thereunto pertaining ; being, after the Example of all
other Bifhopricks in this Province, willing that
all matters of Faith fhould be judged of by the
fame Court, or by fuch Perfons as it fhall depute : And notwithftanding the faid Holy Office
has not hitherto, by reafon of this Church's having been feparated, and had little or no cor-

neither fuffers its Prifoners to know the particular Crime where-of they are accufed, nor the Perfons that accufe them, nor the Witneffes that depofe againft them, *Acts* 25. v. 16. I referr thofe that have a mind to be fatisfied of the Juftice of this Court, to the Hiftory of the Inquifition of *Goa*, which was the Inquifition this Synod put the Church of *Malabar* under, publifhed by a *French* Papift who was himfelf a Prifoner in it; tho' I muft tell them that as bad as his Treatment was there-in, that it was but Play to what it would have been, had he profefs'd himfelf a Proteftant, or not to have been of the *Roman* Communion,tho'he had once been of it.

Bulenger, tho' otherwife a fierce Papift, gives this following account of this Holy Office. *Inter hæc actum à Pontifice cum Hifpaniæ Rege, ut Inquifitio Hifpanica Mediolanum inferretur, quod tam acerbè tulêre Infubres, ut defectionis confilia ini-erint. Ea quæftio in Hifpaniâ Mauris deprehendendis inftituta eft, per cujus caufam, & nomen, crebrò innocentes ac fceleris integri cuftodiæ mancipan-tur, opibus evertuntur, vitâ & dignitate falfis criminibus circum-venti fpoliantur. Si vocula fortè à Delatoribus excepta eft, Majeftatis illico poftulantur, in ultimæ fortis hominibus crimina prætentata, mox in Viros Principes diftricta funt. Jacent plerumque tres annos in fitu & pædore carceris, priufquam libello aut noto crimine arceffantur: alii nullius criminis comperti judicio affli-guntur: quidam in fqualore carceris ignorati contabefcunt. Auricularii, frumentarii, quadruplatores fubdolè graffantur, qui rei faciendæ Studio in Divitum capita involant, & non tam crimina judicio, quàm objectamenta jurgio prolata quærunt. Sermones inter familiares habitos in rem non modo feriam,fed capitalem ducunt.*

And *Mazeray* a Papift too, in the Life of *Henry* II. calls the Inquifition a *Dreadful Monfter*.

respondence with the Apostolical See, or with
any of the Churches that are subject to it, med-
led with any Persons belonging to this Bishoprick, yet now for the benefit of their Souls, as
to Absolutions in cases of Faith, which are known
to be reserved to that Court; This present Synod doth beseech the Lords Inquisitors to Authorize some Learned Men within this Bishoprick, or
the Jesuits of the College of *Vaipicotta*, and of
other residences of the same Religion in the said
Diocess, to Absolve all such as shall stand in
need thereof, and that with such limitations as
they shall think fit; considering how difficult it
is for the People inhabiting the *Serra*, to have
recourse to the Tribunal at *Goa*; neither can it
be otherwise, considering that they live in the
midst of Infidels, but that such necessary Cases
will sometimes happen, and especially to rude
and ignorant People.

Decree XXIII.

THe Preservation of the Purity of the Faith,
and the prevention of Peoples being corrupted with false and strange Doctrines, being
a thing of the greatest importance; this Synod
doth therefore command all Persons, of what
Quality or Condition soever in this Bishoprick,
that whensoever they shall happen to know of
any Christians doing, speaking, or writing any
thing that is contrary to the Holy Catholick
Faith, or of any that shall give assistance or

coun-

countenance thereunto, to * dilate them with all
poſſible Expedition and Secrecy to the Prelate,
or to the Vicars of the Church, or to ſome o-
ther faithful Perſon, who will immediately give
an account thereof, that ſo ſuch a courſe may
be forthwith taken, as the neceſſity of the Matter ſhall require ; the Synod in virtue of Obedience commanding the ſaid Vicars, and Perſons to
whom ſuch things ſhall be denounced to intimate
them with all poſſible ſpeed.

* What a Confuſion muſt this   is newly and forcibly converted to
practice needs make in a place that   the *Roman* Church.

Action IV.

Of the Sacraments of Baptiſm, and Confirmation.

THe Holy Sacraments of the Goſpel, inſtituted
by our Saviour and Redeemer Jeſus Chriſt
the Son of God, for the Remedy and Salvation
of Men, and to which he hath applyed the Virtue of his Holy Paſſion, and infinite Merits, and
by which all true Holineſs begins in us, and being begun, is encreaſed, and being loſt is reco-
vered, are † Seven, to wit, *Baptiſm, Confirmation,*
the *Euchariſt, Penitence, Extream Unction, Or-*

† Seven.] The Doctrine of   who lived above a thouſand years
the Seven Sacraments is ſo great   after the Apoſtles, being the firſt
a Novelty in the Church of *Rome,*   he quotes for it. This is a long
(for it is in no other Church)   time for an Apoſtolical Traditi-
that *Bellarmine* with all his read-   on to run under ground; and
ing, was not able to produce the   which is yet more wonderful,
teſtimony of one Father for it,   that it ſhould break out in an
Greek nor *Latin : Peter Lombard,*   Age that knew nothing of Ec-
                                        der,

der, and *Matrimony :* All which do differ much
from the Sacraments of the Old Law, which did
not caufe, but did only fignifie the Grace that
was to be given by the Paffion of Chrift, whereas our Sacraments do contain Grace, and give it
to all thofe that receive them worthily ; the
firft *five* were ordained for the Spiritual perfe-
ćting of every Man only with relation to himfelf, the *two laſt* were appointed for the good
Government and encreafe of the Church ; by
Baptifm we are fpiritually born again to God;
by *Confirmation* we are advanced in Grace, fortified in the Faith, and being Regenerated and
ſtrengthened, we are fupported by the Divine
Food of the *Eucharift,* and Sacrament of the Altar; and when we chance by Sin to fall into any diftemper of Soul, we are Spiritually reftored by
Penitence, and both Spiritually and Corporally
by *Extream Unćtion* ; by the Sacrament of *Order,* the Church is governed, and Spiritually
multiplied, and by *Matrimony* Corporally : All
thefe Sacraments are perfećted by three Caufes ;
that is, Things as their matter, Words as their
form, and the Perfon that is to adminifter them
with an † Intention of doing what the Church

clefiaftical Antiquity, or indeed
of any other fort of Learning ;
but this was the common fate of
all the *Roman* Doćtrines and Rites,
which they pretend to have received from the Apoftles, only
by the way of the dark and uncertain conveyance of Oral Tradition.

† *Intention*] This Doćtrine
after all their talk of the neceffity
there is of an infallible certainty
in all matters of Religion, muft
make them to be very far from
having any fuch certainty of their
being Chriftians, or of their having either a Prieft, or a Bifhop
in their Church. For as they

doth ;

doth ; and where any of these three Causes are wanting, they are not perfect, neither indeed is any Sacrament administer'd ; all the Ceremonies and Rites, approved and made use of by Holy Mother Church, in the administration of the Sacraments are holy, and cannot be despised, neglected, or * changed for others without a great Sin, notwithstanding they do not appertain to the In-

cannot be infallibly certain of any Bishop or Priest's Intention in the Administration of the Sacraments, so they may be certain that it is possible that Bishops and Priests may be so wicked as not to intend what the Church does in such administration, nay, to intend the contrary ; for there was a Parish-Priest burnt not many Years ago at *Lisbon*, who confessed at his Death, that whenever he baptized, or consecrated, he had a formed Intention not to administer those Sacraments.

* **Changed.**] This is very strange, considering that most of those Rites are but new even in the *Roman* Church, that of the Elevation of the Host not excepted : Of the Elevation of the Host, Cardinal *Bona* in the 13*th*. Chap. of his 2*d*. Book of Liturgies, saith, *Non enim liquet quæ prima Origo fuerit in Ecclesiâ Latinâ, elevandi Sacra Mysteria, statim ac consecrata sunt ; in antiquis enim Sacramentorum libris, & in codicibus Ordinis Romani, tam excusis quàm MSS, nec in priscis rituum Expositoribus, Alcuino, Almario, Walfrido, Micrologo & aliis, aliquod ejus vestigium reperitur.*

As to Peoples being present at Mass, that did not communicate at the same time, the same Cardinal saith in the 14*th*. Chap. of his first Book, *Primi & Secundi post Christum sæculi fœlicitas hæc fuit, cum multitudo credentium, quorum & erat Cor unum, & anima una, ardentissimo Dei amore succensa, nihil impensius desiderabat, quàm ad hoc supercæleste convivium accedere, in quo anima de Deo saginatur, ut loquitur Tertullianus ; at propè finem Tertii cœpit fervor ille languescere, & numerus communicantium imminui, quam tepiditatem ægrè ferentes Patres Concilii Illiberitani, Cap. 28. Statuerunt, Episcopum non debere munera ab eo accipere qui non communicat. Patres item Conc. Antioch. Can. 2. Omnes qui ingrediuntur Ecclesiam, & se à perceptione Sanctæ Communionis avertunt, ab Ecclesiâ remover decreverunt : Patres denique Conc. Tolet. Cap. 13. Eos abstineri præceperunt, qui intrant Ecclesiam, & non Communicant.* What the Cardinal saith here of these two Practices, makes almost the whole *Roman* Worship at this time to be a meer Novelty, the whole of that Worship con-

consisting almost now in Peoples going to Mass upon *Sundays* and Holy-days, which the Church obliges them to, not obliging them at the same time to communicate above once a Year, and in adoring the Host when the Priest elevates it. As to the Priest's putting the Sacrament into the mouth of the Communicants, the same Cardinal in the 17*th*. Chap. of his second Book, saith; *Sacra Communio antiquo ritu, non ore excipi solebat, ut hodiè fit, sed manu, quam qui susceperat, Ori reverenter admovebat.* As to the Priest's speaking the words of Consecration so low that no body can hear him, in his 12*th*. Chap. of the same Book, he saith; *Græci & alii Orientales verba consecrationis elatâ voce pronunciant, & populus respondet, Amen. Eundem morem servabat olim Ecclesia Occidentalis, omnes enim audiebant verba consecrationis ; postea statutum est, ut Canon submissa voce recitaretur ; & sic desiit ea consuetudo, seculo decimo, ut conjicio.*

As to the usage of her denying the Cup to the People, in the 18*th*. Chap. of his second Book, he saith, *Semper enim & ubique ab Ecclesiæ primordiis usᵹ, ad sæculum duodecimum, sub specie panis & Vini in Ecclesiis communicârunt fideles; cœpitᵹ; paulatim ejus sæculi initio usus calicis obsolescere, plerisᵹ; Episcopis eum populo interdicentibus, & sic paulatim introducta est Communio sub solâ specie panis ; quod à nullo negari potest, qui vel levissimâ rerum Ecclesiasticarum notitiâ imbutus est.*

And as to her making use of Unleavened Bread, in the 23*d*. Chap. of his first Book, he saith; *Quod si Veteres Patres, percurrere & omnem evolvere antiquitatem libeat, inveniemus procaldubio sic à tempore Apostolorum, & de inceps de pane Eucharistica. omnes loqui, ut non nisi de communi, & fermentato commodè intelligi, & explicari queant.*

As to her giving the Sacrament in Wafers, in the 23*d*. Chap. of the same Book, he saith; *Vivente Humberto qui floruit Anno* 1245. *panis consecrandus in Eucharistiâ tantæ magnitudinis erat, ut ex eo consecratæ tot particulæ frangi possent quot erant necessariæ ad populum communicandum, & panis qui tradebatur talis fuit, ut deglutiri non posset, nisi dentibus comminutus.*

And as to her keeping the consecrated Bread, or Hosts as she calls them, after the Communion is over, he saith in the same Book ; *Ne reliquiæ Sacramenti superessent, sæpe decretum est, ut tot particulæ consecrarentur, quot erant parati ad communionem; & si quid residuum foret, à sacerdote, seu Ministris commederetur ; quod si contigerit ut Ministrorum incuria putrescerent, statuit Concilium Arelatense apud Joan. X. 2. Cap.* 56. *ut igne comburatur, & cinis juxta Altare sepeliatur ; idq, in usu fuisse docet Algerus, Lib. 2. Cap* 1.

Now I take this acknowledged change of Rites in the Administration of the Eucharist, to be a very great Evidence, that there has been a Change of belief about it, and indeed to have been the Natural Consequence of such a Change, and so I believe will any body else that shall consider it impartially.

tegrity

tegrity or Eſſence of the Sacraments; there are
three that imprint a Spiritual ſign on the Soul,
that can never be blotted out; it is called a
Character, which is the reaſon why thoſe Sacraments are never to be repeated; they are *Baptiſm, Confirmation* and *Orders;* the other four,
that is, *Penitence,* the *Euchariſt, Extream Unction,* and *Matrimony,* imprint no Spiritual Sign
in the Soul, and ſo may be repeated with due
Order; but tho' theſe ſeven Sacraments are all
Divine, and do contain Grace, and diſpenſe it
to their worthy Receivers, deſerving our moſt
profound Reverence and Adoration, on the account of the Majeſty of their Inſtitutor, who
was our Lord Jeſus Chriſt the Son of God, as
alſo for the aſſiſtance of the Holy Spirit, who
operates in conjunction with them; and for the
virtue that is in them for the curing of Souls,
the Treaſure of the Paſſion of our Lord Jeſus
Chriſt, being depoſited in them, and diſpenſed
to us by their means; Nevertheleſs this does not
hinder, but that in ſome reſpects, ſome of them
may be more worthy than others, and may de-
ſerve a greater reverence and veneration. Theſe
Sacraments were all inſtituted by our Lord Jeſus Chriſt before his Aſcention into Heaven, that
ſo by their means he might communicate Grace,
and other Spiritual Benefits, he had merited for
us by his Death on the Croſs, confirming them
to the faithful by his Word and Promiſes, that
ſo by uſing them lawfully, and with due diſpo-
ſitions, we might be aſcertained of his communicating

nicating himfelf, and all the fruits of his Paffion
to us, in every one of them, in fuch a manner as
he reprefents himfelf in them.

The Doctrine of the Holy Sacrament of Baptifm.

THe firft of all the Sacraments is that of *Baptifm*, which is the Gate of the Spiritual Life,
and that whereby we are made capable of the
other Sacraments, of which without it we are no
ways capable; for as a Man muft firft be born,
before he can enjoy the good things of the Natural Life, fo Men before they are born again
in Baptifm, are not capable of enjoying the heavenly advantages of a Spiritual Life, it being by
Baptifm that we are made Members of Chrift,
and are incorporated into the Chriftian Com-
mon-wealth, and the Myftical Body of the
Church; for as by the firft man Death came upon all, for the Sin of Difobedience committed
by him and us, for which Sin we were exclu-
ded the Kingdom of Heaven, and were born
Children of Wrath, and feparated from God,
fo that without being born again of Water and
the Spirit, we cannot enter into the Kingdom of
Heaven, as Chrift himfelf has taught us; fo that
as we were born Children of Wrath, by Baptifm
we return to be Children of Grace, and as we
were born in fin the Sons of Men, in Baptifm
we are born the Sons of God; all that are baptized

tized in Chrift, as St. Paul hath it, having put on Chrift: The Matter of this Sacrament, is true, natural, and common Water, as of the Sea, Rivers, Fountains, Lakes, or Rain, and no other, tho' never fo pure and clean; all others being Liquors, and not natural Water: The Form is, *I Baptize thee in the name of the Father, and of the Son, and of the Holy Ghoft.* The Minifter of this Sacrament is a Prieft, to whom it belongs by virtue of his Office; but in cafe of neceffity, not only a Prieft or Deacon, but a Lay-man, or Woman, nay an Infidel, a *Mahometan*, a Heretick, or *Jew*: In a word, any Perfon that can Baptize, ufing the Form of the Church, and intending to do what fhe does, may adminifter this Sacrament: For feeing none can be faved without being Baptized, therefore as our Lord ordained Water, than which nothing is more ready at hand, to be the matter of this Sacrament, fo he would exclude no Man from being the Minifter thereof; the effects and virtue of this Sacrament, is, the pardon and remiffion of all fins Original and Actual, and of all punifhments due to them; for which reafon there is no Penance to be enjoyned thofe that are Baptized, for any fin they committed before Baptifm, all that die after Baptifm, before they have committed any fin, going directly to Heaven, where they enjoy the Divine Vifion for ever.

𝔇𝔢𝔠𝔯𝔢𝔢

Decree I.

WHereas in the Examination of the Forms of the adminiſtration of the Sacraments of the Church in this Dioceſs, made by the moſt Reverend Metropolitan in his laſt Viſitation, he found that in divers Churches there were different Forms uſed , and written in the Baptiſteries, ſome Curates uſing the Form following ; * N. *is Baptized and perfected, in the name of the Father, Amen ; in the name of the Son, Amen ; in the name of the Holy Ghoſt, Amen* : Others uſing the *Greek* Form, ſaying, *Baptizetur ſervus Chriſti, in nomine Patris, Amen ; in nomine Filii, Amen ; in nomine Spiritûs Sancti, Amen.* The Synod in virtue of Obedience, and upon pain of Excommunication to be *ipſo facto* incurred , doth command, that no Perſon ſhall preſume hereafter to uſe either theſe, or any other Forms , but that which is uſed in the Holy *Roman* Church ; *I Baptize thee in the name of the Father, and of the Son, and of the Holy Ghoſt* ; and that all other Forms be blotted out of their Baptiſteries, and Books, and this be put in their place.

* The Ancient Form of Baptizing was by Prayer.

Decree II.

THis Synod being informed, That at divers times they have uſed different Forms of Baptiſm in this Dioceſs , which were introduced by by Schifmatical and Ignorant Prelates, fome of which were not Legitimate, neither was the Sacrament adminiftred by them, as was declared by the moft Illuftrious Metropolitan, and others, after a ftrict Examination; and others were very doubtful, doth therefore in the name of the Holy Ghoft, defire and command all the faithful Chriftians of this Diocefs to declare to the faid Metropolitan at the Vifitation he intends to make of the Churches of this Diocefs, or to Perfons deputed by him, the time when they were Baptized, that fo according to the Form that was then ufed, a faving remedy may be provided, in conformity to what fhall be ordained therein, and that all fubmit themfelves to whatfoever he fhall be pleafed to order.

Decree III.

FOrafmuch as the Synod is informed, that there are many Perfons in this Diocefs, and efpecially among thofe that live in the Heaths, and are far from any Church, who tho' they are not Baptized, yet being of a Chriftian race, do profefs themfelves Chriftians, and when they come where there is a Church, do go to it and receive the Holy Sacraments with others, and out of meer fhame of letting it be known that they are not Chriftened, do die without Baptifm; and others becaufe they will not pay the Fees, which are Simoniacally demanded of them: It doth therefore command all Vicars of Churches

ches to make diligent inquiry through their whole
Parishes and the Heaths, to see if there are any
that are not Christened, besides the search that
the most Illustrious Metropolitan does intend at
his next Visitation, as he did at his former; and
that the said Vicars on the high Festivals, upon
which those that live in the Heaths do usually
come to Church, shall admonish them all in general, that in case there are any among them that
have never been baptized, or that have some
reason to doubt whether they have or not, that
they go to them and acquaint them therewith
in private, that so they may be secretly Christened, and without paying any Fee, letting them
know that they are not Christians, nor capable of
inheriting Eternal Life, nor of receiving the Holy
Sacraments without being baptized; and all Preachers shall frequently give the same admonition,
and all Confessors must be careful to ask all rude
Christians that live in the Heaths, whether they
have been baptized, and in case it appear doubtful, they shall then baptize them privately. The
Synod grants the same License to all Priests within or without this Diocess, to baptize all such secretly, in what place soever they shall think fit.

Decree   IV.

THE Synod being informed that there are
some small Villages in this Diocess, which,
by reason of the great distance they are at from
any Church, and through the negligence of their
Pre-

Prelates and Priests, tho' they call themselves
Christians of St. *Thomas*, becaufe defcended of
fuch, yet are not Baptized, having nothing of
Chriftians but the bare name, doth command a
diligent enquiry to be made into this matter,
recommending the fame to the moft Reverend
Metropolitan, and commanding all Vicars of
Churches to fearch all places bordering upon
their Parifhes, and to oblige all fuch to be Baptized : The Synod doth likewife command Chap-
pels to be built in or near to all fuch Villages,
and to be provided with fuch Curates as may inftruct them in all matters of Faith, that fo there
may be none in all thefe parts that call themfelves Chriftians of St. *Thomas*, but what are
Baptized ; and of fome Parifh where they may
receive the Sacraments.

Decree V.

BY reafon of the great negligence that is fo
vifible in the Chriftians of this Bifhoprick,
in bringing their Children to be baptized within
eight days after they are born, according to the
Cuftom of the Church, but chiefly among thofe
that live at a confiderable diftance from any
Church, whofe Children are many times fome
Months or Years old before they are Chriften'd ;
the Synod doth ftrictly command, That all Children be baptized on the 8*th*. day after they are
born, according to the cuftom of the Univerfal Church, without there fhould be fome danger

ger of their dying before, in which cafe they ought to be Chriftened immediately, or that it fhould fo happen, that if they are not baptized fooner, they cannot be in a long time, in which cafe alfo they ought to be prefently Chriftened; and for thofe that live in *Heaths*, and far from any Church, if they fhould not be able to bring their Children to be baptized on the eighth day, they muft not fail to bring them betwixt the fifteenth and the twentieth; and all that are found to be negligent herein, let them be punifh'd feverely; and whofoever fhall neglect to bring their own Children, or others that they have the charge of, tho' their Slaves, to Baptifm for above a Month, let them be thrown out of the Church, neither fhall it be lawful for any Prieft to go to their Houfes, or to give them the *Cafturi*, or a Vifit, no not in order to perfwade them to bring their Children to Baptifm: But if it fhould be probable that the length of the Way might endanger the Child's Life, then let the Father or Guardian fignifie fo much to the Vicar of the Church to which they belong, that a fit remedy may be taken therein, that the *Baptifm* of the Infant be no longer deferred; and in fuch Cafes the Synod doth command all Vicars either in Perfon, or by fome other Prieft, to haften to go; the doing thereof with diligence being one of the higheft Duties of their Function.

O

Decree

Decree VI.

THe prefent Synod doth condemn the Cuftom or Abufe which has hitherto obtained in this Diocefs, of not Baptizing the Infants of Parents that are Excommunicated, for fear of having fome Communion with them, by which means it often happens, that Children continue unbaptized for many Years, thereby running a great hazard of dying without Baptifm; and ordaining the contrary, commands the Children of Excommunicated Parents to be Chriften'd as well as others, and to that intent declares, That they that go into fuch Families to fetch fuch Children, or fhall carry or accompany them to Church, fhall incurr no cenfure or punifhment whatfoever for fo doing; neverthelefs, the Perfons that are Excommunicated fhall not be fuffer'd to go along with them, nor fhall others go to any Feaft or Banquet at their Houfes which they may have made on that occafion.

Decree VII.

THe Synod doth exhort and admonifh all Fathers and Mothers, and all other Perfons that are prefent at Womens Labour, to be careful not to fuffer any Infant to die without Baptifm: Wherefore if they fhall perceive the Child when it is born, to be weak, or in danger of dying prefently, they fhall then, if it can be

done,

done, call the Vicar, or in his abfence any other
Prieft, to come immediately to Baptize the Infant ; but if the danger fhall be fuch as not to
admit of any delay, in that cafe any Perfon that
is prefent fhall Baptize it in the Church ; throwing Water upon its Face, and faying, *I Baptize
thee in the name of the Father, and of the Son,
and the Holy Ghoft, Amen :* which fhall be done
by Ecclefiafticks, if any are prefent, rather than
Laicks, and by Men, rather than Women, if they
know the *Form* ; but if they do not, then any
one that knows it may perform it ; and when
Infants are in danger of dying in the birth, in
cafe the Head or any other principal Member doth
appear, tho' the whole Body fhould not, they
fhall fprinkle the Member that appears with Water, ufing the *Form.* And as for thofe that have
been Baptized in this manner, if they fhall happen to live, and it fhall be proved that they were
Baptized on the Head, or the greater part of the
Body, they fhall not then be Chriften'd again, but
fhall only be carried to the Church to be anointed
with the Holy Oils ; but if the Baptifm was performed on any other part, they fhall then be Baptized again, but with a Condition, faying, *If thou
art not Baptized, I Baptize thee in the name of
the Father, and of the Son, and of the Holy Ghoft,
Amen :* And after the fame manner Priefts, and
others fhall behave themfelves, as to fuch Perfons of whofe Baptifm they have any reafon to
doubt ; provided, if there are any other prefent, it fhall not be lawful for the Parents of
fuch

fuch Infants to Baptize them, that they may not
contract the Spiritual Relation of Godfather, or
Godmother; but in .cafe there fhould be no
body elfe prefent, and the Child fhould be in
apparent danger of Death, in fuch a cafe of neceffity, the Father or Mother muft Baptize it.

Decree VIII.

THe Synod doth earneftly recommend to all
People, to procure Chriftian *Daia's* or
Midwives in all their Towns, and fuch as know
the Form of Baptifm, and are able to fuccour
the neceffities of Infants when born in danger :
And whereas Infidel *Daia's* do ufe a great many
Ceremonies and Superftitions with Infants, which
are foreign to the purity and integrity of the
Gofpel, and efpecially fuch of them as are *Mahometans*; the Vicars fhall therefore take care
frequently to inftruct all their People, but efpecially the *Daia's*, in the Form of Baptifm, that
fo every body may know how to fuccour the
neceffities of Infants when they are born ; and
the Confeffors of the *Daia's* muft be fure to examine them as to the faid Form, and having inftructed them therein, fhall acquaint them how
much it is their duty to be perfect in it.

Decree IX.

THe Synod doth command, That no Person presume to keep an Infidel Slave without Baptizing him; whom, if they are Infants, they shall Baptize presently; and if come to years of discretion, they shall take care to instruct in the Faith, in order to make them Christians, but without any manner of Compulsion, besides that of continual Persuasion; and whosoever should be found to have an Infidel Child that is not Baptized, or one that is of Age and does desire to be, shall be severely punished by the Prelate, and the Parties shall be Christened; In this the Vicars ought to be extreamly vigilant, and especially when they make the Roll of Confessions, and inquire what Persons are in every Family, and who are not Christians, and why they are not.

Decree X.

THere being some Christians so unmindful of their Christian Obligations, as to sell Christians to Infidels, contrary to the Holy Canons, who by that means are certainly constrained to Apostatize from the Faith; wherefore the Synod in virtue of Obedience, and upon pain of Excommunication to be *ipso facto* incurred, doth command, That no Christian presume to Sell any of the Faithful to Infidels; and that whosoever shall be found to have done it, shall be forthwith

O 3

decla-

declared Excommunicate, and fhall not be Abfolved, until he hath redeemed the faid Chriftian, tho' he fhould coft him more than what
he fold him for; or until it fhall be manifeft
to the Vicar of the Church, and to other Curates,
and the whole People, that it cannot be done;
in which cafe he fhall not be Abfolved until by
way of Penance he has refunded the Money
that he received, with which the Vicar and
Church-wardens fhall buy an Infidel, whom
they fhall *Chriften*, great numbers of fuch
being fold daily in *Malabar*; and the Perfon
fo bought fhall have his liberty, and fhall be
cemmitted to the care of fome devout fubftantial Chriftian that will Educate him for God's
fake. Moreover, the Synod in virtue of Obedience, doth prohibit all Chriftians to Sell any Boys
or Girls, tho' they are not Baptized, to any *Mahometan, Jew, or Heathen*; it being certain, that
fuch when fold to Infidels, will never come to
the knowledge of the Faith; tho' when it is neceffary, and they are their lawful Slaves, they
may fell them to other Chriftians: Whofoever
fhall tranfgrefs herein, fhall be feverely punifhed, except the Perfon that was fold was Twenty
Years of Age; and it is manifeft to the Vicar,
to whom he fhall be carried before he is fold,
that he refufed to be Baptized.

Decree

Decree XI.

THe Heathens of thefe Parts being fo ftrangely addicted to *Auguries*, and Superftitions,
as fometimes to kill their Children which are
born on thofe days which they reckon to be Unlucky, imagining they muft be miferable if they
live, the Mothers, that they may not Murther
them with their own hands, leaving them in
Heaths, or at the bottom of fome Tree, or in a
Ditch, there to perifh; wherefore the Synod
doth command all the faithful Chriftians of this
Bifhoprick, That whereas living among fuch Heathens, and being their Neighbours, they cannot
for the moft part but know what paffes in their
Houfes, to be very watchful in this cafe; and
whenfoever they fhall know of any Infants being thus expofed, or fhall find them at any time
in the Heaths, to carry them home to their
Houfes, and cherifh them with Chriftian Charity,
either Baptizing them themfelves, or procuring
it to be done; and if when they find them,
they fhall apprehend them to be near dying,
notwithftanding they may know that their Parents will take it ill of them, who by thus ex-
pofing them have loft their dominion over them,
they fhall Baptize them immediately, whereby
the Church will acquire a right in them, and as
a Holy Mother, is glad to receive them; and if
it fhould fo happen that thofe by whom they are
found, are not in a condition to breed them

O 4 up,

up,they fhall then carry them to the Vicar,and the
other Curates of the Church, whom we command in the name of Chrift, to call together the
chief Men of the Parifh, to take fome courfe a-
bout the bringing up of the Child ; and if there
is no well-difpofed Perfon that will for the love
of God, take the charge thereof upon him, they
fhall then procure a Nurfe, and whatfoever elfe
is neceffary, if there can be no other way found,
out of the Alms and Fabrick of the Church.

Decree XII.

THe Synod commands, That the Infants
that are left at the Gates of the Churches,
or in any other place, if it does not manifeftly
appear that they are already Chriftned, fhall be
Baptized, and fhall be brought up in the fame
manner as is prefcribed for the Children of Infidels that are found expofed in the Heaths, the
Vicars doing all they can to prevail with fome
to undertake the charge of their Education for
God's fake.

Decree XIII.

ALL that fhall be converted from Heathe-
nifm to Chriftianity, being of Age, fhall
be well inftructed in the matters of Faith, before they fhall be admitted to Baptifm, and fhall
know at leaft how to Crofs themfelves, and be
able to fay the *Pater Nofter*, *Ave Mary*, the
Creed,

Creed, and the *Commandments,* as well as they can
be taught; in which Matter there has been hitherto a great Neglect, commanding the Vicars
to examine all such in the Faith before they Chri-
ſten them, without they ſhould happen to be in
danger of Death before they have learn'd thoſe
things; in which caſe their making a profeſſion of
Faith, and the neceſſary Myſteries thereof, and
ſignifying a deſire to be Baptized, ſhall be ſufficient: And whereas the Synod is inform'd, that
great numbers of Infidels living among Chriſtians, have long deſired Baptiſm of them, but
through the coldneſs of Prieſts and others, have
had none that would be at the pains to inſtruct
them, it doth therefore charge the Conſciences
of the Vicars therewith, ſpeedily to ſet about
inſtructing ſuch, according to the fervour of thoſe
that deſire it, that ſo they may be brought to
the Sacred Font of Baptiſm, deſiring all other
Chriſtians likewiſe to be diligent and zealous in
that Matter.

Decree XIV.

THe *Holy Oils* having hitherto not been uſed
in this Biſhoprick in any of the Sacraments,
and if any have been uſed, it having been without any diſtinction, and without being Bleſſed
by the Biſhop; wherefore for remedy thereof,
the moſt Illuſtrious Metropolitan, in his Reformation of the Affairs of this Church, having on
the *Thurſday* of the laſt Holy Week bleſſed the
Oils,

Oils, and furnished all the Churches therewith, instructing them in their Holy Uses and Distinctions; the Synod doth therefore command all Vicars in virtue of holy obedience, to use the said *Oils* in Baptism, Anointing all that are Baptized therewith on the Breast, and the Sides, and after they are Baptized, anointing them with the Holy *Chrism* on the Head, and making the *sign of the Cross* thereon with their Thumb dipt in the Holy *Oils*, or with a Feather kept in the Vessel for that use, wiping the *Oil* off afterwards with a Cloth or Towel, which shall likewise be kept in the same place : The Synod doth also command under the same Precept, That all Curates and Vicars do celebrate this Sacrament, with the Rites and Ceremonies, Exorcisms and Prayers, that are contained in the *Roman Ceremonial*; which the most Illustrious Metropolitan has order'd to be Translated into *Syrian* for the administration of all the Sacraments, and is to be kept in all Churches; and that the Priests when they administer Baptism solemnly in the Church, shall have on a *Surplice,* and a *Stole* about their Necks, for the more decent administration of that Sacrament, and shall not perform it in their ordinary wearing Habit, as they have done hitherto.

Decree XV.

WHereas hitherto the ancient Custom of the Church of having Godfathers and Godmothers, has not been in use in this Bishoprick, by which

which means there has been no knowledge
therein, of the Spiritual Affinity that is contracted betwixt the Party Baptized, and the Parents
thereof, and the Godfathers and Godmothers;
therefore the Synod does command, That all
that are Baptized, fhall have one or two Godfathers and Godmothers, to prefent them in the
Church, and to touch them on the Head before
Baptifm, and ,to receive them from the Holy
Font: The Men muft be fourteen Years of Age
at leaft, and the Women twelve; neither fhall
any be admitted under thofe Ages. The Synod
doth likewife declare, That there is fuch a clofe
Spiritual Affinity betwixt the Godfathers and
Godmothers, and their God-children, and the
Parents of the Children, that they can never
Marry with one another, without a Difpenfation
from the Pope, or from one empowered by him,
and which is feldom granted, and never but
when there is a very urgent caufe for it; and
that fuch Marriages celebrated without a Difpenfation, are void, and of no effect. The Synod
furthermore declares, That this Spiritual Affinity
reacheth no further than to the one or two Godfathers, and one Godmother, but not to thofe
that fhall ftand for them, tho' they touch the
Heads of the Children, neither fhall the Prieft
admit above two.

Decree

Decree XVI.

SEeing that by our Lord Jefus Chrift, and his Death, we are paffed from the *Old Law*, to the *New Law* of Grace, it is therefore reafonable, that we fhould in all things be ingrafted into the fame: and whereas in this Bifhoprick Chriftians do take feveral of the Names of the Saints of the *Old Teftament*, as alfo feveral of the Names of the Country, infomuch that there are but very few called by any of the Names of the *Law of Grace*; wherefore the Synod doth command the Priefts to do all they can to have the Names of the *Law of Grace* given in Baptifm, but chiefly thofe of the Holy Apoftles, and of the Saints that are moft celebrated in the Church, not intending hereby to take them from any Devotion that feveral among them may have for fome of the Saints of the *Old Teftament*, whofe Names have been hitherto very common in the Diocefs, fuch as *Abraham, Jacob, Zacharias,* and others; nevethelefs from henceforward they fhall not prefume to take the Name of *Hijo*, which has been very common among them, neither fhall the Priefts ever give it to any, it being the moft fweet * Name of *JESVS*, to

* **Name of Jefus.**] The *Portuguezes* had the leaft reafon of any Chriftians that I know of, to be offended with fuch a Name; *Emanuel* being by much the moft common Name in *Portugal.*

which

which that Refpect and † Reverence is due,
that none ought to take it upon them; for that
in the naming thereof, *all Knees both in Heaven*
and Earth, and under the Earth, ought to bow them-
felves, and every Tongue ought to confefs, that it
is from that Divine Name that we defire all the
good things that we enjoy on Earth; commanding all that are called by that Name, to change
it for another when they come to be Confirmed; and as for the common Names of the
Countrey, they may ftill retain them, if they
are fuch as have been ufed only among Chriftians, but not among the Heathens, for as to
thofe Names which the Heathens have ‖ in common with Chriftians, the Synod will not have
them to be given in Baptifm, charging the
Vicars and Priefts that Baptize, to take care
thereof.

† **Reverence**] *Francifco Roz*,
and the other Jefuits, ought to
have had their Order excepted
here; for if the Synod's Reafon
why none ought to be called by
that Bleffed Name holds good,
it will reach their Order no lefs
than particular Perfons.

‖ **In common.**] The Popes,
among whom we have had fo
many *Alexanders* and *Julius's*,
have had little regard to this
Rule.

Decree

Decree XVII.

THe Synod being informed, That there are
some Chriftians fo far unmindful of their
Duties in this Matter, as to give other Names
to their Children, than the * Chriftian Names
they received in Baptifm, and fometimes fuch
as are not ufed among Chriftians ; it doth therefore ftrictly command, that no Chriftian fhall
prefume to give their Children, or to call them
by any other Names, than thofe that were given
them when they were Chriftened ; or when
there fhall happen to be any juft caufe for the
changing of their Baptifmal Names, it fhall be
done only at their Confirmation, and whofoever
fhall tranfgrefs herein, fhall be feverely punifhed
by the Prelate ; and the Priefts muft not be wanting frequently to admonifh their People thereof.

* **Chriftian Names.**] This left their Baptifmal Names which
is what feveral Popes have done, were Chriftian, and have taken
who upon their Creation, have thofe that were rank Heathen.

Decree XVIII.

THe Synod being informed, That when many Children are brought together to be
Baptized, there are great heats, which fhall be
firft Chriftened ; and that after having lay'd Wa-
gers, they give Money to the Curates for the
pre-

preference, all which are intolerable diforders, and fuch fcandalous abominations as the Church ought not by any means to give way to, and which might be eafily prevented, if People could but be perfwaded to bring their Children to be Chriftened upon the eighth day, it being their deferring of their Baptifm fo long, that is the caufe of fo many coming together ; wherefore for the removing of thefe diforders in the Church, the Synod doth command that the Children be baptized as they come, without any diftinction of firft or laft, and that the Priefts do accuftom themfelves, either to baptize the pooreft firft, or all indifferently; and the Vicar or Prieft that fhall be found to have taken Money, or any Fee, before or after Baptifm, tho' it fhould be voluntarily offer'd, and of never fo fmall value, or only what is to be Eat, fhall be condemned of Simony, and punifhed according to the Canons.

Decree XIX.

IN all Parochial Churches there fhall with all poffible expedition be Fonts provided for Baptifm, which may be built with the Fabrick Money, or with the Alms Money of the Church, or by a Collection among the Parifhioners ; it muft be erected in a decent place, in a corner of the Church, and fhall have a hole in the bottom, through which the Water may be conveyed away, that fo it may not be thrown

out

out where it may be trod upon, or treated with any irreverence, it shall also be close covered at top, and locked up, and until such time as a Font shall be provided, they shall have a Vessel of some Metal or other, which shall be put to no other use, and shall be always kept in some decent place in the Church, or Sacrifty; neither shall they hereafter make use of any common Vessel, as has been the Custom hitherto; and the Water they have baptized with, shall be thrown in some place of the Church, where it will not be trod upon, and all the Water that shall be made use of in Baptism, whether it be in a Font, or a Vessel, shall be blessed with the Holy Chrism, according to the *Roman* Ceremonial, which they are to make use of.

Decree XX.

THis Synod, conforming it self to the Decrees of the Holy Council of *Trent*, and the Universal usages of the Church, doth command every Parish-Church to provide a Book, wherein the Vicar shall register the Names of all that are baptized, together with the Names of the Parents, and of the place where they live, and of the Godfathers and Godmothers, naming the place also where they were Christened, the day of the Month, and the Year, in this Form: On such a day of the month, in the Year *N*, I *N.* Vicar of the Church of *N.* baptized there, or in such a place, *N.* the Son of *N.* and of *N.* naming

the

the Father and Mother Natives of such a place, and the Godfathers and Godmothers were *N.* and *N.* the Vicar signing his Name to it at the bottom ; and when any Priest that is not the Vicar shall Christen a Child, which shall never be done without the Vicars leave, he shall Register it thus : I *N.* Curate, with leave from the Vicar of such a Church, naming both the Vicar and the Church, did Baptize *N.* and so on as above, signing his Name at the bottom ; which Book shall be always kept in the Church, and the Vicars shall be obliged to give an account thereof, and at every Visitation to shew it to the Prelate, out of which the Curates are to give Certificates of the Age of such as are to be Married, or to receive Holy Orders, that so their Age may be certainly known ; and that such Matters may not be so in the dark, as they have been formerly, when there was no certain way of coming to the knowledge of Peoples Age, which must needs create great scruples in the Minds of such as were to be Married or Ordained.

The Doctrine of the Sacrament of Confirmation.

THe Second Sacrament is *Confirmation*, which our Lord Christ instituted, in order to the confirming and establishing of Christians in the Faith, so that nothing might be able to separate them from it through the Power of the

P   Holy

Holy Ghost which is given therein, particularly
to that effect; besides the sanctifying Grace which
it gives in common with the other Divine Sacraments; the Matter of this Sacrament is the
Holy Oyl of Chrism, made of the Oyl of the
Olive-tree, signifying the light and purity of the
Conscience; and of Balsam, which signifies the
sweet smell of a good Name, both mixed
together, and blessed by the hand of the Bishop;
the Form are the words spoke by the Bishop
when he dips his Thumb into the said Chrism,
making therewith the Sign of the Cross on the
Forehead of the Person that is confirmed, saying,
*I sign thee with the sign of the Cross, and do con-
firm thee with the Chrism of Health, in the Name of
the Father, and of the Son, and of the Holy Ghost*;
to which the Bishop subjoyns three holy and
wholsome Prayers, wherein he beseeches God to
fill those that are confirmed with his Divine Spirit. The ordinary Minister of * Confirmation is the
Bishop, for tho' simple Priests may perform several other Unctions, this can be done only by

* The *English* Jesuits, who could not endure that the Pope should put a Bishop over them here in *England*, in their Books wherein they laboured to prove that there was no need of one, spoke very slightingly of Confirmation; affirming it to be a Sacrament that was not enjoyned but only where it might be had very easily; that the effects thereof might be abundantly supplyed by the other Sacraments, nay by or-dinary Assistances, that the Chrism in Baptism had not only the signification, but all the effects of Confirmation, so far at least as to make it not to be very necessary. In a word, that Confirmation was not simply necessary, neither *Necessitate Medii*, nor *Necessitate Præcepti*; so that it was not likely, that the want of it in *England* was the cause of so many Peoples apostatizing from the Catholick Faith: So little do either

a

a Bishop, the Bishops being the Successors of the Apostles, by the imposition of whose hands the Holy Ghost was given; in the place of which imposition of hands the Church gives Confirmation, Christ having so ordained it, wherein the Holy Ghost is given likewise; Nevertheless, by a dispensation from the Holy See, and by no other way, when there is any very urgent Occasion, or when it happens to be necessary for the good of the Faithful, simple Priests may confirm with Chrism, that has been consecrated by a Bishop in the forementioned Form; the effect of this Sacrament is, that therein the Holy Ghost is given, to the strengthening

the Sacraments, or the Hierarchy, not excepting the Papacy it self, signifie, when they stand in the way of the Jesuits ambition.

I do not except the Papacy, because when it was generally believed that *Clement* the VIIIth. was resolved to condemn *Molina's* Book of *Scientia Media*, the *Spanish* Jesuits endeavoured to ward off that blow, by affirming in their publick Conclusions in their College at *Complutum*, that it was not a matter of Faith, to believe that *Clement* the VIIIth. was true Pope; for which *Luisius Turrianus* the President of the Disputation, the Rector of the College, and *Vasquez*, who were present at the Act, were all summoned to appear before the Inquisition of *Toledo*, as *Gaspar Hortadus, Gregory de la Camara,* and *Alvarez de Villegas*, were to appear at *Rome* before the Pope, for having defended the same Conclusion publickly in the said University much about the same time; so that had *Clement* the VIIIth. condemned *Molina's* Book after the whole order of the Jesuits had espoused the merits thereof so publickly, which the *Dominicans* say he would certainly have done, had he but lived a few Months longer, *Ignatius Loyola* appearing to some Jesuits in *Spain*, and assuring them that *Molina's* Book would never be condemned by any Pope notwithstanding; we should have had Simony, or some other Nullity found in his Election by the Jesuits before this time: By this we see that Jesuits have wherewith to intimidate Popes, as well as Princes and Bishops.

and

and fortifying of the Soul, as it was given to the Apoftles on the day of *Pentecoft*, that Chrifti-ans may with boldnefs confefs the **Name of** Chrift and his Catholick Faith, for which rea-fon the Perfon confirmed is anointed on the forehead with the Sign of the Crofs, that being the moft open place of the Body, and the Seat of Shame and Confufion, which is very diffe-rent from what is done to People when they are baptized, who are anointed on the Head ; Peo-ple are confirmed on the forehead, that they may not be afhamed to confefs the Name of Je-fus Chrift and his Crofs, which as the Apoftle faith, is *to the Jews an Offence, and to the Heathens foolifhnefs* ; this Sacrament differs much from that of Baptifm, for as by Baptifm we are born into the Faith, fo by this we are confirmed therein ; for as in the Natural Life, to be born is different from growing, fo in the Spiritual Life it is one thing to be born to Grace and Faith, which is done in Baptifm, and another to encreafe and grow ftronger therein, which is done in Confirmation, and fo in Baptifm we are born to a Spiritual Life, and are afterwards prepared and confirmed for our Warfare, and do receive fo much ftrength, that no dangers or terrors of Punifhments, or Loffes, or Torments, or Deaths are able to fepa-rate us from the Confeffion of the Name of Chrift, and of the true Faith we profefs.

Decree

Decree I.

FOrafmuch as hitherto there has been no ufe, nor fo much as Knowledge of the Holy Sa-crament of *Confirmation* among the Chriftians of this Bifhoprick, the Heretical Prelates that go-verned it, having neglected to feed the People in a great many cafes with wholfome Catholick Food; therefore the Synod doth declare, That all Perfons who are come to the ufe of reafon, ought to receive this Holy Sacrament, having the opportunity of receiving it at the hands of a Bifhop, and that all Mafters of Families, and o-thers having the Charge of Children, are in Du-ty bound to command their Children and Slaves to receive the faid Sacrament, and that all who out of contumacy or contempt fhall refufe to re-ceive it, or to order fuch as belong to them to go to it, are guilty of a Mortal Sin, and if they neglect it out of a conceit of it's not being a Sa-crament, they are Hereticks and Aliens from the true Catholick Faith; wherefore the Synod doth command, that in the Vifitation that is to be made fpeedily by the moft Illuftrious Metropoli-tan in the Churches of this Bifhoprick, all Men and Women that are above feven years old do come to be Chriften'd or Confirmed, thofe on-ly excepted who were confirmed by the faid Lord in his former Vifitation, or at fome other, or on fome other occafion, by fome other Bifhop; this Sacrament as well as that of Baptifm being ne-

ver

ver to be repeated, in so much, that all that receive it a second time wittingly, are guilty of a
great piece of Sacrilege, besides, that they receive no Sacrament thereby : But in case any are
doubtful whether they have ever been confirmed or not, or should not remember that they
were ever, they shall declare so much to the said
Lord, or to the Bishop that is to confirm them,
that they may order the matter according to the
merit of their doubts : But if any, which God
forbid, should sacrilegiously· and obstinately despise the said Sacrament, it being proved upon
them, they shall be declared Excommunicate
until such time as they have done condign Penance, and·shall be punished at the pleasure of
the Prelate.

Decree II.

THe Synod, to its great sorrow, having been
informed, that some ignorant Persons in
Sacred Matters and the Doctrine of the Holy Sacraments of the Church, being instigated by the
Devil to persist in their cursed Schism, did in several places resist the most Illustrious Metropolitan in his former Visitation of these Churches,
so far as not only to refuse to receive the Holy
Sacrament of *Confirmation* from him, but did also oppose him publickly in the Churches, and
that many did absent themselves, some whereof
excused themselves by pretending, that it was an
unnecessary thing, and that they had never seen nor
heard

heard of it before, and others that they fhould
be affronted by the Holy Ceremony of the Prelates touching their Cheek , fcurriloufly upbraiding thofe that had received it, with bafe pro-
voking words, telling them that they had fuffer'd themfelves to be affronted and buffeted,
with other fuch Sacrilegious Expreffions, full of
Infidelity and Herefy , arifing from the Schifm
wherein they have been brought up: Whole
Towns confpiring together fo far in this Mutiny,
that the defpifing or receiving this Holy Sacrament, became the Teft of their obedience or
difobedience to the faid Metropolitan, doth
therefore (notwithftanding it knows they have all
in common, and every one in particular repented of this, and being fenfible of the greatnefs
of the error they committed therein, have beg'd
pardon for it, and upon their having confefs'd their
Ignorance, have been gracioufly received by the
faid Lord Metropolitan, and having fubmitted
themfelves to the obedience of the Holy *Roman*
Church, are ready to do all that fhall be enjoyned them, to prevent the life however, that none
for the time coming may commit the like faults
or Sacrileges) command, That if any (which God
forbid) fhall dare to do or fay any fuch thing
againft this Sacrament or the Holy Ceremonies
and Rites wherewith it is adminiftred to the
Faithful, that they be declared Excommunicate,
and be feparated from the Church and the Communion of the Faithful, until fuch time as they
have undergone condign Penance at the plea-

fure

sure of the Prelate, and shall demonstrate their
due subjection to the obedience of the Holy
Church, and have taken the Oath of the Faith
contained in this Synod, and declared that all
that reject and despise the Rites and Ceremonies
approved of, and received in the Church, in the
solemn administration of this and the other Sacraments, are Hereticks and Apostates from our
Holy Catholick Faith, as was determin'd in the
Holy Council of *Trent*, and ought to be proceeded against and punished as such, according
to the Sacred Canons.

Decree III.

THe Synod doth declare, That in the Sacrament of *Confirmation* or *Chrism*, there must be
a Godfather and Godmother as well as in *Baptism*,
to present such as are to be Confirmed according
to the ancient Custom of Holy Mother Church,
but there shall be but only one Godfather and
Godmother , who must themselves have been
Confirmed ; it being very indecent, that any
Person should present one to have that done to
him, which they have not had done to themselves ;
and that the Man shall be above 14, and the Woman above 12 Years Old, or one of them at
least shall be of that Age ; and in this Case the
Godfathers and Godmothers do contract the same
Spiritual Affinities and the same Impediments that
the others do in *Baptism*, the said Spiritual Affinity being equally contracted in both these
Sacraments.   ACTI-

ACTION V.

Of the Holy Sacrament of the Eucharist, *and of the Holy Sacrifice of the* Mass.

The Doctrine of the Holy Sacrament of the Eucharist.

THe third Sacrament in the Order of the *Spiritual Life*, is the Holy *Eucharist* , tho' in Veneration, Sanctity and Dignity, it is the first and most excellent, for containing in it *the true, real and substantial Body and Blood, together with the Soul and Divinity of our Lord Jesus Christ, the Son of God, true God, and true Man, our Saviour and Redeemer; which was instituted by him the day before he suffer'd for us, as the most sweet Remate, or Conclusion of all his Works, and a Memorial of his Passion, the fulfilling of all the ancient Figures, the greatest of all the Miracles that ever he wrought, and for the singular Consolation of the Faithful in his absence.* The Matter of this Sacrament is Bread of *Wheat*, and Wine of the *Grape* only; so that all that Consecrate in Bread made of *Rice*, or of any thing else but the Flower of *Wheat*, or of Wine that was not pressed out of the ripe *Grape* of the Vine do not make the Sacrament; there must also be *Water* mixed with the Wine before it is Consecrated, but in a much smaller quantity than the Wine, that so it may easily * turn it self into Wine before the Con-

---

* **Turn.**] For Water to turn   Miracle as for the Priest to turn
it self into Wine, is as great a   Wine into Blood.

secration:

fecration : which mixture is therefore made, becaufe from the Teftimony of Holy Fathers, Holy Mother Church believes that our Lord Chrift himfelf did fo, whofe having mixed Water with the Wine that he Confecrated, makes it a great Sin to omit to do it. It is alfo agreeable to the reprefentation of the Myftery of what paffed on the Crofs, and of our Lord Chrift, out of whofe precious Side flowed *Water* and *Blood* ; as alfo to fignifie the Effect of this Sacrament, which is the *Union* of the Faithful with Chrift, the *Water* fignifying the Faithful, and the *Wine* our Lord Chrift, and the converfion of the *Water* into the *Wine*, the Union of our Souls with Chrift by means of this Divine Sacrament, according to what our Lord faid ; *He that eateth my Flefh and drinketh my Blood, dwelleth in me, and I in him.* The *Form* of this Sacrament is the words of our Saviour, by which the Sacrament is made ; for tho' the Prieft pronounceth many and divers words in the *Mafs*, and makes many Prayers and Petitions to God, yet when he comes to Confecrate, he ufeth only the words of Chrift, none others belonging to the fubftance of Confecration ; fo the Prieft fpeaking in the Perfon of Chrift, makes this Divine Sacrament, becaufe by virtue of thofe words, he turneth the fubftance of *Bread* into the fubftance of the Body of Chrift, and the whole fubftance of the *Wine* into his *Blood*, there remaining nothing of *Bread* and *Wine* after that, but only the Accidents or Species of them ; and that after fuch

a

a manner, that the whole of Chriſt's Body and Soul, and Divinity, are contained under every Particle of both, tho' never ſo ſmall when ſeparated; ſo that in every crumb of the *Hoſt*, tho' never ſo ſmall, there is Chriſt intire, and in every drop of the Species of Wine that is ſeparated there is Chriſt entire, ſo that in each of the Species whole Chriſt, God and Man is received, as alſo the true Sacrament; for which reaſon Holy Mother Church does not uſe to Communicate the Faithful but † under one Species, becauſe in that they receive Chriſt entire. To this Divine Sacrament the Worſhip, Veneration and ‖ Adoration of *Latria* is due, or the

† 𝕌𝔫𝔡𝔢𝔯 𝔬𝔫𝔢 𝔖𝔭𝔢𝔠𝔦𝔢𝔰.] What makes the Sacrilege of denying the Cup to the People in the Sacrament to be ſomething the greater, is, that moſt of the *Roman* Doctors do hold, that there is more Grace convey'd to People by communicating under both the Species of Bread and Wine, than under that of Bread only, *Vaſquez Cap.* 2. *Quæſt.* 80. *Art.* 12. *Diſp.* 215. Nay, Pope *Clement* the VIth, in his Bull to the King of *England* in the Year 1341, acknowledgeth as much, wherein he tells that King, that he granted him the privilege of communicating under both kinds, that he might receive the more Grace by receiving the Sacrament ſo.

‖ 𝔄𝔡𝔬𝔯𝔞𝔱𝔦𝔬𝔫.] The Primitive Chriſtians muſt have been People of a ſtrange confidence in triumphing as they did over the ſtupidity of the Heathen Worſhip, for being directed to Objects that were ſubject to all the Accidents and Caſualties, that any other Bodies are ſubject to, had they themſelves at the ſame time Worſhiped the Hoſt, which is ſubject to more Accidents than the Stone, Wood, or Braſs of the Heathen Images; for they that do Worſhip it cannot deny, but that the Hoſt may be Stole, Burnt, eat by Mice, or other Vermine, and if kep' too long, will of it ſelf Mould and Corrupt. They muſt certainly have the privilege of believing what they have a mind to, that can believe, That if the Primitive Chriſtians had had any ſuch Doctrine as this of *Tranſubſtantiation* among them, conſidering how many, eſpecially in times of Perſ-

ſame

fame that is due to God who is contained therein, and is really prefent there. The Effect that this Sacrament worketh on the Souls of thofe that receive it worthily, is the *Union* of the Man with Chrift, and by it, through Grace, the Man is incorporated into Chrift, and joyned to his Members: Moreover by this Sacrament, Grace is increafed in all fuch as receive it worthily, fo that whatever effects Carnal eating and drinking works upon a Man as to his Corporal Life, the fame are wrought upon Man by this Divine Sacrament as to a Spiritual Life.

fecution, apoftatized from the Faith, that it was poffible for them to have concealed it from *Celfus*, *Lucian*, *Porphyry*, and above all, from *Julian* the Apoftate; or that thofe Heathens, if they had but had the leaft inkling thereof, would not have made the World to have rung with the noife of it; wherefore their having never mentioned any fuch thing, confidering the Wit and Spite of the Men, is a demonftration, that there could be no fuch Doctrine among Chriftians in their days; neither can *Schelftrat's Doctrina Arcani*, confidering the great numbers, quality, and temper of Renegado's, do any fervice in this cafe.

Decree I.

THere being nothing fo neceffary for the Faithful, as the acknowledgement of, and thankfulnefs for fo profound a Bleffing, and fo excellent a Mercy as that which our Lord Chrift did for us, in leaving himfelf under the Sacramental Species, to be the true Food of our Souls, and for the confolation, fupport, and remedy of the Spiritual Life of Believers; we ought therefore wholly to occupy our felves in the Veneration

tion of that Divine Myſtery : In order whereunto,
Holy Mother Church, beſides the continual
Thanks and Veneration which ſhe always gives
and ſhews, hath ordained a particular Day in
the Year for the celebration of the Memory of
ſo great a Bleſſing : which not being * obſerved
in this Dioceſs, the Synod deſiring that in all
things this Church may conform her ſelf to the
Cuſtoms of the Holy Mother, the Univerſal
Church of *Rome* doth command the Feſtivity of
the moſt Holy Sacrament to be Celebrated in all
the Churches of this Dioceſs, on the *Thurſday*
after *Trinity Sunday,* according to the Stile of
theſe Parts, and the ſaid Day to be kept by
all ſorts of People ; and that thereon, either before or after *Maſs*, they make a *Proceſſion* through
the Town, or in ſome convenient place with
all poſſible Solemnity, in the ſame manner as
they do upon *Eaſter-day.*

---

* **Obſerved in this**] This
Feaſt is of later ſtanding by at
leaſt 100 Years, than the Doctrine
of *Tranſubſtantiation* : It was Inſtituted in the Year 1240 by Pope
Urban, as is commonly ſaid upon
a Viſion a Nun had, of the Church's
being Imperfect for want of it ;
but the *Spaniards* will have a Miracle that was wrought in *Spain* at
that time, which is both too long
and too ridiculous to relate, to
have given occaſion to the Pope's
inſtituting it. The Indulgences
granted to it by Pope *Urban,*
Martin, and *Eugenius,* are 500 days
Pardon to all that ſhall be preſent at its firſt *Veſpers,* 500 to
all that ſhall be preſent at the
Maſs of the day, 500 to all that
ſhall be at its ſecond *Veſpers,*
and 500 to every day of its
Octaves, as alſo 500 to every
hour of them ; and whereſoever
it finds any place interdicted, it
takes off the Interdict for eight
days.

Decree

Decree II.

THe Synod doth declare, That every faithful Chriſtian ſo ſoon as he attains to the
Years of perfect Diſcretion, that is to ſay, Men
at the Age of fourteen, more or leſs, according
as their Confeſſors ſhall think fit, and Women
having a Capacity to know what they do at the
Age of twelve, are obliged to receive the moſt
Holy Sacrament of the *Euchariſt*, once a Year in
Lent, or at *Eaſter*, from the hands of their own
Vicar or Curate of their Church, and that whoſoever does not receive it, being capable, betwixt
the beginning of *Lent*, and the ſecond *Sunday*
after *Eaſter*, ſhall be declared Excommunicate
on the third *Sunday*, and be held as ſuch untill
they have confeſſed themſelves, and Communicated. Neverthelefs the Synod gives Licence to
ſuch Vicars as know their Pariſhes to be of that
Nature, that it is not poſſible for the People to
comply with this Obligation in ſo ſhort a time,
to wait 'till *Whitſuntide*, and then to declare
them; provided that before they declare thoſe
that live on the Heaths, they ſhall firſt take care
to admoniſh them, either by themſelves, or by
others of known fidelity, that ſo they may do
their Duty herein, letting them know if they
fail, that they muſt be declared Excommunicate.
The Curates muſt alſo be ſure to obſerve who
have complyed with this Obligation, putting
their Names in a Roll as is ordered in Confeſſion.

on. But notwithstanding the Sacred Canons do oblige the Faithful only to confess and communicate once a Year at the time aforesaid, nevertheless the Vicars shall advise their Parishioners to do it oftner, namely at *Christmass* and *Whitsuntide*, and the *Assumption of our Lady*, giving warning thereof still the *Sunday* before.

Decree   III.

THe Synod doth declare and teach, That no Christian, how contrite soever for his Sins, may lawfully come to receive the Divine Sacrament of the *Altar*, being guilty of any Mortal Sin, without having first confessed all his Sins entirely, to some approved Priest that has Authority to receive his Confession, that being the Tryal and Examination that the Apostle speaks of, and faith a Man ought to make of himself, and being so approved and confessed, let him eat of the Divine Bread, and drink of the Divine Cup; *For he that eateth and drinketh unworthily*, and with a Conscience of Sin, *eateth and drinketh Judgment* and Condemnation *to himself*; for which reason this Divine Sacrament must not be given to publick Sinners, without they have left their Sins, as publick Witches, and common Women, and such as keep Concubines publickly, and such as are in open malice, before they are reconciled, and all other open Sinners whatsoever. In which Matter the Vicars must be extreamly careful, being sensible, that as it is a grievous

vous Sin in such to receive the Divine Sacrament, before they have forsaken their Sins; so it is likewife a grievous offence in them to give the Sacrament to such publick Sinners, and who are known by all to live in such Sins, and not to have forsaken them, notwithstanding they should have been confessed by others, and should bring a Note of their being absolved. This matter ought to be laid home to the Consciences of the Vicars by reason of the great dissoluteness that there is in this Bishoprick in giving the Communion to publick Sinners, and especially to those that keep Concubines, and are Married, but will not live with their Wives, and to others who live in open Malice, without any Body to hinder them, of all which the Vicars muft give a strict Account to God; but at the point of death they may give the Divine Sacrament even to such as have been publick Sinners, if they are not finally impenitent.

Decree IV.

THe Synod teacheth, That this Divine Sacrament ought to be received Fasting, as Holy Mother Church commands, and that upon the day on which people are to communicate, they are neither to eat nor drink any thing from Midnight untill after they have received the
Com-

Communion, not to do fo being * a moft grievous Sacrilege, fuch only excepted as are under
any great infirmity, or much fpent with Sicknefs, who may take Electuaries, and other light
things to ftrengthen them, of which the Confeffor muft be judge.

* **A moft grievous Sacri-**
lege.] Tho' the cuftom of receiving the Sacrament Fafting is
very laudable, yet confidering
that it was not fo received by our
Bleffed Saviour himfelf, nor his
Apoftles when he firft inftituted it,
nor by the Faithful for fome Ages,
they muft needs carry the matter
too far, that call the receiving it
otherwife than Fafting, a grievous
Sacrilege.

Decree V.

CHriftians are not only bound to receive the
moft Holy Sacrament of the *Altar* once a
Year, at *Eafter*, but as often as they are in probable danger of Death, and efpecially in any
great Sicknefs, for which reafon this Divine
Sacrament is called the *Viaticum*, that is to
fay, the Support in the way from a Mortal to
an Eternal Life, wherefore the Synod doth command all Sick People, whofe Diftempers are any
thing dangerous, to receive it with much Devotion ; and as they that look after the Sick
ought to give the Vicars timely Notice, fo the
Vicars themfelves muft be diligent to enquire
what Perfons are fick in their Parifhes, that fo
before they come to be too weak, at a time when
it will do them no prejudice, they may be
brought in a Palanquin, or in fomething elfe that

Q covers

covers them, to the Church, there to receive the Holy Sacrament; for which ufe there fhall be a *Palanquin*, or Net, made commodious with Carpets, in every Church, in which the Sick fhall be carried with due care, which fhall be bought within a month after the publication hereof out of the Fabrick money of the Church, all which the Synod doth recommend earneftly to the Vicars, this being truly the chief Duty of their Office; and if it fhall any time happen that a Parifhioner fhall die without having received the Communion, thro' the Vicars default, the faid Vicar fhall be fufpended for fix months, from his Office and Benefice, and if it happen thorow the Vicars not having been advifed thereof, then thofe that attended the Sick Perfon, fhall be feverely punifhed by the Prelate.

Decree VI.

WHereas Women are many times in danger of Death in Child-bed, a great many dying therein, the Synod doth therefore declare, That all Women with Child ought about the time when they reckon they are to be delivered, to confefs themfelves, and receive the Holy Sacrament, but efpecially before the Birth of their firft Child, in which the danger is greateft, recommending it to them to be careful to do it in time, that they may not be prevented by their Labour from going to Church. Such alfo as defign to undertake any long and dangerous Voyage,

age, ought to do the fame, to whom the Synod recommends it much, and requires it of them.

Decree VII.

FOrafmuch as there are feveral Priefts and *Cazanares* of this Diocefs that do never celebrate, fome by reafon of their having been ordained when they were but Boys, and fo do wait till they come to be of a due Age, and others through other Impediments, therefore the Synod doth command all fuch to receive the Holy Sacrament upon all the folemn Feftivities, and at leaft once a month, wifhing they would do it every *Sunday* with a due preparation and reverence; and as often as any Prieft doth communicate, he fhall be in a *Surplice* and *Stole*, with a *Crofs* on his Breaft to diftinguifh him from other People, by reafon of the Reverence and Refpect that is due to the Sacerdotal Office which he bears.

Decree VIII.

SEeing as is aforefaid, it is not lawful for any Perfon to come to the moft Holy Sacrament of the Altar, having the leaft fcruple of any Mortal Sin about him, without having been Sacramentally confefs'd, the Synod doth declare, That even to Priefts it is not lawful, and that none finding in themfelves the leaft fcruple of Mortal Sin, and having an opportunity of a Confeffor,

Q 2   fhall

shall say *Mass*, tho' under an Obligation to do it, without having first confessed themselves: But besides, that such when under any scruple are obliged to confess, for the greater purity of their Souls, tho' under no scruple the Synod commands all Priests to confess at least once a Week.

Decree IX.

THe Synod doth furthermore command all Deacons and Sub-Deacons, that Minister solemnly in the solemn *Masses* on *Sundays* and Saints-days, to receive the most Holy Sacrament at those times, and on the Festivity of our *Lord Christ*, our *Lady*, and the *Holy Apostles*, all the *Chamazes*, or Clergy that are in the Church; of which the Vicars ought to take special care, and the Prelate in his Visitations is to make diligent Inquiry, how these things are observed.

The Doctrine of the Holy Sacrifice of the Mass.

THe great Love of God to Mankind, does not only appear in the Institution of the Holy Sacrament of the *Eucharist*, and in the putting of his Divine Body and Blood under the Sacramental *Species*, to be the heavenly Food of our Souls, by which the Spiritual Life is maintained and preserved, but in his having likewise so instituted it, that the *Catholick Church Militant*

tant might have a perpetual and vifible Sacrifice
for the purging away of our fins, and for turning the Wrath of our Heavenly Father, who is
many times offended with our wickednefs into
Mercy, and the rigour of his juft punifhment into Clemency : So in the *Mafs* there is offered
unto God a true and proper Sacrifice, for the
pardon both of the Living and of the Dead, by
the offering of the which Sacrifice the Lord is
fo far appeafed as to give Grace, and the Gift of
Repentance to Sinners, and by means thereof
does forgive Men their Sins and Offences, tho'
never fo enormous ; the *Hoft* that is offered by
the Miniftry of the Prieft on the Altar of the
Church, being one and the fame that was offered
for us on the Crofs, with no other difference befides that of the reafon of their being offered : And
fo it is not only offered for the Sins, Punifhments, Satisfactions, and other Neceffities of the
Faithful that are Living, but alfo for the Dead,
departed in Chrift, and that are in the Torments
of *Purgatory,* being not as yet fully purged by reafon of their not having made a compleat fatisfaction
for the punifhments due to their fins, it being but
juft and reafonable, that all fhould be benefited by a
Sacrifice, which was inftituted for the Remedy and
Health of all Mankind'; which Oblation is of
that purity, that no indignity or wickednefs in
the *Offerers* is able to defile it : fo that as to the
fubftance, value, and acceptation, it is the fame
when offered by a wicked and unclean finner,
as when by a pure and holy Prieft, becaufe it

Q 3   doe

does not derive its Dignity from the *Offerer*, but from the Majesty and excellency of what is offered, neither does the Eternal Father accept thereof for the Merits and Vertue of the Priest that offers it, but for the value of the Sacrifice it self, and the infinite Merits of *Christ*, who is offered therein; so that our Saviour being about to offer himself to God the Father on the Altar of the Cross, could not possibly have given us a greater expression of his immense Love for us, than by leaving us this visible Sacrifice in his Church, in which the Blood which was presently to be once offered upon the Altar of the Cross, was to be renewed every day upon the Altar of the Church, and the Memory thereof to our great profit, was to be adored every where in the Church until the end of the World; which Divine Sacrifice is offered to God only, notwithstanding it is sometimes celebrated in Memory and Honour of the *Martyrs*, and other *Saints* in Bliss; it not being offered to them but to God only, who has been pleased to Crown them with Immortal Honour, rendring him thereby our bounden thanks for the notable Victory of the *Martyrs*, and the publick Mercies and Blessings he has vouchsafed to other *Saints*, and for the Victories which by these means they obtained over the World, the Flesh, and the Devil; beseeching the said Saints to be pleased to intercede for us in Heaven, whose Memories we celebrate on Earth: and tho' the Divine *Eucharist* does still continue to be a Sacrament, yet it is never a Sacrifice, but as it is offered in the *Mass*.

Decree

Decree I.

FOrasmuch as it is of great moment, that all
things belonging to the Sacrifice of the *Mass,*
should be preserv'd pure and undefiled, and whereas this Church has been for *1200 years from under
the Obedience of the Holy *Roman* Church, the Mi-
stress of all the other Churches, and from whence
all good Government and true Doctrines do come,
all the Bishops that came hither from *Babylon* having been Schismaticks and *Nestorian* Hereticks,
who have added to, and taken from the *Mass*
at their pleasure without any order ; from whence
it has come to pass, that several things are foisted
into the *Syrian Mass* which is said in this Diocess,
without any consideration, and such things too
as may give occasion to many Impious and Heretical Errors: For which, if due Order were
observed, all the *Missals* of this Bishoprick ought
to be burned, as also for their having been of *Ne-*
storian use, and compiled by *Nestorian* Hereticks ;
but being there are no other at present, they
are tolerated , until such time as our *Lord* the
Pope shall take some Order therein, and there

* 1200 **Years.**] It would
puzzle them to prove that they
had ever been at any time under
her obedience; however this shows
what a Cheat that submission of
the *Patriarch* of *Babylon,* in his own
name, and in the name of all the
Churches that were subject to him,
to the *Pope* at the *Council* of *Trent,*
was; which Father *Paul* tells us
made a mighty noise in the World,
the Court of *Rome* boasting thereupon , that the *Pope* had got
more new Subjects by that submission, than he had lost by the *Re-*
formation.

Q 4   shall

shall be *Missals* sent by him printed in the *Chaldee* Tongue, which is what this Synod humbly and earnestly defires may be done: And in the mean time it doth command, that the *Missals* now in ufe be purged and reformed as to all the following Matters, and that till fuch time as they are fo purged, which the moft *Illuftrious Metropolitan*, with the affiftance of fome Perfons well verfed in the *Chaldee* Tongue will fee done the next Vifitation, no Prieft shall prefume to make ufe of them any more.

Whereas from the above declared Doctrine of this Sacrament it is evident, that the Prieft does not Confecrate with his own words, but with thofe of our *Lord Chrift*, the Author and Inftitutor of the faid Divine Sacrament; it is not therefore lawful to add any Claufe, how good foever in it felf to the Form of Confecration, or to what our *Lord Chrift* faid therein; in which we do not comprehend the word *Enim*, which the *Church of Rome* adds to the Confecration of the Body and Blood; for befides that, there is the † *Tradition* of the Holy *Apoftles*, for our *Lord Chrift's* having ufed it in the Confecration

† *Tradition*] This is what she confidently pretends to have for all her Novelties. Cardinal *Bona* in the 24 Chap. of his firft Book of *Liturgies*, paffeth the following true judgment upon the common practice of the Church of *Rome* in all fuch Matters; *Orta deinde eft 4 ferè feculis poft 6. Synodum controverfia de & Azymo fermentato, & diu agitata inter Græcos & Latinos, partium potius quam veritatis inveniendæ ftudio, ut in fimilibus fieri folet, atque hinc factum eft ut pertinaciter contenderint fuam quifque confuetudinem, à Chrifto & ab Apoftolis ad noftra ufque tempora derivari: fed fi omiffis hac de re Scholafticorum fubtilitatibus & argumentis quæ apud*

of

of the *Body*; and that St. *Matthew* alſo relates
it in the Conſecration of the *Cup*, it is no Clauſe
or diſtinct Sentence, but a conjunction to a Sentence of the words of Chriſt which immediately
follow. As alſo the word *Æterni* in the Conſecration of the *Cup*; and the words *Myſterium Fidei*,
which tho' not mentioned by the Evangeliſts,
yet as it is proved by *Apoſtolical Tradition*, were
uſed by our *Lord Chriſt* in the Conſecration of
the *Cup*, and for that reaſon the *Holy Church*
continues to uſe them in the ſame; but as for
the words added to the Conſecration of the *Cup*
in the *Syrian* Miſſal, *Et hoc erit vobis pignus in
ſæcula ſæculorum*, they being no where in any of
the four Evangeliſts, nor in any Book of the New
Teſtament; and it not appearing to the Church
by *Apoſtolical Tradition*, that Chriſt uſed them in
that Conſecration, the Synod doth prohibit them
to be uſed therein any more; but the words in
themſelves being good and Holy, and agreeable

*ipſos legi poſſunt, veritatem ſincerè &
ſine affectu ad alterutram partem ex
veterum Patrum monumentis & ex
praxi Eccleſiæ inveſtigare volueri-
mus, inveniemus proculdubio, quam
parvi momenti ſint in re, quæ à facto
pendet, Doctorum ſpeculationes; tum
perſpicuè cognoſcemus multum inter-
eſſe inter tempora quæ præceſſerunt,
& quæ poſtea ſecuta ſunt, eiſque
turpiter errare, qui ex præſenti rerum
ſtatu omnem æſtimant antiquitatem*;
which is what the *Church of Rome*
has done above theſe 600 Years,
and will do for all that Cardinal
Bona or any body elſe can tell her
of the unreaſonableneſs of it. But

the Cardinal goes on, *Quis non vi-
det Scholaſticos ad hanc rem per-
tractandam præoccupatis mentibus
acceſſiſſe, cum enim ab infantia ſola
azyma offerri viderint, eaque ſola in
ſcholis & in exedris prædicari audi-
erint, ea ſola ſemper in uſu fuiſſe cre-
diderunt, & hoc poſito varias ſubin-
de convenientias, variaque argumenta
excogitârunt, ut quod ſemel concepe-
rant, firmius ſtabilirent.* Never
was there a truer deſcription given
of any thing, than this the Cardinal gives of the *Genius* of the
People that defend the *Novelties*
of the *Church of Rome*.

to

to what *Holy Church* fingeth of this Divine Sacrament, that it is the *pledge of the Glory that
we expect*, that we may keep to the Old *Miffal*
fo far as the fincerity of the Faith, and the purity of this Divine Sacrifice will permit, the Prieft
fhall fay them after the elevation of the *Cup*,
where making a profound Reverence, he fhall
begin the following Prayers with them, only
changing the word *Vobis*, which was ufed as
fpoke by Chrift, for *Nobis*, as fpoke by himfelf,
faying, *Hoc erit nobis pignus* ; and for the words
in fæcula fæculorum which follow, they being
commonly faid in the Church of fuch Matters
only as are to laft for ever, or are wifhed
to be Eternal, feeing the ufe of this Divine Sacrament as well as of the reft, is to continue but
to the end of the World, (they having been inftituted only as a remedy for our Spiritual neceffities in this life, for in the other we are to fee our
Lord no more under Sacramental *Species*, but
clearly as he is, neither fhall we in Heaven eat
this Divine Bread of Angels Sacramentally, but
fhall eat as the Angels do in the Vifion of the
Divine Word.) The words *in fæcula fæculorum*
fhall be therefore left out, and inftead thereof
fhall be put *ufque ad confummationem fæculi*, faying, *hoc erit nobis pignus ufque ad confummationem,
fæculi*, the Sacrament being a pledge only for
fo long as we do not fee the Glory that we
hope for, but is and ever will be fuch a pledge
in this life, Chrift having promifed to his Church,
that he will be with her to the end of the World ;

fo

ſo that the Divine Sacraments, which were inſtituted for our benefit, can never fail till then;
after theſe words the Prieſt ſhall go on with
what immediately follows in the *Maſs*, *Gloria
tibi, Domine, gloria tibi*, and ſo on.

Furthermore in the Conſecration of the *Cup*
there is added to the words of Chriſt, *novi teſtamenti qui pro vobis*, &c. *novi & æterni teſtamenti
myſterium fidei, qui pro vobis & pro multis*, &c.
Therefore the Synod doth command, That the
words of Conſecration of the *Body* and *Blood* be
reformed, and put in all their *Miſſals*, according
to the Canon of the *Roman* Miſſal uſed in the
Univerſal Church without the leaſt addition or
diminution, and with the ſame Adorations, In-
clinations, and Ceremonies as are in the *Roman*
Miſſal.

Furthermore, where the Prieſt ſaith *Dominus
Deus noſter quando ſpirabit in nobis odor ſuaviſſi-
mus*, it is ſaid in the ſame Prayer, *& cum animæ
noſtræ veritatis tuæ ſcientiâ fuerint illuſtratæ, tunc
occurremus dilecto filio tuo*, &c. ſpeaking of the
day of Judgment, it ſhall be ſaid, *Cum corpora
noſtra veritatis tuæ ſplendore fuerint illuſtrata, tunc
occurremus dilecto filio tuo*, the Souls of the Juſt
being illuminated and glorified in Heaven before
the day of Judgment, which is the time when
the Bodies receive their Glory; this Paſſage
ſeeming to allude to the *Neſtorian* Hereſie, which
teacheth that the Souls of the Juſt do not ſee
God, nor are Glorified, nor are in Bliſs, before
the day of Judgment.

Further-

Furthermore, where the Deacon faith, *Orando pro sanctis patribus nostris Patriarchâ nostro pastore universalis totius Ecclesiæ Catholicæ*, meaning the Schifmatick of *Babylon*, & *Epifcopo hujus Metropolis*; it fhall be faid *Pro fanctis Patribus nostris, beatissimo Papâ nostro totius Ecclesiæ Catholicæ pastore*, naming him by his Name, & *Epifcopo hujus Metropolis*, naming him alfo, & *Ministris ipforum*; and a little lower where the Deacon praying, faith, *præcipuè nos oportet orare pro incolumitate Patrum nostrorum fanctorum, domini Patriarchæ totius Ecclesiæ Catholicæ pastoris*, naming the *Patriarch* of *Babylon* by Name, instead thereof he fhall fay, *Præcipuè oportet nos orare pro incolumitate patrum nostrorum Domini Papæ*, naming him alfo, & *Epifcopi hujus Metropolis*, naming him alfo.

Furthermore, when the Deacon a little before faith, *Commemoramus autem beatissimam Mariam, virginem Matrem Christi & falvatoris*, it fhall be faid *Sanctam Matrem Dei vivi*, & *falvatoris*, & *Redemptoris nostri*, &c. becaufe the perverfe *Nestorians* do impioufly deny the Blessed *Virgin* to be the *Mother of God*, as has been obferved.

Furthermore, when the Deacon a little lower faith, *Commemoramus quoque Patres nostros fanctos & veritatis Doctores Dominum & Sanctum Nestorium*, &c. all which is Heretical, it being an impious thing facrilegioufly to pray to God to preferve the Doctrine of *Nestorius*, and of other Hereticks his followers in the Church, all the forementioned having been fuch except St. *Ephraim*; wherefore instead of them he fhall fay,

Com-

*Commemoramus quoque Patres nostros sanctos veri-
tatis Doctores S. Cyrillum,* &c. And tho' in some
Missals the Names of *Nestorius, Theodorus,* and
Diodorus are already left out, yet they do still
remain in some, and the Names of *Abraham* and
Narcissus, two of the Ringleaders of that cursed
Sect are in all of them. Wherefore there must
be care taken to have them also left out.

Furthermore, in the beginning of the Prayer
wherein the Deacon saith, *Oportet nos orare &
exaltare unum Deum Patrem Dominum omnium
adoratione dignissimum, qui per Christum fecit nobis bonam spem,* it shall be said, *Qui per Jesum
Christum filium suum Dominum nostrum fecit nobis
bonam spem.*

Furthermore, where the Priest pouring the
Wine into the Cup saith, *Misceatur pretiosus
Sanguis in Calice Domini nostri Jesu Christi,* it shall
be said, *Misceatur Vinum in Calice Domini nostri,*
that no occasion may be given to the Error of
calling the Wine before it is consecrated, *The
Precious Blood of Christ,* alluding to the condemned Custom of the *Greeks,* who as they offer
the Bread and Wine before they are consecrated,
so they adore them too, saying they do it for
what they are to be; and presently after where the
Priest saith, *Expectans expectavi Dominum, Corpus
Christi & sanguinem ejus pretiosum super sanctum
altare offeramus,* it shall be said for the same reason, *Panem Sanctum & Calicem pretiosum offeramus*;
and immediately after where the Deacon saith,
Edent pauperes & saturabuntur, Corpus Christi &
San-

Sanguinem ejus pretiosum super sanctum altare offe-
ramus : He shall say for the same reason, *Edent*
pauperes & saturabuntur, Panem sanctum,& Calicem
pretiosum, &c.

Furthermore, where the Prieſt with a low
Voice in the Prayer, which begins, *Offeratur &*
gloriæ immoletur, ſaith, *& Chriſtus qui oblatus eſt pro*
ſalute noſtrâ, he ſhall ſay, *Jeſus Chriſtus Dominus*
noſter Dei filius qui oblatus eſt, &c. And where the
Prieſt raiſing his Voice ſaith, *Gloria Patri,* &c.
Fiat Commemoratio Virginis Mariæ Matris Chriſti,
he ſhall ſay, *Fiat commemoratio Virginis Mariæ*
Matris ipſius Dei & Domini noſtri Jeſu Chriſti ;
And a little lower, where the Deacon ſaith , *In*
ſæcula uſque in ſæcula, Amen, Amen, Apoſtoli ipſius
filii & amici unigenti; he ſhall ſay , *Apoſtoli*
ipſius filii Dei & amici. And where the Prieſt
begins, *Puſilli cum majoribus* , and ſaith, *Reſur-*
rectione tuâ ſuperglorioſâ reſuſcitabis eos ad gloriam
tuam, he ſhall ſay, *Per Reſurrectionem tuam ſuper-*
glorioſam ſuſcitabis eos.

Furthermore , where the Deacon ſaith, *Ef-*
fundite coram illo corda veſtra, jejunio, oratione,
& pœnitentia, placaverunt Chriſtum, Patrem quoque
& Spiritum ejus ſanctum, where in ſaying, *Spiri-*
tum ſanctum ejus, they ſeem to allude to the Error
of the *Greeks,* that the Holy Spirit proceedeth only
from the Father, and not from the Father and
the Son , as from one principal, as the Catholick
Faith confeſſeth, and becauſe the *Neſtorians* by reaſon of the great Communication they have had
with the *Greeks* , have imbibed ſome of their Errors,

rors, that there may be therefore no countenance
given to such an Error, it shall be reformed thus,
Placaverunt Patrem Filium, & Spiritum Sanctum.

Furthermore, In the Prayer where the Priest
saith, *Dominus Deus fortis, tua est Ecclesia sancta Catholica, quæ admirabili Christi tui passione
empta est;* it shall be said, *Quæ admirabili Christi
filii tui,* &c.

Furthermore, near the end of the Gospel taken out of that Chapter of St. *John,* which, as
has been observed, is corrupted in the *Syrian*
Translation, where it is read *quoniam venit hora
in quâ omnes qui in monumentis sunt audient vocem
ipsius,* it shall be read *audient vocem filii Dei,*
as it is in the Gospel.

Furthermore, in the *Creed* that is sung in the
Mass there are wanting several substantial words,
where speaking of our *Lord Christ,* and saying
that *he was born of the Father before all Worlds,*
there is wanting *God of God, light of light, very
God of very God,* all which shall be added to it :
as also the word *consubstantial to the Father,* leaving out the words that are in its place, in the
Syrian, filius essentiæ Patris, and the whole shall
be reformed and translated into the same words,
as it is sung in the Catholick Church in the *Roman* Missal.

Furthermore, presently after the Creed, where
the Deacon praying for, and making a Commemoration of the Holy *Apostles, Martyrs* and *Confessors,* desires of God that he would raise them up
that they may be Crowned with Glory at the Resurrection

surrection of the Dead, saying, *Oremus, in quam, ut resurrectione quæ est ex mortuis à Deo coronâ donentur*, which besides that it is not the Custom of the Church to pray for the Holy *Apostles*, *Martyrs*, and *Confessors*, nor to desire any good thing for them, whom we believe to be in possession of Bliss, but much rather to * Pray to them, to intercede for us, and to obtain for us of God, whose familiar Friends they are, all that we stand in need of, and is of importance, both as to all our Spiritual and just Temporal Concerns; it seems to allude to the *Nestorian* Opinion, That the Souls of the *Saints* are not to see God, until after their Bodies are raised at the day of Judgment, and that till then they are in a *Terrestrial Paradise*, which is Impious and Heretical; wherefore the Synod doth command, That since there are no such Prayers used in the Church, nor any such Petitions made to God in behalf of the Saints, notwithstanding they are said in the *Revelation* to make them for themselves, that those words be blotted out, and what follows be joined with what went before, saying, *& Confessores hujus loci & omnium Regionum, oremus, inquam, ut det nobis ut efficiamur socii eorum*, &c. leaving out the fore-mentioned words; and at the end of the Prayer where it is said, *per gratiam*

---

* **Pray to them.**] The *Malabar* Custom in this is much the ancienter, as appears from all the ancient *Liturgies*; in all which Petitions Christians prayed for the Dead no otherwise than as we pray for them in the *Lord's Prayer*, in the Petition *Thy Kingdom come*; and in the Office for the *Burial of the Dead*, where we *beseech God of his gracious goodness, shortly to accomplish the number of his Elect, and to hasten his Kingdom.*

Christi

Chriſti, it ſhall be ſaid *Per gratiam Dei, & Domini noſtri Jeſu Chriſti.*

Furthermore where the Prieſt begins *Confite-mur & laudamus, Domine Deus noſter,* where he ſaith below *Dignos nos feciſti diſpenſatione ſacra-mentorum ſanctorum corporis & ſanguinis Chriſti tui,* it ſhall be ſaid *Chriſti filii tui ;* as alſo before where the Prieſt ſpeaketh to thoſe on the right ſide of the Altar, and they anſwer with the Dea-con *Chriſtus exaudiat orationes tuas, hoc ſacrificium quod tu offers pro te, pro nobis, & pro toto orbe à minimo uſque ad maximum,* the laſt words *& pro toto orbe à minimo uſque ad maximum,* muſt be left out, for the *Maſs* being a publick Prayer of the Church, *Infidels, Schiſmaticks* and *Hereticks* are not to be prayed for therein, but only *Catholicks,* and ſuch as are united to the Church ; wherefore inſtead thereof it ſhall be ſaid, *quod tu offers pro te, pro nobis, & pro univerſà Eccleſià Catholicâ, & omnibus orthodoxis, atque Apoſtolicæ & Catholicæ fidei cultoribus.*

Furthermore, where the Prieſt begins *Etiam Domine Deus Exercituum,* where he ſaith, *& pro Sacerdotibus, Regibus, & Principibus,* it ſhall be ſaid, *& pro Regibus & Principibus Catholicis,* the Chriſtians of this Church being ſubject to *Infidel* Princes ; and a little lower, where the Prieſt be-gins *Tu Domine cui propter,* &c. where he ſaith, *recordatione corporis & ſanguinis,* it ſhall be ſaid, *Chriſti filii tui ;* and a little lower in the ſame Prayer, near the end, it ſhall be ſaid, *ſanguine Chriſti filii tui redempta.*

R   Further-

Furthermore, where the Deacon and Clergy praying, do say, *Et pro omnibus Patriarchis, Episcopis, & Presbyteris*, &c. it shall be said, *& pro beatissimo Papâ nostro*, naming him, *& pro omnibus Patriarchis & Episcopis*.

Furthermore, in the Hymn said by the Clergy and the Deacon *alternatim* after the elevation of the most Holy Sacrament, in the Verse where the Priest saith, *Quando ad sanctum altare ingreditur, manus suas purè protendit in cælum, & invitat spiritum qui de superis descendit & consecrat corpus & sanguinem Christi*, in which words the Priest seems to call upon the Holy Ghost, to come down from Heaven to consecrate the Body of Christ, as if it were not the Priest that consecrated it; whereas in truth it is the Priest that does it, tho' not in his own words, but the words of Christ; wherefore that no colour may be given to such an error, it shall be said, *manus suas purè protendit in cælum & consecrat corpus & sanguinem Christi*, leaving out the words of *& invitat spiritum qui de superis descendit*, &c. and the following words *à sæculo usque in sæculum*.

Furthermore, in the Prayer said by the Deacon, which begins *Omnes timore pariter & amore accedamus*, where it is said, *unigenitus Dei mortale corpus & spiritualem, rationalem, immortalemque animam ex filiis hominum suscepit*, that there may be no countenance given to an error held by some, and followed by several *Nestorians*, that the Soul as well as the Body, is *ex traduce*, or derived from the Parents; whereas in truth it is created by by God out of nothing, and infufed into the Body when it is perfectly formed ; it fhall therefore be faid *unigenitus Dei mortale corpus ex filiis hominum, & fpiritualem, rationalem, immortalemque animam fufcepit.* As alfo where the Deacon after the Communion of the Prieft, inviting the People to communicate, faith, *fratres mei fufcipite corpus ipfius filii*, he fhall fay *ipfius filii Dei.*

Furthermore, in the firft word of the Benediction of the People, where he faith, *Ille qui benedicit nos in cælis, per filium Humanitatis,* he fhall fay *Per filium fuum*; and in the firft Bleffing which the Prieft gives to the People, at the end of the *Mafs* , where he faith, *Cathedra gloriofa Catholicorum orientalium,* meaning Schifmatical *Babylon,* he fhall fay *benedicatur Cathedra gloriofa Romana,* and in the following verfe of the fame Bleffing, where fpeaking of the Bifhop of the Diocefs, he faith, *Dominus totius gregis epifcopus plenus fobrietate cuftodiatur à malo,* &c. he fhall name our Lord the Pope, faying, *Dominus totius gregis catholici Papa N. plenus fobrietate cuftodiatur à malo, una cum bono Doctore, & Epifcopo noftro N.* naming him by his Name: And a little after in the fame Bleffing, where he faith, *Illuftris in congregatione Sanctorum religiofus Hormifda, fanctitas fanctitatum,* &c. the name of *Hormifda,* who as has been obferved, was a *Neftorian* Heretick, fhall be left out, and inftead thereof he fhall fay, *Illuftris in congregatione Sanctorum S. Apoftolus Thomas,* &c. all that follows

agree-

agreeing very well with that glorious Apostle, who first taught the Faith in these parts, and not to that false Heretick.

Furthermore, in the first Verse of the Blessing of the Solemn Days, where it is said of the Divine Word, *Qui factus est homo, & operuit speciem suam in filio hominis,* for fear of the *Nestorian* Doctrine it shall be said, *Qui factus est homo, & operuit Divinitatem suam humilitate nostrâ;* and a little lower where it is said, *Benedic Ecclesiam tuam quæ patitur, & in ovili pessimi Dæmonis ecce comprehenditur,* it shall be said, *Quæ patitur infestationes a pessimo Dæmone, libera illam,* &c. for the Catholick Church tho' it be infested and persecuted by the Devil, is not held nor overcome by him, our Saviour having promised, that *all the Powers of Hell shall never prevail against her.* And afterwards where it is said, *Benedic dextrâ tuâ, Christe, congregationem hanc,* it shall be said, *Benedic dextrâ tuâ, Jesu Christe,* &c. and in the same Blessing, where it is said, *Salva Reges nostros & Duces nostros,* it shall be said, *Salva Reges nostros & Duces nostros Catholicos,* all the Kings and Princes of this Church being *Infidels,* and so ought not to be prayed for in the publick Prayers of the *Mass*; and a little after, where it is said, *Sicut decet coram ipso Jesu Salvatore,* it shall be said, *Coram ipso Jesu Deo Salvatore,* because of the *Nestorian* error; and in the last Verse but one of that Blessing, where it is said, *Qui comedit corpus meum & bibit ex sanguine meo sanctificante liberabitur ab inferno per me,* the words

words of Chriſt, *Habet vitam æternam,* ſhall be
uſed inſtead of *Liberabitur ab inferno;* and in the
end of the third Bleſſing, where it is ſaid, *Gloria illi ex omni ore Jeſu Domino,* it ſhall be ſaid,
Jeſu Domino Deo, becauſe the *Neſtorians* do impiouſly affirm, That *the name of Jeſus is the name
of a humane Perſon, and does not agree to God.*

All the above-mentioned particular the Synod
doth command to be Corrected, as is here ordered,
with ſuch caution as is neceſſary in theſe Matters,
wherein the curſed *Neſtorian* Hereticks have
ſown ſo many Errors.

Decree II.

WHereas in the *Miſſals* of this Dioceſs there
are ſome *Maſſes* that were made by *Neſtorius,* others by *Theodorus,* and others by *Diodorus,*
their Maſter, which are appointed to be ſaid on
ſome certain days, and which, carrying thoſe
Names in their Titles, are full of Errors and
Hereſies; the Synod doth command all ſuch *Maſſes,* entire as they are, to be taken out, and burnt,
and in virtue of Obedience, and upon pain of Excommunication *Latæ Sententiæ,* doth prohibit all
Prieſts from henceforward to preſume to uſe
them, ordering them to be forthwith cut out
of their Books, and at the next Viſitation to be
delivered by them to the moſt *Illuſtrious Metropolitan,* or to ſuch as he ſhall appoint to correct
their Books, that ſo theſe *Maſſes* may be burnt.

Decree

Decree III.

WHereas in the *Masses* of this Bishoprick, there is an impious sacrilegious Ceremony, which is the Priests, after having dipt that part of the *Host*, after his having divided it, which he holds in his right hand, and has made the sign of the Cross upon the other part that is upon the *Patin*, opening this latter part that was upon the *Patin* with the Nail of his right Thumb, to the end, according to their Opinion, that the Blood may penetrate the Body, that so the Blood and Body may be joyned together, which is ignorantly done in allusion to the Heresie of *Nestorius*, or of his Followers, who do impiously affirm, That *under the Element of Bread is only the Body of Christ without Blood, and under the Element of Wine the Blood without the Body:* Wherefore the Synod doth command in virtue of Holy Obedience, and upon pain of Excommunication to be *Ipso facto* incurred, that no Priest presume to use any such Ceremony, and that they throw it out of their Masses, for that besides it alludes to the forementioned Heresie, it contains a great ignorance in supposing that the *Species* can penetrate the Body and Blood of Christ.

Decree

Decree IV.

FOrafmuch as the *Syrian Mafs* is too long for Priefts that have a mind to celebrate daily, the Synod doth grant Licenfe for the tranflating of the *Roman Mafs* into *Syrian*, defiring the Reverend Father *Francifco Roz*, of the Society of *Jefus* to undertake the Work, which *Mafs* together with all the *Roman* Ceremonies the Prieft may fay on particular Occafions, but the folemn and fung *Maffes* of the day fhall be always the *Syrian*, as they fhall be emended by the moft *Reverend Metropolitan :* and fuch Priefts as are able to fay *Maffes* both in *Latin* and *Syrian* in the Churches of other Dioceffes, may fay it in *Latin*, but not in this Bifhoprick, in which to avoid confufion, it fhall be faid only in *Syrian*. Wherefore the Synod defires the Bifhops of thofe parts to give Licenfe, that the Priefts of this Diocefs, having *Letters dimiffory* from their Prelate, that do not know how to fay *Mafs* in *Latin*, may be permitted to fay the *Syrian Mafs* in their Churches, or at leaft the *Roman* tranflated with all its Ceremonies into *Syrian*; the Schifm which this Church has been in, being now thorow the goodnefs of God removed, entreating the moft *Illuftrious Metropolitan*, the Prefident of this Synod, that he would be pleafed to prefent this Petition in behalf of the Priefts of this Diocefs to the firft Provincial Council that fhall be cele-

R 4   brated

brated in the Province, that so if the *Fathers* shall
think fit, it may pass into a Decree.

Decree V.

WHereas the Power of handling the Holy
Vessels is given particularly to the order
of the *Subdeacon*, this Synod doth command that
from henceforward if the Minister that assists at
the *Mass* be not a *Subdeacon*, that the Priest shall
not put the *Patin* into his hand, when he is ordered by the *Syrian Mass* to do it, such a one
having no Authority to touch it; but he may
lay his hand only on the stone or wood of the
Altar, so as not to touch the *Patin*, which is
according to the *Rubrick* of the *Missal*, which
supposes the Person that assists at the *Mass* to be
a *Deacon*, ordering expresly that the *Priest shall
put the Patin into the hand of the Deacon.*

Decree VI.

WHereas the *Stole* that is thrown over the
Shoulders is the particular Badge of the Order of *Deacon*, it is not lawful therefore for any
Person that has not taken the said Order, to use
the Stole in the Church with any publick Ceremony; and whereas hitherto all of the Clergy
that have assisted at *Mass*, tho' but in *inferior Orders*, or without them, have wore the said *Stole*
over their shoulders, no less than the *Deacons*,
contrary to the *Ceremoniale*, which supposeth him
that

that affifts at the *Mafs* to be a *Deacon* ; the Synod doth therefore ordain and command, that
from henceforward the *Chamazes*, who do affift
at the *Mafs*, and are not *Deacons*, be not permitted to wear the *Stole* ; it would alfo be decent for the *Deacons* when they wear the *Stole*,
to be in a *Surplice*, and to have a *Towel*, and not
to have it over their ordinary wearing Cloths,
as has been hitherto the Cuftom.

Decree VII.

THe Synod doth command, That in all
Churches there be *Stamps* of *Hofts* (or Inftruments wherewith to print the Wafers that
are to be Confecrated) which fhall be bought
forthwith out of the Fabrick-money, or the Alms
of the Church ; and that the Vicars take care to
be always provided of the flour of Wheat, for
the making of them, which they muft be fure
not to mix with any thing elfe, as is done commonly in other Bread, for fear there fhould be
no Confecration therein ; wherefore they muft
either make them themfelves, or employ fuch as
are of known Skill and Fidelity to do it, and
the fame care fhall be taken of the Wine that it
be no other than that of *Portugal*, and that it be
not mixed with the Juice of *Raifins*, or with any
other Wines of the Countrey for the fame danger.

Decree

Decree VIII.

THe Synod doth earneſtly recommend it to the Prieſts of this Dioceſs to take heed in what Wine they celebrate, having been inform-ed, That as ſome Churches, by reaſon of their Poverty, are without *Portugal* Wine, ſo where it is that the Prieſt keeps it in Glaſs Bottles, where being in a ſmall quantity, and kept a long time, it muſt neceſſarily decay and turn to Vi-negar, with which they celebrate notwithſtand-ing, not conſidering the danger there is of there being no Conſecration ; for remedy whereof the Synod in the ſtricteſt manner that it can, doth command, That in every Church there ſhall be in the Vicars keeping a ſweet pipe, or ſmall Run-let of Wood, or a Fraſk, in which the Wine for the *Maſſes* ſhall be kept, and that the Vicars be extreamly careful, that the Wine do not decay or turn to Vinegar ; which if it ſhould happen ſo as to have loſt the eſſence of Wine in the Opi-nion of thoſe that have good Palates, they ſhall not then celebrate therewith, it being a great Sacrilege to do it, ſeeing there can be no Conſe-cration.

Decree IX.

WHereas for want of *Portugal* Wine, it ma-ny times falls out that there are no *Maſ-ſes* celebrated in this Dioceſs, to the great prejudice

judice of the Faithful Chriſtians, who for that
reaſon are ſeveral months without hearing *Maſs*,
and without an opportunity of receiving the
moſt Holy Sacrament, and the Sick of receiving
the Holy *Viaticum*; wherefore the Synod, for
remedy hereof, doth entreat his *Majeſty* the King
of *Portugal*, out of his great Piety, and as he is
Protector of the Chriſtians of theſe parts, once a
Year to ſend us as an Alms, a Pipe and a half,
or two Pipes of *Muſcatel* Wine of *Portugal*, to be
diſtributed among the Chriſtian Churches of
this Biſhoprick, and of the whole *Indies*; and
till ſuch time as an Anſwer ſhall be returned to
this Petition, the moſt *Illuſtrious Lord Archbiſhop*
of *Goa, Dom ffray Aleixo de Menezes*, Metropolitan of this Church, Primate of *India*, and Preſident of this Synod, is pleaſed to give the ſaid
quantity of Wine to be diſtributed among the
Churches of this Biſhoprick, the diſtribution
whereof ſhall be made by the Prelate according
to the Informations he ſhall receive of the Neceſſities of every Pariſh, and whereas all the ſuc-
ceſſes of this Life are uncertain, if this ſhould
happen to fail at any time, the Prelate ſhall then
at his Viſitation take ſo much out of the ſtock
of every Church as ſhall ſuffice to purchaſe what
Wine is neceſſary, and the Wine ſhall be committed to the Vicar, who ſhall make uſe of it only
in the *Maſſes* that are ſaid in the Church, and
order ſhall be taken that the *Maſs* of the day,
which belongs to the whole Pariſh, and is the
chief obligation of the Church, ſhall be celebrated without fail.　　　　　　　　　　**Decree**

Decree X.

THis Synod being very doubtful whether the
Stones of the Altar, on which the *Masses*
are said in the Churches of this Diocess, be consecrated with Holy Oil, or truly Blessed, by reason of the small care and knowledge which the
former Prelates coming from *Babylon* had of such
Matters ; doth command, That all such as are
not well known to have been lawfully Consecrated, shall be brought to the most *Reverend Me-*
tropolitan that they may be Consecrated by him,
whom the Synod doth intreat to provide such
Churches with Stones as want them : Commanding likewise, all Cups that are not of Gold, Silver, Copper or Tin, to be broke, and * no Cups
to be used but what are made of one of these
Metals, and that *Mass* be never said in any of
these after they are broken ; and seeing there
are many Churches that for want of Cups have
no *Masses*, the *Lord Metropolitan* is desired to
give order, that all Churches be furnished with
Cups.

* **No Cups.**] In the Primitive Church they thought it no
such Crime to make use of wooden
Chalices in the celebration of the
Sacrament. So *Honorius* in the
89 Chap. of his 3. Book *De gemma*
animæ, saith, *Apostoli & eorum*
successores in ligneis Calicibus Missas
celebrârunt : And *Boniface* Bishop
of *Mentz*, being asked in the
Council of *Triburis*, whether it
were Lawful to celebrate in
Wooden *Chalices*, answered,
Quondam Sacerdotes aurei ligneis
Calicibus utebantur, nunc è contra
lignei Sacerdotes aureis utuntur
Calicibus.

Decree

Decree XI.

WHereas there are many poor Churches in this Bishoprick, and especially in the *Heaths*, that have no consecrated Vestments for the saying of *Mass*, and for that reason have but few said in them, to the great prejudice of the faithful Parishioners; therefore the Synod doth command, That out of the Alms of the Parish the most *Reverend Metropolitan* may provide all Churches with Holy Vestments, so that none may be without them, and for that reason be without having *Masses* every *Sunday*; and in those Parishes where the Alms shall not be found to be sufficient to do it, the said Lord *Metropolitan* is desired to take such order therein, that they may be some way or other provided, and have so great a want supplied.

Decree XII.

WHereas the Christians of this Diocess have not hitherto heard *Mass* as upon obligation, having never imagined that the not hearing thereof upon some particular days was a mortal sin; for which reason, some have without any scruple neglected going to hear it, and others have not stayed to hear it out; therefore the Synod doth declare, That it is the Precept of the Universal Church, and that upon penalty of a mortal Sin, that all Christians, Men and Women, having no
lawful

lawful impediment, do hear an entire *Mass* upon
every *Sunday* and Holy-day that is commanded
to be kept, if they have the opportunity of a
Prieft to fay it to them.   As alfo, that all Mafters of Families are obliged by the faid Precept,
to make their Children, and fuch of their Servants
and Slaves as are Chriftians, and all other Perfons
living in their Families, to go every *Sunday* and
Holy-day to hear *Mass*, which every one fhall
endeavour to hear at his own Parifh-Church, or
at the place where he then happens to be; and
as for thofe who with juft reafon are afraid to
leave their Houfes alone without any body in
them, and efpecially fuch as live in *Heaths*, and
are a great way from any Church, they fhall
fo order the matter, that all in their Families
fhall take their turns of going to *Mass* and ftay-
ing at home on *Sundays*; and the Vicars of the
Churches muft be careful to mark all fuch as
are negligent herein, and reprove, admonifh, and
punifh them, fo as they fhall judge neceffary:
and where there is any number of *Clergy*, they
fhall fing the *Mass* on *Sundays* and Holy-days:
and when there is not a competent number, there
the *Mass* fhall be faid at a convenient hour, the
whole Parifh being prefent; and he fhall at the
fame time Preach, publifh their Admonitions,
the Banes of Matrimony, and whatfoever elfe is
neceffary in the Church.

Decree

Decree XIII.

THe Synod being informed that moſt of all
the Chriſtians that live out of Towns and
Villages in the *Heaths* , being a great way from
Church, do go to Church but once a Year, on the
three days before *Lent*, which they call *Monorbo*,
and then rather to fill their Bellies with what is
given by Chriſtians at that time, than to hear
Maſs; and that there are others who content
themſelves with going to hear *Maſs* twice or
thrice in the Year, and ſo have no opportunity of
being inſtructed in matters of Faith and Religion
as they ought to be, nor of complying with their
Obligations, doth command all Chriſtians living
within two Leagues of the Church to go to *Maſs*
at leaſt once a Month, and on the principal
Feſtivities of our *Lord* and *Lady*, commanding
the Vicars alſo to conſtrain them to do it; and
all ſuch as are but one League, to hear *Maſs* once
a Fortnight, and ſuch as are leſs than a League, to
hear it every *Sunday* and Holy-day; commanding all that ſhall trangreſs herein, being obſtinate, after the third Admonition, to be thrown
out of the Church when they come thither;
neither ſhall the Prieſt go to their Houſes, or give
them the *Caſture*, or Bleſſing, until they ſhall come
to hear*Maſs*, more or leſs, in the Form afore-
ſaid; and beſides, they ſhall be puniſhed by the
Prelate as he ſhall think good.

Decree

Decree XIV.

WHereas upon several Festivals of the Church there are Muficians called to the celebration thereof, according to the cuftom of the Country, who are all *Heathens*, fmall care being taken in what part of the Church they are placed, or to hinder them from playing during the time of the Holy Sacrifice, at which no Excommunicate Perfon or Infidel ought to be prefent, therefore the Synod doth command, that great care be taken not to fuffer them to remain in the Church after the Creed is faid, or the Sermon, if there be one, is ended, that fo they may not behold the Holy Sacrament ; the Vicar fhall alfo be careful to drive all Heathens who may come upon fuch occafion, from the Doors and Windows of the Church.

Decree XV.

WHereas there is nothing that is fo great a help to the Souls of the Faithful that are in the Fire of * *Purgatory* as the Holy Sacrifice of the *Mafs*, of which there is no memory remaining in

* **Purgatory**.] I fhall give in the matter of *Indulgences* to the Reader one inftance out of a Souls in *Purgatory*. hundred of the Popes liberality

Indulgencias

" Ndulgencias Concedidas pello
" Papa Adriano VI. de boa Me-
" moria ás contas, ou graos que
" benzeo á Inftancia do Illuftrif-
" fimo Cardeal Laquinaues Tri-
" germano Barbarino no Anno de
" 1523. E. Confirmadas pelo
" Santiffimo Padre Gregorio De-
" cimo tercio aos 26 de Mayo
" de 1576. E bien affi confirma-
" das pelo Sanctiffimo Padre Papa
" Paulo quinto no anno de 1607.
" E. tambem agora confirmadas
" por noffo fantiffimo Papa Ur-
" bano Octavo no quarto anno de
" fue Pontificado.

" Primeiramente, quem tiuer
" huma deftas contas, rezando hum
" Pater Noter, et huma Ave Maria
" cada dia tira tres Almas das
" penas do Purgatorio & de for
" em Domingo, ou em Dia fe fe-
" fta rezando dobrado tira de is.

" Item, Cada fexta feira re-
" zando finco vezes O Pater No-
" fter, & Ave Maria à honra das
" finco chagas, de Chrifto, gan-
" ha fetenta mil annos de per-
" dam, et remiffam de todos fe-
" us peccados.

" Item, em cada Sabbado re-
" zando fete Pater Noftres, et fete
" Ave Marias, aos fete gozos de
" noffa Senhora, ganha indulgen-
" cia fem numero.

" Item, Quem nano poder cor-
" rer as eftaçoens de Roma na
" Quarefma rezando finco Pater
" noftres, et finco Ave Marias
" diante da imagem de hum Cru-
" cifixo ganha as ditas eftaçoens
" dentro et fora, dos muros de
" Roma & Jerufalem.

" Item, Trazendo configo huma
" deftas contas confeffado, et
" comungado ganha indulgencia

" plenaria, et remiffam de todos
" feus peccados.

" Item, O Sacerdote, que con-
" feffa et comunga ganha indul-
" gencia plenaria, et remiffam de
" todos feus peccados, et alem
" difto ganha tam bem todas as
" indulgencias, que eftam den-
" tro, et fora de Roma, & Hieru-
" falem.

" Item; avendo comungado,
" quantas vezes rezer O Pater No-
" fter, & à Ave Maria, tantas almas
" tira do Purgatorio.

" Item, Concede fua Santidade,
" que eftas contas, qua fua Santi-
" dade benzeo, poffam tocar a
" outras, as quaes tocadas ficam
" com as mefmas graças, falvo
" que eftas tocadas nam poffam to-
" car as outras Dada em Roma a
" 15 de Janeiro de 1607.

" Nos Joano Ambrofio Referen-
" dario Apoftolico Vifto eftar
" conforme com o Original, po-
" de correr efte Summario de In-
" dulgencia Lisboa 11. de Junho
" de 1642. Er. Joano de Valcocel.
" Franc. Card. de Torn.Sebaftiano
" Cæfar de Menefes.

" Com. Licença. Em. Lisboa
" Na Officina de Domingos Carney-
" ro Anno 1660.

Indulgences granted by Pope A-
drian VI. of Bleffed Memory, to
fome Beads or Grains which he
bleffed at the inftance of the moft
Illuftrious Cardinal Laquinaues Tri-
germano Barbarino, in the Year
1523. and which were confirmed
by the moft Holy Father Gregory X,
on the 26 of May 1576. and were
alfo

*also confirmed by the most Holy Fa-
ther Pope* Paul V. *in the Year* 1607.
*and were now again confirmed by
our Holy Father Pope* Urban VIII.
in the 4th *Year of his Pontificate.*

*First. Whosoever shall have one
of these Beads, and shall recite a*
Pater Noster *and an* Ave Mary *e-
very day, shall take three Souls out
of the Torments of* Purgatory; *and
if he shall double them upon a* Sunday *or* Holy-day, *he shall take out six.*

2. *If he shall say five* Pater Nosters *and five* Ave Maries *to the
honour of the five Wounds of Christ
upon a* Friday, *he shall gain seventy
thousand Years Pardon and Remission
of all his Sins.*

3. *If he shall every* Saturday *say
seven* Pater Nosters, *and seven* Ave
Maries *to the seven Joys of our
Lady, he shall gain* Indulgences
without number.

4. *He that cannot go the* Stations
at Rome *in* Lent, *if he shall say
five* Pater Nosters *and five* Ave
Maries *before a* Crucifix, *he shall gain
the said* Stations *within and without
the Walls of* Rome *and* Jerusalem.

5. *He that shall bring one of these
Beads along with him, and shall
Confess and Communicate, shall gain
a plenary* Indulgence *and remission
of all his Sins.*

6. *The Priest that shall Confess
him, and give him the Sacrament,
shall likewise gain a plenary* Indulgence, *and the remission of all his
Sins; and moreover, all the* Indulgences *which are within and without* Rome *and* Jerusalem.

7. *Having Communicated, as often as he shall say a* Pater Noster
and Ave Mary, *so many Souls he
shall take out of* Purgatory.

His Holiness *does likewise grant,
That these Beads which have been
blessed by his* Holiness, *may touch
other Beads, which being touched by
them, shall have the same Graces,
saving that those which are touched
cannot touch others.*

Dated at Rome *the* 15th. *of*
January, An. 1607.

We John Ambrosio, Referen-
dary Apostolick, *having seen this
summary of* Indulgence *to be conformable to the Original, it may be
Published.*

Er. Joan. de Vasconcel. Franc.
Card. de Torn. Cæsar de
Meneses.

With Licence. In Lisbon *in the
Shop of* Domingo Carneyro, 1660.

this Diocess; that Holy Sacrifice having been instituted for the health and remedy of the Living
and of the Dead: Wherefore the Synod doth exhort all the Faithful of this Bishoprick to accustom
them-

themfelves to procure * *Maffes* to be faid for the Souls of their deceafed Friends, and to leave fomething by Will that they may have *Maffes* faid for their own Souls, which will be much more profitable for them than the Feafts that they ufed to make for their Kindred and others invited to their Funerals; which Cuftom fhall be left off, and inftead thereof, they fhall give a

* **Maffes.**] Private *Maffes* are not only a flat contradiction to the Primitive Practice, but to the very Office wherein they are celebrated, all that Office being made in the name of a Congregation, not only as prefent, but as communicating. A demonftration that the Offices of the *Roman* Church are older than her Errors; it is plain likewife from the very *Canon* of the *Mafs*, that when that Office was compofed, *Tranfubftantiation* was not fo much as dreamt of in the *Roman* Church; but as to the thing in hand, Cardinal *Bona* in the 3 Chap. of his 1 Book of *Liturgies*, faith, *Ab initio Sacrificium principaliter inftitutum fuit, ut publicè ac folemniter fieret, Clero & populo aftante ac communicante, ipfe tenor Miffæ & veteris Ecclefiæ praxis evincunt; omnes enim Orationes atque ipfa Canonis verba in plurali numero tanquam plurium nomine, proferuntur: hinc facerdos populum invitat ad Orationem dicens* Oremus, *& poft Communionem ait quod ore fumpfimus*, &c. *Suntque ferè omnes ejufdem tenoris Orationes quæ peractâ Communione recitantur:* And in the 18*th* Chap. of the fame Book he faith, *Solenne hoc fuit in utrâque Ecclefia* Græca & Latinâ, *ut unum & idem Sacrificium a pluribus interdum Sacerdotibus celebraretur;* Epifcopo *enim five Presbytero celebrante, reliqui quotquot aderant* Epifcopi *feu* Presbyteri *fimul celebrabant ejufdemque Sacrificii participes erant*, &c. And a little after he adds, *Cur autem defierit ille mos caufa mihi videtur fuiffe primo quidem quod fundatis ordinibus mendicantibus & longè latèque propagatis, multiplicata funt onera Miffarum; atque adeo neceffe fuit fingulos Sacerdotes, ut iis fatisfacerent fingulis diebus privatim celebrare, deinde quia charitas multorum refrixit, ceffavit etiam frequens acceffus ad hoc Sacramentum adeo ut hodie nec ipfi quidem miniftri in plerifque Ecclefiis Communicent, licet Sacrificio cooperantur.* To which the Cardinal might have added the Introduction of the *Doctrine* of *Purgatory*, and the confequent *Doctrine* of *Maffes* being the moft effectual means of delivering the Souls out of the Torments thereof. So *John* the IV. of *Portugal*, ordered ten thoufand *Maffes* to be faid for his Soul, as foon as he was dead.

　　　　　　　　　　　　　　　　　　Dole

Dole to the Poor, which is alſo very profitable to the Souls of the departed. And that the Decree relating to ſuch *Maſſes* may have its due effect, the Synod doth command, That all that ſhall be found to have died worth 2000 *Fanoins*, and have left nothing for a certain number of *Maſſes* to be ſaid for their Souls, ſhall have ſo much taken out of their Eſtates before they ſhall be divided among the Heirs, as ſhall procure the ſaying of five *Maſſes* for their Souls, which ſhall be depoſited by the Executors in the hands of the Church-wardens, by them to be diſtributed among five Prieſts, that they may be the ſooner ſaid ; and where there are more than five Prieſts, the Alms ſhall be given to the five Eldeſt, there not being ſufficient to divide among them all ; and where there is only the Vicar of the Church, the whole ſhall be given to him : which Cuſtom of procuring *Maſſes* to be ſaid for the Souls of the Faithful departed this Life, as it is uſed in the Univerſal Church, ſo it is what this Synod is extreamly deſirous to introduce into this Biſhoprick, wherein it has been totally diſuſed, recommending this Matter earneſtly to the Preachers and Confeſſors, to perſuade all Chriſtians to it in their Sermons and Confeſſions, and to the Vicars to do the ſame in their Admonitions.

ACT I-

A C T I O N VI.

Of the Holy Sacrament of Penance *and* Extream Unction.

THe Fourth Sacrament is that of *Penance*, in which the Acts of the Penitent are, as it were, the Matter, and are diftinguifhed into thefe three parts, *Contrition of Heart, Confeffion of the Mouth*, and *Satisfaction for Sins, according to the direction of the Confeffor*. It belongs to the *Contrition of the heart*, that the Penitent be forry at his Soul for the Sins that he has committed, and detefting them, is firmly refolved not to commit them any more : which *Contrition*, tho' it fometimes happen to be perfect through Charity, fo as to reconcile one to God even before he has actually received the Sacrament of *Confeffion*, yet it can never be perfect, nor a means of reconciliation with God, if not attended with a readinefs and purpofe of mind to confefs thofe very fins which it is converfant about ; fuch fins being no lefs fubject than others, to the Keys and the ingagements to *Confeffion*. It belongs to the *Confeffion of the mouth*, that the Penitent Confefs himfelf entirely to his own Prieft, as to all the fins that he remembers, ufing all due diligence according to the length of the time, fince he laft Confeffed himfelf ; and this *Confeffion* is not to be only of fins in general, nor only of the

S 3   *Species*

Species of them, but of every fin in particular,
and as far as the Penitent is able to remember
of their number; declaring withal, all the ag-
gravating Circumftances, and all fuch as change
the *Species*; in a word, all *mortal* fins, how fe-
cret foever, tho' only in thoughts and wicked
defires; as alfo all faults committed againft the
two laft Commandments; *Thou fhalt not covet
thy Neighbours Wife*; *Thou fhalt not covet any
thing that is anothers*; fuch fins being at fome
times more dangerous for the Soul, than others
that are open; all which we are commanded to
do by the Divine Law; our Saviour when he
afcended into Heaven, leaving the Priefts for
his Vicars upon Earth, and conftituting them
Judges, before whom all *mortal* fins committed
by Chriftians, were to be brought, that by the
power of the Keys, which he committed to them
to forgive or retain fins, they may pronounce
Sentence, which cannot be juft and Righteous,
neither can the punifhments they impofe be e-
qual or proportionated to the Nature of the Faults,
without their having a full knowledge of the
fame, as of the matter that they pafs Sentence
upon; which knowledge cannot be had but by
the Penitents confeffing all and every *Mortal* Sin,
whereon Judgment is to pafs, not only in general, but in *fpecie* and number, making mention
of every fuch Sin in particular, with all its neceffary circumftances, that fo a juft fentence of
abfolution or retention may be pronounced upon them. And as to *Venial* Sins which we frequently

quently fall into, and for which we are not ex-
cluded from the Grace of God, tho' the confeffing of, and being abfolved from them, is very
profitable to the Soul, yet we are not under
any fuch precife obligation of confefling them,
there being other ways by which they may be
pardoned, fo that it is no fin not to difcover
them.   The third part of *Penitence*, is, *Satisfa-*
ction for Sins according to the judgment of the Con-
feffor ; which *fatisfaction* is chiefly performed by
Prayer, Fafting and Alms, the Penitent being
obliged to comply with the Penance impofed
upon him by the Prieft, who being as a Judge
in the place of God, ought to impofe what he
thinks to be neceffary, not only with refpect to
the amendment of Sin for the future, but chiefly with refpect to the *Satisfaction* and *Penance*
of paft Sins.   The Form of this Sacrament is, *I*
abfolve thee, to which neceffary words the Church
has thought fit to add the words following, *from*
all thy Sins, in the Name of the Father, of the Son,
and of the Holy Ghoft.   There are alfo fome Prayers which the Prieft faith immediately after o-
ver the Penitent, which, tho' they are not effential to the form, yet are very profitable and
healthful for the Penitent.   Now by pronouncing
the form, not only all the Sins that are confeffed, but all thofe likewife which after a due diligence and Examination of the Confcience do
not occurr to the Memory, fo as to be difcovered, all fuch being included in the faid Confeffion, are all pardoned ; tho' with an obligation of

confessing them, if they should ever after come to be remembred, sins being as it were chains to the Soul, from which it is delivered by the absolution of the Priest, which is applicable to such, as by virtue of contrition joyned with a desire of confessing, have obtained pardon of God for their Sins, which they were under an obligation to have confessed : as also to those Sins which were never confessed, because not remembred after a due diligence, and to those likewise which having been once lawfully confessed and truly pardoned, are by the Penitent of his own accord, and for the greater Penance confessed and submitted to the Keys several times. The Minister of this Sacrament is a Priest, *who hath Authority to absolve*, and is either the *Ordinary*, as the Prelates, or such as are commissioned and approved of by them. The effect of this Sacrament is, *The absolution and pardon of Sins*, and for that reason it is by the Doctors properly called the *Table after Shipwrack*, because the Grace which was given to us in Baptism, being lost by the commission of *Mortal* Sin, by which we make Shipwrack thereof, and of all the other Vertues and Gifts, which together therewith were poured down upon us, there remains no other remedy or means whereby we can be saved, but only by the plank of *Penance*, or the Sacrament of *Confession* ; for that without this either actually received, or firmly purposed according to the command of Holy Mother Church with contrition, wherein such a purpose is always

ways included, we cannot be faved nor enter into the Kingdom of Heaven ; for which reafon this Sacrament ought to be much reverenced and frequented, as the only remedy that finners have for all their evils.

Decree I.

WHereas an entire Sacramental *Confeffion* is of Divine right, and neceffary to all thofe who after Baptifm fall into any *Mortal* Sin, and Holy Mother Church doth command all faithful Chriftians who are come to the ufe of Reafon, upon pain of *Mortal* Sin, to confefs at leaft once a Year in the time of *Lent*, or at *Eafter*, when all that are capable are bound likewife to receive the moft holy Sacrament of the Altar, declaring all that negleƈt to do it, to be excommunicate ; and notwithftanding, this Precept has not hitherto been in ufe in this Bifhoprick, in which no Chriftian has ever confeffed upon Obligation, and a great many not at all, which was occafioned through their ignorance of this healthful precept, and of the neceffity of this Divine Sacrament, this Church having been governed by Schifmatical *Chaldæans*, and *Neftorian* Hereticks, the particular Enemies of this Sacrament, being the caufe of their being totally unacquainted with the Virtue, Efficacy, and Neceffity thereof. Some not ufing it all, others being perfwaded by the Devil into a vain and fuperftitious Opinion, That if they fhould confefs

fefs themfelves, they fhould die immediately, all which having been made known to the moft *Illuftrious Metropolitan* in his firft Vifitation of thefe Churches, he at that time perfwaded a great many that had never done it before to confefs themfelves, having undeceived them as to the unreafonable and pernicious miftakes which they lay under, therefore the Synod the more to further this, doth declare that it is the Duty of every faithful Chriftian, upon penalty of *Mortal* Sin, to obferve the precept of the Church concerning *Confeſſion*, at the time by her determined and founded on the Divine precept of *Confeſſion*, for all fuch as are fallen from Grace, by the Commiſſion of any *Mortal* Sin, and doth command all faithful Chriftians Men and Women, that are arrived at the Years of Difcretion, to confefs themfelves to their own Vicar, or to fuch Priefts as are licenfed by the Prelate to hear Confeſſions, at the time of *Lent*, or againft *Eafter*, and that whofoever fhall not have complyed with this Precept, or is not confeſſed fometime betwixt the beginning of *Lent*, and the fecond *Sunday* after *Eafter*, fhall be in the Church declared Excommunicate by the Vicar without waiting for any order from the Prelate to do it, until he has effectually confeſſed himfelf, and has undergone the punifhment due to his Rebellion ; and if the Vicar fhall for fome juft reafon think fit to wait any longer, for fome that have been negligent, and who being bufie have defired to be difpenfed with till *Whitfuntide*, *suntide*, it shall be in their power to bear with them, according to what is determined in the 2*d. Decree* of the 5*th. Action*, of the Sacrament of the *Eucharist*, having first admonished those that live in the *Heaths*, or are at Sea, or engaged in Business in such places where there are no Churches to confess in, that when they return home, they are bound to do it within a month.

And that the whole of this may be executed, with the more ease, and be performed as is reasonable, the Vicars of the Churches shall be obliged a month or more before *Lent*, if it be necessary to go to all the Houses of their Parishes belonging to Christians, however remote in the *Heaths*, either in Person, or by some other Clergyman, whom in Conscience they can trust with such a business, and taking the Names of all the Christians even to the very Slaves in every Family that are nine Years old and upward, and of those too that are abroad, observing whether they do return home after the time of the Obligation, and having made a Roll of Parchment of all that are of Age to confess themselves, they shall afterwards make a mark at their Names as they come to Confession, that so they may know certainly who have, and who have not complyed, that the Disobedient may be Excommunicated, which we declare to be the precise Obligation of their Office, the Pastor being bound to know his Sheep, that he may give them Food, and so far as he is able, supply all their necessities,

sities, Temporal as well as Spiritual, and to have
their number, that he may know when any are
lost ; and for the perfecting of such a Roll the
Vicars may take the advantage of the *Monoibo*,
at which time all Christians do flock to the
Churches, at which time likewise they may hear
of many that live in the *Heaths.* And as to
those that have confessed themselves to some other
approved Confessors, they shall bring a Note
signed by them of their having been confessed,
which they shall deliver to their Vicar, who
shall thereupon mark them in his Roll ; but tho'
it is lawful for them to confess themselves to
Confessors that are Strangers, yet they cannot
receive the most Holy Sacrament, nor the Communion upon Obligation in *Lent* any where, but
in their own Parish Churches, and the Prelates
in their Visitations shall call for those Rolls, in
order to inform themselves how this Decree is
observed.

Decree II.

WHereas the Precept of *Confession* obligeth
all that have the use of Reason, and conscience of *mortal* Sin, which happens sooner to
some than others, the Synod therefore taking the
most safe and probable way, according to the
knowledge it hath of the People of *Malabar,*
doth ordain, That at eight Years old and upward, all People shall Confess themselves, and
that without prohibiting such as are younger and
capable

capable to do it fooner; on the contrary, the
Vicars, if they fhall underftand that there are
any under eight, of fo much Judgment and
Difcretion, as to be capable of committing a
mortal Sin, they fhall immediately conftrain them
to come to *Confeffion*, as being oblig'd to it, which
muft be left to the difcretion of the Parifh Priefts.

Decree III.

THe Synod doth admonifh all Mafters of Families, and all that have the charge of o-
thers, to be careful to make all the Perfons in
their Families to confefs themfelves at the time
of Obligation, and particularly their Servants
and Slaves, both Men and Women, who if they
do never come to *Confeffion*, their Mafters and
none elfe muft be certainly in the Fault, in having neglected to put them in mind of it, and to
order them to do it, it being their Duty, and
that upon penalty of *Mortal* Sin, to call upon
them to do it, of which they muft give a ftrict
Account to God, the Apoftle St. *Paul* affirming,
That *he who does not take care of his Servants, has
denied the Faith, and is worfe than an Infidel*;
which words are chiefly to be underftood of the
Spiritual Neceffities of thofe of his Family, and
of Matters appertaining to their Salvation; about
which matters the Vicars ought to be very careful, and muft obferve whether the Slaves, whofe
Names as well as others, they muft have down
in their Rolls, do come to *Confeffion*, declaring
fuch

such of them as have not complied with their obligation at the time appointed, Excommunicate, having first admonished their Masters to command them to come, and acquainted them with the Declaration that will be made if they do not: and the Vicars that shall be found negligent herein, shall be punished at the discretion of the Prelate.

Decree IV.

ALL faithful Christians are not only obliged to Confess themselves once a Year, under penalty of *mortal* Sin, but also as often as they are in any probable danger of Death, or are very Sick, they are under the same obligation; wherefore the Sick Persons or those that attend them, so soon as ever they shall apprehend any danger, where-ever they live, tho' in the *Heaths*, shall send to call a Confessor, and shall advise the Vicar of the Church thereof, who shall either go himself, or send another to hear their Confessions. The Vicars are also to understand, that it is their indispensible duty to enquire after the Sick, and either to go to Confess them themselves, or to send another to do it, whensoever they shall be sent for, that so none may die without the Holy Sacrament of *Confession*, they being guilty of the Condemnation of such of their Sheep as go to Hell for not having confessed their Sins before they died, if it was through their fault or negligence it was not done. And
the

the Vicar, through whofe fault or negligence
any of the Parifh fhall die without *Confeffion*,
fhall be fufpended from his Office and Benefice
for a whole Year without any difpenfation, and
another fhall be appointed to fupply his Cure,
and the Perfons that attend the Sick, that fhall
neglect to fend for the Parifh-Prieft, fhall be
feverely punifhed at the difcretion of the Prelate;
and fuch as die in *Hamlets* or in *Heaths* without
Confeffion, if they did not fend to call a Confeffor,
if their death was not fo fudden as to prevent
them, fhall not be buried in Holy Ground, neither fhall the Clergy go to their Houfes, or fay
the Office of the Dead for them, nor fo much as
the *Chata.*

Decree V.

NOt only fuch as are dangeroufly Sick, but
all that are any ways in danger of Death,
are obliged to Confefs themfelves; wherefore
fince all Women in Child-birth are in danger
thereof, they fhall before they are in Labour,
Confefs themfelves, but efpecially before the
birth of their firft Child, at which time the
danger is known to be the greateft; and fhall
likewife, if capable, receive the moft Holy Sacrament; and if any fuch, not being furprized
by their Labour, fhall die without *Confeffion*,
or being in vifible danger, did not defire it, their
negligence being proved, and efpecially if they
lived in Towns, they fhall be proceeded againft

in

in the same manner, as those are who through their own fault die without *Confession* as is above decreed.

Decree VI.

THe Synod being informed that the greatest part of those that die of the Small-Pox, tho' they lived in Towns and desired *Confession*, do die without it, that Distemper being so very dangerous and infectious, that the Priests are afraid of coming near those that have it; doth command all Vicars to be careful, that none such do die without *Confession*, and either to go themselves, in Person, or to send one to Confess them; a due regard being still to be had to their own health, either by confessing them at some distance, or so that the Wind shall blow the steams from them, and by having taken preservatives against the Distemper; that so none may die without *Confession*, which is what the Synod doth very earnestly recommend to them in the Lord.

Decree VII.

THe Synod doth earnestly recommend to all the faithful Christians Inhabitants of this Bishoprick, not to satisfie themselves with having confessed their Sins once a Year at *Easter*, when they are bound to it upon the penalty of *mortal Sin*; but that they do frequently make use of this Sacrament, in proportion to the Sins they fall

into

into daily, and not to fail to Confefs themfelves
on the Feftivities of the *Nativity* of the *Holy
Ghoft*, and the *Affumption of our Lady*, and at the
Wake of their Parifh, and the Vicars muft not
fail to admonifh their People thereof on the
Sunday before thofe Feftivities.

Decree VIII.

THe Synod doth declare, That notwithftanding the power of pardoning Sins is
annexed to the Sacerdotal Order, neverthelefs
that all Priefts cannot hear *Confeffions*, but only
fuch as are Licenfed by the Prelate; for the Act
of Abfolution being an Act of Jurifdiction, and
Judicature, cannot be without Subjects, which
the Prelate only can give when he appoints Confeffors with fuch limitations as he thinks neceffary; fo that a Prieft having no Licence, or tranf-
greffing the bounds that were fet to him by his
Prelate, if he fhall prefume to hear Confeffions
and Abfolve, his Confeffions and Abfolutions are
void and of no force; neither are the Sins of
the Penitents pardoned, who are therefore bound
to Confefs themfelves again to a Confeffor that
has power to Abfolve, as if they had not Confeffed before; but when any one is in probable
danger of Death, and cannot have a Prieft that
is Licenfed, any Prieft, tho' he is not Licenfed,
may Confefs and Abfolve him in that cafe.

T   Decree

Decree IX.

WHereas it belongs to the good Government of the Church and the Faithful, that Crimes of a heinous nature fhould be judged not by every Prieft, but by Prelates or Bifhops, becaufe for that reafon Chriftians will be the more fearful to commit them; befides that, it has always been the Cuftom of the Church, to referve to the Prelates, and even to the Pope as the Univerfal Head of the Church, fome Crimes from which they and none elfe can Abfolve, or not do it without their leave : therefore the Synod doth declare, That notwithftanding this Doctrine has not hitherto been underftood or practifed in this Bifhoprick, by reafon of the great Ignorance of the Church and facred Canons that has reigned therein : Neverthelefs, that the ordinary Confeffors have no power to Abfolve in cafes referved to the Prelate, and leaft of all in thofe that are referved to the Pope, namely, thofe contained in the *Bulla Cœnæ Domini*; which all Confeffors ought to be acquainted with ; neither can they Abfolve in the Crime of Herefy, or in any cafes wherein the Faith is concerned; all which do belong to the Court of the *Holy Office of Inquifition*, or to fuch as are Commiffioned by them, or to the Bifhop who by himfelf may Abfolve in the Form of the Holy Council of *Trent*; and according to the Ordinations of the Holy Fathers : Neither

ther can ordinary Confeſſors diſpenſe with or
change the Vows of Penitents, becauſe that belongs to the Prelate, or ſuch as are deputed by
him, or that have obtained Apoſtolical Privileges to that effect.   Only at the point of Death,
not only approved Confeſſors, but alſo all ſimple
Prieſts, there being no other to be had, are obliged to hear *Confeſſions*, and may alſo Abſolve
in all Caſes and from all Cenſures to whomſoe'er
reſerved.   Tho' as to the Cenſures with this
Obligation, that if the Sick Perſon ſhall recover,
they ſhall return to the Perſons again to whom
they were before reſerved, from whom they
ſhall receive ſuch healthful Penance as ſhall be
thought meet.

Decree   X.

THat Confeſſors may the better know in
what Caſes they may, and in what Caſes
they may not abſolve their Penitents, having no
Authority to do it, the Synod doth command the
Bulla Cœnæ Domini, and all the Caſes reſerved in this
Biſhoprick to be paſted on a Board, and ſet up in
all *Sacriſties*, and where there are no *Sacriſties*, in
the chief Chapel in every Church in the *Malabar*
Tongue, for the direction of the Confeſſors, and
doth furthermore in its regulation of the reſerved Caſes in this Dioceſs, declare, That willful
Murther, publickly committed with violence on
the Perſon of an Eccleſiaſtick, the voluntary
firing of Houſes, or of any Goods belonging to
Chri-

Christians, formal Simony both in the givers and receivers, marrying without the Vicar and two Witnesses, Schism and Disobedience against the Prelate, in all that are guilty thereof, or that favour such as are, the having of any of the Books condemned by this Synod in their Houses, or the reading of any of them, the performing of the publick Ceremonies called *Taliconum Coliconu*, the having of *Pagods* or Idols in their Houses, and the giving them any Veneration, have all the censure of Excommunication annexed to them, of which tho' some are * reserved by Law, yet that they might be the better known, it was thought fit to have them expressed here.

* **Reserved.**] This is what destroys all Discipline in the Church of *Rome*, and what the Bishops thereof complain of so much. *Didacus Abulensis* in the 73*d.* page of his Book of Councils, gives the following account of it, *Est in urbe Romanâ perniciosis abusus qui dissimulatione quâdam jam diu toleratur, nam sceleratissimi homines Episcoporum & aliorum Judicum ordinariorum, justissimam punitionem effugientes tanquam ad tutissimum asylum Romanam accedunt curiam, nihil aliud cogitantes quam quod eo ipso sint à gravissimis maximâ cum Justitiæ jacturâ immunes: Hinc sanè passim videmus Clericos Criminum atrocissimorum autores, ab ordinariis Judicibus fugientes in Romanam Curiam, propriis beneficiis, quæ obtinebant, æquissimè privatos, brevi compendio temporis in Hispaniam pa-*

triamque redire ita liberos, ut non tantum beneficia, quibus ob scelera privati fuerant, cum maximo dedecore & justitiæ, contemptu, favore & importunis precibus obtinuerint iterum apud Romanam Curiam; sed & aliis pinguioribus honorati in præmium criminum, liberam iterum millies peccandi licentiam ferè impetraverint; sunt enim in Curiâ Romanâ tot Officiales, quorum munus potissimum est præ avaritiâ maximâ & voracitate ab ipsis litigantibus & aliis extorquere, ut tandem jam nihil obtineri apud eandem curiam possit, aliter quam ingenti pecuniâ, veluti in pretium rei impetratæ impensâ. And in the 62*d.* Page he gives the Pope himself the following wholsome advice: *Cavere debet summus ipse Pontifex, ne dum agitur de morum censura, quæ ad Clericos, Episcopos & alios Christianæ professionis homines, omnino in ipso omni-*

omnium capite requirantur, ea morum correctio atque inflitutio quæ à fub-diti exigenda eft : præfertim verò illud eft ab eo poftulandam, ac deni-que fummopere petendum, ne in cu-ria Romana ofcitanter tot contractus Simoniaci, tot manifeftæ fraudes,

tot adverfus naturalia & Divina jura fcelera, palam in totius orbis fcandalum permittantur ; id enin adeo jam in omnium aures devenit, ut à nemine, nifi is prorfus à fenfu alienus judicari cupiat, taceri poffit.

Decree XI.

THe Sentence of Excommunication being the laſt and moſt rigorous puniſhment of the Church, and which for that reaſon ought not to be inflicted but with great Caution and Conſide-ration, the Synod doth therefore condemn the facility wherewith it has been uſed in this Dio-ceſs upon very ſlight and impertinent occaſions, commanding it not to be inflicted hereafter, but for weighty cauſes, and with great conſiderati-on, and never by word of mouth, but always in Writing. The Synod doth likewiſe condemn what has been formerly commanded in this Bi-ſhoprick, which was, that in certain Caſes Pe-nitents were not to be abſolved, but at the hour of Death, and in ſome not then neither, which is contrary to Chriſtian Charity, and the Rules of the Church, who as a Pious Mother at all times receives true Penitents, and never ſhuts the Gates of Salvation againſt any of her Chil-dren : So that let their Crimes be never ſo enor-mous, yet upon their doing Penance, and ex-preſſing a deep ſorrow for their Sins, and yield-ing the ſatisfaction that is impoſed upon them, they are graciouſly received, and made free at

T 3 leaſt

leaft in the Internal or Sacramental **Court** : But
being there is no other punifhment in this **Church**,
by reafon of its being under Kings that are *Infidels*, beyond that of Excommunication or Exclufion from the Church, fome who are abfolved in the Internal Court may ftill continue excommunicate in the External, fo as not to be
permitted to enter the Church; and tho' the
Priefts may go to their Houfes, they fhall not
give them the *Cafture*, until fuch time as the Prelate fhall order it to be done, having a regard to
the heinoufnefs of their Crimes, and the length
of time from the Commiffion of them, that by
this means the facility wherewith the Chriftians
of this Diocefs commit feveral Crimes, namely
Murther, and the Ceremonies of the *Taliconum*
may be removed.

Decree XII.

FOrafmuch as the Ignorance of Confeffors is
the deftruction of Penitents, and thorow the
Error of the Key, there is nothing done, and
it being known to the Synod that in this Diocefs
there are many Confeffors that are fuch Idiots,
as not to know what they do in Confeffion, all
the Priefts exercifing themfelves therein without ever having been examined as to their fufficiency; it doth therefore command, that from
henceforward no Prieft fhall prefume to hear
Confeffions without being Licenfed thereunto in
writing by the Prelate, which Licenfe fhall not
be

be granted to any, but what have been first examined by Learned Persons, as to their sufficiency for such an Employment, and until such time as this Church is provided of Prelates to regulate all such matters to the best of their understanding, the Synod doth commit the Examination and Approbation to the * Fathers of the Society of *Jesus*, of the College of *Vaipicotta*, upon

Fathers.] This is what the Bishops and other Orders in the Church of *Rome* complain of so much, that the *Jesuits* every where in the *Indies* ingross all Jurisdiction and Advantages to themselves. Of their ingrossing all to themselves to the exclusion of all other orders in *China*, *Japan*, and the other parts of the *East-Indies*, we have large complaints in the Apologies of *Diego Collado* a *Dominican*, and in the Letter of Father *Luis Sotela*, a *Franciscan*, written to *Urban* VIII. and as to the *West-Indies*, Bishop *Pallabox* in his Defence of Ecclesiastical Jurisdiction against the *Jesuits*, who had worryed him out of his Archbishoprick, after twenty more such charges, sayeth, 'En las 'provincias del Peru ha setenta 'annos que se quez an las Cathe-'drales, de que las Religiosos de la 'Compania com immoderadissi-'mos adquisiciones les despoian de 'los diesmos, ellos callando y pas-'sando y comprando, haziendos 'con grandissima paz y silencio 'van desnudando a los ocispos de 'sus rentas, a los pohes de su so-'corro, a los Cabildas de su con-

'grua sustentacion lo mismo hazen 'ein la nueva Espana, quanto mas 'corre et tiempo, tanto mas crece 'eldano legan ya con la navaia 'hasta clehuello. That is, *In the Provinces of* Peru, *the Cathedrals have complained these* 70 *Years of the Jesuits robbing them of their Tithes, by their vast purchases, they hold their Tongues, and go on purchasing Estates, without any noise, thereby stripping the Bishops of their Rents, the poor of their Alms, and the Chapter of a convenient maintenance; they do the same in* New Spain, *and this evil has gone on increasing daily, so that they are now come to the bone with their Rasor.* 'Revego a Dios, *saith the same Bishop,* 'Que ne sean las pincas 'de un tabardillo peligrosissimo, 'que necessite de sercurado en 'algunos hijos desta Religion por-'lamano del pontifice sumo com 'repitidas sangrias de tanto poder; *And I pray God that these things be not the spots of a most dangerous malignant Feavour, not to be cured in some of the Sons of that Religion, any otherways than by repeated bleedings from the Chief Pontiff.*

whose

whofe Examination and Approbation, and a Licence granted by the Governour whom the moft *Illuftrious Metropolitan* will leave in this Bifhoprick, the Priefts may hear Confeffions with the limitations expreffed in the faid Licences, and all fuch as are at prefent Confeffors, fhall be examined by order of the *Lord Metropolitan* at his next Vifitation, and fuch of the Clergy as fhall be made Parifh-Priefts, or Vicars, fhall be firft examined, and approved of in the fame form to be Confeffors, that fo fuch as are not qualified to be Confeffors, may not be admitted Vicars, whofe precife Obligation it is to confefs their Sheep: And all Confeffors that are not approved of by the faid *Lord Metropolitan* in the form aforefaid, this Synod doth fufpend from the Office of Confeffor till fuch time as they fhall be effectually examined and allowed of, and if any Prieft, which God forbid, fhall be found hearing Confeffions without fuch a Licence, except in the cafe of danger of Death, and where no Confeffor is to be had, he fhall be fufpended from his Office and Benefice for a Year, and be further punifhed according to the degree of his Contumacy, and the Penitents fhall be admonifhed to confefs themfelves again to fome approved Confeffor.

Decree

Decree XIII.

BY reason of the great want there is of knowing and able Confessors in this Bishoprick,
the Synod for the sake of the Sheep thereof doth
approve of all such Confessors as understand the
Malabar Tongue, and are Licensed Confessors
in any other Diocess, of whom also the Prelate
may make use for the assistance of the Parish-
Priests in *Lent*, where it shall be judged necef-
sary, and especially of the Priests of this Diocess
residing at *Cochim.*

Decree XIV.

THe Synod doth grievously condemn the
Sacrilegious Ignorance of those Priests,
who when they have confessed any at the command of the Prelate, or of any other by whom
they are authorized, after having heard the Sins
of their Penitents, do carry them to the said Prelate, to be absolved by him in the Sacramental
Court; which was what happened to the most *Illustrious Metropolitan* in these parts; the Synod
doth therefore teach and declare, That none
can absolve the Penitent in the Sacramental
Court, but the Priest only that heard his Sins;
for whereas he is the Judge, it is he that ought
to pass sentence and absolve, in conformity to
what he has heard confessed, the contrary being a gross and manifest Error.

Decree

Decree XV.

FOrafmuch as there are fome ignorant Clergymen, who being defired by Chriftians to
read the Gofpels and Prayers to them, or to
give them the Blefling on their heads, do igno-
ran˙ly ufe the form of Sacramental Abfolution,
faying, *I abfolve thee from thy Sins in the Name
of the Father,* &c. wherefore the Synod doth
advertife and admonifh them not to commit fuch
an Error, it being a moft grievous Sacrilege to
apply the Sacramental form, where it ought not
to be, wherefore they fhall only read the Gofpels and Prayers allowed, ending with the
Blefling *In the Name of the Father,* &c.

The Doctrine of the Sacrament of Ex-
tream Unction.

THe fifth Sacrament of *Extream Unction* has
for its matter, *the Oyl of Olive blefled by a
Bifhop,* it is called *Extream Unction,* becaufe it
is the laft of all the Holy Unctions, inftituted by
our Lord Chrift in his Church, and the laft that
is received by a Chriftian; this Sacrament is to
be adminiftred to an adult Perfon that is fick,
when apprehended to be in probable danger of
death, who is to be anointed by the Prieft the
only minifter of this Sacrament, on thofe parts
wherewith he hath offended God chiefly ; that
is to fay, on the Eyes, becaufe of Sins committed

ted by the fight ; on both the Ears, becaufe of
Sins committed by hearing ; on the mouth, becaufe of Sins committed by tafting and fpeaking ;
on both the hands, for the fins committed in feeling
and touching ; on both the Feet, for the Sins committed in walking ; on the Loins and Reins, for being the chief feat of Carnal pleafure ; every one of
which parts muft be anointed by the Prieft, making
the fign of the Crofs upon them with his Thumb
dipt in Holy Oil, and at the fame time repeating
the words of the form, which are, *By this Holy
Unction, and his moft tender mercy may our Lord
forgive thee all the Sins thou haft committed by
thy fight* ; and fo on, naming every part or fenfe
as it is anointed : The effect of this Sacrament, is
the Health of the Soul, and of the Body alfo, fo
far as it is convenient and neceffary to the Soul,
which is the chief ; moreover, it wafheth away
the Reliques of fin, if there are any remaining
in the Soul, comforting the Soul of the Sick
withall, and confirming and exciting in it a
great confidence in the Divine Mercy, by virtue of which Confolation it fuffers the troubles
of Sicknefs with the more patience, and with
the greater eafe refifts the Temptations of Satan,
whofe cuftom it is to affault the Soul with extraordinary violence in its laft Hour : It likewife cherifhes and fuccours the Body, fo far as
it is convenient for the falvation of the Soul, as
S. *James* teacheth us in his Canonical Epiftle,
faying, *Is any one Sick, let him call for the Priefts
of the Church, and they fhall pray over him, anoint-*
ing

ing him with *Oyl in the Name of the Lord,* and
the *Prayer of Faith shall save the Sick,* and the
*Lord shall give him ease, and if he be in Sins, they
shall be forgiven him:* The Apostle in saying *they
shall be pardoned,* demonstrates it to be a Sacrament, whose Virtue and Nature is to conferr
Grace, that pardoneth Sins; and in saying, *If
any are sick among you,* he declares the time when
this Sacrament is to be received, that is in time
of dangerous Sickness; and in saying, *they shall
call the Priests of the Church,* he sheweth that the
Priests are the only Ministers of this Sacrament,
and in saying, *they shall be anointed with Oil in
the Name of the Lord,* he sheweth, that Holy Oil
is the matter of this Sacrament; and in saying,
they shall pray over the Sick, anointing, he sheweth, that the form of this Sacrament is to be pronounced by way of deprecation, or Prayer; and
in saying, *the Lord shall give him ease,* he sheweth also, that the effect of this Sacrament is to give
health to the Body, so far as it is convenient and
necessary to the health of the Soul. And whereas this Sacrament was instituted for the use of the
Sick, none but what are dangerously so must take
it, and a Person who shall recover after having
received it, may when dangerously sick receive
it again, it having been instituted by our Lord
for that end; and to prepare, defend and fortifie us at the time of our departure out of this life,
whensoever it is.

Decree

Decree I.

WHereas in this Bifhoprick there has not been hitherto any ufe of the Sacrament of *Extream Unction*, in which for want of Catholick Inftruction, there has been no knowledge of the Inftitution, Effects, or Efficacy thereof; therefore the Synod does moft earneftly recommend the ufe of this Sacrament, commanding the Vicars to be vigilant over the Sick of their Parifhes, where-ever they live, whether in the Villages or in the *Heaths*; and whenever they fhall hear of any in danger of Death, to carry the moft Holy Sacrament of *Unction*, and adminifter it to them according to the *Roman* Ceremonial, which is to be tranflated into *Syrian*, and kept in all Churches, anointing them with Oil, and making the fign of the Crofs with Holy Oil on both their Eyes fhut; doing the right firft, and then the left, upon the Eye-lafhes, and upon both the Ears, the Noftrils, and the Mouth, being fhut, on both the Lips; but if the Diftemper fhould be fuch, that the Sick Perfon's Mouth cannot be fhut, or not without danger, then the upper Lip fhall be anointed, making the fign of the Crofs upon it; as alfo both the Palms of the Hands, the Balls of the Feet and the Loins, ordering the Sick Perfon to be moved gently; neither is it neceffary that any more of thefe parts fhould be anointed than what is convenient for the making the fign of the
Crofs

Crofs with the Holy Oil; and the Prieft muft
be fure to remember in this , as in all other Sacraments, to join the Form with the Matter, repeating the words of the Form as he anoints the
parts : If the Sick Perfon fhall happen to ex-
pire while the Prieft is anointing, the Prieft being fatisfied that he is dead , fhall proceed no
further with the Office; and the Vicar, through
whofe negligence any Parifhioner fhall die without having received this Sacrament , fhall be
fufpended from his Office and Benefice for fix
Months.

Decree II.

FOrafmuch as the Troubles the Sick are in,
together with the want of good Inftructi-
ons in matters appertaining to their Salvation,
do but too often make them unmindful of the
Holy Sacraments; wherefore the Synod doth
command and earneftly recommend it to all
Confeffors that are called upon to Confefs any
Sick Perfon to inftruct them in the Doctrine and
Efficacy of this Sacrament of *Unction*, admonifhing, perfuading and intreating them when they
fhall come to ftand in need of it, to have it
adminiftred to them; and they fhall alfo admonifh the People, and particularly thofe who attend the Sick Perfon, not to fail to call the
Vicar when it is neceffary, that is, when they
apprehend the Sick Perfon to be in any danger,
and before he has loft his Senfes, to give him
                                                    the

the Holy *Unction*; and fuch as fhall be negligent
therein, befides the offence they do to God and
the Sick Perfon, fhall be punifhed feverely at
the pleafure of the Prelate.

Decree III.

THe Synod doth command the Priefts that
go to anoint the Sick, tho' it fhould be to
the *Hamlets*, to go in their Surplice and Stole,
carrying the Veffel the Holy Oil is in, in their
hands, covered with a piece of Silk, with great
reverence, having the *Chamus* or Parifh-Clerk
before them with the Crofs of the Church in his
Arms, who, or fome other Perfon, fhall alfo carry a Pot of Holy Water, and if it is in the Night,
a Lanthorn or fome other Light before him, that
fo all People may know what he is going about;
and if the Sick Perfon is in a condition, he fhall
perfuade him to Confefs himfelf again, and be
reconciled, notwithftanding he fhould have Confeffed himfelf the day before; letting the Sick
Perfon know that it is neceffary in order to his
receiving the Holy Sacrament of *Unction* with
the greater purity; and when the Prieft fhall be
to carry this Sacrament a long way to thofe that
live in *Heaths*, he fhall go in the beft Form he
can, and fhall carry the Surplice and Stole along
with him, that fo when he comes to adminifter the
Sacrament, he may do it with all due reverence; he fhall likewife, if the Sick Perfon has
not a **Crucifix** of his own, leave one upon his
Pillow,

Pillow, exhorting him to fix both his Eyes and confidence thereon at his laſt minute, begging by it the pardon of his Sins of our Lord, who for our ſake died thereon.

A c t i o n VII.

Of the Holy Sacraments of Order *and* Matrimony.

The Doctrine of the Sacrament of Order.

THe ſixth Sacrament is that of *Order*, which was inſtituted by our Lord Jeſus Chriſt the day before he ſuffered for us, after that he had made an end of inſtituting the Sacrament of the Euchariſt, that ſo he might inſtitute the Sacrifice and the Prieſts that were to offer it together; at which time he created the Apoſtles Prieſts, giving them withal power to conſecrate others, that ſo the Sacrifice and the Prieſthood might be continued in the Church till the end of the World. The Matter of this Sacrament is that which is delivered to the Perſon that is ordained, for the exerciſe of that Order he has received; to the Prieſts, a Cup with Wine in it, and a Patten with Bread; to a Deacon the Book of the Goſpels; and to a Sub-Deacon an empty Cup and Patten, and ſo as to the other inferiour Orders: The Form of the Prieſthood and other Orders, are the words ſpoke by the Biſhop when he
deli-

delivers to every one that which belongs to
his Miniftry and the exercife of his Order. The
Minifter of this Sacrament is only a Bifhop, to
whom only Chrift committed the power of
Confecrating Priefts ; the effect of it is the encreafe of Grace, to the end that the Perfon ordained may be a fit Minifter.   This Sacrament
was inftituted by Chrift as highly neceflary in his
Church ; for a Sacrifice and Priefthood are fo joined, that the one cannot be without the other ;
wherefore fince under the New Teftament the
vifible Sacrifice of the Holy *Eucharift* was to be
inftituted, it became therefore neceflary, that
there fhould be a new, vifible and eternal Priefthood in the fame Church, whereby the ancient
Priefthood of the Old Law was tranflated ; and
there were Priefts provided accordingly for the
Offering of the Divine Sacrifice ; which Priefts being lawfully ordained , our Lord Jefus Chrift has
given them power over his true and real Body, to
Confecrate, Offer, and Adminifter it, as alfo o-
ver his Myftical Body the Church ; giving them
power to pardon and retain Sins ; to which power
it likewife belongs to rule and govern all Chriftian People, and to lead them in the way to
Eternal Life.   Now the Priefthood being fo high
an Office, that it may be exercifed with the
more decency and veneration, it was convenient that there fhould be different Orders or
Minifters, who are bound by their Function to
ferve the Priefthood, and to be divided in fuch
a manner, that after having received the *Clerical*
V   *Tonfure,*

Tonsure, they are to ascend through the lower to the higher Orders. The * lower are the *Ostiary, Reader, Exorcist, Acolythus*. The higher those which are called *Holy*, and are the *Sub-Deacon, Deacon*, and *Priest*, to which degrees there is joined that of *Bishops*, who succeeded in the place of the Apostles, and as St. *Paul* saith, are ordained to *govern the Church of God*; so that they are in a higher degree than the Priests, and to them only it belongs, by virtue of their Office, to administer the Sacrament of *Confirmation*, to Consecrate the Holy Oil of *Chrism*, and to Consecrate Altars and Churches, and ordain Priests and other Bishops. The Church enjoins *Continency* and *Chastity* to all that take *Holy Holy*, that so being disingaged from all other business they may employ themselves wholly in the Ministry of the Altar, and be intent only on matters appertaining to our Lord, and Divine Worship. The Church does not admit *Slaves* to be Priests, because it is necessary to the Divine Worship, that the Ministers thereof should be free and not subject to others, and

---

* **Lower.**] That there was none of the lesser Ecclesiastical Order in the Primitive Church is acknowledged by Card. *Bona* in his Book of *Liturgies*, *Tertia classis Ministrantium*, saith the Card. *Clericos minorum ordinum complectitur, Acolythos, scil. Exorcistas, lectores & Ostiarios, quos antiquissimos esse & ab Apostolis vel ab immediatis eorum Successoribus institutos, Doctores Scholastici asserunt, sed non probant, dicendum igitur cum St. Thoma, quod temporibus Apostolorum, omnia Ministeria quæ ordinibus minoribus competunt, non à distinctis personis, sed uno duntaxat Ministro exercebantur, contingit nimirum Ecclesiæ quod hominibus solet, qui dum tense patrimonium habent, uno servo contenti sunt, qui solus omnia administrat, si vero reditus augeantur, servorum etiam augetur numerus, eoque modo crescit familia.*

that

that they fhould not have been guilty of Murther or Blood, neither muft they have been born
out of lawful Wedlock, nor have any blemifh
or maim, nor have been twice Married, nor
have married a Widow, nor be Boys that are
not come to perfect Age; all which is ordered
for juft Reafons and Confiderations, and out of
refpect to the high Myftery wherein they are
exercifed.

Decree I.

WHereas it has been hitherto the Cuftom
of this Diocefs to ordain *Boys* even
Priefts, and that without examining their Lives
and Manners, having for Money and not for
any extraordinary fufficiency, all the Orders Inferiour, as well as Holy, conferred upon them
in one day, contrary to the Holy Canons and
the Laws of the Church: Therefore the Synod
doth command, That from henceforward, none
be ordained but what have firft been examined
as to their Sufficiency, Lives, and Manners, which
fhall be done by the Prelate, or by fome appointed by him, fearing God, and who are ob-
fervers of the Holy Canons, and the Forms of
the Holy Council of *Trent*. And whereas in
the faid Council it is commanded, That none
be ordained Sub-Deacon under Two and Twenty, nor Deacon under Three and Twenty, nor
Prieft till they are Five and Twenty, this Synod doth command the fame to be inviolably

obfer-

obferved; declaring, that no Prelate can difpenfe
therewith without being particularly impowered
and authorized thereunto by the Apoftolical See.
And forafmuch as there are great numbers in
this Diocefs that have been ordained before they
were at that Age, the Synod fufpends all fuch,
whether Priefts, Deacons, or Sub-Deacons, from
the exercife of their feveral Functions, until fuch
time as they have perfectly attained to it, they
fhall neverthelefs hold their Places, and reap the
benefits thereof, in the fame manner as if they
were in the exercife of their Functions: And as
to their Sufficiency, the Synod doth declare, That
as the Council of *Trent* requires, that all that are
ordained do underftand *Latin*, fo in this Diocefs
it is required, that all that are ordained if they
do not underftand *Latin*, fhould underftand *Syrian :* Neither fhall any *Syrian* that does not underftand it fo well, as to be able to read and
fing it, fo as to underftand what they fay in the
Offices, be admitted into Orders, or at leaft not
into thofe that are Holy.

Decree II.

ALL that are in Orders in this Diocefs having
been Simonaically ordained in having pay'd
a certain price, upon a formal Bargain for their
Orders, have thereby incurr'd the grievous punifhments of the Law. Neverthelefs in confideration of their Ignorance, and the falfe Doctrine wherein they have been educated by their
former

former Prelates, the *Moft Reverend Metropolitan,*
both by his ordinary Authority, this *See* being vacant, and the Apoftolical Authority committed to
him over this Church, doth Abfolve all that have
been fo ordained, from all Penalties and Cenfures
which by the Law they have incurr'd, by having
been Simonaically ordained, commanding them
to have no further fcruples about that matter,
and difpenfing with them all as to the exercife
of their Orders, fo that they may lawfully officiate, as in right they may and ought to do.

Decree III.

THe Synod being informed that there are
feveral Priefts, who tho' infected with the
Leprofie, and miferably deformed thereby, do
prefume to Celebrate, to the great loathing of
the People, and to handle the Holy Veffels and
Veftments, to the endangering of the health of
others, doth command, That none that are
notorioufly Leprous, do prefume to Celebrate,
all fuch being irregular according to the Law
of Corporal defects, on the account of the
difguft they give to People when they fee them
Celebrate in fuch a condition, and receive the
moft Holy Sacrament of the Altar at their
hands.

Decree

Decree IV.

WHereas it is the cuſtom to receive the *Caſture* or Bleſſing from the hands of the oldeſt Clergy-man that officiates in the Quire, and for all that are preſent to return it to him; which according to the uſage of this Dioceſs, contains in it a Symbol of Charity, Communion, and Brotherly Love; the Synod being informed that there are thoſe, who not being in Charity with their Neighbours, do not ſpeak to them, nor take them by the hand, and do neither give nor take the *Caſture* from them, thereby diſcovering that they live in malice with their Neighbours, denying them the ordinary Eccleſi-aſtical Salutation uſed in the Church of this Dioceſs; doth command, that all that ſhall re-fuſe to give or receive the ſame, be puniſhed by the Prelate as Perſons living in hatred or out of charity with their Neighbours; and that un-til ſuch time as they ſhall give the ſaid *Caſture*, they ſhall not be ſuffered to come to the Altar, according to the command of our Lord Jeſus Chriſt: Neither ſhall they be permitted to offici-ate or Miniſter in the Church; neither ſhall the Bleſſing be given them until they have effectu-ally reconciled themſelves to their Brother.

Decree

Decree V.

WHereas it is the Precept of the Universal
Church, that all that are in Holy Orders
do recite the whole Divine Office, and the usage
of this Diocess is, to recite it only when they
go to Church, and there, tho' it happen to be
near ended before they come, having heard a
little to go away immediately, reckoning they
have complied with their Obligation, tho' they
do not say over what they were not present at,
there being very few that recite the Divine
Office in their Houses, some imagining that they
are not bound to do it any where but in the
Church, and others excusing themselves for want
of Books, there being but very few, and those
that are, are in Manuscript in this Bishoprick ;
therefore the Synod doth declare, That all that
are in Holy Orders, are obliged upon pain of
Mortal Sin, to recite the whole Divine Office as
it is recited in the Church ; and that all such as
shall come late, shall be obliged to recite what
they have missed; and if they do not recite it in the
Church, they shall do it at home in their Houses,
having the conveniency of a Book, which being
what a great many do want, the Synod obligeth
all such to recite the said Divine Office by Beads,
that so there may be none but what perform
this duty either by Book or Beads : And tho'
the Divine Office consists of seven distinct Canonical hours, yet in this Church, in conformity

to

to the *Breviary* thereof, they shall only recite one part at two times in the Morning, and the other part in the Evening, without making any other difference in the Divine Office, besides that of repeating one part thereof in the Morning and the other in the Evening; and whereas they who have no Books are to recite with Beads, such beginning in the Morning as the Divine Office is begun in the Church, shall say Thirty-three *Pater Nosters*, and as many *Ave Maries*, with the *Gloria Patri*, &c. in the Morning; and when they are ended, they shall moreover say twelve *Pater Nosters*, and twelve *Ave Maries*, for the Souls of the Faithful departed, and one *Pater Noster* and one *Ave Mary* for the Pope, and the same for the Bishop, instead of the Prayers that are said for them in the Church: and instead of the Prayers that are to be recited by them in the Evening, they shall say Thirty-three *Pater Nosters*, and as many *Ave Maries*, with the *Gloria Patri*, &c. as in the Morning; and when they are ended, they shall say *nine *Ave Maries* to our Lady, and one *Pater Noster* and one *Ave Mary* for the Pope, and another for the Bishop as in the Morning, provided that

---

* *Nine.*] It would have been no true *Roman* Devotion, had not the *Ave Maries* exceeded the *Pater Nosters*; for one may speak within compass, and say, that the blessed *Virgin* has ten Prayers and an hundred Vows made to her in the Church of *Rome*, where Christ has one made to him; and of this the *Tabulæ Votivæ* in their Churches, are a clear demonstration, there being few or none of these Tables (and there are vast numbers of them in several Churches) but what are dedicated solely to the honour of the blessed *Virgin*.

such

fuch as have Books fhall recite by them, and
not by Beads, and fuch as recite by Beads, if
they have faid any of the Prayers either in the
Morning or Evening at Church, fhall not be obliged to recite them again, but fhall only recite
thofe which they may have omitted there.

Decree VI.

THe Synod doth command the Creed of St.
  Athanafius, *Quicunque vult*, to be tranflated
into *Syrian*, and to be put into all the *Brevia-*
ries, and Books of Prayer of this Diocefs, and to
be read every *Sunday* in the Church immediately
after Morning Service, defiring the Reverend
Father *Francifco Roz*, of the Society of *Jefus* to
tranflate it, and all the Curates and Clergy to
learn the faid Creed by Heart, which is what the
Holy Canons recommend to them, for as much
as that Creed contains in it fummarily the chief
Myfteries of our Faith, and is ufed and fung in
the Univerfal Church.

Decree VII.

THe Synod doth earneftly recommend it to
  all the Clergymen and Curates, not to be
abfent from Church at the time of Divine Service, Morning nor Evening, and that none offer to talk or divert themfelves there any other
way, as has been the Cuftom, or to difpofe
themfelves to fleep whilft others are reciting,
who

who are alfo to take notice, that in reciting they ought not to begin a new Verfe before the Congregation has done with the former, and that tho' it has hitherto been the cuftom for the oldeft Clergyman that was prefent at Divine Service to give the *Cafture*, that from henceforward the true Vicar of the Church being prefent, fhall in every thing be preferr'd to all others as he is the particular Paftor of the Church.

Decree VIII.

THere being no reafon why they that do not minifter in the Church, fhould be equally rewarded with thofe that do ; it feems juft to the Synod that the Curates and other Clergymen, that are abfent either from Morning or Evening Service, or from the *Mafs* of the day on *Sundays* and Holydays, be marked by the Vicar, or the oldeft Clergyman in his abfence, that when the Dividend comes to be made, for every time they have been abfent fo much may be deducted from their fhare, as they that make the diftribution fhall think fit, in proportion to the quantity of the Dividend, which fhall be done only when they are not hindred by fome lawful Impediment, as Sicknefs, or are not otherwife employed in the Service of the Church, or by the Prelate, in all which cafes they are to be excufed : and the *Sconfes* fhall be equally divided among the reft.

Decree

Decree IX.

THe Synod being informed, that great numbers of Clergy-men do ufe fuperftitious
and Heathen Exorcifms, taking words out of an
impious and prohibited Book called *Parifman*,
for the cafting out of Devils, doth command in
virtue of Holy Obedience, that none prefume
to ufe any other exorcifms to that effect, but fuch
as the *Roman* Church makes ufe of, and have
been approved of by the Holy Fathers, which
are to be bound up with the Offices of the Adminiftration of the Sacraments, and all Clergymen,
that fhall be found to ufe any other, or to ufe
any unknown fuperftitious words or Ceremonies with fuch as are poffeffed, fhall be fufpended
from their Office and Benefice for a Year, and
be fubject to what other penalties the Prelate
fhall be pleafed to lay upon them, according to
the quality of the Superftitions they have made
ufe of; and in cafe they fhall after they have
been admonifhed and cenfured, perfift therein,
they fhall then be Excommunicated; and when
it fhall appear that any have acted thus upon
any compact or contract with the Devil, which
God forbid, as it is faid fome do, they fhall be
declared Excommunicate, until they have done
the condign Penance, which the Prelate fhall
have impofed upon them, and fhall be moreover fufpended from their Office and Benefice
during their Lives, without any hopes of a difpenfation,

penfation, and fhall be yet further punifhed, as the Law requires they fhould be, who are guilty of fuch Crimes, and are convicted of having had a compact with the Devil.

Decree X.

WHereas there are feveral Clergymen, who according to the fuperftitious Cuftom of the Heathens, do give good days for Marriages, and do feveral other things, at the requeft of Chriftians for the Heathens, and for that end keep an account of the lucky and unlucky days of the *Gentiles* in their Books, and do ufe fome of their Prayers, and do make Schemes after the manner of *Aftrologers*, as appears from feveral even of their Church-books, the Synod doth command in virtue of Holy Obedience, and upon pain of the greater Excommunication, that no Ecclefiaftical or Secular, or *Caffanar*, fhall dare to give good or bad days for Marriages, or on any other occafion, or to draw any thing out of a Book of Lots, and namely out of that which is generally bound up with the Book called *Pariffman*, or out of any other place, or by whomfoever invented ; and whofoever fhall tranfgrefs herein fhall be declared excommunicate, and fhall be fufpended from their Office for a Year, and fix Months from their Benefice ; it being the duty of the Priefts rather to admonifh the People to avoid all Heathen Superftitions, and to chufe the folemn days of the Church, or the

Saints

Saints days, who may intreat God for them, for
the celebration of their Marriages, or any other
days they pleafe, all days being good to thofe
that do good upon them, being all equally the
work of Gods hands.   Thofe only which are
fpent in the greateft works and the higher celebration of the Divine Myfteries, being the days
that are to be moft reverenced.

Decree XI.

WHereas it is decent that Priefts being the
Mafters, from whom the People are to
learn good Manners fhould themfelves give good
example, the Synod is therefore much concerned for the fcandal fome give by their being dif-
orderly in their eating and drinking, to the
great difgrace of the Sacerdotal Office among fo
many *Infidels*, and does recommend Moderation
to them, ordering fuch as fhall be found at any
time overtaken with drink to be fharply reproved by the Prelate, and if it appear that they
are frequently fo drunk, as to lofe their Judgment, they fhall be fufpended from the Exercife
of their Orders for ever, tho' not from reading
Prayers with others in the Church, nor from
the profits they may receive from thence.   The
Synod doth likewife command, That no Prieft
fhall dare to eat or drink in a Tavern or Publick Eating houfe, it being very unbecoming the
gravity of the Sacerdotal Office fo to do,
and is therefore forbid the Priefts by Law: it
doth

doth likewife prohibit all Priefts to eat with *In-fidels*, whether *Heathens*, *Mahometans*, or *Jews*, upon pain of being fufpended for four Months, from their Office and Benefice.

Decree XII.

IT being convenient that Clergymen fhould always go in a habit different from that of the Laity, and in fuch a one as becomes their Function, wherefore the Synod doth command, that no Clergymen prefume to go abroad in Doublets with their Skirts flanting out, as has been too cuftomary, or with any open Linen: but when they fhall go into Town, or to the Church, or when they travel upon the Road, they fhall wear a white and black, or blew Veftment, according to Cuftom, and a Hat or Bonnet on their Heads; neither fhall they at any time go difguifed, no not at Nights, nor when they go a hunting, or Fifhing: and all that fhall tranfgrefs herein fhall be feverely punifhed; neither fhall they wafh themfelves, or if they do, it fhall not be in the Company of Women, according to the cuftom of the Country, it being a thing very unbecoming the gravity of the Minifters of the Church: and as for their Beards, they fhall be left to their liberty to do what they fhall think fit, only fuch as are Young fhall not fuffer their Beards to grow, but fhall ftill keep them fhaved, and they that wear them

very

very long, fhall take care to * cut off the Hair,
that grows near their Lips, that fo they may not
be a hinderance to their receiving the Blood of
the Cup in the *Mafs*, by being fo long as to touch it.

* **Cut**] This is one of the | the belief of *Tranfubftantiation* has
many fuperftitious Cautels that | introduced into the *Roman* Church.

Decree XIII.

WHereas the Apoftle S. *Paul* faith, That the
Perfons that are particularly dedicated to
the fervice of God and the Divine Worfhip, ought
not to entangle themfelves in fecular Affairs;
for which reafon all Clerks are by the Sacred Canons prohibited to Merchandize, a thing very little obferved in this Diocefs, therefore the Synod
doth prohibit all the Clerks thereof to go upon
the publick Exchange, or to Farm any of the
Revenues, or to be Factors or Agents, or to farm
any Contracts fingly, or in Company: or to fell any
forts of Merchant Goods publickly in their houfes,
or any fort of Victuals, or to bear any * fecular
Office, all that fhall tranfgrefs herein, fhall be moft
rigoroufly punifhed by the Prelate, and if they do
not reform, fhall be fufpended from their Orders,
and fuch as are *Tarcgas*, if they fhall not renounce
that Office within a month, fhall not be fuffered to enter the Church, and fhall be fufpended
from their Office and Benefice, until fuch time as
they have effectually abandoned it.

* **Secular.**] There are feve- in 5 years was made the Supream
ral Cuftom-houfes, where you fhall Governor of the *Indies*, could not
feldom fail to find *Jefuits* difpatch- but execute this Decree with a
ing Sugar, Tobacco, and other very good Grace.
Goods: The Archbifhop who with-

Decree

Decree XIV.

WHereas several Priests in this Diocess not having the fear of God or of the Church, or of their Prelates, before their eyes, and without having a due regard to the high Station and Dignity they are in, do occupy themselves in Secular Business and in publick Merchandize, and that they may do it the more securely, do neither wear the Sacerdotal Habit, nor the *Tonsure*, nor any manner of Crown, but do wear their Hair long like the Laity : Therefore the Synod doth command in vertue of obedience, and upon pain of Excommunication, That all Clerks in Holy Orders, do wear the Habit *Tonsure* and shaved Crown, and not long Hair after the fashion of the Laity ; and that whosoever shall transgress herein, shall be declared Excommunicate, until they have put on the said Habit and *Tonsure*, and shall have their Crown shaved as other Ecclesiasticks.

Decree XV.

WHereas there are several Ecclesiasticks, as well *Cassanars* as *Chamazes*, who being unmindful of their obligations, to free themselves from some vexations of *Infidel* Kings ; or, which is yet more scandalous, to be favoured and protected by such Princes against their Prelates, that they may not punish them for their faults, do

receive

receive Pay from the faid Kings as the Natives
do, whereby they are obliged to take the Field as
Souldiers, and Fight when commanded, which
is exprefly contrary to the Holy Canons and Ecclefiaftical Laws : Therefore the Synod doth
command in virtue of obedience, and upon pain
of Excommunication to be *ipfo facto* incurred,
That no *Caffanar* nor *Chamaz* do from henceforward
prefume to receive pay from any King as a Soul-
dier ; and that whofoever fhall tranfgrefs herein,
fhall be immediately declared Excommunicate, and
fhall not be Abfolved before they have renounced
the faid pay, and all the obligations thereof, and
have undergone condign punifhment for their
fault.

Decree XVI.

IT having been the Univerfal cuftom from the
beginning of the Church, for all that are
in Holy Orders, and efpecially Priefts, to keep
Chaftity and Continency, as is evident from all
the ancient Councils, *Eaftern* and *Weftern* ; and
tho' in the beginning of the Church, as well for
the want of Priefts, as for the making ufe of
feveral Learned Men who were Married when
they turned Chriftians, but not having been
twice Married, feveral who were Married were
not only confecrated Priefts but Bifhops alfo ;
which cuftom ftill remains both in the *Greek*
Church, and in fome that are fubject to the
Apoftolical *See*, by which it is tolerated for juft
Reafons : Neverthelefs the Church Catholick did
never confent that Priefts fhould Marry after

they are in Orders, but was much rather for having such as were Married to leave their Wives, that that they might serve the better in the Holy Ministry : And whereas in this Diocess (which the Synod has taken notice of with great sorrow) through their vile ignorance of the Law, and the abounding iniquity of the Times, and their having been governed by Schismatical Prelates, Priests have Married after they were in Orders, nay have taken Orders on purpose that they might Marry the better, and have frequently Married Widows, and some have Married three or four times, making no account of the impediment of Bigamy, so strictly observed in the Church from the beginning, but did, notwithstanding that, go on still exercising their Function, some few excepted, who after they had been twice Married, gave over celebrating and performing all other Exercises and Ministeries of Priests; all which they thought they might do lawfully by virtue of a Licence granted by their Prelates, who notwithstanding they prohibited them to Marry upon pain of Excommunication, and had declared them Excommunicate, did neverthelefs Absolve them for a sum of Money, or upon some Simonaical contract; so that notwithstanding that Excommunication, they did all Marry and continued in Wedlock, reckoning themselves safe in Conscience upon their having obtained a Licence after such a manner: All which being detested by the Synod as the inventions of the Devil, and devised by the covet-

oufnefs

ousness of Schismaticks, and desiring to restore this Church to its due purity, and the usage of the *Roman* Church, doth command, in virtue of obedience and upon pain of Excommunication *latæ Sententiæ*, that henceforward no Clerk in Holy Orders presume to Marry, nor shall any *Caſſanar* Marry any such, nor shall any presume to be present at any such Marriage, nor give Council, Favour, or Assiſtance thereunto: And whoever shall offend in any of these particulars, muſt know that they are Excommunicate and Curſed, and are to be declared as such by the Church; and as to those who are already Married, the Synod suspends them all, whether Married once or oftner, from the Miniſtery of their Orders, and all Sacerdotal Acts, until such time as they have put away their Wives effectually, which is what the Synod intreats them in the Lord to do: And to those who have been twice Married, or have Married Widows, or Women that were publickly diſhoneſt, the Synod doth command all such as being *Bigamiſts*, and having Married contrary to their conſciences, as it appears several of them have done, by their giving over thereupon to Celebrate, notwithſtanding their having obtained a Licence from their Biſhop, in virtue of obedience and upon pain of being declared Excommunicate, ſo ſoon as this Decree shall come to their knowledge, to turn off the said Women, not only as to Bed and Board, but ſo as not to dwell in the ſame Houſe with them; declaring, that until they

have

have done it they are in *Mortal* Sin, and do live
in Concubinate, fuch Marriages having never
been true or valid; but on the contrary, void
and of no force: neither can any Prelate or
Bifhop grant Licences in fuch cafes, having no
Authority to do it, by reafon of its being contrary to the Rules of the Church, that have been
always punctually obferved, and contrary to the
Holy general Councils received all over the
World; and as to thofe who have been but
once Married, the Synod will confult the moft
Holy Pope and Bifhop of *Rome*, that he as
Prelate and Head of the whole Church of God,
and Mafter and Doctor of the fame, may teach
and command what ought to be done therein,
and whatfoever his *Holinefs* fhall ordain, fhall
be punctually obferved.

Decree XVII.

THe Synod doth declare, That thofe Priefts
who as obedient Sons fhall follow the advice of the Synod in turning away their Wives,
may, after they have fo done, continue in the
exercife of their Functions; and if not otherwife hindered, may Celebrate, notwithftanding
they have been twice Married, or may have
Married Widows, fince by fuch Weddings not
being true Marriages, they did not incurr the
irregularity of Bigamy: All which the Synod
grants out of pure Grace, being extreamly defirous to have them turn away fuch Women, and
out

out of refpect to their Ignorance, and the
Cheat that was put upon them by their Prelates,
who inftead of inftructing them better, granted
them Licences : And whereas all Priefts that Marry are Irregular, according to the Holy Canons,
the moft *Illuftrious Metropolitan* by the Ordinary, as well as the Apoftolical Authority, that he
has in this Church by reafon of the *See's* being
vacant, doth difpenfe with the Priefts and all
the other Clergy-men in Holy Orders that fhall
yield obedience to the Synod, in turning away
their Wives, and fhall defire to continue to officiate, as to the faid irregularity which they have
incurred, granting them Licence as to this freely and without fcruple, to exercife their Orders.

Decree XVIII.

WHereas the Wives of Priefts who are called *Catatiaras* or *Caffaneiras*, have not
only the moft Honourable place in the Church
for their being fuch, and are the more reverenced, but do moreover partake of the profits of
the Churches wherein their Husbands miniftred
equally with the furviving Priefts, and have
fometimes a greater fhare of them than any of
the Priefts, by reafon of the Seniority and Prehe-
minence that their Husbands had in the Church;
therefore the Synod doth ordain, That fuch of
them as do not from henceforward depart from
their Husbands, fhall receive no fuch benefit :
but if obeying the admonition of the Synod

they

they ſhall leave their Husbands, they ſhall then immediately receive their proportion as an Alms to help to ſuſtain them and their Families, and ſhall injoy the ſame place and Honour in the Church, and every where elſe which they did before.

Decree XIX.

THe Synod doth declare, That notwithſtanding it has received the Holy Council of *Trent*, with all its Decrees, relating both to the good Government of the Church and Manners, neverthelefs that what was declared therein relating to Prieſts Baſtards, not being permitted to Miniſter in the ſame Church, wherein the Fathers have Miniſtered before, is not to be extended to the Sons of the Married Prieſts in this Dioceſs that are now born, by reaſon of the great numbers there are of ſuch at preſent in all Churches, and of other great inconveniencies that would follow thereupon; it is therefore permitted to ſuch to Miniſter, nay to be Vicars of the Churches wherein their Fathers have officiated; but this is to be underſtood of ſuch only as were born of Marriages, that were reputed true, the proviſion of the forementioned Holy Council being to take place, as to all that ſhall be born hereafter.

Decree

Decree XX.

WHereas the fin of * *Simony* is one of the greateſt offences in the Church, and a pernicious plague therein, which God has always puniſhed with great rigour, it being the ſelling of Spiritual things for Money; and this Biſhop-

---

* **Simony.**] This noiſe of Simony was raiſed for no other reaſon, but to throw Dirt on the Memory of their former Biſhops, whoſe Fees at their Ordination were not in all probability ſo great as they are at *Goa*, and had as little in them of a formal Bargain: But the truth is, Simony, as well as Hereſy, is a Stone the Church of *Rome* throws blind-fold at all that diſpleaſe her, tho' at the ſame time ſhe's the Church in the World that's moſt guilty of it; ſo when ſhe was crying ſhame of the Emperors as Simoniacks, *Petrus Clemangis* tells us, ſhe her ſelf was *totius negotiationis, latrocinii & rapinæ officina, in quo venalia exponuntur Sacramenta, venales ordines.* And *Didacus Abulenſis*, a learned *Spaniſh* Biſhop, and who was no ſtranger at *Rome*, at the ſame time ſhe was thus reproaching the poor Church of *Malabar*, tells us in his Book of Councils, that *vitium Simoniæ frequens eſt & veluti res honeſtiſſima in uſum deducitur in Curiâ Romanâ, nulla unquam punitione hujus ſceleris à judicibus Eccleſiaſticis præmiſſâ,* I do not deny but the Canons and Bulls of that Church are ſevere againſt all

forts of *Simony*, namely, the Bull of *Julius* the II. publiſhed in the Year 1553, againſt *Simony*, in obtaining the Papacy; I ſhall here ſet down the ſubſtance of that Bull, and then leave it to any to judge, whether according to that Bull we have had ſo much as one true Pope ſince it was made, or are likely ever to have one ſo long as the Papacy continues ſo great a preferment.

Si Papa eligatur per Simoniam, nempe aliquo Cardinale quomodo libet, ſuffragium ferente, datâ vel acceptâ vel promiſſi pecuniâ, vel bonis cujuſlibet generis, Caſtris, Officiis, Beneficiis, Promiſſionibus, vel Obligationibus, vel per ſe, vel per alium, pro Pontifice non habeatur, item etiamſi duarum partium ſuffragiis, vel unanimi Cardinalium concordiâ, etiam per viam aſſumptionis concorditer nemine diſcrepante, & etiam ſine ſcrutinio facto ſit electio, nullus exiſtat & nihil juris electus acquirat, ſive in Spiritualibus, ſive in Temporalibus, & contra electum per Simoniam opponi criminis exceptio poſſit, ſicut contra electum poteſt opponi vera & indubitata hereſis, & electus Simoniacè à nullus pro Papâ habeatur.

X 4   rick,

rick, which the Synod takes notice of with great
regret, having hitherto abounded with it, Money having been publickly taken for the adminiftration of the Holy Sacraments, and after
fuch a manner that none of them were given,
before the Money was either put into the Prieft's
hands, or into the Church Box, to be divided
among them, no, not fo much as the Holy Sacrament of the Eucharift, at which all pious Ears
do tremble, nor any other Sacraments or Difpenfations for Marriages, nor Abfolutions from Excommunication, nor the Confecrations of Stones,
nor any of the leffer Orders, nor Licences, nor
Reverenda's, to go to receive thofe Orders in a-
nother place, nor Letters Dimiffory for Clerks,
to go to other Diocefles ; all which was done
at a Rated Price, or by a Publick Agreement :
All which the Sydod detefting as a moft execrable
and horrid abomination, doth therefore in virtue
of Holy Obedience, and upon pain of Excommunication to be *ipfo facto* incurred, command,
That no Money, nor nothing elfe, be taken for
any of the forefaid things ; and that no Priefts
fhall dare to take any thing for the adminiftration of any of the Sacraments, nor to give them
upon any fuch confideration to any Perfon whatfoever, but fhall give the Holy Sacrament *gratis*
to the Faithful, according to the Precept of our
Lord Chrift, who faid, *Freely you have received,
freely you fhall give* ; neither fhall they fo much
as receive Alms that the Faithful would give
voluntarily, though not given with any refpect
                                    to

to the Sacrament, if offered at the fame time
when the Sacrament is adminiſtred: And the
Prieſt that ſhall be found to tranſgreſs herein,
beſides being Excommunicated, ſhall be ſuſpended from his Office and Benefice for three Years,
and the Vicars muſt take care to advertiſe
the People thereof. The Synod being moreover informed, That a great many poor People
who live in the *Heaths*, do not bring their Children to be Baptized, becauſe they have not ſo
much Money as is demanded, doth order the
Prieſt to be ſatisfied with the profits ariſing from
the Dead, the Alms they receive for their *Maſſes*,
in which the Synod declares there is nothing of
Simony; but only a congruous maintenance for
the Prieſt that Celebrates, given by the Perſon
that he recommends, and with the other Alms
which the Faithful are accuſtomed to give;
which being Juſt and Holy, ſhall be divided after the ſame manner as they have been formerly: And the Synod doth declare further, That
ſuch as are abſolved from Excommunication, if
it was for any great Crime that they were under
that Cenſure, though there can be nothing taken
for their Abſolution, yet for the Fault that they
have committed, they may, by way of Puniſhment,
be Condemned in a Pecuniary Mulct, if Authorized by the Prelate, which Money muſt be put
to ſome Pious uſe, or employed in the building
of a Church; and the Offender being Poor, he
may be employed in Perſon to do ſome work
about a Church, for ſo long as ſhall be thought
fit,

fit, and in that Cafe no Money fhall be required
of him.

Decree XXI.

THe Synod defiring by all means poffible to
deftroy and root out of this Diocefs the
pernicious Vice of *Simony*, which it underftands
to have been encreafed in part by the want the
Minifters of the Church are in of a neceffary
maintenance, doth therefore moft earneftly entreat the People of this Bifhoprick to apply a
certain Yearly Summ to be raifed by the way of
Alms, Collection, or Affeffment, or by the way
of Tithes, according to Peoples Abilities ; for
the fupport of the Vicar and Curate of their
Souls, and the other Minifters that are neceffary
to the Divine Service in the Church, which the
moft *Reverend Metropolitan* may treat about in
every Parifh; for they muft know, that Chriftians are bound both by Divine and Humane
Laws to maintain the Priefts which pray to God
for them, and give Spiritual Food to their Souls,
of which they are to render an account to God
and their Prelates.

Decree XXII.

THat this Synod may by all ways poffible fupply the Neceffities of the Minifters of the
Church, and by that means extirpate *Simony* ;
befides what it defires the People to contribute
towards

towards their maintenance, underſtanding their
Poverty to be ſuch, that they are not able to ſup-
ply them with ſo much as is neceſſary, it doth
further beſeech his Catholick *Majeſty*, the King
of *Portugal*, that as Protector of the Chriſtians of
theſe parts, and the only Chriſtian King and Lord
in the *Indies*, he would be gracioufly pleaſed to
provide the Vicars of this Church with a ſufficient
Maintenance, as he does in all the other Churches of the *Indies*, allowing them at leaſt fifteen
thouſand *Cruzado's* to be divided among them
all, beſides what ſhall be gathered for them in
their reſpective Pariſhes; which as the Synod is
informed, is the Summ that was formerly deſired of his Majeſty in the third Provincial Council of *Goa*, in order to the reducing of this Church
to the Obedience of the Church of *Rome*, and
the extirpating of *Simony*. The Synod doth
moreover intreat the moſt *Illuſtrious Metropolitan*
to preſent this their Petition to his Majeſty, in
the Name of this Church, repreſenting therewith
the great Neceſſities of the Miniſters thereof,
and that until ſuch time as they ſhall have his Majeſty's Anſwer, the ſaid Lord Archbiſhop, Metropolitan of this Church, and Preſident of the Synod,
Dom fray Aleixo de Menezes, underſtanding how
effectual a courſe this will be for the rooting
the Peſtilential Sin of *Simony* out of this Dioceſs,
and for the tying of Vicars to their Churches,
there to govern the Faithful, and adminiſter the
Holy Sacraments to them, would be pleaſed to
give the ſaid Summ of fifteen thouſand *Cruzado's*
Yearly

Yearly out of his own Revenues, and to pay it Quarterly at *Goa*, to be divided among the said Vicars, the diftribution whereof the Synod orders to be made in all Churches according to the Allotments, in the Inftrument paffed, and figned and fealed by the faid Lord Arch-bifhop, under the Great Seal of his Chancery, every Church being to receive fo much, as was now read in the prefence of the whole Synod.

Decree XXIII.

WHereas this Diocefs is not only provided with a fufficient number of Clergy, but has a great many more than are neceffary, and the Holy Council of *Trent* having prohibited that any more fhould be ordained than what are neceffary for the Churches, the Synod doth therefore command, that during the vacancy of this *See*, none fhall be put into * Holy Orders, neither fhall any *Reverenda's*, or Licences be granted for that purpofe, fuch only as are in Holy Orders may go afcending therein, as the Governour, who is to be left in this Diocefs by the moft *Illuftrious Metropolitan* fhall judge convenient: The Synod doth alfo put fuch as do afpire to Priefts Holy Orders in mind of not failing to learn the Doctrine of the Sacraments, and the Form of Sacramental Abfolution, fo as to

---

* If this was one of the Grievances of this Church, the Arch-Bifhop did not do well in Ordaining above a Hundred Priefts among them in lefs than three Months time.

be

be ready to ufe them on all occafions, and in all
Cafes of Neceffity, as alfo the abfolution from
Cenfures, or at leaft the Conditional one, which
always goes before the Sacramental Abfolution
from Sins in Confeffion.

The Doctrine of the Sacrament of Matrimony.

THe feventh Sacrament is that of *Matrimo-
mony*, which according to the Apoftle is
the fignification of that Union which is betwixt
Chrift and his Church. The efficient Caufe of
Matrimony regularly, is the Confent of both parties declared by Words or Signs *de præfenti*. This
Sacrament our Lord Jefus Chrift Founded on the
Matrimonial Contract, which has always been in
the World, and in all Religions, from whence it
is that Matrimony is to be confidered in two
refpects; either as a Natural Contract, or as a
Sacrament inftituted by our Lord Jefus Chrift:
The Bond of Matrimony God hath made to be
perpetual, infomuch that it cannot be diffolved
by any thing but Death, according to what
Chrift faid, *Whom God hath joined let no Man
put afunder*; which is alfo in it felf very convenient. As it is a Sacrament, there is Grace received therein, as in other Sacraments, our Lord
Chrift, who was the Author and Inftitutor of
the Divine Sacraments, having by his Paffion
merited Grace for us, whereby the Natural Love
which is betwixt the Married couple is perfected, and the conjunction that is betwixt them is
con-

confirmed, and made Perpetual, and the Husband and Wife are Sanctified. There are two
Reasons or Ends for which Matrimony was ordained and instituted; the first and principal is
the Procreation or Generation of Children, for
the conservation of the World, and the multi-
plication of the Faithful, and Servants of God.
The second is, for a remedy for Uncleanness;
and that such as are inclined to that Vice, might
have a remedy given them by God, so that living with their Wives, they might not fall into
that Sin, from whence it is that People may not
only Marry once, but as often as one of the
Parties dies, because this end of Matrimony may
not only be compassed in the first, but equally
in the subsequent Marriages; wherefore the
Church detests those as Hereticks, who condemn
second Marriages, holding them to be unlawful,
as some Hereticks did anciently, and as some of
the most Superstitious Heathens do at this day in
these Parts; from whence it may also be collected,
that this Sacrament may not only be lawfully celebrated betwixt Persons capable of having Children, but also betwixt those, who according to
the ordinary course of Nature, cannot have any,
because the second end may be answered in
such Marriages; but where neither the one nor
the other end can be answered, as in Children,
for whom the Church has set a certain time, and
in such as are under a Natural Impotency that
will last as long as they live, as to Matrimonial
Acts, Matrimony is not to be celebrated: And
tho'

tho' both under the Law of Nature and of *Moses*, there were Difpenfations whereby Matrimony was made to deviate from its firft Original, fome of the Patriarchs having had feveral Wives at once by a Divine Difpenfation, and the Law of *Moses* having permitted Divorces, or the repudiating of Wives, yet under the Evangelical Law, by which Matrimony was perfected and reftored again to its firft Eftate and Purity, it is prohibited for a Man to have more than one Wife at a time, and to turn away his Wife and take another fo long as fhe lives. The Benefits of Marriage are three principally ; the firft is the Generation and Education of Children for the Worfhip and Service of the true God ; the fecond is the Fidelity which the Married couple ought to keep to one another ; and the third is the Perpetuity of Matrimony, which, in that it cannot be diffolved, fignifies that infeparable Conjunction and Union that is betwixt Chrift and his Church : And notwithftanding for the caufe of Fornication or Adultery, it is lawful for the Married couple to part as to Cohabitation, yet it is not lawful to Marry with any other, becaufe the Bond of Matrimony, being once lawfully tied, is Perpetual, and cannot be diffolved by any thing but the death of one of the Parties.

Decree

Decree I.

HOly Mother Church has always so ordered the celebration of *Matrimony*, as to make it to be understood to be a Holy thing, and that as Holy, it ought to be Holily treated; wherefore for the removing of several inconveniencies, and those especially that attend Clandestine Marriages, she has ordained and commanded, that *Matrimony* be celebrated in the face of the Church by the Vicar, or Parish-Priest, or some other Priest, Licensed by him or the Prelate, and in the presence of two or three Witnesses at least; and that all Marriages that are not celebrated with this Solemnity by the Parish-Priest before two Witnesses, are void and null: And that the Priest, who without leave from the Parish-Priest, and the Parish-Priest who without two Witnesses shall presume to Marry any couple, shall be severely punished. Now the Synod understanding that this Rule is not observed in this Diocess, but that the Persons who are to be married do imploy any Priest, and are married where they please, from which great Inconveniencies and Disorders do many times follow, different Rites and Ceremonies being also used in divers places in the celebration thereof, doth command, that all that is above related be punctually observed according to the Decrees of the Holy Council of *Trent*, which has been received by this Church in this Synod; declaring all Marri-

ages

ages not celebrated in this Form, or not by the
Parish-Prieſt before two Witneſſes, to be null, and
the Parties not to be Married, neither are they
to be permitted to live together as Man and
Wife : And the Prieſts who ſhall preſume to
Marry without leave from the Pariſh-Prieſt or
Ordinary, ſhall be ſuſpended from their Orders
and Benefices for one Year without Indulgence,
and the Marriage ſhall be declared void, and
the Parties ſhall be obliged to Marry again in
the foreſaid Form. The Synod doth furthermore
declare, That the Contracted may be Married
by the Pariſh-Prieſt of either of the Parties,
tho' the ordinary Cuſtom is to be Married by
the Pariſh-Prieſt where the Woman lives.

Decree II.

WHereas *Matrimony* ought to be celebrated
with words ſignifying a preſent Conſent,
and in many places of this Dioceſs, it is commonly celebrated with words ſignifying only a
Conſent for the time to come: Therefore the
Synod doth command, That when the Perſons
that are to be Married, come to the Door of the
Church, the Pariſh-Prieſt, or ſome other Prieſt,
having his or the Prelates Licence, being in his
Surplice, with his *Stole*, and at leaſt two Witneſſes preſent, ſhall ask them, if they are pleaſed
to Marry; and if they ſay they are, or expreſs
their Conſent by ſome other evident ſigns, the
Prieſt then ſhall take one end of his *Stole*, and
Y laying

laying it on the Palm of his left Hand, shall take the right Hand of the Bride and lay it on the *Stole*, and lay the Palm of the right Hand of the Bridegroom on the Palm of the right Hand of the Bride, in form of a Cross, and covering both their Hands with the other end of the *Stole*, and laying his own right Hand upon all, so that the Hands of both Parties, and both the ends of the *Stole* are betwixt the Priest's Hands; after having blessed them with the sign of the Cross, he shall say, *In the name of the Father, and of the Son, and of the Holy Ghost, Amen*; and shall make the Bride say first, *I N. receive thee N. for my lawful Husband, so as the Holy Mother Church of* Rome *doth command*; and shall afterwards make the Bridegroom say the same words, *I N. receive thee N. for my lawful Wife, so as the Holy Mother Church of* Rome *doth command*; and after they have both said these words, the Priest shall say, *I, by the Authority I have, do join you in Matrimony in the name of the Father, and of the Son, and of the Holy Ghost, Amen*; after which he shall sprinkle them both with Holy Water, saying, *By this sprinkling of Holy Water, the Lord give you Health and Blessing, Amen.* And if neither of the Parties was ever Married before, they shall then be carried before the High Altar, where being upon their Knees, the Priest shall give them the Blessings, as they are in the *Roman* Ceremonial of the administration of the Sacraments, which is to be translated into *Syrian*, and to be used in all Churches; but if either
of

of the Parties have been Married before, he
ſhall not then give them the ſaid Bleſſings, but
diſmiſs them, after having ſaid a Prayer in the
Church.

Decree III.

THat there may be no Frauds in Matrimony,
and that the Impediments, which, if they
were known, would hinder the ſame, may be
diſcovered; and that in all things we may conform our ſelves to the Decrees of the Holy Council of *Trent*, the Synod doth command, That
what is ordained by the ſaid Holy Council,
be punctually obſerved; to wit, That the Parties to be Married, ſhall have their Banns publiſhed by the Vicar, or by one appointed by
him, on three *Sundays* or Holy-days in the
Churches where the Bridegroom and Bride live,
when the People are aſſembled at *Maſs*, in this
Form; N. *born in ſuch a place, does purpoſe to Marry*
N. *the Daughter of* N. *and* N. *born in ſuch a place;*
wherefore if there be any that know any Impedi-
ment, they muſt declare it upon pain of Excommu-
nication : And the Vicar, in caſe he has any
lawful Impediment declared unto him, ſhall not
Marry the Parties before he has made the Prelate acquainted therewith, that ſo he may determine what is juſt to be done therein; which
Publications cannot be diſpenſed with by any
but by the Prelate, or one repreſenting him:
And in caſe it is probable that if ſuch Publi-

cations are made, there are those that will maliciously endeavour to hinder the Marriage, tho'
in such a case the parties may be received without them, yet for the better discovery of other
Impediments that may happen to be therein, they
cannot be joined together, nor receive the Bleffings, tho' capable thereof, before the publications are made in the Churches, without the Prelate should be pleased to dispense therewith, to
whose Prudence and Judgment the Holy Council of *Trent* has committed the whole of this
Matter, and the Priest who shall receive any
couple without a License from the Prelate, before such publications have been made, shall be
suspended from his Office and Benefice for six
months.

Decree IV.

THis Synod conforming it self in all things to
the Holy Council of *Trent*, doth command that in every Parish there be a Book, as
was ordered as to *Baptism*, wherein the Vicar
of the Church shall write the Names of the Married Persons, and the Place, day of the Month
and Year, and the Names of the two Witnesse
commonly called the *Padrinhos*, where they
were Married, registring them thus, *On such
Day of such a Month and Year, I N. Vicar of the
Church*, naming the Saint to whom it is dedicated, *in such a part*, naming where the said Church
is, *did joyn* N, *the Son of* N, *and* N. *to* N. *the
Daught*

Daughter of N. *and of* N. *born in such a place, both* at the gate of the Church according to the Holy Council of Trent, *the Witnesses were* N. *and* N. to which
the Vicar and the two Witnesses shall sign their
Names, and when any Priest shall by a License
from the Vicar, or Prelate, marry any couple,
he shall write, *On such a day of such a Month, and
Year, I* N. *a Priest, by a License from the Vicar of such
a place, or from the Bishop,* if he granted the License, *did receive at the gate of the Church* N. naming him, *the Son of* N. *and* N. naming his Parents, *born in such a place,* naming the Town according to the Holy Council of *Trent, the Witnesses were* N. *and* N. to which the said two
Witnesses and Priest shall put their Names;
which Book shall be kept among the Registers of
the Church, and the Prelate at his Visitations
shall see that there be no fault or neglect therein.

Decree V.

AS Holy *Matrimony* is a Sacrament, and as
such conveys Grace, it ought therefore to
be received with great Purity and Holiness, wherefore this Synod conforming it self to the Holy
Council of *Trent,* doth exhort and admonish, and
command all that are to be Married, that at least
three days before the celebration of this Sacrament, they do confess themselves, and being capable do receive the Holy Sacrament of the *Eucharist,* neither shall the Vicars receive them be-
Y 3 fore

fore they have complyed with this Obligation,
concerning which they shall make diligent Enquiry.   The Synod doth furthermore command,
That all Marriages be celebrated in the Church,
and that the Parish-Priest do not accommodate
himself to the negligence of those who do not care
to be seen to marry in the Church ; but declaring
withall that wheresoever Matrimony is celebrated, if it be done by a Parish-Priest, and in the
presence of two Witnesses, it is true and valid,
tho' the Parish-Priest ought not to Marry any
out of the Church, but upon very urgent Reasons.

Decree VI.

THere have been always in the Church, even
under the Old Law prohibited degrees of
Kindred, within which Matrimony was not to be
celebrated, and being celebrated, was null ; and
that not only as to such as were prohibited by a
Divine Natural Law, as betwixt Persons in the first
degree, and betwixt Brothers and Sisters, but as to
others also who are prohibited by a Divine positive Law ; wherefore the Synod doth declare,
that the degrees at this time prohibited in the
Church, without which *Matrimony* cannot be
celebrated without a Dispensation, and being
celebrated, is void, are only to the fourth degree inclusive of Consanguinity, and of Affinity
only to the second degree, as first Cousins, second Cousins, third Cousins, fourth Cousins, by
Fa-

Father and Mother, and the fame degrees are prohibited in the Kindred of Affinity, betwixt the Kinsfolk of the Husband and Wife, with whom either of the Parties have been Married; and befides, that the Kindred in the firft and fecond degree only with fuch, or of thofe with whom either of the Parties have at any time had unlawful Carnal Knowledge, beyond which degrees there are no other of Carnal Kindred that can hinder *Matrimony*, but in all thefe that have been mentioned, all Marriages that are made, are null, and of no force, and all thofe that have Married fo, do live in the *Mortal* Sin of foul Fornication: but if any upon juft and reafonable accounts fhall defire to Marry within any of thefe degrees that are prohibited only by a pofitive Law, they muft have * recourfe to the Holy Apo-

---

* **Recourfe.**] The Church of *Rome* feems to have multiplied prohibitions in Matrimonial matters for no other end, but to get the more Money by Difpenfations. *In Romana Curia*, faith *Didacus Abulenfis*, *adeo frequentes difpenfationes ad Matrimonia contrahenda inter Confanguineos, ut juris Canonici prohibitiones hæc in parte nullis fint impedimento, nifi his qui pauperes funt, nec patrimonium habent unde poffint aliquam fummam pro obtinenda difpenfatione erogare.* I have a rate by me of Matrimonial Difpenfations, which is too long to be here inferted. I had it from a Proteftant Merchant, who upon receiving the rated fumm in *Portugal*, had the Difpenfation difpatched at *Rome*, and fent to him by the *Jews* that live there, who by reafon of their general Correfpondence, have in a manner ingroffed the whole trade of *Difpenfations*, fo little is the honour of Chriftianity regarded by fome People, where it clafheth with conveniencies. *Emanuel* King of *Portugal*, with a difpenfation Married two Sifters, notwithftanding his having had a Son by the firft; and I knew a Nobleman in a certain Popifh Country that was both Uncle and firft Coufin to his Wife.

ftolick

stolick See for a Dispensation, or to their Prelate, having power from the said *See* to do it, declaring the degree of Kindred wherein they desire to be dispensed, together with the Causes why they do desire it, in which the Prelate shall do what he shall judge convenient in the Lord, and so the Prelate being impowered by the Holy *See* to do it, shall do it *gratis*, without taking any thing for the dispensation, tho' the Parties of their own accord should offer to pay him for it.

Decree VII.

BEsides the Carnal Kindred of Consanguinity and Affinity, which hinders *Matrimony* in certain degrees, there is also another sort of Kindred that does the same, which is called Spiritual Kindred, and is contracted in *Baptism* betwixt the Godfather and Godmother, and the Child that is Baptized, and the Parents of the said Child, and in *Confirmation* or *Chrism* betwixt those who offer and present the Person that is confirmed, as was ordered in the Decrees of *Baptism* and *Confirmation*; which Spiritual Kindred of Godfathers and Godmothers, and Gossips, does so hinder the celebration of *Matrimony*, that without a Dispensation from the Apostolick *See*, or from some authorized by the Pope to that purpose, the *Matrimony* is null, and of no force, all that live therein living in Fornication, and a state of Damnation; and if any that are

are thus a kin have a mind to marry together, they shall preferr a Petition, as they shall be directed hereafter, but are to know that the Church does very seldom or never, but for weighty Causes dispense in Cases of Spiritual Affinity.

Decree VIII.

WHereas hitherto the prohibited degrees, and the reservation of dispensing with the same to the Apostolical *See*, has not been understood in this Diocess, the Prelates thereof having dispensed in all degrees, prohibited only by a positive Law, without having had Authority for what they did, so that great numbers by virtue of such Dispensations, have lived many Years in a Married Estate, without any scruple concerning what was granted by their Prelates; for which reason the Synod for the greater security of the Consciences of such People has thought fit that the most *Reverend Metropolitan* should dispense with them in all the said degrees, by virtue of the Apostolick Authority granted to him in these parts to that effect, and particularly by the brief of *Gregory* the XIII. of glorious Memory, obtained at the instance of the *Jesuits*, and confirmed by our Holy Father *Clement* the VIII, at this time presiding in the Church of God; wherefore for the quieting of the Consciences of such as have been Married with the forementioned Dispensations, the said Lord with the approbation of the Fathers of the Society,

doth

doth by the Authority of the said Brief, effectually difpenfe in all and every one of the said degrees of Spiritual as well as Carnal Kindred and Affinity, which are prohibited only by a pofitive Law, and with all Perfons who have Married within the fame with fuch difpenfations fo far as of right can or ought to be done, as much as if they were here particularly named ; commanding them for the further fecurity of their Confciences to be * Married again privately in their Houfes, or elfewhere, as they fhall judge moft convenient, by any Prieft they pleafe, there being two Witneffes prefent, according to the form of the Holy Council of *Trent* : And the Synod doth command that henceforward fuch Difpenfations be not granted any otherwife than in form of the Briefs of the Holy Apoftolick *See* in thefe parts to that effect, declaring all that fhall be granted otherwife to be null, and of no force ; and the Marriages that are celebrated by virtue of them, to be void, and the Parties not to be Married.

* **Married.**] By this Decree all the Children born before fuch Marriages were born Baftards ; now how many thoufand Baftards would fuch a Decree make in any Country, where fuch Prohibitions concerning Natural and Spiritual Affinity are not regarded ?

Decree

Decree IX.

THe Synod recognizing for the time to come the ancient prohibition, obferved in the Univerfal Church of not Marrying, from the firft day of *Advent* until the *Epiphany*, and from *Afh-wednefday* until the *Sunday* of the *Octaves* of *Ea-fter* inclufive, doth command the fame to be inviolably obferved in this Diocefs, adding to thofe days the time from *Quinquagefima Sunday* forward when by ancient cuftom *Lent* is begun in this Church, but that at all other times, tho' of Fafting, marriage may be celebrated as People fhall think fit.

Decree X.

WHereas in this Diocefs there has hitherto been no refpect had in the celebration of *Matrimony* to the Age of the Parties that the Law appoints, therefore the Synod doth command, that no Man fhall be Married hereafter, until he has attained the Age of fourteen Years at leaft, nor no Woman before fhe is full twelve, declaring that herein the Prelates have no power to difpenfe, but can only, if any that are under that Age fhould pretend to marry, judge in their Confciences whether they are ripe for *Matrimony*, and judging them to be fo, may grant them a Licenfe, and difpenfe with their marrying ; neverthelefs, for feveral juft refpects, and the

greater

greater fecurity of Peoples Confciences, and to remove as far as is poffible for the Synod to do it,
the imitations of the marriages that are fo much
in ufe among the Heathens, who marry people
very young, there being alfo great numbers in
this Diocefs who have been married at nine or
ten Years old, or under, the Synod will not
have the faid Difpenfation or Anticipation of
time to exceed four months as to men, and fix
as to Women ; nor to be granted by any but
the Bifhop ; and if any man hereafter fhall prefume to marry without fuch a Difpenfation, before he has attained the Age of fourteen, or any
Woman while fhe is under twelve, all fuch marriages fhall be void, but may be refolved into
Contracts *de futuro,* and the Priefts that fhall
marry any fuch, fhall be fufpended from their
Office and Benefice, for fix months, and the Parties fhall be kept afunder until they are of a due
Age.

Decree XI.

THe Synod being informed, that great numbers of married people in this Diocefs do,
without any fentence of the Church, (to which
all Matrimonial caufes do belong) forfake their
Wives, and, to the great offence of God, abfent themfelves from them for a long time together, doth command that there be no fuch fepa-
rations made without the order of the Church,
and if any fhall prefume to make them, that
they

they be conftrained to come together again, upon pain of Excommunication, or whatfoever o-
ther Penalty the Bifhop fhall think fit to inflict;
and in cafe they refufe to comply, they fhall be
declared Excommunicate, until fuch time as they
return to one another; and in cafe they have any
juft Caufe to feparate, they fhall carry it before
the Prelate to be Judged according to Law, and
what is Juft, and fhall be obliged by Cenfures
to ftand to his laft determination. The Synod
doth furthermore declare, That the non-payment
of the Portion that may have been promifed, is
no juft Caufe to leave their Wives, which they
might have been careful to have fecured before
they were Married to them; and that whofoever fhall forfake their Wives on that account,
fhall be punifhed and conftrained by Excommunication to live with them.

Decree XII.

THe Synod being informed that the Black
Slaves that are Chriftians, and even fuch
of them as live in the Mountains with Chriftians,
do Marry without a Prieft, by only tying a Thred
about the Brides Neck, according to the ufage
of the Heathens, doth declare, That all fuch
Marriages are void and null, and that all that
live fo, do live in Uncleannefs; commanding
all that have been fo Married, to be brought
to the Church, there to be Married by the Vicar,
according to the Form of the Holy *Trent* Council,
and

and as is above ordered. The Vicars muſt take
pains to inform themſelves of the Marriages of
all ſuch Slaves, in order to make them obſerve
the ſaid Decree inviolably ; and the Maſters who
have conſented that their Slaves or Servants
ſhould be thus Married , and have celebrated
ſuch Marriages themſelves, and ſhall not ſend
them to Church to be Married, tho' they deſire
it, ſhall be ſeverely puniſhed at the pleaſure of
the Prelate, and ſhall be told of the great wrong
they do to their own Conſciences therein, and
of the Scandal they give to Chriſtianity.

Decree XIII.

THe Synod being informed that ſome
of the Chriſtians of the Mountains have
been Married to ſeveral Women in the face of
the Church, their firſt Wife being ſtill alive, to
the great affront and injury of the Holy Sacrament of *Matrimony* ; doth command all Vicars
and Curates at their firſt inſtitution into their
Churches, immediately to make ſtrict enquiry
into this Matter , and to force all ſuch to live
with their firſt Wives ; and, in caſe they refuſe,
to declare them Excommunicate, until ſuch time
as they comply, and do turn away all their other
Wives, removing them from the place where
they live, which ſhall be done to all, who during the life of their firſt Wife have preſumed
to take others until they ſhall be brought to
live only with the firſt ; and beſides, they ſhall
be

be punifhed with other punifhments at the pleafure of the Prelate, or of the Holy Office of
* *Inquifition* to which this doth belong.

* There are two Crimes which both the *Inquifition* and Civil Courts take cognizance of, that is, *Polygamy* and *Sodomy*. The Civil Courts punifh both with Death, the *Inquifition* only with Penances: This makes, that all that are guilty of either of thofe Crimes, when they apprehend themfelves in any danger of being accufed of them before the Civil Judges, do take Sanctuary in the *Inquifition,* where having confefs-ed their Fault, and fubmitted themfelves to Penance, they are in no further danger, and fo by that fhift fave their lives. Now this Politick piece of Clemency, for it is no other, quite drowns the noife of all the barbarous Cruelties of the Court of *Inquifi-tion,* and alone gains it the repu-tation of being a much more merciful Tribunal than the Civil.

Decree XIV.

WHereas it is a thing unworthy of a Chriftian to obferve the Superftitious Ceremonies of the Heathens, from whence it is imagined good Succefs may be derived, the Synod
being informed that there are fome ill Chriftians,
that, in imitation of the Heathens, do go to fome
of them, and others to fome of their own Superftitious Priefts, to learn which are the beft
Days and Hours to be Married on, after the
manner of the *Infidels*; and do furthermore on
their Wedding-day make certain Circles, into
which they put Rice, and certain Perfons ufing
feveral Superftitious Ceremonies, which are plainly Heathen; and do moreover make certain
Figures behind their Doors to make their Marriage Fortunate, and ufe feveral Prayers with Ceremonies,

remonies, which they call the *Ring of Solomon*;
all which being Devilish, Superstitious, and Heathenish Ceremonies, condemned by Holy Mother Church: Wherefore the Synod doth command and exhort all Faithful Christians, neither
to practise any such Ceremonies themselves, nor
to suffer others to use them in their Houses; and
that all who shall presume to practise them themselves, or permit others to do it in their Houses,
shall be denied the Sacrament for a whole Year,
and be rigorously punished at the pleasure of
the Prelate: and the same shall be done to
those that go to Heathens, to learn what Days
are Fortunate.

Decree XV.

THe Synod having been informed, that when
Contracts *de futuro* are celebrated among
the Christians of this Diocess, or Marriages are
concerted, that it is performed with some Heathenish and Superstitious Ceremonies, and that
many times when the Parties contracted are not
of Age, or have not Judgment enough to give
their consent, doth command, that no such Contracts be made, but when the Parties contracting
are of sufficient Age to understand what they
do, and are capable of giving their consent *de
futuro*; and, if the Parents will make such Matches,
they shall do it by a simple Writing, or by
shaking Hands, or by any other way that has
nothing of Superstition in it; neither shall they
use

ufe any Superftitious Ceremonies, upon pain of
being feverely chaftifed at the pleafure of the
Prelate; commanding the Priefts, in virtue of
Holy Obedience, not to be prefent at Contracts,
where any fuch damnable Superftitions are performed, that fo they may not feem to Authorize them by their Perfon and Dignity.

Decree XVI.

THe Synod doth condemn the Cuftom, or
abufe that has obtained in this Diocefs of
the new-married couple's not going to Church
till after the fourth day after their Marriage,
when they ufe to Wafh themfelves, which is according to the *Judaical* Ceremonies condemned
by the Law of Chrift, but on the contrary, doth
exhort all new-married People, without refpect
of Days, to go to Church and fay their Prayers,
knowing for certain, that if any of the Days
that they ftay from Church, fhould happen either
to be a *Saint's-day* or a *Sunday*, upon which all
People are obliged to hear *Mafs*, that they fin
mortally in not hearing it, if hindred by no o-
ther caufe: Neither are they to imagine, that
fuch Wafhings do any way contribute to the
Spiritual Health of their Souls, the Worfhip of
God, or the Reverence of the Church.

Z   ACTI-

A C T I O N VIII.

Of the Reformation of Church-Affairs.

Decree I.

WHereas the Univerſal Catholick Church is
Ruled, Inſpired, and Taught by the Holy
Spirit, by whoſe direction, for the betterGovern-
ment of Chriſtians, and the more commodious
adminiſtration of the Sacraments to the Faithful,
it has divided the Provinces of the whole World
into Dioceſſes, which are all ſubject to their
ſeveral Biſhops ; and the Dioceſſes into Pariſhes,
which are all ſubject to their Pariſh-Prieſts, ſo
that as the Dioceſſes and all the faithful Inhabitants of the ſame are ſubject to their ſeveral Biſhops, and through them to the Biſhop of *Rome*,
*the Univerſal Paſtor and Head of the Church, and
Chriſt's Vicar upon Earth* ; ſo all the faithful Inhabitants in every Pariſh are ſubject to their
Rector or Vicar, that adminiſter the Sacraments
to them, and are the particular Paſtors and Curates of their Souls, through whom they are
ſubject to their Biſhop, and through the Biſhop
to the Pope, and through the Pope to Chriſt ;
which Order has been at all times preſerved in
the Church all over the World, and for want
whereof, this Church is ſo Confuſed and Diſ-
orderly as it is ; every one doing what ſeems
                                                    good

good in his own eyes, without ever being called to an Account for what they do, having
none that are under any obligation to take care
of their Souls, nor no particular Paſtor to aſſiſt
them in their Neceſſities, nor diſtinct Pariſhes,
unto which every one is bound to reſort; therefore this Synod conforming it ſelf to the Government of the whole Catholick Church, doth ordain, that this Dioceſs be alſo divided into Pariſhes, allotting ſuch a number of People to each
Pariſh as ſhall be found moſt convenient, and
furniſhing them with particular Vicars and Curates, to watch over the Souls of the Faithful ;
and as for other Prieſts and Curates that ſhall
be in any Church, they ſhall be therein as Be-
neficed Perſons, and Co-adjutors to the Vicars in
the adminiſtration of the Sacraments to the People, as alſo in the Divine Service and Worſhip
of the Church, as they have hitherto been, having the ſame Profits and Dividend they had
formerly, ſave that the Synod intends to deprive
them of thoſe Fees which formerly they Simonaically received for adminiſtration of the Sacraments, as to which they ſhall obſerve what is before
decreed, as the Vicars and Pariſh-Prieſts are to
have what is allotted for their maintenance in
the Twenty-firſt and Twenty-ſecond Decrees;
and the ſaid Vicars ſhall make a Roll of all the
Inhabitants of their ſeveral Pariſhes, that ſo they
may be acquainted with their Cuſtoms and way
of living, and may adminiſter the Sacraments
unto them, and comfort them in their Troubles

and Necessities; neither shall the Faithful receive the Sacrament from any but their own Vicar, without his Licence in Form.

Decree II.

THe Synod doth declare, That the Division of Parishes, and the laying of People to them, has at all times belonged to the Prelate; so that he may at any time Divide or Unite Parishes at his pleasure, and as he shall find to be most convenient for the administration of the Sacraments to the Faithful, to whom it also belongs to provide Vicars and Curates for Churches, whom he may Institute or Depose as often as he shall judge it to be necessary, to the better feeding of the Flock of Christ, which he is charged with, and is to give an account of; and for the present the most Reverend *Metropolitan* shall make such a reparition of Parishes and People in this his Visitation, Uniting or Dividing them as shall seem to him to be most commodious for the administration of the Sacraments to the Faithful, who at the end of the Synod will name Vicars for every Parish: And the Synod, for the just Respects and the better Government of the Church, will not have any Vicars so Established, as not to be removable at the pleasure of the Prelate.

Decree

Decree III.

THe Synod doth furthermore declare, That
no Prieſt ſhall hold Two Churches with
Cure, or receive the Fruits of them according to
the Holy Canons ;   And whereas in this Dioceſs
there are many that have two or three Churches,
which they have had commended unto them in
ſeveral parts, either becauſe they were built by
their Relations, or for ſome other Reaſon ; all
which being a great Abuſe, the Synod doth declare, That after the diviſion of the Pariſhes is
made, none ſhall have any Juriſdiction therein
beſides their proper Vicars, to whom only it ſhall
belong to order all the Affairs of their Churches,
and to whom whoſoever ſhall deny to yield
Obedience, ſhall be declared Excommunicate,
and ſhall be puniſhed at the pleaſure of the Prelate as diſturbers of the Church ; and all ſuch
Prieſts as are in preſent poſſeſſion of the Churches,
if qualified, and there be no juſt Impediment,
the Synod will have it be inſtituted Vicars of
one of their Pariſhes, as the moſt Reverend *Me-*
tropolitan ſhall think fit ; not that the Synod intends to prohibit the Prelate, in caſe he is not
provided of a ſufficient number of able Prieſts,
or where there is not a ſufficient maintenance,
to recommend two Churches to one Vicar, provided they are at ſuch a diſtance that he can
look after both, without any wrong to the
adminiſtration of the Sacraments. However,

this

this shall never be done, but when there is an urgent and necessary Reason for it.

Decree IV.

WHereas there are a great many Churches in this Diocess that have no Priests, to the great detriment of the Faithful, who by that means are for several Years without *Mass*, or any to administer the Sacraments to them, as has appeared to the Reverend *Metropolitan* in his Visitation of the Churches, in some of which he found there had been no *Masses* said in five or six Years, and that there are Children of that or a greater Age, that have never been Baptized; therefore the Synod both command, That there be no Church that is made Parochial, how poor and inconsiderable soever the People may be, for any long time without a Curate or Vicar to administer the Sacraments to the Faithful, of which the Prelate is to take special care; and if it should so happen, as it does too often, that he cannot have a Priest to supply such Cures, in that Case, the Synod declares, that the Prelate may oblige whomsoever he pleaseth, by Penalties and Censures to serve such Churches, that so the Necessities of the Faithful may be provided for, giving them whereon to subsist in the said Churches.

Decree

Decree V.

THe Synod being informed that there are many Villages in this Diocefs, which, by reafon of their great diftance from any Church, have little of Chriftianity left in them befides the Name of the Chriftians of St. *Thomas*, which has been occafioned through the great negligence of the former *Schifmatical* Prelates of this Bifhoprick; wherefore the Synod doth, in virtue of Holy Obedience, command all Priefts that are nominated Vicars, fo foon as they fhall come to their Churches, to make a ftrict inquiry into the Chriftians that live in the Skirts of their Parifhes, and to report what they fhall difcover as to this Matter to the moft Reverend *Metropolitan*, that fo he may take fuch courfe therein as fhall be moft for the Service of Chrift, and the Benefit of Souls; and the fame diligence fhall be ufed in all Parts, where there are fuch People found, and have never been Baptized, and where it is thought neceffary, there fhall be New Churches built, and Vicars appointed for the reducing fuch to true Chriftianity, and the ufe of the Holy Sacraments of the Church.

Decree

Decree VI.

WHereas the Church of *Travancor* is at this time totally demolished, the greater part of its Parishioners having above forty Years ago turned perfect Heathens, all which has happened through the negligence of sending Priests among them by reason of their great distance from any other Church, there being nevertheless several good Christians there still, therefore the Synod doth command, that a Vicar be forthwith collated to that place, who shall set immediately about rebuilding the Church; there shall likewise be some Preachers sent along with him to reduce the said People into the bosom of Holy Mother Church, and to the Holy Catholick Faith of Christ, according to the Orders given therein by the most Reverend *Metropolitan*, and the Vicar shall continue there baptizing and receiving all, according to the necessity of the Church, for which an *Olla*, or Licenfe has been already obtained from the King of *Travancor*, and shall from henceforth continue in the Church according to the necessity thereof.

Decree VII.

THe Synod being informed, That upon the borders of the Territories belonging to the *Samorim* King of *Calecut*, at the distance of four leagues from any Church in this Bishoprick, there

there is a Country called *Tadamalla*, in which
there are certain Villages of Chriftians, who
were anciently of this Church, but at prefent
have nothing of Chriftianity but the bare Name,
doth command that Priefts and Preachers be fent
thither immediately from this Church to reduce
them to the Catholick Faith, and baptize them,
in which matter, through the diligences that
have been ufed by the moft Reverend *Metropolitan*, they will meet with no difficulties on the
part of thofe who have loft their Chriftianity
only for want of Inftruction, and the Synod
doth recommend this People, as a Member of
their Church to the Spiritual Care of the moft
Reverend *Metropolitan*.

Decree VIII.

WHereas the ufe of the Holy Oils was inftituted by Chrift in the Church, who
made the Oil of *Chrifm*, the matter of the Sacrament
of *Confirmation* and *Extream Unction* ; and did furthermore appoint other Holy Unctions for the *Catechumeni*, delivering the Doctrine of the Confecration of fuch Oils in his laft Supper to his Difciples, as
we are taught by Holy Tradition from the Apoftles
and the Doctrine of the Holy Fathers of the Church,
and there having notwithftanding this been no
fuch thing in ufe, or known in this Church to
this day : Therefore the Synod doth command,
that in all Parifh Churches there be a Box that
fhall hold three Veffels of Plate, Tin, or Glafs,

in

in which the Holy Oils shall be kept with due
Decency and Reverence, with their several
Names upon each Vessel, so that they may not
be used one for another, commanding the Vicars
that are to be nominated, not to go from hence
without carrying these Boxes along with them,
to their respective Churches, which the most Reverend *Metropolitan* will furnish them withal,
and with the Holy Oils which he consecrated on
Holy *Thursday* last for this purpose in the Church
of *Carturte* in this Diocess, which Boxes they shall
put under Lock and Key in their Repositories,
either in the chief Chapel of the high Altar, or
in their Vestries, or near to the Font, having
them always decently covered with Silk, or in
case the Vicars live at a considerable distance
from their Churches, or in the *Heaths*, in some
decent place in their Houses for fear of Infidel
Robbers, and that they may be always at hand,
when they shall be called to administer the Sacrament of *Unction*, and whensoever they are
carried to Church for Baptism, or are carried
to the Sick, they shall be always carried by a
Priest, if it is possible; but at least by one in
Holy Orders ; and upon Holy *Thursday* they
shall either burn all the Oils that remain of that
Year in the Lamps of the Church, or pour them
into the Font, so as after that day not to make
use of any Oils but such as are new, which after *Easter* they shall either go or send to the
Prelate for, or to the place where he has ordered them to be distributed, and in case the

See

See be vacant, they shall then by order from
the Governour of the Diocess, have recourse to
the Bishop of *Cochim*, and the Vicars that shall
neglect to go or send for the said Holy Oils for
the use of their Churches, so as not to have them
within a month after *Easter*, shall be suspended
by the Prelate, who is desired to be very watchful in this matter, from his Office and Benefice
for six months, and be obliged to fetch them,
and the Children that shall be baptized during
that time, shall be anointed with the Holy Oils
of Baptism when they come, neither shall the
Vicars depart from hence, until they are fully
instructed in the use of the Oils by Persons appointed by the Synod to teach them, that so they
may not be mistaken in the administration of the
Holy Sacraments.

Decree IX.

THere being a great Confusion in this Bishoprick as to the Holy days that are to be
kept under the Obligation of a *Mortal* Sin, as
well as to the hearing of *Mass*, as to the doing
of Work; wherefore the Synod doth declare
that they are these following, to wit, all the *Sundays* in the Year.

In *January*, the first day being the *Circumci-
sion of our Lord*, and the sixth being the Feast of
the *Epiphany*.

In *February*, the second day being the *Purification* of our *Lady*, and the twenty fourth being
the

the Feaſt of the Apoſtle St. *Matthew*, which in the Biſſextile is to be celebrated on the twenty fifth.

In *March*, the twenty fifth day, being the *Anunciation* of our *Lady*.

In *April*, the twenty third being the Feaſt of St. *George* the Martyr, according to the cuſtom of this Biſhoprick.

In *May*, the firſt being the Feaſt of the Apoſtles St. *Philip* and St. *James*.

In *June*, the twenty fourth being the Feaſt of St. *John* the Baptiſt, and the twenty ninth being the Feaſt of St. *Peter* and St. *Paul*.

In *July*, the ſecond being the *Viſitation* of our *Lady*, and the third being the Feaſt of the glorious Apoſtle St. *Thomas*, which by ſome is ſaid to be the day of his Tranſlation, by others of his arrival in theſe parts, and which has by ancient cuſtom been ſtill kept in this Biſhoprick; and the twenty fifth being the Feaſt of the Apoſtle St. *James*.

In *Auguſt*, the ſixth being the *Tranſfiguration of our Lord*, according to the cuſtom of this Biſhoprick, the fifteenth the *Aſſumption* of our *Lady*, and the twenty fourth the Feaſt of St. *Bartholomew* the Apoſtle.

In *September*, the eighth being the *Nativity of our Lady*, the fourteenth the Feaſt of the *Holy Croſs*, according to the cuſtom of this Biſhoprick. The twenty firſt the Feaſt of St. *Matthew* the Apoſtle, the twenty ninth the Feaſt of St. *Michael* the Archangel.

In *October*, the twenty ſeventh being the Feaſt
of

of the Apoſtles St. *Simon* and St. *Jude*.

In *November*, the firſt being the Feaſt of *All Saints*, the thirtieth of St. *Andrew* the Apoſtle.

In *December*, the eighth being the *Conception of our Lady*, the eighteenth being the day where-on the * Holy Croſs of the Apoſtle St. *Thomas* did ſweat : the twenty firſt being the Feaſt of the ſame Holy Apoſtle St. *Thomas*; the twenty fifth the Feaſt of the *Nativity* ; the twenty ſixth the Feaſt of St. *Stephen* the Protomartyr, the twenty ſeventh of St. *John* the Evangeliſt, the twenty eighth of the *Innocents*.

The *Thurſday* of our Lord's Supper, from the time the Offices are begun in the Church until midnight, according to the cuſtom of the Church. *Eaſter*, and the three days following, notwithſtand-ing they may have hitherto obſerved only two days. The day of our Lord's *Aſcenſion*, the moſt Holy Feaſt of *Pentecoſt*, with the two following days.

The moſt Holy Feaſt of the *Body of God*, or of the moſt Holy Sacrament, which, according to the cuſtom of theſe parts, they celebrate on the *Thurſday* after *Eaſter*.

* **Holy Croſs.**] The ſtone Croſs that was found under ground at *Maliapor*; with the Blood of St. *Thomas*, and the Sword wherewith he was Mar-tyr'd , by *Gabriel de Ataide*, a *Portugueze* Prieſt, as he was dig-ging a Foundation for a Church, about the Year 1547. is reported to have ſweat at a moſt prodi-gious rate upon the day of our *Ladies Expectation*, being the 18th of *December*, in the Year 1557. and to have continued always to ſweat upon the ſame Feſtivity un-til the Year 1566. to which pious Fraud, for that is the beſt that can be ſaid of it, the Archbiſhop and Synod it ſeems gave ſo much credit, as to dedicate the 18th. of *December* to the Memory there-of.

Alſo

Also the days of the Confecration of their Churches, and the Feasts of the Saints, to whom they were Dedicated, in their own Parishes only.

The Synod doth furthermore declare, That the *Fridays* from *Christmas* to *Lent*, which ufe to be obferved in fome Parts, fhall not be kept hereafter, the Saints that were Celebrated on fome of them, having their particular Feasts; and others of them being Dedicated to Hereticks, as is above obferved, whofe Memories ought not to be Celebrated; and the Vicars fhall not fail on *Sundays* at *Mafs*, to warn the People of all the Holy-days of the Week, that fo they may be advertifed to keep them.

Decree X.

NOt only what Holy-days were to be kept, were uncertain, and not uniformly obferved in this Bifhoprick, but the fame alfo happened to the Fafting-days, which Chriftians are under an obligation to keep; wherefore the Synod doth declare, that the Fafting-days, as well the Ancient ones, as thofe that are now commanded, are thefe following.

The Holy and Solemn Faft of *Lent*, which according to the Cuftom of this Bifhoprick, begins upon the *Monday* after *Quinquagefima*.

The Holy Faft of *Advent*, which is kept in this Bifhoprick with great rigor from the *Sunday*, that is next to the firft of *December*, until *Chriftmas.*

The

The firſt day of *February*, being the Vigil of the *Purification* of our *Lady*, the 23*d.* being the Vigil of St. *Matthias* the Apoſtle.

The 23*d.* of *June*, being the Vigil of St. *John* the Baptiſt, and the 28*th.* of St. *Peter* and St. *Paul.*

The 24*th.* of *July*, being the Vigil of St. *James* the Apoſtle.

The 12*th.* of *Auguſt*, being the Vigil of the *Aſſumption* of our *Lady*, and the 23*d.* of St. *Bartholomew* the Apoſtle.

The 7*th.* of *September*, being the Vigil of our *Lady's Nativity*, the 13*th.* of the *Holy Croſs.*

The 27*th.* of *October*, being the Vigil of St. *Simon* and *Jude*, and the laſt, of *All-Saints.*

The 29*th.* of *November*, being the Vigil of St. *Andrew.*

The 2*d.* of *December*, being the Vigil of the Glorious Apoſtle St. *Thomas*, on the 24*th.* of our Saviour's *Nativity*, notwithſtanding theſe two do both fall in *Advent.*

And that this Dioceſs may be in all things conformable to the Cuſtoms of the Univerſal Church, the Synod doth command, the *Faſt of the four Times* to be publiſhed and obſerved therein; they are the firſt *Wedneſday, Friday,* and *Saturday* after the firſt *Sunday* in *Lent*; and the the firſt *Wedneſday* and *Friday*, and *Saturday* after *Whitſuntide*; and the firſt *Wedneſday, Friday*, and *Saturday* after the Feaſt of the *Holy Croſs*, in *September*; and the *Wedneſday, Friday,* and *Saturday* after the Feaſt of the *Holy Croſs*, on the 13*th.* of *December*, which falls in with the *Advent* Faſt.

　　　　　　　　　　　　　　　　And

And the Synod doth furthermore declare, That the Faſt of our *Lady's Aſſumption*, which begins on the firſt of *Auguſt*, and laſts to the day of the Feſtivity, and the Faſt that is called the *Apoſtles*, which begins on the firſt day after *Whitſuntide*, and laſts fifty days, notwithſtanding they are Holy and Laudable, it wiſheth they were not kept as they are by the Chriſtians of this Dioceſs, after the ſame manner as the ancient Faſts are; neverthelefs, ſince they are obſerved by ſome and not by others, that there may be no Scruples nor Diſorder, the Synod doth declare, that the keeping of them is not commanded under the Precept of a *Mortal* Sin, though they may be kept out of Devotion by thoſe that have a mind to't, neither are People under any obligation to a *Lent* Fare on theſe Days; and as to the three Faſting Days of the Prophet *Jonas*, called *Mononebo*, which begins eighteen days before the firſt day in *Lent*, the Synod, out of reſpect to its Antiquity and Holineſs, doth permit it to be obſerved with great ſtrictneſs: But whereas People do aſſemble together in the Churches on thoſe days, there to eat the *Nercha's* that are diſtributed, the Synod, tho' it is not willing to oblige People to Faſt on thoſe three days under the obligation of a *Mortal* Sin, doth neverthelefs oblige them to a *Lent* Diet at leaſt upon them; and the Vicars ſhall be obliged to give notice to the People of all the Faſts of the Week upon *Sundays*, that ſo all may be warned to obſerve them.

Decree

Decree XI.

THe Synod doth approve of the Holy and Laudable Cuſtom obſerved by the Chriſtians of this Dioceſs, of eating neither Eggs nor Cheeſe, nor any thing made of Milk, nor of Fiſh, and of abſtaining totally from Wine, and from their Wives during the whole time of *Lent*; all which it deſires them to continue to obſerve inviolably, as alſo to begin the Faſt upon the day after *Quinquageſima Sunday*; and ſome Abuſes being reformed, it doth declare, That Faſting doth not only conſiſt in Peoples abſtaining from ſome ſorts of Meat, but alſo in their not eating ſo often as they may deſire, the Integrity of the Precept of Faſting obliging People not to eat above one Meal a day; and that at * an hour appointed, and at Night they that ſhall ſtand in need of

* The Faſts of the Church of *Rome*, as they are now obſerved, are little elſe than a Mockery of the Duty, of which Card. *Bona* in the 21ſt Chapter of his firſt Book of *Liturgies*, complains as loud as he durſt: *Ita factum eſt*, ſaith the Cardinal, *ut non prorſus veneranda vetuſtas interierit, dum ordo à ſanctis patribus præſcriptus, ſaltem in publica officiorum recitatione, retinetur, quamvis legitimus horarum punctus nullo modo attendatur, neque enim hora nonæ officium, tertia vel quarta poſt meridiem in Vigiliis pſallimus, neque veſperas in Quadrageſima, circa ſolis occaſum, ſed una vel duabus horis ante meridiem, quæ anticipatio, ut doctiſſimus Francolinus ſcribit Cap. 34. quædam eſt noſtri temporis calamitas, ne dicam abuſus: Cæpit hæc horarum præventio poſt ſæculum duodecimum introduci, cum priſtina ſeveritas paulatim relaxata, mollior diſciplina ſucceſſit, de quâ ſatius eſt tacere quam loqui.* And ſo that they may obſerve the ancient Rule of not eating upon a Faſting-day till after *Veſpers*, they have turned the Morning into Evening, and ſay the *Veſpers* at Ten a Clock, that they may go to Dinner at Eleven.

A a   it,

it, and have an appetite to drink for their Healths-fake, may eat a light Collation, according to the permiffion of the Church; but if they fhall exceed either in the quality or quantity of the faid Collation, or eat oftner than twice after this manner, they do violate the Faft, and Sin Mortally; and if through infirmity or weaknefs, they fhould break the Faft upon any day, they fhall not, as fome imagine, be releafed by their having broke *Lent* once: from continuing the Faft, but on the contrary, they fhall be guilty of fo many *Mortal* Sins, as there are days of Obligation, on which they neglect to Faft: They are alfo bound to Faft on all the Saints days, tho' never fo Solemn, that fhall fall in *Lent*, *Sunday* only excepted, upon which it is not lawful for any Chriftian to Faft, as to which matter there are great Abufes introduced in to this Diocefs.

Decree XII.

THe Synod doth declare, That notwithftanding Fafting is of great benefit, that it doth not intend to oblige any that are under one and Twenty, nor fuch as are very ancient, or weak, or fickly, nor Women with Child, nor thofe that give Suck, nor thofe that cannot Faft conveniently by reafon of fome hard Labour they are obliged to, to Faft any otherwife than by eating a *Lent* Diet on Fafting-days, as to which too the weak and fick are excepted, who may

at

at all times eat what is neceſſary to their health ;
and it ſhall alſo be lawful for Women with
Child to eat whatſoever they long for, to prevent Abortion.

Decree XIII.

THe Synod doth very much condemn what
ſome ignorant obſervers of Heatheniſh Su-
perſtition imagine, *viz.* That if they do not waſh
their Bodies betimes in the Morning on a Faſt-
day, their Faſt will be of no worth; and that
if they happen to touch any of a baſe Race, or
a *Naires* , they muſt waſh themſelves to make
their Faſt to be of any Merit; and declares,
that all ſuch Waſhings and Superſtitious touches,
are commanded neither by God nor the Church,
and are no ways proper for Chriſtians; and doth
furthermore command the obſervers of all ſuch
Superſtitions to be puniſhed ſeverely by the Prelate, as followers of * Heatheniſh Vanities, condemned by Holy Mother Church, earneſtly deſiring that all ſuch things may be totally rooted
out of the hearts of the very *Infidels* in this Dioceſs.

*Heatheniſh Superſtitions.] The Church of *Rome* has little rea-ſon to condemn any practiſe pure-ly for being Heathen, her *Crea-ture Worſhip*, with all the Ceremo-nies thereof, being viſibly of ſuch extraction; for it was a true judg-ment that the Fathers of the Coun-cil of *Conſtantinople* under *Leo Iſau-rus*, paſſed upon the endeavours of thoſe who were for introducing Images into the Chriſtian Church; *That to do it would be to reſtore Heatheniſm again under a Scheme of Chriſtianity.*

Decree

Decree XIV.

NOtwithstanding the Synod doth approve of
the laudable Custom that has obtained in
this Diocess, of beginning the Holy Fast of *Lent*,
upon the *Monday* following *Quinquagessima Sunday :* Neverthelefs in conformity to the ufage of
the Univerfal Church, it doth ordain and command, that on the *Wednefday* following, they confecrate Afhes in the Church, which fhall be fprin-
kled on the Heads of the People by the Prieft
that celebrates *Mafs*, ufing thefe words, *Remember Man that thou art duft, and that to duft thou
fhalt return*, as he is directed by the *Roman* Ceremonial tranflated into *Syrian*, by the order of
the moft Reverend *Metropolitan*, leading by this
Holy Ceremony the Faithful to a deeper Repentance, for their Sins, and a fenfe of their own
vilenefs in that Holy time ; which Afhes fo far
as it can be done, fhall be made of the branches
that were bleffed the former Year upon *Palm
Sunday*, which is called *Ofana* in this Diocefs, as
it is likewife ordered in the faid Ceremonial, but
at the fame time the People fhall be told that
this is only a Holy Ceremony of the Church, and
not a Sacrament.

Decree

Decree XV.

THat this Bilhoprick may in all things be conformable to the Cuſtoms of the Catholick Church, the Synod doth command all the Members thereof upon pain of *Mortal* Sin, not to eat Fleſh upon *Saturdays*, in memory of our Lord's Burial, but Eggs, Milk, Butter or Cheeſe they may lawfully eat upon *Saturdays*, as alſo upon all Fiſh days that are not Faſts, and ſince the cuſtom of not eating Fleſh on *Wedneſdays* is not obſerved over the whole Dioceſs, but only in ſome parts thereof, and that but by a few ; the Synod doth declare, that albeit that cuſtom is Holy and Laudable, and it were to be wiſhed that it were univerſally obſerved by all Chriſtians, it doth not think fit to oblige People thereunto upon pain of Sin, ſo that all that liſt may eat Fleſh upon *Wedneſdays*.

Decree XVI.

THe Synod doth declare, That the Obligation of not eating Fleſh on prohibited days, laſts from midnight to midnight, beginning at the midnight of the prohibited day, and ending at the midnight of the day following, ſo that the Obligation of not eating Fleſh upon *Frydays* and *Saturdays*, begins at the midnight of *Fryday*, and ends on the midnight of *Sunday*, and the Obligation of ceaſing from labour begins at

the

the midnight of the faid day, and ends at the midnight of *Monday* : being to underftand that in beginning the Fafts and Feftivities on the Evening of the former, and continuing them to the Evening of the latter day, they do conform themfelves to the Cuftoms and Rites of the *Jews* condemned by Holy Mother Church, in which days and their obfervances are not reckoned from Evening to Evening, but from midnight to midnight.

Decree XVII.

WHereas it is the Cuftom of the Univerfal Church, to have * Holy Water at the entrance of the Churches, that fo the Faithful by fprinkling themfelves therewith, may have their *Venial* Sins pardoned, and the Holy Water that has been hitherto made ufe of in this Diocefs has not been bleffed by the Prieft, nor by any Prayer of the Church, the *Sextons* only throwing a little of the Clay into it, that is brought by Pilgrims from the Sepulchre of St. *Thomas*, or from fome other Holy Place relating to him, and where fuch Clay has been wanting, the faid *Sextons* have thrown fome Grains of Incenfe into it: Whereupon without any further Confecration, it has been efteemed Holy: Therefore the

* **Holy.**] This Ceremony of fprinkling the people with Holy Water, is no lefs of Heathen Extraction than the wafhings condemned in the former Decree, as is acknowledged by the Learned *Valefius*, in his Annotations on the 6 Ch. of the 6 Book of *Sozomen*.

Synod

Synod doth declare, that such Water is not Holy, and that the Faithful ought not to make use of it; and albeit that all the Earth of Holy places, and of the Sepulchres of Saints approved of by the Church, ought to be kept with much Veneration, yet that the Earth of the Holy places belonging to St. *Thomas*, has not the virtue of such a Consecration in it: for which reason it commands all Priests to bless the said Water, by throwing Holy Salt into it, according to the custom of the Universal Church, as is directed by the *Roman* Ceremonial translated into *Syrian* by the order of the most Reverend *Metropolitan*, according to the Form whereof the true Vicars shall take care to consecrate Water, and every *Saturday* Evening, or *Sunday* Morning to furnish the Water-pots therewith; and upon *Sundays* the People being assembled, the Priest being in his *Surplice* and *Stole*, but without his *Planet*, shall before he begins *Mass*, sprinkle the whole Congregation, repeating the *Antiphona*, and the Prayer contained in the said Ceremonial: and at *Masses* at which the Deacon and Sub-Deacon officiate, the Deacon may repeat the *Antiphona*, but the Prayer shall always be said by the Priest. The Vicars must also instruct the People at their entring into the Church, to take Holy Water and bless themselves therewith, in the form of a Cross, and to give over the saying the Prayer to the impious Heretick *Nestorius*, which they used to do when they took Holy Water as they entred into the Church, the Synod condemning the same as Heretical and Blasphemous. A a 4   Decree

Decree XVIII.

WHereas the greateſt part of the People of this
Biſhoprick are not inſtructed in the *Doctrine*, and they that are, know only the *Pater
Noſter*, and *Ave Mary* in the *Syrian* Tongue,
which they do not underſtand, and moſt of the
Children know not how to bleſs themſelves, nay
the Clergy themſelves are ignorant thereof, not
being able to ſay the *Commandments* ; therefore the Synod doth command, that in all Pariſh
Churches in the Morning and Evening, as the
Vicar ſhall think mcſt convenient, one of the
Boys or the Bell-man ſhall ring the little Bell to
call the Boys and Girls together in the Church,
where being aſſembled, the Vicar, or ſome o-
ther Clergyman that he ſhall appoint, ſhall inſtruct them in the *Doctrine*, that is to ſay, the
Sign of the Croſs, the *Pater Noſter*, *Ave Mary*,
the *Creed*, and the *Commandments of God*, and
the Church, the *Articles of Faith*, and other Chriſtian Doctrines in the *Malabar* Tongue, that ſo
all may underſtand them, and not in the *Syrian*, which the People do not underſtand, it being the cuſtom of the Church to teach the *Doctrine* to Children, and to the People in their
Mother Tongue, and furthermore upon all *Sundays* and Holydays, either before or after *Maſs*,
the Vicar ſhall teach the ſaid *Doctrine* in the
Congregation, that ſo all may be inſtructed therein, and ſhall alſo after having called the people
toge-

together with a Bell, teach it on the Evenings
of *Sundays*, and as for the Churches that are in
the *Heaths*, the Vicars shall give orders that the
Children, or at least such of them as are nighest
to the Church, shall upon a certain day of the
Week come to learn the *Doctrine*, employing o-
thers persons to instruct the rest therein, and
the Schoolmasters that teach *Syrian*, or that
teach to read and write, shall every day before
they begin School repeat the said *Doctrine* to
their Scholars in *Malabar*, neither shall any inferior Orders, no not the *first Tonsure*, be given
to Children before they can say the whole *Doctrine* in *Malabar*, in which they must be examined according to the Holy Council of *Trent*, and
in all Churches there shall be a Book of the * *Doctrine* in the *Malabar* Tongue, for the instruction of Children: which the Synod doth entreat
the Father Rector, of the College of Jesuits of
Vaipicotta, to order to be translated by some of
that College, commanding all the Churches of
this Diocess, as also exhorting all the Christians

* **Doctrine.**] The Christians of *Malabar* would certainly
lose the second Commandment,
by receiving this *Roman Doctrine*,
in which that Commandment never appears, no not as part of
the first, nay in the *Tridentine* Ca-
techism, tho' writ in *Latin*, and
for the use of Parish-Priests, there
is only the three first words of it
mentioned, and I do not believe
there is one Priest of a thousand
in *Spain* or *Portugal*, who if they
should have the whole Second
Commandment repeated to them
would not say, what I have heard
more than one, and those very
grave Priests too, say of it, *That
it might be* John Calvin's, *but they
were sure it was none of God's Commandments.*

thereof at Night to caufe the faid *Doctrine* to be taught in their Houfes to their whole Families, that fo their Servants and Slaves may be inftructed therein, and the Confeffors in their Confeffions muft not fail to examine their Penitents in the *Doctrine*, and to exhort them to learn it.

Decree XIX.

THat the Faithful Chriftians in this Diocefs may in their Common Prayer be conformable to the whole Catholick Church, they muft not from henceforward fay the *Ave Mary*, as they have been taught by the Perfidious *Neftorians*, but muft fay it thus, *Ave Mary full of Grace, the Lord be with thee, bleffed art thou among Women, bleffed is Jefus the fruit of thy Womb ; Holy Mother of God pray for us Sinners, now, and at the hour of our Death, Amen, Jefus.* And in this form it fhall be inferted into all the Prayer Books of this Diocefs.

Decree XX.

WHereas the Chriftians of this Diocefs do not fhew the leaft Reverence to the moft Holy Name of *Jefus* when it is mentioned, which arifeth from the falfe Doctrine of the *Neftorian* Hereticks, who do impioufly affert, That it is not worthy of Reverence, being the Name of a Humane Perfon, teaching falfly that there are two Perfons

ſons in Chriſt, therefore ſince that Divine Name
contains in it ſo many Divine Myſteries, being
the Name of our Redemption, and the Name
above all Names, *At which* St. *Paul* ſaith, *every knee
in Heaven and in Earth, and below the Earth ought to
bow*, the Synod doth command, that as often either
in the Goſpel or Prayers of the *Maſs*, or Offices, or
any where elſe that that Name is mentioned, all
People do reverently bow their Body, whether they
be ſitting or ſtanding, and the Clergy and other
Chriſtians, having their Caps on ſhall take them
off, and the Vicars and Preachers muſt not neglect to put their People frequently in mind thereof; and whereas the Name *Lyo* is the ſame with
the moſt ſweet Name of *Jeſus* in the *Malabar*
Language, and is commonly given to Children
in Baptiſm; the Synod doth ſtrictly prohibit the
giving of that Name to any body for the future,
commanding all that are called by it, to take
another Name in Confirmation, or at any other
time, it being a great irreverence for any one to
be called by ſo high and Divine a Name.

Decree XXI.

WHereas it is neceſſary that the Feaſt of
Chriſt's *Nativity* ſhould be celebrated
with great ſolemnity and uniformity through the
whole Catholick Church; the Synod doth command that on the Eve of that Feſtivity, all the
Clergy and People do aſſemble together in the
Church, there to ſay the *Matins*, with the greateſt

eft Solemnity poffible; and that after they have done thefe Prayers, which fhall end about Midnight, they fhall make the cuftomary Proceffion, which being over, a Solemn *Mafs* fhall be faid, with all poffible Feftivity, after which the Prieft may fay a *Mafs* at break of day, and a third at the ufual time of *Mafs*; for the Prieft muft know, that for the greater Solemnity of this Feftival, they are permitted to fay three *Maffes* upon it, that is, one at Midnight, one at break of day, and a third at the ordinary time; or being private *Maffes*, all three together after break of day, but being publick, fhall be all faid in the fore-mentioned Order; neither fhall they after the firft two take the *Lavatory*, but after having received the Blood, fhall go on with the *Mafs* without taking the *Lavatory*, that fo they may be Fafting to celebrate the third; and they fhall be very careful to have the Cups well fcoured, and their Fingers wafhed clean with Water, which fhall be preferved in a particular Veffel in order to its being afterwards either thrown into a Pond, or poured under the Altar, or into the Baptifmal Water that is in the Font; and if any Prieft through carelefsnefs fhould in either of the two firft *Maffes* take the *Lavatory*, after that it fhall not be lawful for him to fay any more, becaufe the *Mafs* is not to be celebrated but Fafting, which the taking of the *Lavatory* breaks.

Decree

Decree XXII.

THe Synod doth command, That the Priests in the solemn administration of the Sacraments of *Baptism*, *Matrimony*, and *Extream Unction*, or when they administer the Holy *Eucharist* without the *Mass*, for the greater decency and reverence for what they are about, do wear a *Surplice* with a *Stole* about their Necks : And whereas hitherto there has been no such thing as a *Surplice* in this Bishoprick, the most Reverend *Metropolitan* having been pleased to provide such Vestments as are necessary in this Bishoprick, no Vicar shall go from hence without taking a *Surplice* along with him, which he is to wear in the administration of the Holy Sacraments, wherein the Synod commands them likewise to use the Rites and Ceremonies prescribed in the *Roman* Ceremonial, which the said Lord *Metropolitan* has commanded to be translated into *Syrian* and to be kept in all Churches, which contains the Forms of Baptizing, of Anointing the Sick, of Marrying, of Sacramental Absolution, with the customary Prayers therein ; of administring the Holy Sacrament of the Altar, of the Exorcisms of the Church, for People possessed with the Devil, the Blessings of Holy Water, of Ashes, of Chains and Branches, as also the Form of Burying the Dead, Old and Young, and of reconciling Churches and Church-Yards. Which Books being Bound, shall be kept in all Churches ;

neither

neither shall any Priest presume to apply them
to his own private use, or to take them out of
the Church: And the Synod doth earnestly recommend it to the Rector of the College of the
Jesuits of *Vaipicotta*, to have always some of these
Books Translated by some of the said College by
him, in order to the supplying of the Necessities
of these Churches.

Decree XXIII.

THe Synod desiring that this Church may in
all things be conformable to the Holy *Ro-*
man and whole *Italian* Church, doth command,
That on the second of *February*, being the day
of our Lady's *Purification*, before *Mass*, the Wax
Candles which are in the Church, be Blest, as
also all the Candles that shall be brought by the
People out of Devotion, according to the *Ro-*
man Ceremonial , translated into *Syrian*; and
after the publick and solemn Benediction is over,
there shall be a Procession in or round the Church,
in which all the Clergy shall carry Blessed Candles lighted in their hands, as the People shall also
do that have any, in Memory of the Mystery of our
Lord Jesus Christ, the Divine Light and Splen-
dor of the Father, first entrance into the Temple, there to offer himself to his Eternal Father,
cloathed with our Humanity: So likewise upon
the *Monday*, *Tuesday*, and *Wednesday* before the
Feast of our Lord's Holy *Ascension*, in the Morning, either before or after *Mass*, there shall be

a

a Proceffion in the Church, or where the Vicar
fhall appoint, in which the *Litanies* fhall be faid
according to the cuftoms of the Church, which
fhall alfo be tranflated in the faid *Roman* Ceremonial, expunging the Names of all the Hereticks, who according to the cuftom of the *Ne-*
ftorians, were commemorated in this Church;
and it is the defire of the Synod, that the ufe
of the faid *Litanies* be brought into this Church
to be read in their Neceffities, or when they defire to implore the Divine Mercy.

Decree XXIV.

THe Synod being informed, that in the remote parts of this Bifhoprick, as well towards the *South,* as towards the *North,* the Chriftians that dwell in the *Heaths* are guilty of
Working and Merchandizing on *Sundays* and Holy-days, efpecially in the Evenings, doth command the Vicars to be very vigilant in this
Matter, and to admonifh and reprehend all that
they fhall find fo doing; and if after three particular Admonitions, they fhall not reform, they
fhall after that be thrown out of the Church,
and have the *Cafture* denied them; neither fhall
any Prieft go into their Houfes until they have
yielded Obedience.

Decree XXV.

WHereas in this Dioceſs there are many Churches dedicated to *Marxobro* and *Marphrod*, who are commonly ſtiled *Saints*, of whom there is * nothing known, only it is commonly ſaid, *That they came into theſe Parts and wrought*

* Nothing known.] At *Compoſtella*, the moſt famous place of Devotion in all *Spain*, the People pray to ſome that they know as little of, as the *Malabars* do of *Marphrod*.

For the famous *Spaniſh* Antiquary *Ambroſius Morales*, in the 9*th*. Book of his Chronicle, gives us a particular Account of an Altar with ſome Names upon it that he met with there, and that had great Devotion paid to it.

In the famous Monaſtery of the Benedictine *Nuns that joins to the Holy Church of St.* James, ſaith Morales, *and is dedicated to the Glorious Martyr* Pelayo, *whom in that Country they commonly call St.* Payo, *there is an Ara on the Altar, which they affirm to have been Conſecrated by the Apoſtles, and that they themſelves ſaid Maſs on it, and that it was brought thither with the bleſſed Body of St.* James. *Now there is not*, ſaith Morales, *not only no foundation for the Truth of this Story, but there is juſt cauſe to believe, that that Stone, which is at preſent in the ſame ſtate it was in when it was firſt made, could never be an Altar. I obſerved it with great attention in the company of ſeveral great and learned Men, who had all the ſame thoughts of it that I had, the thing indeed being too clear and manifeſt for any ſuch to doubt of; for it is viſible, that the Stone is the Grave-Stone of ſome Heathens, with this following Inſcription.*

D M S
ATIAMO ET AT-
TE T LVMPS AO
VIRIA EMO
NEPTIS PIANO XVI
F. T S. E. C.

The words are very plain and clear, there not being a Letter wanting; ſo that notwithſtanding the Blunders committed by the Graver in Spelling it, they may be with great eaſe Tranſlated, which I will do as well as I can into Spaniſh.

" This Stone is Conſecrated to " the Gods of the Dead, and De- " dicated to the Memories of " *Atiamo*, and of *Atte*, and of " *Lumpſa*, as alſo to her Memory " who Erected it, *Viria Emoſa* " their pious Grand-child, being " 16 Years of Age.

This

This is what the Stone contains, therefore, they that Consecrated it an Altar, would have done well to have defaced the Letters, by which means they would have removed the indignity that stares all People in the face, that consider what a thing it is to have the most Holy Body and Blood of Christ our Redeemer, consecrated and placed upon the Tomb-Stone of Heathens, whereon the Devils are invocated. Thus far Morales.

But as this Stone has had a great deal of Honour done it, in coming to be Consecrated an Altar in such a famous place of Devotion, so the Persons whose Names are upon it, have had no less done to them, who are all great Saints in that Country, and particularly *Piano*, who in all probability is the St. *Payo*, to whom the Church and Monastery is dedicated.

For first, *Salazar* in his *Spanish* Martyrology upon the 30th. day of *December*, gives this following Account of the said Stone and Persons. Don Didacus Sequinus, *Bishop of* Auria, *who has Epitomized the Life of his Predecessor* Serrandus, *gives therein the following Exposition of the Inscription that is upon this Altar Stone, in the* Galecian *Language, which History I have now by me in* MSS.

Confegrada a Deos Maximo,

Atiamo, Erato, Telumpsa Viriamo Nepotispiano, Xuuito, Teliforo,

Forem Martyres e padezeron em Galizia, no Pago *Sarense* antes que ô Apostolo se fose a *Jerusa-*

lem, e por isto deyxon esta Ara, a seus Discipolos, paraque sobre de la dixiesem Missa, en membraza destes Santos : así dexou escrito ô Bispo Don *Serrando* : *That is to say,*

' Consecrated to the greatest God,

' *Atiamo, Erato, Telumpsa, Viriamo,*
' *Nepotispiano, Xuuito, Teliforo,*

' Were all Martyrs, and suffered
' in *Galecia* in the Village of *Sarep,*
' before the Apostle went to *Jeru-*
' *salem,* who for that reason left
' this Altar to his Disciples to say
' Mass on in memory of those
' Saints, as Bishop Don *Serrando*
' has left upon Record.

Lobarinus tells us, that Don *Serrandus* after having given a description of the Altar, subjoins the following Account of it
' Este he ô Retrayto de Ara
' que deyxo escripta o Apostol
' Santiago, a seus discipolos, e he
' un tanto da que trouxa con sigo
' nó mar, sobre que, pausaran
' o santo corpo e sobre de la deria
' nissa Arcadio 1 Bispo do Orenes
' en san Maria Madre ; autro tanto
' como este esta en san Payo, de
' Santiago com istas mismas letras
' destos Santos Martyres. That is
to say : *This is the Portraiture of the Altar which the Apostle* St. James *left, with an Inscription upon it, to his Disciples, who carried another of the same Dimensions, and with the same Inscription, along with him to Sea ; upon which his Holy Body was laid, and* Arcadius *the first Bishop of* Orenes *said Mass upon it in the Church of* St. Mary *the Mother of God ;*

God; *the other which is the same
with this, is in the Church of St.*Payo
of Compostella, *with the same
Names of these Holy Martyrs.*

I hope the Reader will pardon
me, if I offer one or two more
instances of the same Nature.

In the *Spanish* Martyrology upon the 22*d.* of *May*, it is said,
*Sanctius Publius Bebius Venustus
Martyr qui pontem in honorem templi beatæ Mariæ condidit, petente Ordine Oretanorum ut pateret aditus ad
Templum*, XX. CHS. *in quo ponte
suæ Pietatis, hujusmodi in visceri-
bus lapidis Monumentum reliquit.*

P. BÆBIUS VENUSTUS P.
EÆBIIVENETIEP. BÆSISCERIS
NEPOS ORETANUS. PETEN-
TE ORDINE ET POPULO, IN
HONOREM DOMUS DIVINÆ,
PONTEM FECIT EX HS XXC.
CIRCENSIBUS EDITIS.
D. D.

This needs no Commentary, it
being plain from the Monument
it self, that this *P. BÆBIUS* was
a Heathen, and that *Domus Divina* herein mentioned, was not
a Church dedicated to the blessed
Virgin, but to some Heathen god.
And at *Ebora* in *Portugal*, St.
Viarius, who infallibly cures all
pains in the Loins, and for that
reason is very much prayed to,
was raised out of such another
Heathen *Roman* Monument,
whereon *Viarum Curator* was writ,
as *Resendius* tells us.

But as in some places they
have made Saints of Heathens, in
others they have made Heathens
of Saints: For in the Castle of *Li-
ria* in *Portugal*, there is over the

Inner Gate a Stone Statue, with
a long inscription under it, of
which there is nothing legible
from the ground but the word
Veneris, which is very plain, the
Portugueze who shewed us the
place, for we were several Protestants in Company, told us very
gravely that the Castle was built by
the *Romans*, and that the Statue
we saw so much defaced, the
Head and Arms being broke of,
and the Body very much malled
with Stones, was the Statue of
the *Roman* Goddess *Venus* : we
kept our Countenances as well
as we could, perceiving plainly,
that neither the Castle nor the
Statue were *Roman* work, and
the Letters of *Veneris* were perfectly Gothick, so I and two more
having industriously lost our *Portugueze*, we resolved if possible to
find out the truth of the matter,
and after some poring, we began to discover some more Letters, and with some pains spelt
out the word *Ante* after *Veneris* ;
whereupon we concluded, that
Veneris there must be a *Verb*, and
not a *Substantive*, and that *Veneris ante* must be the end of a Mon-
kish Verse : and we were quickly satisfied that it was so by what
followed, which was,

*Pertransire cave, nisi prius dixeris
Ave
Regina cœli mater,*

What followed was so defaced
that we could make nothing of
it, neither indeed were we soli-
citous about it, being abundantly
satisfied from what we had read,
that it was a Statue of the most
Blessed

Bleffed Virgin; when we returned to our *Portugueze*, we asked
him as we did the People alfo at
our Inn, how he came to know
certainly that it was the Statue
of a Heathen Goddefs, and we
found him and them all in the
fame Story, that the Name of
the Goddefs was written under it,
and that it was the conftant Tradition of the City and Country.

wrought Miracles, and returned afterwards to
Babylon, from whence they came, others affirming that they died in *Coulaon*, there being nothing writ of them that is Authentick, neither
does it appear that they were ever canonized
by the Church ; but on the contrary, fince they
came from *Babylon*, there is juft caufe to fufpect
that they might be Hereticks: Wherefore the
Synod doth command, That all the Churches
which are dedicated to them, be dedicated to
all the Saints, and that the Feftivities ufed to
be kept to their Honour , and the *Ner-
chas* that ufed to be given upon their days,
fhall be given on *All Saints* day, being the firft
of *November* : and for the future there be no
more Churches dedicated to them, Churches and
Feftivities being never to be dedicated, nor Prayers made to any but to Saints canonized and approved of by the Church.

Decree

Decree XXVI.

WHereas Experience has demonſtrated that many Churches have been Robbed by reaſon of the Poors Box being kept in them and not opened in many Years, no not when the neceſſities of the Churches did require it ; therefore the Synod doth command , That in every Church upon the firſt of *January* there be choſe four ſubſtantial and conſciencious Men to be Overſeers of the Poor, and to take care of the Church, who at the end of the Year ſhall open the Poors Box and take out all the Alms they find therein, which ſhall be put down in a Book by one of the four Overſeers, and the ſaid Alms ſhall be afterwards put into a Cheſt Locked with three different Keys, which ſhall ſtand in any one of their Houſes as they ſhall agree, of which Keys the Vicar ſhall have one, and the other two the two Overſeers, who are not the Scrivener, nor in whoſe Houſes the Cheſt is not kept: He that's the Scrivener ſhall alſo have a Book, in which he ſhall ſet down the Expences of the ſaid Alms, how much has been laid out upon the Fabrick of the Church, and in the reparation of the Walls and Roof, how much in adorning it, and in neceſſary Linen, and in Pictures, and in keeping it clean : And when-ſoever there is any great extraordinary Expence, it ſhall not be made without the conſent of the four Overſeers, according to cuſtom ; neither
ſhall

ſhall the Cheſt be opened but when they are all
five preſent, or ſome one in the place of him
that is lawfully hindred ; and when new Overſeers are choſe, the old ones ſhall deliver the
ſaid Cheſt to them, for which the Elect ſhall give
a Receipt, that ſo it may always appear how
much has been received and how much is remaining : And the Prelate in his Viſitation ſhall
look over the ſaid Books and inform himſelf
of the Expences, and may order the Alms to be
diſpoſed of as he ſhall think fit and neceſſary.
And the Synod intreats the moſt Reverend *Me-*
tropolitan to ſee that this Decree be put in execution at the Viſitation he intends to make, it
being a thing of great advantage to the Churches.

Decree XXVII.

WHereas moſt of the Churches of this Dioceſs are kept very Naſty, being full of
Duſt and Cobwebs, for want of an Officer to
keep the Church clean, therefore the Synod
doth command, that the Overſeers appoint a *Capiar,*
who ſhall be paid out of the Alms, for Sweep-
ing the Church and keeping clean the Lamps
and Candleſticks ; and the *Capiar* ſhall take care
that the Church be Swept at leaſt three times a
Week, and there be always one Lamp at leaſt
lighted before the High Altar, and the Veſſels
wherein the Lamp-Oil is kept, without they be
ſo ſmall as not to be ſeen, ſhall not be kept in
the Church, nor the *Bategas* or Kettles, nor any

thing elſe that is undecent, but ſhall be kept in
the *Capiar*'s or Overſeers Houſes, that ſo the
Church may be kept clean and decent.

Decree XXVIII.

THe Synod doth command, That in all
Veſtries of Churches there be Cupboards
and Cheſts with Locks, to keep the Cups, Corporals, and Ornaments in; and where there is
no Veſtry until one ſhall be built, they ſhall be
kept ſome where in the Church; except in the
Heaths, where the Churches are in danger of being
robbed, where the Vicars ſhall keep them in
their Houſes, and ſhall by no means leave any
of them upon the Altars, as has been the cuſtom,
which was the occaſion of the Ornaments being ſo dirty, and of the Altars being ſo much
out of order: And whereas moſt of the chief
Chapels are extreamly dark, they ſhall take
care to have Windows opened, and fortified
with Iron to let in Air and Light, which muſt
nevertheleſs be ſo contrived, that the Heathens
when they come may not ſee the Divine Myſteries thorow them.

Decree XXIX.

WHereas almoſt all the Churches of this Dioceſs are without Pictures, which was the
effect of their being governed by *Neſtorian* Hereticks, who do not allow of the healthful uſe

of

of Sacred Images; therefore the Synod doth command, That in Churches that are finished, the first work that shall be done after that of the Baptismal Font out of the Alms of the Parish, shall be to set up some Images, according to the directions of the Prelate, who shall always be consulted about every Picture; and after that of the High Altar is once set up, if the Church has any Side-Altars, they shall also have Images set up in them, and on every Altar besides an Image, there shall be a Cross or some Matter or other set up; and in all Churches that are large enough, and yet have no Pulpits, Pulpits shall be erected for the Preaching of the word of God; and they shall also put Bells in their Steeples to be rung at meet times, and to call the People to Church, which shall not be hung within the Church, where besides that they cannot be rung as they ought to be, they do take up too much room; and in places where there is danger of having their Bells stole, they shall have their Steeples fortified and shut up after the manner of Towers; and where the Kings and *Bramens* of the *Pagods* will not consent to their having a Building higher than the Church, which often happens through their imagining that the *Pagods* are made melancholly by the hearing of such Bells; they shall hang them within the Church but at such a height, that they may ring them without touching them with their hands, and that they shall take up no room below in the Church; and in those Churches where

they

they have no Bells, the Synod grants Licence until such time as they can procure some, to make use of Boards, as they have done formerly, to call the Faithful together, and to give the Signal at the *Mass*.

Decree XXX.

THe Synod doth teach and declare, That by ancient Right always observed in the Church, Churches may be so violated in certain Cases, that it is not lawful to Celebrate in them, nor to bury the Dead until they are reconciled, which through ignorance of the Canons has not hitherto been observed in this Bishoprick; the Cases are, *when humane Blood is injuriously* shed in the Church, or there is a Natural Cause given of such shedding, or of Death; as if one has a Mortal Wound given him in the Church, or a Wound that fetches Blood, notwithstanding the Wounded Person shall be got out of the Church before any Blood is shed; but if the Wound was given without the Church, notwithstanding the Blood thereof should come to be shed therein, the Church is not violated thereby; and by a Wound that is injuriously given in the Church, whereby Blood is shed, tho' the Wound should not prove Mortal, the Church is violated. The second Case is, *when humane Seed is voluntarily spent in the Church*, tho' in conjugal Copulation: The third is, *when one that is Excommunicated is buried in the Church:* The fourth,
when

when an Infidel is buried in it; in which Cafe
the Church is not only to be reconciled, but the
Walls are alfo to be fcraped : The fifth is`, *when
the Church has been Confecrated or Bleffed by
a Bifhop that was publickly Excommunicate*; in
all which Cafes the Church is to be reconciled,
which reconciliation being to be done to a Church
that was Confecrated by a Bifhop, none but a
Bifhop can perform it : But having been only
Bleffed by one, or by a Prieft, the Vicar may
perform the Reconciliation, according to the
Form, and with the Prayers and Ceremonies
contained in the *Roman* Ceremonial Tranflated
into *Syrian*; and it is to be obferved, that when
a Church is violated, the Church-yard that belongs to it is violated alfo, if they are not
at fome diftance the one from the other; but
when the Church-yard is violated in any of the
forementioned Cafes, the Church it belongs and
is joined to, is not violated thereby.

Decree XXXI.

IT being of mighty moment that Confecrated
Churches be had in great Reverence; and
whereas in this Diocefs it is a common thing for
Sick People out of Devotion to lie in Churches
with their Wives and Families for feveral days,
hoping thereby to be cured of their Diftempers,
which cannot be done without many Services;
wherefore the Synod doth command, That no
Perfon whatfoever, tho' never fo Sick, do lie
in

in the Church with his Family, the time of War
only excepted, but the Sick having performed
their Devotion , ſhall lie at home at their own
Houſes, or if they ſhall deſire it may Lodge
in ſome Houſes that are near to the Church, or
in the Porches thereof, but by no means within
the Church.

Decree XXXII.

WHereas there is a great neglect in carrying
the Corps of thoſe that die in the *Heaths*
to the Church, which are ſometimes buried without a Prieſt, and in unconſecrated Earth ; wherefore the Synod doth command, That the Kindred,
or thoſe in whoſe Houſes Chriſtians do die, do
carry their Corps, how far ſoever they may live
off, near to the Church, where the Vicars ſhall go
to fetch them, with the Croſs of the Church, and
in their *Surplice* and *Stole*, praying all the way
they go with the reſt of the Clergy, and Interr
them, which all, tho' never ſo poor, ſhall be
oblig'd to do: And if at the time when they
bring the Corps they ſhall meet with no Prieſts
in the Church, they ſhall then aſſemble as many
Chriſtians together as conveniently they can, and
bury the Corps in the Church-yard, praying for
their Souls with Chriſtian Charity: And whoſoever ſhall neglect to bring their Dead to the
Church, and ſhall bury them in Profane Ground,
ſhall be ſeverely puniſhed by the Biſhop.

Decree

Decree XXXIII.

WHereas the Small-Pox is looked upon in thefe parts as a very dangerous and infe-ctious Diftemper, for which reafon a great many Chriftians dying thereof are not carried to the Church, nor buried in Holy ground; here-fore the Synod doth very much recommend it to the Vicars to take order, that the Corps of fuch as die of that Sicknefs may be brought with due caution to the Church-yard, where they with the reft of the Clergy at fome diftance are to recommend them, and pray for them, as they do for others, and to fee them interr'd: all which Chriftian Charity will teach them to do, according to the Obligation of their Office.

Decree XXXIV.

THe Synod doth order that no Town or Vil-lage, wherein there is a Church dedicated to any Saint, fhall dedicate the fame to any o-ther, or if they do, they fhall appoint another *Orago,* or Wake, fo as to have two Feftivals to prevent thofe Emulations that are common in thefe parts. The Synod alfo condemns the * Ig-norance of thofe Chriftians who imagine that they

* *Ignozance.*] Upon S. *Te-refa* being joyned with St. *James,* in the Patronage of *Spain* by Pope *Urban* the VIIIth. how loud did a great many people complain of the Indignity done to St. *James,* their old Patron and General in all their Wars, by that Partner-

do

do an injury to a Church, in dedicating a New one in the same Country to a different Saint, from whence it is that all the Churches in the same Country are as it were called by the same Name, and doth furthermore command, That upon the *Orago's* of Churches where there are Sermons, people having no Sermon in their own Parish, do repair thither that so there may be no divisions among Churches, to the prejudice of Charity and Christian Unity, as the Synod is informed there is in many places, all which it is desirous to remove, as not becoming Christians, and for the further service of the Church commands Fraternities to be erected, but especially for the festivities, by which means such things as are necessary for the Church may be greatly advanced.

ship. Among others, *Quivedo*, as in Honour bound, being a Knight of the Order of St. *James*, drew his pen in his Patron's Quarrel, and having laid down this as an undeniable position, *That St. James must necessarily be disparaged by having one joyned with him, and especially a Woman, in a Patronage he had enjoyed solely for so many Ages*; did manfully maintain that, its being said in the Pope's Bull, *That nothing was granted therein to S. Teresa that should be in any wise to the prejudice or diminution of St. James*, did make that whole grant null and void, for that joyning her with St. *James* in such an Office must necessarily lessen him : 2*dly.*

That the Saints in Heaven did resent such Affronts. 3. That it was monstrous Ingratitude in *Spain* to treat a Patron thus, who had fought personally on Horseback for her in all her Battels with the Moors, among whom to this day the Captain on the Whitehorse was formidable. As to the Text in Scripture urged by S. *Teresa's* Friends for such a partnership. *viz. It is not good for man to be alone; I will make him an help meet for him.* He saith, That considering what was the true intent of those words when they were spoke, such an application of them was profane and Heretical.

Decree

Decree XXXV.

THe Synod doth very much recommend it to
the Vicars of Churches, and other Priests
to labour much in the Conversion of *Infidels*,
and that by just and gentle methods, namely,
by the preaching of the Gospel to bring them to
the Catholick Faith, and to omit no opportunity of instructing as well the *Naires* as the *Chegos*,
or baser sort of People in the knowledge of the
Truth ; but above all, the poor *Malleans* who
live in the Heaths, who as the Synod is informed, are less wedded to their Errors, particularly that of the Adoration of Idols, and are much
better disposed to receive the Evangelical
Doctrine than others ; and whensoever any
Infidel is converted, the Priest shall advise the
Prelate thereof, that he may take such order
therein as he shall judge most convenient, and
to be most for the service of Christ, earnestly
entreating that the Conversions that are begun
in some parts by the most Reverend *Metropolitan*, may be carried on by the Clergy of this
Diocess, by providing themselves continually of
such Priests as are fit to advance the same, and
where-ever there is any considerable number of
Converts, they shall immediately build Churches, and appoint Vicars to take the Cure of their
Souls.

Decree

Decree XXXVI.

WHereas the Synod is informed, That the meaner fort of People are much better difpofed to receive the Faith than the *Naires*, or Nobles, and being extreamly defirous to find fome way whereby fuch well difpofed People may be made Chriftians, fo as to affemble toge-ther with the old Chriftians, as why fhould they not, fince they all adore the fame God, with whom there is no diftinction of Perfons, and are all of the fame Faith, and do all ufe the fame Sacra-ments, and whereas after mature deliberation, and having oftentimes recommended the matter to God, and conferred about the moft proper me-thods for the effecting of it in the Congregati-ons, we have not been able to find any that are effectual, by reafon of the Heathen Kings and Lords to whom all the Chriftians in thefe parts are fubject, who, if they fhould obferve that we withdraw their common Subjects from their Religion, would correfpond with us no longer to the lofs of the Trade and Commerce we do at prefent maintain with them, all which being ob-ferved by the Synod, it doth command that if any of the poorer fort of People fhall defire to turn Chriftian, that they be received to Baptifm, and the Prelate fhall be advifed thereof, that he may give order for the building of diftinct Churches for them, and may appoint Priefts to take the Cure thereof, that fo the meaner fort of

People

People may not have the Gate of Chriſtianity
and Salvation ſhut againſt them, as it has been
hitherto in this Church; and in caſe they have
not a Church to themſelves, they ſhall then hear
Maſs without doors in the Porch, until Chriſt
ſhall provide ſome better way for them, and the
Heathen Kings ſhall be brought to allow the
mean People that turn Chriſtians to be eſteemed
as Noble, upon the account of the Relation that all
Chriſtians ſtand in to one another: and the Synod doth beg it of His Majeſty the King of *Portugal*, that by means of the great Power he has
in theſe parts, he would procure this privilege
of the Kings and Lords of *Malabar.*

Decree XXXVII.

THe Synod being deſirous that the Church of
the *Serra*, ſhould in all things be conformable to the *Latin* cuſtoms, or Holy Mother
Church of *Rome*, unto which *See* ſhe has now
yielded a perfect Obedience, and whereas in the
Roman Church, the cuſtom is to make the Sign
of the Croſs and Bleſſings from the left to the
right, ſo that in ſaying, *In the Name of the Father, and of the Son, and of the Holy Ghoſt*, they
put their hand on their Forehead, and after that
deſcended to their Breaſt, where after having
croſſed themſelves, they go next to the left Shoul-
der, and from thence to the right, thereby ſignifying among other Myſteries, that by virtue
of the Croſs of Chriſt the Son of God, we are
tran-

tranflated from the left hand, the place of Repro-
bates, to the right, the place of the Elect; and the
cuftom of this Diocefs is to make the faid fign from
the right to the left; wherefore the Synod doth
command that all Children and all other People be taught to crofs and blefs themfelves from
the left to the right, according to the *Latin* cuftom, which fhall alfo be obferved by the Priefts
in the bleffings they give to the People, and in
the Croffes they make in the Holy Sacrifice of
the *Mafs*, and the Adminiftration of the other
Sacraments.

Decree XXXVIII.

THe Synod doth declare, That the Execution of Laft Wills lawfully made by deceafed Chriftians does by the Canon Law belong to
Prelates and Bifhops, who are to take care that
they be obferved; and that whatfoever Chriftian has made a Will that is valid according to the
cuftom of the place, if it is not complyed with
in a Year after the Death of the Teftator, the
Bifhop fhall by cenfures, and other Penalties, if
found neceffary conftrain the Heirs, or others,
whofe Duty it is to fulfill the fame.

Decree

Decree XXXIX.

WHereas it often happens that Persons dying who were under the scandal of having committed some grievous Sin, tho' never
proved upon them, are upon that account denyed the Prayers, and other Offices of the Dead,
especially if they desired Confession, and were
confessed at their Death, which is contrary to the
order and custom of the Church, which deprives
none of her publick Prayers, but such as die Excommunicate, or in the Act of some Mortal Sin,
without having given any sign of Contrition :
Therefore the Synod doth command, that whatsoever Sins one may have committed, if the censure of Excommunication was not annexed to
them ; or unless the Person died in the very Act
of some Mortal Sin, without giving any sign of
Contrition, or slowly in his Bed, without desiring to be confessed, or to have a Priest called to
him to that effect, as is appointed by the Decrees
of the Sacrament of *Penance*, they shall pray and
perform the Office of the Dead for him, and bury him in Holy Ground with the same Prayers
they do other People.

Decree XL.

THe Synod having thanked the *Jesuits* of
the College of *Vaipicotta* in this Diocess,
and of the other Residencies, for the pains they

have been at in inftructing the Chriftians of thefe
parts, does for the greater benefit of the Souls of
the faid Chriftians, grant Licence to the faid Religious, as well of the College, as of their other
greater Refidencies to preach and hear Confeffions, and adminifter the Sacraments in all Churches where-ever they come, without ftanding in
need of any further Licence, the Sacrament of
Matrimony only excepted, which it fhall not be
lawful for them to adminifter without leave from,
or at the requeft of the Parifh Priefts, commanding all Vicars and Curates of Churches, and all
the People to receive the faid Fathers chearfully, and to entertain them with great Kindnefs
and Thanks, for the great trouble they are at
in travelling continually over the Mountains only
for the Salvation of their Souls, and rejoyce to
learn from them how to adminifter the Sacraments, and to have their Flocks inftructed by
them in all fuch Doctrines as are neceffary to
their Souls, and their Vicars fhall oblige their
People to come to Church, to hear them, whenever they preach, the Syned being very confident, that the faid Fathers will exercife all the
faid Functions in great Love and Charity with
the Parifh, and all the other Priefts of the
Church.

Decree

Decree XLI.

WHereas the Conftitutions of the Bifhoprick of *Goa* have been received in the Provincial Councils thereof, and have been ordered to be obferved thorow the whole Province, of which this Church being a *Suffragan*, is obliged by the faid Councils, and to which this Synod yielding a due Obedience, doth command, That in all things that can be obferved in this Bifhoprick, or concerning which there is no provifion made in this Synod, the faid Conftitutions be kept and obeyed, and doth likewife command, That Appeals whenfoever made from Sentences given in this Bifhoprick to the *Metropolitan*, fuch Appeals being made in fuch Cafes wherein the Canons allow them, fhall be granted ; neverthelefs not intending hereby to alter any thing in that mild method of the Prelate, and four or more Perfons compofing Matters amicably to the prevention of many Difcords, but if the Parties fhall not fubmit to fuch determinations, but will appeal to the *Metropolitan*, it fhall not be denyed them, being done in due form.

ACTION IX.

Of the Reformation of Manners.

Decree I.

WHereas of all the evil Cuftoms that are to
be rooted from among the Faithful, thofe
are the moft dangerous which have fomething of
the Heathen Superftition in them, of which this
Bifhoprick is full ; therefore the Synod defiring
that all fuch cuftoms were totally extirpated, that
fo Chriftians may enjoy Chriftianity in its purity,
doth in order thereunto command, that all Superftitious wafhings which are by fome moft fuperftitioufly practifed as Holy Ceremonies be utterly abo-
lifhed, fuch as the wafhing of Dead Corps the Day
after they have given a *Dole*, reckoning it a Sin
to negleċt fuch wafhings, the making of Circles
with Rice, into which they put the Parties that are
to be Married, having given Rice before to Children, as alfo the taking a thred out with great Superftition when they cut a Web of Cloath, and the
taking two grains of *Nele* back again, after they
have fold and meafured it : all which Heathenifh
Vanities the Synod totally prohibits, commanding
all that fhall ufe them hereafter to be feverely
punifhed.

Decree

Decree II.

THo' it would much rejoice the Synod to
see the Superstitious and absurd Customs of
the Heathen *Malavars* of the better sort not
mixing with the lower, and of having no communication or correspondence with those that
have but touched any of them, totally abolished
among the Christians of this Bishoprick ; yet forasmuch as the Christians thereof, by reason of
their being subject to Infidel Princes, whom they
are forced to obey in all things, wherein the
Faith is no ways concerned ; and that Christians,
if they should but touch those of the baser rank,
could not after that, according to the Laws, have
any Trade or communication with the better
sort of People, and so would not be able to live
among them; for which reason the Synod doth
declare, That the custom of not touching any
of the baser sort, being observed only in com-
plyance with the Heathens, and looked upon as
a Superstitious Heathen Vanity, and not voluntarily observed, is no Superstition, nor for the above-
mentioned Reasons any matter of scruple, and
that Christians may in all places thus lawfully
observe it, where there are *Naires* or any of
the better sort, or where it is likely they may
be, or may come to hear of it : But in all places
where these Causes do not concurr, or in secret,
or among the *Portuguezes*, this Superstition cannot
be observed without doing a great injury to

their

their Confciences; on the contrary, the Synod
doth admonifh all the Faithful to receive all
fuch with great Love and Charity, tho' never fo
poor and mean, and efpecially if they are Chriftians, knowing that there is no diftinction of
Perfons with God, who is Lord of all: And
albeit they do not touch the bafe fort of People upon the forementioned account, yet if they
fhould happen to touch any of them, they fhall
not wafh themfelves thereupon, that being a thing
that can never come to the knowledge of the
Heathens, and would therefore be a manifeft
Superftition; thofe alfo that will not touch the
Naires, or if they fhould, do wafh themfelves,
which, as the Synod is informed, is what the
Chriftians in the _Southern_ parts do obferve, where
the forementioned impediment is not among the
Heathens, who are rather fcandalized by fuch a
contemptuous Carriage: Therefore the Synod
doth command all that fhall be found guilty of
forbearing to touch fuch, or having touched
them, fhall wafh themfelves, to be feverely punifhed as Superftitious followers of the Heathen
Cuftoms, and commands the Preachers and Confeffors to admonifh them thereof in their Sermons and Confeffions.

Decree

Decree III.

THe Synod being informed, that in some parts when any one of the baser sort do but touch the Cisterns of Christians, that Christians do * *Disempolear* or *Purify* them, by performing certain Ceremonies after the manner of the Heathens, which is very contrary to the Purity of the Christian Religion, being an intolerable Superstition, doth with great rigour command those that make the said *Disempoleamento* or *Purification*, or use the said Ceremonies, to be thrown out of the Communion of the Church, and to be denied the *Casture* during the Prelate's pleasure, or at least for one Year, and to be punished with the Penalties that such Ceremonies do deserve.

* This word *Disempolear*, comes from *Isleas*, which is the name | this vile cast of People is called by.

Decree IV.

WHereas in the Feast of the Heathen, called *Ona*, which is Celebrated in *August*, in which they go out one against another with Bows and Arrows, and other Arms, in which conflicts some are killed, and more wounded; and some Christians, unmindful of their Obligations, living among them, and communicating much with them, do go forth with them, and Armed as they are to the said Feasts, and are thereby liable to the same Disasters : Therefore
　　　　　　　　　　the

the Synod doth command all the Faithful Chriftians of this Bifhoprick, in Holy Obedience, and
upon pain of Excommunication, not to prefume
to refort to this or any other Heathen Feftivity,
tho' there fhould be no Ceremony belonging to a
Pagod therein; forafmuch as all fuch Feafts are
dedicated to the faid *Pagods,* and are celebrated
and obferved to their Honour and Veneration ;
which is the rather to be forbore in this of the
Ona, by reafon of the danger of death that there
is probably therein, the Heathens fuperftitioufly
imagining that all that die in that occafion, go
immediately to Heaven ; but Chriftians fhall only
obferve their own Holy Feftivities among themfelves, and that with a due moderation and decency, as becomes the Profeffors of the Law of
Chrift; without having any thing to do with
the Superftitious Feftivals of the Heathens, which
are dedicated to the Honour of the Devil, and
if any Chriftian fhall die in the faid Heathen
Feaft, he fhall be denied Ecclefiaftical Burial.

Decree V.

FAithful Chriftians muft not only avoid the
Ceremonies and Superftitions of the *Heathens,*
but the *Judaical* Rites and Ceremonies alfo, which
were all abrogated by the fufficient promulgati-
on of the Gofpel, for which reafon the Synod,
tho' it doth very much commend the Holy Cuftom of carrying Children to Church forty days
after they are born, to offer them to the Lord,

in

in imitation and praife of what was done by our Lady the moft Holy *Virgin*; nevertheless it condemns the feparating of Women for the faid forty days after the birth of a Male, as if they were unclean fo as not to fuffer them to enter into the Church, imagining they would fin in doing it, and eighty days after the birth of a Female; both which are *Jewifh* Ceremonies, that are now abrogated, and not only ufeless but prejudicial, and as fuch, the Synod doth totally prohibit the obfervance of them; declaring, that if Women have Health and Strength fooner, they fhall be obliged to go to Church to hear *Mafs* upon *Sundays* and Holy-days: and after forty days they may, according to their Cuftom, carry their Sons to Church with Devotion, underftanding that there is no Precept of the Church for it, but that it is only a pious Devotion of faithful Women that are willing to make fuch an Offering of their Sons to God in imitation of the moft Holy Virgin *Mary*, the Mother of God, taking her for the Interceffor of the Children thus offered to God both for Spirituals and Temporals.

Decree VI.

ONe of the greateft Sins in the fight of God, and which he has always prohibited and punifhed above all others, is *the confulting of Witches*, and fuch as hold a correfpondence with the Devil; wherefore the Synod being informed that a great many Chriftians of this Bifhoprick,

and

and especially among those that live in the *Heaths*, by reason of the Communication they have with *Infidels*, and their having so many *Witches* and *Fortune-tellers* about them, when they intend to Marry, have recourse to such People to know what Success they shall have, governing themselves so much by what they are told, as to break off Matches after they are concluded, and to make new ones at the pleasure of the said *Witches*; as also when they are Sick, that they send for such People to perform some Ceremony whereby they hope to have their Health restored; and at other times to help them to Children, and to discover Thefts, and for several other purposes; all which are things repugnant to the Christian Religion, doth command all Christians convicted of having consulted any of the said *Witches* for these or any other purposes, to be thrown out of the Church; neither shall any Priest go to their Houses or give them the *Casture*, during the Prelate's pleasure, or for one Year at least, and shall be punished with such other Penalties as the Ceremonies they performed and consented to shall deserve.

Decree

Decree VII.

THe Synod being informed, that some wicked Christians are not content only to go
to *Witches* to consult them, but do furthermore
send for them to their Houses, where they joyn
with them in the Invocation of their *Pagods*, and
in making offerings and Sacrifices to them, in
killing Dogs, and performing other Ceremonies,
that are contrary to the Faith, namely, one which
they call *Tollicanum, Ollicanum, Bellicorum, Co-
num,* which they do often publickly to the great
scandal of Christianity, as if they were not Christians, and at other times permit the Heathens to
perform them in their Houses, doth command in
virtue of Holy Obedience, and upon pain of
Excommunication to be *Ipso facto* incurred, that
no Christian shall presume to perform any of
the said Ceremonies, or consent to the performing of them in their Houses, and that all that do
transgress therein, shall be declared Excommunicate in the Church, until they shall beg for mercy, and have undergone condign and publick
Punishment in the Church, and tho' upon their
Repentance appearing to be true and sincere, ·
they may be absolved, yet they shall not have
the *Casture* given them, neither shall any Priest
go to their Houses in two Years, save in case of
peril of Death ; and they who shall go to offer
any thing to a *Pagod,* or shall make any Vow to
one, shall be punished after the same manner,
and

and with the fame Penance, and fhall incurr Excommunication *Ipfo facto*, in all which Matters
the Vicar muft be very watchful for the prevention of all fuch Idolatries.

Decree VIII.

A Great many ignorant Chriftians of this Bifhoprick being unmindful of the Purity of
their Chriftian Obligations, do carry Notes a-
bout them which have been given them by
Witches for the Cure of their Diftempers, hoping
for relief from their vertue, hanging them likewife about the Necks of their Cattle to keep
them well, and putting them in their Orchards
to encreafe the Fruit, and communicating them
to feveral other things for various effects; all
which the Synod detefting as Diabolical, doth
command all that are guilty thereof to be feverely punifhed by the Prelate, and all Vicars not to
permit any fuch Offenders to enter into the
Church, nor to give them the *Cafture*, and no
Priefts to go to their Houfes, and they fhall be
compell'd to deliver all fuch Notes to their Vicars to be torn, and all that have ufed any of
them, tho' they fhould never do it more, fhall
be punifhed for the fpace of fix months with the
faid Penalties.

Decree

Decree IX.

THe *Onzena,* or practice of Usury, is a grievous Sin in the sight of God, and is very
much condemned in the Scriptures, Christ commanding us *to lend to others , hoping for nothing again* , and the Synod being very much
troubled to find the greatest part of the Christians of this Diocess entangled therein, through
their ignorance of what gains are lawful, and
what are not, and of what may be kept, and what
ought to be restored, doth therefore admonish
in the Lord, all Faithful Christians to consult
the Learned about these Matters, giving them
an account of all their Contracts, in order to
their being rightly instructed as to what they
may lawfully take for Money they have lent out.
And the Synod doth furthermore declare, that
according to the best Information it has received, the Interest of Money in *Malabar* is Ten *per
Cent.* and whatever is taken more, if the Principal runs no * risk is *Onzena,* or Usury, and as

---

* **Risk.**] Most *Convents* in
trading Cities lend out Money at
6 or 7 *per Cent.* and take as much
care to secure their Principal, as
any Usurer whatsoever, so that
the distinction of *Lucrum Cessans,*
and *Damnum emergens* will either
justifie a legal Interest in general, or it will not justifie what
the lending *Convents* do. But
tho' this Decree falls in exactly
with the common practice of the
Church of *Rome,* the Monks and
Friars not excepted, yet it plainly contradicts the Doctrine of
that Church, which is, that all
sort of Usury is a Mortal Sin ; for
if the taking of 10 *per Cent.* for
Money, and that where the principal runs no risk, is not Usury, it
will be hard to tell what is.

to the Ten they shall likewise consult the Learned, to whom they shall declare how Money may be improved in the place where it is lent, that so they may be able to tell them, whether it be lawful for them to take so much, for it may happen that in some places, there will not be so much to be got by the Negotiating of Money, which must make such an high interest to be there unlawful, and whosoever shall take more than Ten *per Cent.* if his Principal runs no risk, after having been three times admonished by the Prelate or Vicar without Amendment shall be declared Excommunicate, and shall not be absolved until he has dissolved the said Contract.

Decree X.

THe Synod doth condemn the taking of One *per Cent.* by the month, where the Principal runs no risk, being secured by a pledge, and of Two *per Cent.* by the Month, if the one is not payed punctually, such Contracts being very unjust and manifest *Onzena*, or Usury; so that neither the want of a pledge, nor any thing else can justifie the taking of Two *per Cent.* by the month, if the Principal is not in danger, all which Contracts the Synod doth prohibit, and the Vicars to give their consent to any such, and where they are made to dissolve them, compelling all that are faulty therein by Penalties and Censures if it shall be found necessary : The Synod doth furthermore condemn their calling all Gain arising

sing from Money, *Onzena*, becaufe it gives occasion for fome to imagine that all fuch Gain is unlawful, and notwithftanding fuch Gain is lawful, and may be juftly taken in feveral Cafes, to fcruple the taking any.

Decree XI.

WHereas there are great numbers of Chriftians who for want of having the Fear of God and the Church before their Eyes, do cohabit publickly with Concubines, to the great fcandal of Chriftianity ; the Vicars fhall therefore with great Charity admonifh all fuch Offenders, three times declaring to them, That if they do not reform, they muft declare them Excommunicate, and if after fo many Admonitions they do not turn away their Concubines, they muft be Excommunicated until they are effectually parted, and be punifhed with other Penalties at the pleafure of the Prelate, according to the time that they have lived in that Sin , and when it fhall fo happen that their Concubines are their Slaves, they fhall conftrain them not only to turn them out of their Houfes, but to fend them out of the Country where they live, that there may be no more danger of their relapfing, which fhall be likewife obferved as to all other Women where there is the fame danger.

Decree

Decree XII.

THe Synod doth very earneſtly recommend it to all Maſters and Fathers of Families, to be very watchful over the Lives and Manners of their Slaves and Servants, and the rather for having been informed, that moſt of the Black Women belonging to Chriſtians in this Biſhoprick, do lead very ill Lives in being publick Whores, and known to be ſuch by their Maſters, never going to *Maſs* or *Confeſſion*, and being totally ignorant of the Chriſtian Religion, their Maſters taking no care to have them inſtructed therein, or of the good of their Souls, notwithſtanding the Obligation they are under of doing it, St. *Paul* having told us, that *he that does not take care of his Family, is worſe than an Infidel.* Wherefore the Synod doth very much recommend it to the Vicars of Churches to be very watchful over, and to make diligent Inquiry into the Lives of the Slaves that are in their Pariſhes, and as they ſhall ſee occaſion to exhort their Maſters, and oblige them not to ſuffer their Slaves to live in a ſinful State.

Decree XIII.

WHereas ſeveral poor wretched Chriſtians following the Cuſtom of the Heathen among whom they live, when they find themſelves pinched with any want, do, contrary to all right and
reaſon,

reafon, fell their Children : Wherefore the Synod doth in Virtue of Obedience, and upon pain of the greater Excommunication, prohibit all Chriftians to fell their Children, or any of their Kindred, no not to other Chriftians, and doth under the fame Precept and cenfure forbid all Chriftians to buy any fuch, or to keep them as Slaves, except when they fee Parents fo far defpife this prohibition, as to be ready to fell their Children to Infidels, in which cafe they may buy them to keep the Chriftian Children from coming under the power of Heathens, whom neverthelefs they fhall not keep as Slaves, but fhall forthwith fignifie what they have done, to the Prelate, that he may take fuch courfe therein, that the Buyer may have his Money, and the Child its liberty, and the Seller may be punifhed : all that fhall buy fuch Children in any other cafe, as well as thofe that fell them, fhall be held Excommunicate until they have effectually diffolved all fuch Bargains ; and if the Child do happen to be made an Infidel, he that fold it fhall not be abfolved until he has ranfomed the faid Child, or at leaft until the Vicar and People are fatisfied of his having done all that he is able to have redeemed it, and the Synod doth furthermore recommend it to the Vicars and Curates of Churches, and to all Chriftian People, that whenever any fuch thing happens, they do all that is in their power to recover fuch Children, and to ranfom them whatever it coft, by contributing Money towards it, and by complaining thereof

to

to their Kings, and advising the Prelate of it, leaving no means untried to rescue such Children, that so they may not be bred up Infidels.

Decree XIV.

THe Synod doth approve of the laudable Custom of this Diocess of Mens giving the Tenth part of their Wives Portion when they are Married, to the Church; as also of that of making a repartition of the said Alms betwixt the Fabrick of the Church and the Priests thereof; and whereas this Custom does not obtain all over the Diocess, and especially in the *Southern* Parts, the Synod doth intreat and command all People to conform themselves to the same, and willeth that the People among whom this Custom is not as yet introduced, may be obliged to it by their Procurators, there being no reason, since it is observed in the greater part of this Diocess, why it should not be established all over it.

Decree XV.

WHereas by the ancient Custom consented to by the Infidel Kings of *Malabar*, the whole Government of the Christians of this Bishoprick, not only in Spirituals but in Temporals also, is devolved to the Church and the Bishop thereof, who is to determine all differences that are among Christians, and that some dreading the Justice and Judgment of the Prelate in their Con-

Controverfies, do without any fear of God, carry them before Infidel Kings and their Judges, who are eafily bribed to do as they would have them, to the great prejudice of Chriftianity; the faid Kings taking occafion from thence to intrude themfelves into the Affairs of Chriftians, by which means, befides that they do not under-ftand fuch Matters, being Tyrants and Idolaters, they become very grievous and vexatious to Chriftians; for the avoiding of which, and feve-ral other mifchiefs arifing from thence to Chri-ftianity, the Synod doth ftri&ly command all the Chriftians of this Diocefs, not upon any pretence whatfoever, to prefume to carry any of their Caufes before Infidel Kings or their Judges, with-out exprefs Licence from the Prelate; which, whenfoever it fhall be judged necefiary, fhall be granted to them as fhall be thought fit in the Lord; but all Caufes fhall be firft carried before the Prelate, that he may judge or compofe them according to Reafon and Juftice; and all that fhall do otherwife, fhall be feverely punifhed for the fame, at the pleafure of the Prelate, and be thrown out of the Church for fo long time as he fhall think fit.

Decree XVI.

WHereas the Chriftians of this Bifhoprick are fubje& to Kings and Lords that are Infidels, by whom they are many times obliged to handle Bars of hot Iron, or to thruft their

Hand

Hand into boyling Oil, or to fwim thorow Rivers that are full of Snakes; reckoning, that if they are Innocent, none of thofe things can hurt them, but will certainly, if guilty of what they are accufed : And feeing there are not wanting, fome ill-minded Chriftians, who finding themfelves unjuftly accufed, do voluntarily offer themfelves to undergo the faid *Ordeals* for the manifeftation of their Innocency ; and notwithftanding that it is true that God has fometimes concurr'd with Peoples Innocency and Simplicity in fuch Cafes, by not fuffering them to be hurt by fuch things; neverthelefs fince for any to offer themfelves to undergo fuch *Ordeals*, is to tempt God, and to pretend to work a Miracle, which is not lawful, and may fometimes fo fucceed, as to be a great affront to our Catholick Faith ; therefore the Synod doth prohibit all Chriftians to prefume to offer themfelves to undergo any fuch *Ordeals*, knowing that they fin mortally in fo doing, in being guilty therein of tempting God ; commanding all that fhall tranfgrefs therein, to be feverely punifhed. And when it fhall happen that any fuch *Ordeals* fhall be fo impofed upon them by their Infidel Princes, that there is no avoiding it, in fuch Cafes they fhall fubmit themfelves to the Will of God, as to the Injuftices and Violences laid upon them by Infidel Tyrants ; and in cafe of any Oath being tendred to them by Infidels, wherein they muft fwear by their *Pagods*, they muft know that they ought rather to fuffer death, than take any fuch Oath,

the

the taking of an Oath being an act of Worſhip
and Veneration, that is due to God alone: Neither ſhall Chriſtians uſe any *Ordeals* among themſelves, or Oaths, but ſuch as were in uſe in the
Church, the foreſaid Oaths being what Chriſtians
ought to dread more than all the Torments of
the World.

Decree XVII.

WHereas the diſtinction of the Faithful from
Unbelievers, even by outward ſigns and
habits, is a thing which has always been endeavoured, that ſo the one may be known and divided from the other; therefore the Synod having obſerved that there is no diſtinction neither
in their Habits nor in their Hair, nor in any
thing elſe, betwixt the Chriſtians of this Dioceſs
and the Heathen *Naires*, doth command, that
henceforward no Chriſtian do preſume to bore
their Ears, or to do any thing to make them
large, except Women, among whom it is an
Univerſal Ornament; and whoſoever ſhall tranſgreſs herein, ſhall be puniſhed at the pleaſure of
the Prelate, who ſhall not ſuffer them to wear
an Ornament of Gold or of any thing elſe in
their Ears; and whoſover ſhall preſume to wear
any ſuch Ornament, ſhall be thrown out of the
Church, neither ſhall the *Caſture* be given them until ſuch time as they are brought to yield effectual
Obedience, and to leave off all ſuch Ornaments;
but as for thoſe whoſe Ears are bored already,

if

if they are not Children, they may wear what they pleaſe, or what they have accuſtomed themſelves to.

Decree XVIII.

THe Synod being deſirous to rectifie whatever is amiſs in this Dioceſs, and ſo far as it is poſſible, to reform all evil Cuſtoms ; and having obſerved the great Debauchery of many, and eſpecially of the poorer ſort, in drinking *Orraca*, from whence do follow many Diſaſters, Murders, and Wounds ; wherefore in order to the preventing ſuch Miſchiefs ſo far as is poſſible, the Synod doth prohibit the ſelling of *Orraca* in any Chriſtian Inn, neither ſhall Chriſtians Trade in that Commodity upon pain of being puniſhed at the pleaſure of the Prelate, by which means not only Diſorders, but the great Communication the Faithful hath with the Heathen in ſuch Inns, will alſo be prevented.

Decree XIX.

WHereas it is a manifeſt Injuſtice to have diverſe Weights in the ſame Country, the Synod being informed, that in many Markets of this Biſhoprick every one ſells with what Weights they pleaſe, doth command, That there be but one Weight for the ſame Merchandize in a Market and all the Shops thereof, and that it be the uſual Weight of the place ; to which all that do

not

not yield Obedience, ſhall be admoniſhed by the
Vicars, and if they do not reform thereupon, ſhall
chaſtiſed at the pleaſure of the Prelate, who
ſhall conſtrain them to the ſame by Penalties and
Cenſures, if they ſhall be found neceſſary; there
being no other Government among the Chriſtians of this Dioceſs but that of the Church, nor
no other coercive Power but that of Cenſures.

Decree XX.

WHereas an unreaſonable Cuſtom has obtained in this Dioceſs, *viz.* That Males only
inherit their Fathers Goods, the Females having
no ſhare at all thereof; and that not only when
there are Sons, but when there are Daughters
only, and they unmarried, and many times Infants, by which means great numbers of them
periſh, and others ruin themſelves for want of
neceſſaries, the Fathers Goods falling to the
Males that are next in Blood, tho' never ſo remote or collateral, there being no regard had
to Daughters no more than if their Parents
were under no obligation to provide for them;
all which being very unreaſonable, and contrary
to the natural right that Sons and Daughters
have to ſucceed, to the good of their Parents;
the Kindred who have thus poſſeſſed themſelves
of ſuch Goods, are bound to reſtore them to
the Daughters as the lawful Heireſſes to them;
wherefore the Synod doth decree and declare
this Cuſtom to be Unjuſt, and that the next

D d 4.　　　　　a-kin

a-kin can have no right when there are Daughters to inherit their Father's Estate; and being possessed of such Estates, are bound in conscience to restore them; neither is it lawful for the Males to divide the Estate among them, without giving any equal Portion to the Females; or if they have not done it already, they stand indebted for their Portions; or if the Father has disposed of the third part of his Estate by Will, the remaining two parts shall be equally divided betwixt the Sons and the Daughters, the Portions that have been received by those that are married being discounted; all which the Synod doth command to be observed, intreating and commanding all the Christians of the Diocess to receive this Decree as a Law, and observe it intirely, it being laid as a duty upon their Consciences; and if any shall act otherwise, and being a Kinsman, shall seize upon the Goods belonging to Daughters; or being a Son, shall deny to give Portions to his Sisters, or being in possession of the said Goods, shall refuse to make restitution; the Prelate, if it cannot be done otherwise, shall compell them to it by Penalties and Censures, declaring them Excommunicate, without any hope of Absolution, until such time as they shall pay an effectual Obedience, and shall make restitution.

Decree

Decree XXI.

THe Adoption of Sons is not lawful, but in defect of natural Children; which not being underſtood by the Chriſtians of this Biſhoprick through their ignorance of the Law, they do commonly Adopt the Children of their Slaves born in their Houſes, or of other People, diſinheriting their lawfully begotten Children, ſometimes upon the account of ſome differences they have had with them, and ſometimes only for the affection they have to Strangers, all which is contrary to Law and Reaſon, and is a manifeſt injuſtice and wrong done to their legitimate Children; wherefore the Synod doth declare, that the ſaid Adoptions muſt not be practiſed where there are natural Children, and being done are void, ſo that the Perſons thus Adopted are not capable of inheriting any thing, except what may be left them by way of Legacy, which muſt not exceed the third of the Eſtate; no, not tho' the Adoption was made before there were any Legitimate Children to inherit. The Synod doth furthermore declare, That the Adoptions which have been made before the celebration of this Synod, where there are Children, and the Adopted are not in actual poſſeſſion of the Eſtate, are void, neither ſhall the Adopted have any ſhare thereof, or having had any, ſhall be obliged to reſtore it, to which if it be found neceſſary, the Prelate ſhall compell them by Pen-
nalties

nalties and Cenfures; but as to thofe who by
virtue of fuch Adoptions, have for a long time
been in quiet poffeffion of Eftates, the Synod
by this Decree does not intend to difpoffefs
them thereof, by reafon of the great difturbance
and confufion the doing fo would make in this
Diocefs, which is what this Synod pretends to
hinder, leaving every one however in fuch Cafes,
at liberty to take their remedy at Law.

Decree XXII.

WHereas the way of Adopting by ancient
Cuftom in this Diocefs, is to carry the
Parties that are to be Adopted before the Bifhop
or Prelate, with certain Teftimonials, before
whom they declare, that they take fuch a one
for their Son, whereupon the Bifhop paffeth an
Olla or Certificate, and fo the Adoption is perfected; the Synod doth command, That from
henceforward, the Prelate do not accept of an
Adoption from any that have Children of their
own; or in cafe they have none, yet it fhall
be declared in the *Olla*, That if they fhall
afterwards happen to have any, that the faid
Olla fhall be void to all intents and purpofes;
by which means the great Injuftices that
are now fo common in this Diocefs will be
prevented.

Decree

Decree XXIII.

THe Synod being defirous to have all the
Chriftians of this Diocefs to live together
in Villages, by reafon of the great inconveniencies they are under that live in the *Heaths*,
as well by reafon of the great communication
they muft have with Infidels, as for wanting
opportunities of going to Church, and Sacraments, whereby they are kept in ignorance of
Chriftianity, doth in order thereunto very earneftly recommend it to all Chriftians that live
in *Heaths*, to do all they are able, either to
come and live in fome Village, or to build new
Villages with Churches, that fo they may live
more civilly, and be feparated from the communication of Infidels, and be the better inftructed in the Cuftoms of our Holy Catholick
Faith, recommending it earneftly to the Vicars
to perfuade their Sheep thereunto, for the Spiritual profit they will receive thereby: which
the Prelate fhall alfo endeavour with all his
power.

Decree XXIV.

THe Synod having taken into confideration
the manifold Injuftices, Oppreffions and
Grievances wherewith Infidel Kings and Governours do often treat the Chriftians of this Bifhoprick; and that out of enmity to our Holy
Catholick Faith, and obferving the neceffity they
are

are in of Defence and Protection, doth with great inftance defire, That his Majefty the King of *Portugal* would be gracioufly pleafed to take all the Chriftians of this Bifhoprick under his Favour and * Protection , he being the only Chriftian King or Lord in all thefe Oriental Parts ; and the Chriftians of this Diocefs fhall on their

* **Protection.**] By this we fee, the King of *Cochim* was not jealous without reafon, that the Arch-Bifhop had a State defign in the great pains and charge he was at in the reduction of his Chriftian Subjects; and tho' nothing was talked of but the *Pope*, and the *Roman* Obedience, that the King of *Spain*, and the augmentation of his ftrength in the *Indies* by the acceffion of fo many new Subjects, was the main Spring in the Enterprize. I will not fay, tho' it is probable enough, that the Arch-Bifhop by magnifying this Service at the Court of *Spain*, got firft to be Governour of the *Indies*, and afterwards to be Governour of all the Dominions of *Portugal*, and Prefident of the Council of State at *Madrid*; but this we are fure of, that that Service to the Crown of *Spain* was much boafted of here in *Europe* by others. For the Jefuit *Ilayus* in his Book *De Rebus Japonicis*, fpeaking of this very thing, faith, *Cuæ res quanto Regiæ Majeftati emolumento fit latura, nôrunt qui non ignorant, quanti fit momenti, gentem in tota India lectiffimam, à temporibus B. Thomæ Chriftiano cultui deditum, támque numerofum &*

potentem, ut armatos ad Triginta Millia in promptu habeat cum Lufitanis unire, ad Ecclefiæ Romanæ obedientiam revocare, & in Fidem. ditionemque Regis Catholici accipere.

But as it is vifible that the increafing of the *Portugueze* ftrength in the *Indies*, by the acceffion of fo many new Subjects, was what both the Arch-Bifhop and *Spanifh* Government aimed at chiefly in the troublefome and chargeable reduction of this Church : So it is certain, that from this very Year 1599, the *Portugueze* Hiftorians do begin to reckon the declination of their ftrength in thofe parts; who give the following Account of the three Ages of their *Indian* Government ; that it was in its Infancy till the Year 1561, and from that time till the Year 1600, in its Manhood or full ftrength, and ever fince has been in its Old declining Age, and is now in truth become fo decrepid, as to be only the Ghoft of a great Name. Neither is this to be wondred at, confidering how common a thing it is for God to blaft the moft promifing Securities, when obtained by fuch violent and unlawful Methods,

parts be ready at all times to facrifice their Lives
to their Holy Catholick Faith, the prefervation
of Chriftianity , and the defence of Chriftians,
which they fhall be always prepared to do with
their Lives and Fortunes ; befeeching the moft
Reverend *Metropolitan*, Prefident of this Synod,
to prefent this their Petition to his Majefty, and
to let him know how ready all the Chriftians
of this Bifhoprick are to ferve him.

Decree XXV.

WHereas in this Synod ,Matters pertaining to
our Holy Catholick Faith,the Holy Sacraments of the Church, the Reformation of Affairs
thereof, and the Cuftoms of Chriftian People
have been handled ; the Synod doth command
all Vicars of Churches not to fail to have all its
Decrees Tranfcribed from the Original *Malabar*,
and to have a Copy thereof in all their Churches,
Signed by the Reverend the Arch-Deacon of
this Diocefs, and the Rector of the College of
Vaipicotta, and upon every *Sunday* and *Holy-day*,
when there is no Sermon nor no Lecture upon
the *Catechifm* fet forth by the moft Reverend
Metropolitan , that a portion of this Synod be
read to the People ; but on the Seafons when
the faid *Catechifm* is ordered to be read, it fhall
be read on *Sundays*, and the Synod upon *Holy-
days*, that fo all that is decreed therein may
come to the knowledge of the People, and may
be remembred and obferved by them ; the Original

ginal of the said Synod being Signed by the
moſt Reverend *Metropolitan* and all the other
Members thereof, ſhall be put in the *Archives*
of the *Jeſuites* College of *Vaipicotta* in this Dioceſs, from whence ſo many Copies as ſhall be
thought neceſſary, ſhall be tranſmitted to the
Churches; there ſhall alſo be another Original
Signed by the moſt Reverend *Metropolitan*, the
Arch-Deacon, and other Members, kept in the
Archives of the Church of *Angamale*, called the
Arch-Biſhop's *See*, that all Copies may at all
times be Corrected according to either of thoſe
Originals; and the Synod doth furthermore recommend it to all Vicars, Prieſts, and Curates,
and to all and every Chriſtian of this Dioceſs,
and commands them all in the Lord to conform
themſelves to the Decrees of this *Dioceſan* Synod,
and ſo far as is in their power, to obſerve and
cauſe them to be obſerved inviolably, and to
govern themſelves by them in all things; which
the Synod is confident they will do with the
help of *God the Father, Son, and Holy Ghoſt,
who liveth and reigneth for ever : Amen.*

After the Decrees were read, the Biſhoprick
was divided into Seventy-five Pariſhes, whoſe
Bounds were greater or leſſer as was judged to
be moſt convenient for the adminiſtration of
the Holy Sacraments, and the Spiritual Food of
the Faithful; Vicars were alſo nominated to
them all, and the Churches that were not able
to maintain a Vicar were united: The Vicars
after they were named, were brought in one
　　　　　　　　　　　　　　　　　　　by

by one to kiſs the *Metropolitan*'s Hand, who at
the ſame time gave them their Collation, declaring to them the greatneſs of their Authority,
and of the Obligations of their Office, and commanding the People to acknowledge them as
their Pariſh-Prieſts and the Shepherds of their
Souls. After they had all, one after another, performed this Ceremony, they were admoniſhed
all together in the preſence of the People by
the moſt Reverend *Metropolitan,* to comply with
the Obligations of their Function, and being all
upon their Knees before him, he delivered the
following Charge to them.

' Venerable and beloved Brethren, and fel-
' low Prieſts, and particular Paſtors of the Faith-
' ful, We let you all to underſtand, that we, tho'
' unworthy of it, are in the place of *Aaron,* and
' ye of *Eleazar* and *Ehitaman,* the lower Prieſts;
' we are in the place of the *Apoſtles* of our Lord
' Chriſt, ye in that of the Seventy-two *Diſciples*;
' we are to give a ſtrict Account of you at the
' tremendous Day of Judgment, you of the
' People that are now committed to you : Now
' that we may be all found good and faithful
' Stewards in our Maſter's Houſe, we do admo-
' niſh and beſeech you , beloved Brethren in
' Chriſt, to remember what we are about to ſay
' unto you, and which is of moſt importance,
' be ſure to obſerve it and put it in execution. In
' the firſt place we do admoniſh and beſeech you
' in the Lord, to have your Life and Conver-
' ſations unblamable, yielding the ſavour of a
                                             ' good

'good Name, and Example to the People of
'God, in suffering no Women, and especially
'those of which the World may entertain any
'suspicion, tho' Slaves, to live in your Houses;
'neither are you to converse with any of the
'Sex; you must not fail to rise every Night to
'recite the Divine Office in the Church, which
'must be performed at some certain hour; and
'after that is done, none of you must say *Mass*
'otherwise than Fasting, and after Midnight for-
'ward, and in the Holy Habits, which must al-
'ways be kept clean, ye shall receive the Body
'and Blood of our Lord Jesus Christ, with all
'Reverence and Humility, confessing your Sins
'to some approved Confessor, with great con-
'trition and sorrow for them, but especially if
'your Consciences do check you for any fault
'you have committed. The *Corporal* and *Palls*
'must be made of Linen, neither can they with-
'out an Apostolical dispensation, be made of
'any other Cloth, and must be always kept clean.
'The Holy Vessels you are always to wash with
'your own hands, and that in other clean Vessels
'dedicated to that use; putting the Water where-
'in they were washed, either into the Font or
'into some Cistern dug for the purpose in the
'Church-yard, and drying them with all dili-
'gence. The Altar must be covered with clean
'Towels, of which at the time of Celebration,
'there must be at least three with a *Corporal*,
'neither must any thing besides Reliques or Sacred
'things belonging to the Altar be laid upon it.
'The

' The Missals, Breviaries, and Prayer-Books, must
' be perfect and entire: Your Churches must be
' well covered, and both the Walls and Pave-
' ments must be kept clean. In the Sacristy, or
' somewhere near to the High Altar, there must be a
' place to hold Water, wherein the Corporals and
' Holy Vessels are to be washed, as also the Hands of
' those that have touched any of the Holy Oils;
' and in the Sacristy there must be a Vessel with
' clean Water for the Priests and others that
' have ministred at the Altar, to wash their
' Hands, and a clean Towel to dry them; the
' Gates and Porches of the Churches must be
' strong and well shut. None of you shall take
' the cure of a Church upon you without the
' Prelate's knowledge and order, notwithstanding
' you should be called to it by the People;
' neither shall any of you leave the Churches you
' have a Title to, nor be translated to another
' Church without his Order. None shall pre-
' sume to hold more than one Church, contrary
' to the disposition of the Holy Canons. The
' Jurisdiction of no Church shall be divided a-
' mong many, but every Church shall have its
' own Parish-Priest and Pastor. None shall Ce-
' lebrate any where but in a Church, or with any
' sort of Arms. None shall give the Holy Sa-
' crament to any of another Parish, without leave
' from their Parish-Priest. In the celebration of
' the *Mass* ye shall all observe the same Ceremo-
' nies, that there may be no Confusion nor Scandal.
' The Chalice or Patten must be of Gold, Silver,

E e   ' Brass

'Brafs or Tinn, and not of Iron, Glafs, Copper,
' or Wood. The Parifh and other Priefts muft
' vifit and comfort the Sick in their Parifhes,
' Confeffing them and giving them the moft Holy
' Sacrament of the Altar, and the Holy Unction,
' with their own hands, admonifhing the Sick
' when they vifit them to defire thofe Sacraments,
' when they fhall judge them neceffary. None
' fhall take any Fee for baptizing or for the ad-
' miniftring of any Sacrament, or for burying the
' Dead. No Child fhall die without *Baptifm*
' through your negligence, nor no fick Perfon
' without *Confeffion*, and the Holy *Communion*.
' None of you fhall Drink to excefs, or be noted
' for the fame, or for being quarrelfom ; None
' of you muft bear Arms, nor eat and drink in
' Taverns and Inns. Ye fhall not eat with an
' *Infidel, Mahometan, Jew*, or *Heathen* ; neither
' fhall you imploy your felf in Hawking, Hun-
' ting, or Shooting. What you know of the
' Gofpel of Chrift, of the Holy Scriptures, and
' of good Examples join'd with pure Catholick
' Doctrine, ye fhall deliver to the People on the
' *Lord's-day* and Holy-days, preaching the word
' of God, to the edification of your Flocks. You
' muft take care of the Poor, and of Strangers
' and Widows, of the Sick and the Orphans of
' your feveral Parifhes. You muft be fure to keep
' Hofpitality, inviting Strangers to your Tables,
' therein giving good Example to others. Up-
' on every *Lord's-day* before *Mafs* ye fhall Blefs
' the Water with Salt in the Church, with which
                                                    ' you

' you are to sprinkle the People, taking it out
' of a Vessel or Pot made for that purpose. Ye
' shall not pawn any Sacred Vessels or Ornaments
' of the Church, neither to Heathen nor Christi-
' an. Ye shall not take Usury, nor engage your
' selves in Contracts or Farms, nor in any Secular
' publick Office; ye shall not alienate the Goods
' which ye have acquired after ye were in Orders,
' because they belong to the Church; neither
' shall ye sell or change any thing belonging to
' the Church. In Churches where there are Bap-
' tismal Fonts, they shall always be kept clean,
' and where there are none, ye shall have a par-
' ticular Vessel for Baptism, which shall be put
' to no other use, and shall be kept in some de-
' cent place in the Church or Sacristy. Ye shall
' teach your Parishioners, and especially the Chil-
' dren, the *Articles of the Creed,* the *Pater Noster,*
' the Commandments of the Law of God and
' of Holy Mother Church , the Fasts of the
' four Seasons , and the Vigils. And before
' *Lent* ye shall call upon your People to
' Confess, and shall hear their Confessions with
' great charity and zeal, for their Spiritual profit.
' Upon the Feasts of the *Nativity, Easter,* and
' *Whitsuntide,* ye shall exhort all the Faithful to re-
' ceive the most Holy Sacrament of Christ's Body,
' and at *Easter* at least ye shall take heed that all
' that are capable do receive it. All quarrels, diffe-
' rences and enmities that shall arise among your
' Subjects , ye shall endeavour to compose and
' oblige them all to live as Friends in Christian

'Charity; and if there be any that give offence by
'refusing to speak to their Neighbours, being in
'malice with them, ye shall admonish them there-
'of, and so long as they continue to behave them-
'selves so, ye shall not suffer them to receive the
'Holy Sacrament of the Altar. At certain times,
'but chiefly upon solemn Festivities and Fasts, ye
'shall admonish Married Men, according to a
'Holy Council, to abstain from their Wives.
'None of you shall wear coloured Cloaths, or
'any Habit but what is grave and decent for
'Priests to wear. Ye shall instruct your People
'to forbear Working on *Sundays* and *Holy-days*;
'neither shall ye suffer Women to Sing or Dance
'in the Church. Ye shall not communicate with
'any that are Excommunicate, nor presume so
'much as to Celebrate where any such are pre-
'sent. Ye shall admonish your People not to
'Marry with any that are contracted to others,
'nor with their near Kinswomen, nor with any
'they have stole out of their Fathers Houses;
'neither shall ye suffer the solemnities of Mar-
'riage, and of carrying home a Bride, to be at
'a time prohibited by the Church. Ye shall
'constrain Shepherds and other Servants to hear
'*Mass* at least every *Lord's-day*, and shall ad-
'monish God-fathers and God mothers to teach
'their God-children the *Creed* and *Pater Noster*,
'or to appoint others to instruct them. The
'*Chrism* or Holy Oil of the *Catechumeni*, and Sick,
'shall be kept in the Church under Lock and Key,
'and in a decent and secure place, of which ye
                                                    'shall

' shall give none away, no not by way of Alms,
' it being a moft grievous Sacrilege to do it.
' Every one of you muft have a Catechifm, an
' Expofition of the Creed, and of the Prayers
' of the Church, conformable to the Expofition
' of the Holy Catholick Doctors, by which ye
' may both edifie your felves and others. Ye
' muft alfo have this Synod, that fo you may go-
' vern both your felves and your People by its
' Rules. Ye fhall declare the Catholick Faith
' to all that will learn it. The *Introitus* to the
' *Mafs*, the *Prayers, Epiftles, Gofpels,* and *Creed*
' in the *Mafs*, fhall be read with a loud and
' intelligible Voice; but the *Secret Prayers* of the
' *Canon* and *Confecration*, fhall be fpoke flowly
' and diftinctly, but with a low Voice: When
' ye recite in the Quire, ye muft let one Verfe
' be ended before ye begin another, and not
' confound the Service by chopping it up and
' jumbling it together. Ye muft ftudy to have
' St. *Athanafius's* Creed, which contains the Ca-
' tholick Faith, by heart, and repeat it dayly:
' The *Exorcifms*, Prayers, the order of Baptifm,
' Unction of the Sick, the recommendation of
' the Soul, and the burial of the Dead, ye muft
' underftand and practife, according to the Holy
' Canons, and the ufe of the Holy *Roman* Church,
' the Mother and Miftrefs of all the other Churches
' in the World; as alfo the Exorcifms, and the
' confecration of Salt and Water. Ye fhall ftudy
' to underftand Singing, and the things that are
' Chanted in the Church, as alfo the *Rubricks*

' of

' of the *Breviary* and *Missal,* that ye may be able
' to find what you look for; as also the Account
' of the Moveable Feasts, and of *Easter;* in which,
' that you may not be mistaken, ye must be sure
' to have the *Martyrology* of the Saints in all your
' Churches, which we will take care to have
' translated into *Syrian.* All which ye shall ob-
' serve, that so by these and your other good
' Works, ye may, by the help of God, bring
' both your selves and your People to that Glo-
' ry which shall endure for ever, and be bestow-
' ed on you through the Grace of our Lord Jesus
' Christ, who with the Father and the Holy Spirit,
' liveth and reigneth for ever and ever: *Amen.*

The Speech and Admonition to the Vicars and
Priests being ended, the most Reverend *Metro-*
politan commanded them all to Sign the Original Decrees of the Synod, translated into *Mala-*
bar, desiring them, if they had the least scruple
concerning any thing commanded or declared in
the Synod, those excepted that have been decreed and decided already, that they would
signifie them openly before they Subscribed, that
there might be no doubt or controversie about
any thing hereafter: So after several Doubts
had been considered and satisfied, they did all
unanimously Subscribe to the Synod.

Then the Books of the Synod were delivered
to the most Reverend *Metropolitan,* who being
in his *Pontificals,* and seated on his Throne
with a Mitre on his Head, Subscribed the said
Decrees;

Decrees; which being done, a Table was set in
the middle of the chief Chappel, and the Decrees being laid upon it, all that were called
to the Synod, as well Ecclesiasticks as Secular Procurators, Signed and Subscribed them with their
own hands before the whole Synod and People.
The Synod consisted of 813, *viz.* 133 Priests,
besides Deacons and Sub-Deacons, and others
of the Clergy, and 660 Procurators of the People, and other principal Men of the Laity, besides
the Inhabitants of the Town of *Diamper*, where
the Synod was held, and of several other neighbouring Villages; there were likewise present
a great number of *Portuguezes*, who came along
with *Don Antonio De Neronha*, Governour of
Cochim, who together with all the other Magistrates of the City, assisted at the Synod.

The Decrees being Signed, the most Reverend
Metropolitan rose up, and having taken off his
Mitre, kneeled down before the High Altar, and
begun the *Te Deum*, with which, to the great
joy of all that were present, a solemn Procession
round the Church was begun, the Quire singing
that and some other Psalms, the *Latines* in *Latin*,
and the *Native* Priests in *Chaldee*, and the People
their Festivity in *Malabar*: proceeding to praise
God with abundance of tears and joy, in three
Tongues in the Unity of the Faith, and Good-
will among them all, for having at last obtained
that, which they had so long desired of Almighty
God, *Three Persons, and One Nature, the Father,
the Son, and the Holy Ghost, who liveth and reigneth
for ever: Amen.*   E e 4   After

After the Procession was over, the most Reverend *Metropolitan* going to the High Altar, read the Prayer *Exaudi quæsumus, Domine*, as it is in the *Pontifical*; which being ended, he seated himself upon his Throne with the Mitre on his Head, and his Pastoral Staff in his Hand, and directing his Discourse to the People said, *I give many thanks to Almighty God the Author of all good things, for this great favour he has vouchsafed to me and you, and all the faithful People of this Bishoprick, in permitting us to celebrate this Synod maugre all the impediments which Satan the enemy of Souls, had created to obstruct it, by stirring up Contentions and Debates on purpose to separate this Christianity from the Union of the Catholick Church, and to keep them in their old Errors, as you all very well know. I do also give many thanks to God, for his having been pleased to order Matters so, that this whole Affair should end with so much Joy, Peace and Concord, as you all see it does, and so much to the sorrow of Infidel and Idolatrous Kings, and of all the other Enemies of our Holy Catholick Faith. I do also thank you my most dear Brethren and fellow Priests and Coadjutors, and you my beloved Sons the Procurators of the People, and all the other principal Persons who have been present at this Synod, that not regarding the troubles of the Ways and Times, nor the displeasure of the Kings to whom you are subject; you have, as true Christians desirous of Salvation, over-looked all those Inconveniencies, and obeyed our Precept in assembling your selves together to treat about the good*

of

of your Souls, *for which God will reward you with Eternal Life*, *if you persevere in the purity of the Faith you have here profest*, *and which you have been taught by this Synod*, *and shall conform your Lives and Manners to its Decrees. I trust in the Lord that he will carry you back safe to your Houses*, *and bless you and your Families and Posterity for ever* 5 *which God of his infinite Grace and Mercy grant. Amen.*

This Difcourfe being ended, the moft Reverend *Metropolitan* rofe up, and with abundance of tears gave his folemn Bleffing to the People, and after that, the Arch-Deacon with a loud voice faid , *Let us depart in peace* 5 to which the whole Synod anfwered in the name of Chrift, *Amen.* And thus the *Diocefan* Synod ended the 26th of *June*, in the Year 1599, to the Honour and Praife of our Lord Jefus Chrift, *who with the Father and the Holy Spirit*, *liveth and reigneth for ever: Amen.*

The Synod being ended in conformity to what had been ordained therein, there was given to every one of the Vicars that was nominated to any Church by the moft Reverend *Metropolitan*, a Stone Altar, Confecrated by his *Lordfhip* for that purpofe, their former Altars not having been duly Confecrated 5 as alfo a Box with the Veffels of Holy Oils, together with Directions how to ufe them : There was moreover a Book of the Adminiftration of the Sacraments according to the *Roman* ufe , tranflated into *Chaldee* and *Syrian*, given to every Vicar, and

and another which contained the whole Christian Doctrine in the *Malabar* Tongue, for the instruction of Children and others, as also a Surplice to be used in the administration of Sacraments, which was what had never been in use among them; the Churches were also furnished with Corporals, Vestments, Frontals, Cups, and what-ever else was necessary to the Ministry of the Altar, all which were wanting in most Churches; and all the Controversies, whether betwixt Corporations or particular Persons, that were brought before the Synod, were decided by the most Reverend *Metropolitan* and his Assessors, after which they all departed in peace.

The most Reverend *Metropolitan*, as soon as the Synod was ended, begun his Visitation of all the Churches in the Diocess, in order to put the Decrees of the Synod in execution, reciting the principal and most necessary of them in every Church, and delivering the Books, Breviaries, and Missals, as well of the Churches as of particular Persons every where, and burning the Books condemned by the Synod, and correcting others, puting the Vicars in possession of their Churches, who were every where received as such by the People, who settled Revenues upon them; of which, together with what was given them by the most Reverend *Metropolitan*, they made *Ollas*, or Instruments in the Churches, creating four Church-wardens, and opening the Church Boxes, and in a word, ordering whatever was necessary to be done. The Clergy,

who

who had not been prefent at the Synod, made a profeffion of the Faith, the Confeffors were examined, and had Licences given them in writing according to their abilities, and the neceffity of the Church, prohibiting all others to hear Confeffions: Where there was a Font, they alfo Baptized all the Children that they found unchriftened, and had thofe brought in that were in the *Heaths*, where there were many that were Eight and Ten Years old unchriftened. They Confirmed the whole People, and Abfolved all that were Excommunicate; many of which, according to their cuftom, had continued fo for twenty or thirty Years, and efpecially for Murther, for which they never grant Abfolution, no not at the hour of death; the *Metropolitan* preached every day to Chriftians in the Church, and to Infidels (who flocked to fee him) in the Church Porch, treating with them about Baptifm when he came to fay *Ingredimini in Sanctam Dei Ecclefiam*, feveral of which he perfuaded to turn Chriftians, who after having learned their Catechifm, were Baptized by him at other places: He Catechized the Children in the *Malabar* Tongue; and finding there was none of them that underftood their Catechifm, he ordered them to be taught it every day out of Books that were kept in the Church. Finally, where he met with any that were difpofed to Marry, he Married them, and gave Orders about every thing elfe relating to the Synod, which he did in the Form following.

After

After the moſt Reverend *Metropolitan* had been received by the whole People with great Joy and Feſtivity, according to their faſhion, and carried in Proceſſion to the Church, the way as he went being covered with Cloth or Mats, or Boughs of Trees, after the common Ceremony of Bleſſing and Abſolution, the whole People both Men and Women, came with a moſt profound Humility and Reverence to kiſs his Hands, and to yield Obedience to him; he went to Church betimes in the Morning with the whole Clergy and People; where after having Confeſſed himſelf before the High Altar, which he did for the great need there was of having thoſe Chriſtians inſtructed in the Sacrament of Confeſſion, which was in uſe among them but in few places, he ſaid *Maſs*. When *Maſs* was ended, Father *Franciſco Roz*, Maſter of the *Chaldean* and *Syrian* Languages in the *Jeſuites* College at *Vaipicotta*, with the reſt of the Fathers deputed to that Work, and ſome of the moſt learned *Caçanares* aſſembled together in the Sacriſty, or in ſome other place appointed, where in obedience to the Excommunication of the Synod, all the *Syrian* Books were brought before them, as well thoſe that belonged to the Churches, as thoſe belonging to private Perſons; all which were emended, delivering thoſe which were condemned by the Synod to the *Metropolitan*, who burnt them all. The *Metropolitan* having in the mean time put on his *Pontificals*, ſat down and Preached at length to the People, all

all the neceſſary Doctrines of Faith and Manners ; after which Diſcourſe the chief Decrees
of the Synod were publiſhed, and a Proceſſion for the Dead was made round the Church,
to which ſuch vaſt multitudes of Heathens re-
ſorted to ſee the Novelty, and the *Pontifical*
Veſtments, that they filled the Church-yard and
Windows : After the Proceſſion for the Dead
was ended, and the Doctrine of *Purgatory*, and
the benefits of praying for them declared, the
Metropolitan having ſeated himſelf, began a Diſcourſe of the Sacrament of *Confirmation*, according to the neceſſities of the People, and after
that Anointed all that were preſent, then he
Baptized all the Children of Chriſtian Parents
in his *Pontificals*, and ſuch of the adult Heathens as deſired it, who were called together
the day before to that purpoſe. The *Metropolitan* whenever he came to the words *Ingredimini Sanctam Dei Eccleſiam*, beginning a Diſcourſe
to the Heathens and *Naires*, that flocked to ſee
the Ceremony performed, who tho' all Armed
with Bows and Arrows and other Weapons, and
in their own Country remote from the *Portu-
gnezes*, did quietly and chearfully hear all that
he ſaid to them, not only concerning the Faith
of Jeſus Chriſt, but alſo the indignities and hard
words which he beſtowed upon their Idols and
Prieſts in order to undeceive them : When the
Sermon and Baptiſm was over, the Eccleſiaſticks
that were not preſent at the Synod, made a profeſſion of the Faith before the People in the
                                                    hands

hands of the *Metropolitan*, and having called all
the Children together, and ordering them to
kneel round his Chair, he began a *Chamaz*, or set of
Prayers in their own Tongue , which they all
said after him, and having Blessed them all, made
a Discourse to them suitable to their Age, to
the great satisfaction of their Parents, teaching
them the Veneration that is due to the most
sweet Name of *Jesus*, to which, agreeable to the
Nestorian Doctrine wherein they had been educated, they had payed no manner of Respect :
After that he inducted the Vicar in the presence
of the People, charging him with the Flock
which received him for their Pastor, and where
there were any to be Married he Married them ;
great numbers also Confessed themselves to him,
and received the most Holy Sacrament at his
hands, among whom were abundance of Ancient
People, who had never Confessed themselves before : In the Evening the People assembled together and agreed about the Stipend, they determined to settle upon their Vicar, which was
Registred in *Ollas*, that were to be kept in the
Church ; and having opened the Money-Box of
the Church, they distributed such Alms as they
thought necessary. The *Metropolitan* and the
Fathers that were in his Company, having examined the *Caçanares*, to such as he found to be
qualified for it, he granted a Licence in writing to
be Confessors ; after that he heard all the Complaints and Controversies that were among Christians, and having those four principal Men, with the
consent

confent of the Parties, they decided them all
according to the Cuftoms of the Country, and
the Judgment of the *Metropolitan*, fo as to exclude
all farther Procefs or Appeals; he then Abfolved all that were Excommunicate, and feveral
that had lain twenty or thirty Years under that
Cenfure, there being feveral Cafes wherein they
were fo barbarous, as never to grant Abfolution, no not at the hour of Death, injoyning
every one fuch Penances as were fuitable to their
Faults, omitting nothing that he judged neceffary
to the good of the Church and People; in all
which he was accompanied and affifted by five
Jefuites, who were all zealous for the Salvation
of Souls, and well skilled in the *Malabar* Tongue,
and two of them in the *Chaldee* alfo; they were
Father *Hieronymo Cotta*, Father *Jorgye de Crafto*,
Father *Francifco Roz*, who is now the moft worthy Bifhop of that Diocefs, Father *Antonio To-
fcano*, and Brother *John Maria* : Father *Frey Braz
de Santa Maria*, a Divine of the Order of St.
Auftin, was Confeffor to the moft Illuftrious
Metropolitan; there were alfo three Canons of
the *Metropolitan* Church of *Goa*, and the *Metropolitan's* two Chaplains, and feveral *Caçanares*
that were Natives, who celebrated the Divine
Offices both in *Chaldee* and *Syrian*, whom the
moft Illuftrious *Metropolitan* made great ufe of
in feveral Occafions. In the reduction of this
Church to the Catholick Faith, many remarkable
things happened, in which God manifefted how
much that Work was for his Service; and in
the

the Visitation of the Churches there were several Successes of great edification, and that were
much for God's Praise, which shall, God willing,
be written in another place, for his Glory *who
liveth and reigneth for ever. Amen.*

The Letter of *Dom Andre* Bishop of *Cochin*, to the Synod, being Assembled.

BRethren, *in my judgment all you who are called* the Christians *of* St. Thomas, *do owe
much to God, for his having by means of that
Apostle, chose you from among such multitudes of
Infidels as the* East *is filled with, to enlighten
your understandings with the Truth, and for having
made you, as* St. Peter *saith,* a Holy Nation, a
purchased People : *For you are not to imagine
that your Forefathers did deserve more at the hands
of God, than the other Infidels that were their Con-
temporaries, and yet you see how God was pleased
to chuse them, and you by their means, when at
the same time he left others and their Posterity
in their natural Misery ; for which there can be
no other Cause assigned, but that it was the Will
of God to extend that Mercy to you and your
Forefathers, which he denied to all the other People of these Parts ; and what makes this Mercy to
be the greater and more Illustrious, is, That God
was pleased to bring you to the Faith, not by the
Ministry of some obscure Person of small Authority,*
                                              which

*which has been the Case of many other Christians,
but by sending two chosen and beloved Apostles to
you, for your greater Honour, and that this Church
might justly stile it self* Apostolical; *a privilege that
was granted but to few Churches that are now in being
in the World, and which the Metropolitan of* Con-
stantinople *was long ago ambitious of usurping to
himself, if he might have been permitted. But
Satan, the great Enemy to all that's Good, envying
the great Glory of this Church, laboured to sow the
Tares of Errours and Heresies in this Field of
Christ's, and the Apostle St.* Thomas; *and so coming
from* Babylon *and the Land of the* Chaldeans, *he
brought along with him some of the Disciples of
the perfidious* Nestorius *to pervert this Church:
This* Nestorius *was condemned as a Heretick in*
Asia minor, *in the City of* Ephesus, *in a Council
of* 200 *Bishops, and afterwards in a Council of*
630 *Bishops: He was so wicked and perverse an
Heretick, that besides the punishment inflicted on
him for his Sins by Men, God also begun to punish him in this Life, giving him as it were an
earnest of those Punishments and Torments which
he is now suffering in Hell; for besides his being
deposed and deprived of his Bishoprick, and
Condemned by the forementioned and other following Councils, and Banished by the Sentence of the
Emperour* Theodosius *the* II. *who then Reigned,
to the Deserts of* Ægypt, *and his having his Books
burned by the command of the said Emperour before his death, his Tongue with which he had
uttered such great Blasphemies, rotted in his Mouth,*

F f

as

*as did also his whole Body, and being eat up with
Lice he expired, surrendring his Soul to the Devil,
as* Evagrius, *a Noble Writer who lived at the same
time, relates; and the same is reported of him by*
Nicephorus, Cedrenus, *and other Greek Writers.
The Disciples of this cursed Heretick being brought
into this Church by the Devil, sowed their Errours
in it without being observed by you, who were a
simple sincere People; insomuch that St.* Thomas
*when he was on Earth, might have said the same
that St.* Paul *did to those of* Ephesus *, where*
Nestorius *was afterwards Condemned; I know
that after my departure greedy* Wolves *shall
come among you, not sparing the Flock : And
well might the Pastors you have had among you
be called devouring* Wolves *, who being a base
and inconsiderable People, had no other intent but
to rob you of all they could , taking Money for
Orders , * Dispensations, for Absolutions, and for
all Sacraments and Sacred things , as you very
well know ; a thing so abominable in the sight of
God, that St.* Peter *the Prince of the Apostles, for
this Sin only threw* Simon Magus *out of the Church,
and Excommunicated him, as you may see in the
Acts of the Apostles; insomuch, Brethren, that we
see that fulfill'd in you, and in your Prelates, who
came from* Babylon, *which was foretold by God*

---

* **Dispensations.]** What was ever heard of in the *Ro-
could the poor *Malavars* con-   man* Church, or that the Declamer
clude from hence, but that either   was one of a strange assurance
no such thing as the taking of   to condemn the doing of it at
Money for Dispensations , *&c.*   such a Tragical rate as he does.

so many Years before by the Prophet Isaiah, The Shepherds themselves had no understanding, they have all gone out of the Way, and from the first to the last are all turned to Covetousness. *For God's sake, Brethren, tell me what sort of Prelates and Bishops could they be, who sought nothing but their own Interest ; and who gave Orders and Dispensations, and did every thing that belongs to a Bishop, without being Bishops themselves, or so much as Priests or Clerks , but were pure Laicks, as they themselves afterwards confessed : What Dispensation, what Sacrament, what Grace, could he who was dispensed with and ordained, receive from those who were no Bishops, nor so much as Clerks, but pure Laicks, nay* Lascares, *in whose Habit they came out of their own Country. Brethren , this is the Fruit which they send you from* Babylon, *Hereticks and pure Laicks, and Barbarians for Bishops : Tell me what has* Malabar *to do with* Babylon, *and what correspondence is there betwixt the most pure Doctrine of Christ, which was preached to you by the great Apostle* St. Thomas, *and the barbarous Errours which were brought hither by* Arabians *and* Chaldeans *from* Babylon ; *and from their Master the Apostate* Nestorius? *Believe me, Brethren, these are they of whom* St. Paul *spoke in his Epistle to his Scholar* Titus, That there should come Men teaching what they ought not to teach, for filthy lucre: *And so it fell out for these Men, that they might not lose the Profits and Honours they were unjustly possessed of, did all they could to put into your*

heads

*heads: that the Doctrine of St. Peter was different
from that which had been taught you by St. Thomas: It is true that the Doctrine of the Apostle
St.* Peter *is contrary to the Heresies that have been
brought hither from* Babylon*, but not what was
preached here by St.* Thomas: *For what St. Thomas, that also St.* Peter *taught, and Christ himself and all his other Disciples taught; for as St.*
Paul *faith,* there is one Lord, one Faith, one
Baptism, and one Church, of which Christ is the
Head, and that on Earth St. *Peter* and his Successors the Bishops of *Rome: For that St.* Peter
and his Successors are the Head of the whole Church
* *on Earth is plain, from what Christ before his Passion
promised St.* Peter, *as it is recorded in the* 16. Chap.
of St. Matthew, *where Christ, after having examined his Faith, said to him,* Thou art *Peter,*
and upon this Rock I will build my Church,
and I will give thee the Keys of the Kingdom
of Heaven, &c. *Words which he spoke to* ‖*none
of the rest of the Apostles, but to St.* Peter *only.
And St.* John *in the last Chapter of his Gospel
tells us, That Christ, after his Resurrection, having asked St.* Peter *if he loved him more than
all other things, and, St.* Peter *had answered,
that he knew very well that he did, said to him
three several times,* Feed my Lambs, feed my

---

* **On earth.**] Bishop *Andre*
did not so fair in quoting, [*And
on Earth, St. Peter and his Successors, the Bishops of* Rome, &c.]
as St. *Paul's* words.

‖ **None.**] This is a mistake,
for he gave the same Commission to all his Apostles after his
Resurrection.

Lambs,

Lambs, feed my Sheep : *By which words he made
him the univerfal Paftor of his Sheep, and after
him all the Bifhops of* Rome *who were to fucceed
him in that Office*; *for Chrift has but one Fold
for all his Sheep, and one only Church : and fo in
the Creed that is fung in the Mafs, we fay,* I believe in one Holy and Apoftolical Church : *and
fo Chrift her Spoufe faid of his Church in the*
Canticles, My Dove, my perfect, is but one;
*that is to fay, my Dove, my perfect, which is the
Church, is but one :   And St.* John *in his* 10th.
Chapter *tells us, that the Son of God fpeaking to
his Difciples concerning his intent of calling the
Gentiles to his Faith, faid,* I have other Sheep
which are not of this Fold, whom I muft bring
in, that there may be one Fold and one Shepherd. *Now that Fold wherein the Jews and Gentiles were to concurr in one only Faith, is the Catholick Church, and that Shepherd was St.* Peter,
and all his Succeffors the Bifhops of Rome; *every one of which as he is Bifhop of* Rome, *is the
univerfal Paftor of the* * *whole Church of God, infomuch as that all who will not be fubject to him,
are not of the number of the Sheep of Chrift, but
are without the Fold of the Church, being Schifmaticks and Hereticks, for fuch are all who are
difobedient to the* Roman *Church*; *in which* Roman *Church there never was nor will be any error*

---

* **Whole.**] If this had been
the Faith of the whole Chriftian
Church at the time when the
Creeds were made, the compilers | of them would and ought to have
added *Roman* to Catholick in the
Creed.

in Faith, by reason of Christ's promise, who, as
St. Luke *reports, speaking to St.* Peter, *said to*
him; I have prayed for thee, Peter, that the
† Faith of thy Church may never fail : *The*
Faith of other particular Churches, as we have
seen, may fail, but the Faith of the Roman *Church*
has never failed nor never will. Wherefore, Bre-
thren, fasten your selves close to this firm Pillar
of the Roman *Church ; against which, according*
to our Saviour's promises, the Gates of Hell shall
never prevail; *which Gates are the Heresies that*
are, and have been in the World : You ought there-
fore to render many thanks to God, for his having
relieved you at this time, by sending you the Lord
Arch-Bishop *for a Spiritual Pastor and Master,*
who having left his Dwelling, and quiet is at all
this Trouble, only for the sake of your Salvation,
and to rescue you from the errors you have hither-
to lived in : For I know and am certain, that he
is one of those Pastors which God spoke of by
Jeremiah; And I will give you Pastors according to my heart, and they shall feed you with
Knowledge and Doctrine. *Hitherto you have*
been fed with Errors and Ignorances, and your
Pastors have sought gain, and not the Salvation
of your Souls : This Pastor, as you see, does not
come to take any of your Goods from you, but to
spend his own for your profit, and to put you in
the right way to Heaven and Salvation : From

---

† ſaith.] Here the Bishop | ture again in quoting the [*Faith*
makes very bold with the Scrip- | *of thy Church*] as St. *Luke's* words.

‖ *whence*

‖ *whence you may clearly perceive the great diffe-*
rence there is betwixt him and thofe other Paftors,
or to fpeak more properly, thofe Wolves, *which*
you have had hitherto among you, as our Lord
faith, in Sheeps cloathing. *Hitherto your Errors*
have had fome excufe, becaufe you could know no more
but what your Mafters taught you; whereas from
henceforward, you fhall have no manner of excufe,
neither before God nor Man, if you do not become
fuch, as all that love you defire you to be. The
Faith and Doctrine that has been preached to you
by the Arch-Bifhop, is the Faith of all the Chri-
ftians in the Indies, *and of all Clerks and Religi-*
ous in thefe Parts, and which all Portugal, Spain,
and in a word all * Chriftendom *holds. This is*
the Faith that was taught by the Son of God, the
Faith that St. Thomas *preached, and was preach-*
ed alfo by St. Peter *and the reft of the Apoftles;*
and if any fhall teach the contrary, let him be, *as*
St. Paul *faith,* Anathema, *and Excommunicated*
and expelled the Society of the Faithful, as he is
from Chrift, his Faith and Grace. The Lord
give you a perfect knowledge of himfelf, as it is defired
by your Brother in the Lord. Writ at Cochim *the*
28th of June, 1599.

Your Brother in the Lord,
Bifhop *FREY ANDRE.*

‖ **Whence.**] I do not believe
that the Arch-Bifhops of *Malabar*
made half fo much of their Bifhoprick, as Bifhop *Andre* did of
his of *Cochim,* or as Father *Roz*
the *Jefuit* made of *Malabar,* after
he was preferr'd to it by the Pope.

* **Chriftendom.**] The *Re-*
formed, the *Greek,* the *Mufcovite,*
the *Georgian,* the *Armenian,* the *An-*
tiochian, Alexandrian, and *Abyffin*
Church, are it feems no part of
Chriftendom with this Declamer.

F f 4   The

The S Y N O D's Anſwer,

The Lord Aſſiſt Us.

To the moſt Illuſtrious and Reverend Lord
Dom Andre, the moſt worthy Biſhop of
Cochim ; The Dioceſan Synod of the
Chriſtians of St. *Thomas* of the Biſhoprick
of the *Serra*, aſſembled in the Town of
Diamper, wiſheth eternal Health and Pro-
ſperity in our Lord.

OUr *moſt Reverend* Metropolitan *ordered
your moſt Illuſtrious* Lordſhip's *Letter to
this Synod to be read in a full Aſſembly
of the Prieſts and People; and having heard and
underſtood it, we rejoiced exceedingly in the Lord,
to perceive that the Holy Doctrine taught us by
your* Lordſhip, *is the ſame with that our* Metropolitan *has preached in all our Churches, and has
declared in this Synod, as alſo the ſame that is
preached by the Fathers all over this Dioceſs, by
which means we are the more confirmed in the
Catholick Faith, and the Obedience we owe to the
Holy* Roman *Church, our true Mother, and to our
Lord the* Pope, *the Succeſſor of St.* Peter, *and
Chriſt's Vicar upon Earth, as is manifeſt from the
Acts of the ſaid Synod, Signed by Us, as your
Lordſhip may ſee; and if we have hitherto been*
waſting

wanting to our Duty in thefe Matters, it did not proceed
from any Obftinacy of Mind, or from any Inclination
we had to be Hereticks, or Schifmaticks, but purely for
want of the Light of true Doctrine and healthful and
Catholick Food, which was not given us by our Prelates, but who did inftead thereof, poyfon us with the
falfe Doctrines of Neftorius, and feveral other
Errors ; from which we are now, by the Divine
Mercy, refcued ; and by the goodnefs of God, and
the Miniftry of our Metropolitan, enlightened :
from whence alfo rofe the Rebellion which was
made by us, when the Truth began to be firft
preached to us ; as alfo all the Troubles and Vexations that we gave to our Metropolitan, and the
manifeft Dangers we expofed him to ; for all which
we are now heartily forry, and do dayly more and
more lament it : But whereas God has been pleafed to enlighten us with his Doctrine, the Metropolitan being difcouraged by none of thofe things
to go on preaching in our Churches, the light of
the Truth coming to us by that means, we have
cordially embraced, and have with an unanimous
confent and great alacrity, made profeffion thereof
in this Synod ; having alfo put the Affairs of our
Church in the beft Order we were able, and fubmitting our felves to the Judgment of our Metropolitan Mar Aleixo, who as our Mafter, has
inftructed us in all things : But whereas his Lordfhip, after his Vifitation of this Diocefs is over,
is to go to refide in his * own Diocefs, which we

---

* **Own Diocefs.**] The
Arch-Bifhop cured them of thefe
fears, for fome time at leaft, at | the end of his Vifitation, when
he made a folemn renunciation
of the Arch-Bifhoprick of *Goa*,
take

take notice of to our great Sorrow, by which means we
shall want a Special Protection; we do therefore
beg, that until such time as God shall be pleased
to send the Pastor among us, which we expect from
the Holy Apostolical See, your Lordship, as being
the Prelate that lives nearest to us , and from
whom and your Predecessors, this Church has re-
ceived so many Favors, would be pleased to take
us under your protection, and to concern your self
in all our Affairs, and to favour the Prelate, which
the Metropolitan *with his wonted kindness and*
benignity to his Flock, intends to leave among
us. And seeing your most Illustrious Lordship
in your Charity has been pleased to favour us with
a Letter, we take confidence from thence, to beg of
you, That whereas our Priests, both for their Spi-
ritual Consolation, and other Necessities, do frequent-
ly resort to your City and several parts of your
Diocess, where it will be necessary for them to say
Mass, which they have hitherto been hindred from
doing, by reason of their not being in a perfect
Union with the Holy Mother Church of Rome;
we now being in such an Union, as much as can
be desired, the Synod doth humbly beseech your

and as solemn an acceptation of that of the *Serra*, and that judicially and in Form; desiring the Christians of St. *Thomas*, to whom he delivered both those Instruments, to sollicite the Pope and King of *Spain* to give way to the Translation; and promising withal to employ all his own Interest in both to perswade them to it ;

but it seems all would not do, for the next News we hear of him, is, That instead of being gratified with the Arch-Bishoprick of the *Serra*, he was condemned to be Governour-General of the *Indies* for three Years, and after that translated to the Primacy of *Portugal*.

Lord-

Lordſhip that you would be pleaſed to give leave to ſuch of our Prieſts as have a Licence from our Prelate to ſay Maſs in your Churches, at leaſt the Roman *tranſlated into* Syrian, *that it may appear thereby that we are all one in the* Unity *of one only Catholick Church; and that the diviſion which* Satan *had made betwixt us, and moſt other Churches is at an end, all Churches making one onely Catholick Church, as your Lordſhip has clearly taught us, as a vigilant Paſtor, in your learned Letter. The Lord preſerve your Lordſhip's moſt Illuſtrious Perſon, and prolong your Years, for the good of the Church and the profit of the Sheep of* Chriſt. *Writ in the Synod of* Diamper *the* 25th. *of* June, 1599.

Praiſe be to God.

A

A
Preface to a MISSAL.

The Mass that is henceforth to be used by the ancient Christians of St. Thomas of the Bishoprick of Angamale in the Serra of Malabar, in the East-Indies, purged of the Nestorian Errors and Blasphemies it abounded with, by the most Illustrious and Reverend Dom Frey Aleixo De Menezes, Arch-Bishop of Goa, and Primate of the Indies, at the time when he reduced them to the Obedience of the Holy Roman Church. Translated word for word out of Syriack or Syrian, into Latin.

AMong the other things which the most Reverend Arch-Bishop of *Goa,* and Primate of the *Indies,* Dom *Frey Aleixo de Menezes,* put in Order in the *Diocesan* Synod, assembled by him in the Bishoprick of *Angamale* of the *Serra* of *Malabar,*

of

of the Chriſtians of St. *Thomas,* in which
he purged the Church of the *Neſtorian*
Hereſies, and reduced it to the Obedience
of the Holy *Roman* Church; one of the
chief was the reforming the *Syrian* Maſs,
which was ſaid in the *Chaldee* Tongue in
this Biſhoprick, which having been com-
poſed or inlarged by *Neſtorian* Hereticks,
was full of Errors and Blaſphemies both
in the Prayers and Commemorations of
Neſtorius, Theodorus, and *Diodorus,* and ſeveral other *Neſtorian* Hereticks, to whom as
to Saints, they prayed, for to intercede for
them : And whereas this People was in a
profound Ignorance, nay the very Biſhops,
who came from *Babylon,* not knowing the
true Form of Conſecration, all of them
adding to it and taking from it at their
pleaſure; there being no certain particular
Form of Conſecration among them, until a certain Arch-Biſhop came who had
more knowledge than the reſt in Eccle-
fiaſtical Matters, and the Holy Scriptures;
who perceiving that the Form wherewith
they Conſecrated, contained in it ſome
Erro:s,

Errors, contrary to the Truth of the Divine Sacrament, did eftablifh the true Form, adding fome words to it, both in the Confecration of the Body and Blood, in contradiction to the Error and Herefie of thofe who fay that the Sacrament is *only the Figure of the Body of Chrift our Lord.* From whence it is more than probable, the Hereticks of our Times, the revivers of the Errors of all the ancient condem. ned Sects, took this Opinion: The Form eftablifhed by the forementioned Arch-Bifhop was, *This is in truth my Body; this is in truth the Cup of my Blood, which was fhed for you and for many, for the propitiation and remiffion of your Sins; and this fhall be a Pledge to you for ever and ever;* in which Form they have now Confecrated for feveral Years. But the moft Reverend Arch-Bifhop Primate, having removed the words that are not neceffary, e. ftablifhed the proper Form ufed in the Catholick Church, as it is in the *Roman Miffal,* laying afide divers and Sacrilegious and ignorant Ceremonies alfo, which fig. nified

Lightning Source UK Ltd.
Milton Keynes UK
UKHW010637090223
416681UK00006B/1552

9 789354 481499